Vatican II in Ireland, Fifty Years On

STUDIES IN THEOLOGY
SOCIETY AND CULTURE

Series Editors:

Dr Declan Marmion
Dr Gesa Thiessen
Dr Norbert Hintersteiner

Volume 12

PETER LANG

Oxford • Bern • Berlin • Bruxelles • Frankfurt am Main • New York • Wien

Dermot A. Lane (ed.)

Vatican II in Ireland, Fifty Years On

Essays in Honour of Pádraic Conway

PETER LANG

Oxford • Bern • Berlin • Bruxelles • Frankfurt am Main • New York • Wien

Bibliographic information published by Die Deutsche Nationalbibliothek.
Die Deutsche Nationalbibliothek lists this publication in the Deutsche National-
bibliografie; detailed bibliographic data is available on the Internet at
http://dnb.d-nb.de.

A catalogue record for this book is available from the British Library.

Library of Congress Cataloging-in-Publication Data

Vatican II in Ireland, fifty years on : essays in honour of Pádraic Conway / [edited by]
Dermot A. Lane.
      pages cm. -- (Studies in theology, society and culture ; 12)
   Includes bibliographical references and index.
   ISBN 978-3-0343-1874-7 (alk. paper)
   1. Catholic Church--Ireland--History--20th century--Congresses. 2. Catholic Church-
-Ireland--History--21st century--Congresses. 3. Vatican Council (2nd : 1962-1965 :
Basilica di San Pietro in Vaticano)--Congresses. I. Lane, Dermot A., 1941- editor. II.
Conway, Pádraic, 1962- honouree. III. Title: Vatican 2 in Ireland, fifty years on.
   BX1505.2.V38 2015
   262'.52--dc23

                              2015004570

Cover image © Jraytram/ Wikimedia Commons/ CC-BY-SA-3.0.
Advice on cover design: Amanda Dillon

ISSN 1662-9930
ISBN 978-3-0343-1874-7 (print)
ISBN 978-3-0353-0715-3 (eBook)

© Peter Lang AG, International Academic Publishers, Bern 2015
Hochfeldstrasse 32, CH-3012 Bern, Switzerland
info@peterlang.com, www.peterlang.com, www.peterlang.net

This publication has been peer reviewed.

Printed in Germany

Dedication. Dr Pádraic Conway, 1962–2012

The entire University College Dublin community was deeply saddened to learn of the untimely death of Dr Pádraic Conway, Vice-President for University Relations on 5th October last, following a three-year long battle with cancer. During his almost fifteen years at UCD, Pádraic was friend, colleague and mentor to so many of our staff, alumni and students. His enormous capacity to enjoy the companionship of others, his interest in their lives and thoughts and his gift for repartee and anecdote made him a truly unique figure.

Pádraic was born and bred in Sligo Town and he remained throughout his life a proud Sligoman, attributing many of his achievements, his views and his loyalties to his home town and the good common sense of its citizens. Pádraic attended Summerhill College, Sligo from 1974 to 1979 before going on to study French and Philosophy at University College Cork and subsequently Biblical and Theological studies at Trinity College Dublin.

His training was as a theologian, for which he had been elected a Trinity Scholar in 1988. This gave him a rare ability to combine judicious use of scripture with practical management. Pádraic's academic rigour was seamlessly married to his acute emotional intelligence, an alliance of formal intellectual prowess and charisma which the discipline of theological reflection nurtured in him. In religion, Pádraic was just the same, reflexively Catholic and relentlessly critical all at once.

On leaving Trinity, Pádraic spent four years working with Andersen Consulting (now Accenture) as a management consultant. It is a tribute to Pádraic's adaptability and intellectual capability that he was, as a theology graduate, able to quickly and successfully work in the fields of computer technology, business process design and financial modelling.

As always, Pádraic made a host of friends at Andersen Consulting, many of whom remained close to him right to the end.

Obituary taken from the UCD website, 5 October 2012.

Pádraic could be partisan in politics but he was also fearless in making his views known on any subject whether popular or unpopular. One of his central theological concerns was with "table fellowship", with the result that he believed in sitting down to talk. Therefore he spent much of his time resolving and discussing and problematising issues of concern at the table and in convivial settings. He brought all of his endless energy and his force of personality to the table, whatever table it was, every time he met to do business, to do friendship or to celebrate life. His work for Accenture, Trocaire, TCD and subsequently UCD was all about development, about making sure that organisations and the people in them, reached their full potential and explored all of the possibilities open to them.

Pádraic was a master of the deadline, capable of working at lightning speed and with impressive results. More recently, he began to return to his academic roots in language, literature and the Bible. His trick memory for dates and anniversaries meant that he rarely let a good commemorative occasion slip by. His last academic venture, a conference on the fiftieth anniversary of Vatican II, encapsulates so much of his approach to learning. This is no retrospective enterprise but a "critical examination" of the "enduring significance" of the Council. In other words continuing "aggiornamento", typical of Pádraic's reluctance to let sleeping dogs lie.

Among his many interests was a love of all sports. First and foremost among these was Pádraic's lifelong affection for and commitment to the GAA. Although never a great player himself, Pádraic worked tirelessly for Sligo GAA, where he served as President of the Friends of Sligo Football in 2003. Pádraic also loved rugby and was immensely proud of having captained the Sligo under-15 team of 1977.

Constantly on the move, mobile phone pressed to his ear, waving a greeting to one of his many friends, acquaintances and colleagues, Pádraic was a unique figure at UCD. Always entertaining, sometimes combative, never boring, he embodied all of the features of Belfield life, the academic, the sporting, the social and the political. He will be sadly missed by his many friends and colleagues.

We at UCD extend our deepest sympathies to his family and to all who knew him.

Ar dheis Dé go raibh a anam uasal
HRB. JMcC. TC

Contents

Acknowledgements

The publication of this book would not have been possible without the support and collaboration of a number of people.

Foremost, I wish to thank Professor Dermot Moran, Director of the UCD International Centre for Newman Studies, for his invitation and encouragement to undertake this project.

I also thank the Board of the UCD International Centre for Newman Studies for their support.

In particular I wish to record my gratitude to Hazel Rooke, my secretary, for her patience, advice and attention to detail in typing, editing and proof-reading various versions of the text.

I also want to thank the team at Peter Lang for their help along the way, especially Christabel Scaife for her wise counsel at critical moments.

Lastly, I wish to express my personal thanks to all of the contributors who responded generously to the invitation to be part of this publication.

Abbreviations, Dates and Votes in Relation to the Documents of Vatican II (1962–1965)

SC   *Sacrosanctum Concilium*, Constitution on the Sacred Liturgy, 4th December 1963: 2,147 in favour, 4 against

IM   *Inter Mirifica*, Decree on the Mass Media, 4th December 1963: 1,960 in favour, 164 against

LG   *Lumen Gentium*, Dogmatic Constitution on the Church, 21st November 1964: 2,134 in favour, 10 against

UR   *Unitatis Redintegratio*, Decree on Ecumenism, 21st November 1964: 2,137 in favour, 11 against

PC   *Perfectae Caritatis*, Decree on the Up-to-date Renewal of Religious Life, 28th October 1965: 2,325 in favour, 4 against

CD   *Christus Dominus*, Decree on the Pastoral Office of Bishops in the Church, 28th October 1965: 2,319 in favour, 1 against

GE   *Gravissimum Educationis*, Declaration on Christian Education, 28th October 1965: 2,290 in favour, 35 against

NA   *Nostra Aetate*, Declaration on the Relation of the Church to Non-Christian Religions, 28th October 1965: 2,221 in favour, 88 against

OP   *Optatam Totius*, Decree on the Training of Priests, 28th October 1965: 2,318 in favour, 3 against

DV   *Dei Verbum*, Dogmatic Constitution on Divine Revelation, 18th November 1965: 2,344 in favour, 6 against

AA   *Apostolicam Actuositatem*, Decree on the Apostolate of Lay People, 18th November 1965: 2,340 in favour, 2 against

OE   *Orientalium Ecclesiarum*, Decree on Catholic Eastern Churches, 21st November 1965: 2,110 in favour, 39 against

PO   *Presbyterorum Ordinis*, Decree on the Ministry and Life of Priests, 7th December 1965: 2,390 in favour, 70 against

DH   *Dignitatis Humanae*, Declaration on Religious Liberty, 7th December 1965: 2,308 in favour, 4 against

AG   *Ad Gentes*, Decree on the Missionary Activity of the Church,
      7th December 1965, 2,394 in favour, 5 against
GS   *Gaudium et Spes*, Pastoral Constitution on the Church in the
      Modern World, 7th December 1965; 2,309 in favour, 75 against

Introduction

In summer 2012, Pádraic Conway, as Director of the UCD International Centre for Newman Studies, put in place plans for a conference on 11th October 2012, to commemorate the fiftieth anniversary of the opening of the Second Vatican Council on 11th October 1962. Pádraic had briefed the speakers,[1] organised the venue of Newman House in St Stephen's Green, and drawn up the programme: everything was ready to go. It was, therefore, with great shock and sadness that the theological community learned of the untimely death of Pádraic on 5th October 2012 just days before the conference was due to take place.

In spite of the death of Pádraic but in accordance with his wishes, it was decided hesitantly that the conference would go ahead. Ironically, on the day of his burial, 8th October 2012, *The Irish Times* published a *Rite & Reason* column by Pádraic, entitled "Ireland's Ambivalent Relationship with the Second Vatican Council". That short reflection by Pádraic is reproduced, with the permission of *The Irish Times*, as the opening article in this volume celebrating the fiftieth anniversary of the closing of Vatican II.

It was the intention of Pádraic to edit and publish the proceedings. Professor Seán Freyne was subsequently approached and agreed to edit the papers. However, with equal sadness Seán died on 5th August 2013. Pádraic and Seán had served the church, the academy, and society in many different ways with infectious enthusiasm, great courage, and restless imaginations. May they now enjoy the gift of eternal life "in Christ".

---

1   Gabriel Daly, Seán Freyne, Linda Hogan, Dermot Lane, Enda McDonagh, Joseph O'Leary, Andrew Pierce and Ethna Regan.

The Aims of this Publication

Some months later, the current Director of the UCD International Centre for Newman Studies, Professor Dermot Moran, invited me to edit the proceedings. I decided, with the approval of the Director and the Board of the UCD International Centre for Newman Studies, to publish the papers in honour of Pádraic Conway, to solicit some additional papers, and to aim for a publication date in 2015 to mark the fiftieth anniversary of the closing of the Second Vatican Council. All of the contributors were invited to keep an eye on one or other of the following aims: to offer an objective assessment of the reception and implementation of the Council in Ireland, to give some attention to the historical and theological significance of Vatican II for the self-understanding of Catholicism in the twenty-first century, and to offer suggestions for the reform of the Catholic church in Ireland in the present and in the future. The intention of this collection of papers, therefore, is not to offer a commentary on the documents of the Council which is readily available elsewhere. Instead, the aim is to review the impact of the Council on the church in Ireland in the last fifty years, and to explore how the Council could and should shape the church in the future.

The purpose of this publication, therefore, is to honour the life of Pádraic Conway, especially his contribution as Director to the UCD International Centre for Newman Studies and his energetic work as Vice-President for Public Affairs in UCD. Another purpose is to look back at the reception and implementation of the Council in Ireland with a view to moving forward: how can the Catholic church recover and reform itself in the light of recent crises, especially the trauma it has suffered over the last twenty years in the area of child sexual abuse. It should be noted that the decline in faith and church attendance had begun to take place before the revelations around child abuse emerged. Some would say, however, that these scandals have dealt a fatal blow to the church; others, including this author, believe that the church has resources to reform itself. These resources include the living Gospel of Jesus Christ, the gift of the Holy

Spirit to the Christian community, and the vision of the church offered by the Second Vatican Council.

The gravity of the crisis facing the Catholic church was highlighted by the fact that it received a "Pastoral Letter of Pope Benedict XVI to the Catholics of Ireland" in March 2010. This letter from the highest authority in the Catholic church, namely the Bishop of Rome in the person of Pope Benedict XVI, calls for a renewal of the Irish church.

A Church at the Crossroads

The Catholic church in Ireland is at a crossroads. It needs to stand still in prayer and reflection: to examine the recent past, to discern the promptings of the Holy Spirit in the present, and to respond to the call for renewal from Benedict XVI.

In this regard, the church in Ireland could also benefit by paying attention to the examination of conscience issued by Pope Francis to the Curia in December 2014. In that widely covered address Francis listed "Fifteen ailments of the Curia": feeling immortal, working too hard, becoming spiritually and mentally hardened, planning too much, working without co-ordination, "spiritual Alzheimer's", being rivals or boastful, suffering from "existential schizophrenia", committing the "terrorism of gossip", glorifying one's bosses, being indifferent to others, having a "funeral face", wanting more, forming closed circles, seeking worldly profit and showing off. This wide-ranging examination of conscience could be applied to many organisations and certainly to all Christians, and not just the Curia.

If the reform of the Catholic church is to take place, it will be necessary to retrieve something of the vision, the principles, and the change of style that occurred at the Second Vatican Council. The church in Ireland needs to undergo a process and experience of learning comparable to the process and experience of learning that took place at the Second Vatican Council.

The church is called to a radical conversion from being an authoritarian, clericalised, and male-centred institution to becoming a more humble, lay-shaped, and inclusive reality "so that the sign of Christ may shine more brightly over the face of the church".[2]

It would be naïve to suggest that the Second Vatican Council has answers for all of the challenges facing the Church in the twenty-first century. Vatican II, however, does have principles and it does have a vision that has the potential to reinvigorate the life of the church and to communicate the Gospel in a new and fresh language in the twenty-first century.

Whither the Catholic Church in Ireland in the Twenty-First Century?

Other national churches are also examining the legacy of Vatican II for renewal and reform of their churches in the twenty-first century.[3] With the current emphasis by Pope Francis on the importance of the local church, and with talk in Ireland by bishops, theologians, and the people of God about the possibility of a National Synod, and with the announcement of a diocesan Synod in Limerick, it is more and more likely that the teaching of Vatican II will be invoked as a point of departure. It is worth noting in this context that the Council recommended that bishops should recover the ancient practice of holding Synods at national, regional, and diocesan levels.[4] The Irish theologian Gerry O'Hanlon SJ has called for a national Synod or Consultation or Assembly on a number of occasions. His proposals

2   *LG*, a. 15.
3   Examples include Neil Ormerod, ed., *Vatican II: Reception and Implementation in the Australian Church*, 2012; *Vatican II: Experiences Canadienes/Canadian Experiences*, Sous la direction de/edited by Michael Attridge, Catherine E. Clifford and Gilles Routhier, Presses de Université d'Ottawa/University of Ottawa Press, 2011; O. Ernesto Valiente, "The Reception of Vatican II in Latin America", *Theological Studies*, December 2012: 795–823.
4   See *CD*, 36.

are informed by his experience of leading listening days of discernment in many dioceses throughout Ireland. His views, both pastoral and theological, have been presented persuasively in a number of publications.[5] It is hoped that *Vatican II in Ireland, Fifty Years On* might become a source of ideas for diocesan and National Synods/Consultations/Assemblies in the coming years in Ireland.

   Vatican II in Ireland, Fifty Years On builds on other, earlier reflections on the significance of the Council for the church in Ireland over the last fifty years. These include *Freedom to Hope: The Catholic Church in Ireland: Twenty Years after Vatican II* (1984), *Vatican II Facing the Future: Historical and Theological Perspectives* (2006), *Reaping the Harvest: Fifty Years after Vatican II* (2012).[6] Other equally important reflections can be found in the pages of *The Furrow* and *Doctrine and Life* over the last fifty years, since both journals have been dedicated amongst other things to the mediation of the fruits of the Council.

The Church in a Postmodern World

Although the world today, marked by globalisation, driven by technology and economics, and stamped by a plurality of views, is different to the world of the 1960s, nonetheless there are some similarities: how does the church reform itself, how does the church change with the times while

5   See for example his book *A New Vision for the Catholic Church: A View from Ireland*, Dublin: Columba Press, 2011; his contribution to Sue Mulligan ed., *Reaping the Harvest: Fifty years after Vatican II*, Dublin: Columba Books, 2012; and a number of articles in *The Furrow* over the last three years.
6   See Alan Falconer, Enda McDonagh, and Seán Mac Réamoinn, eds, *Freedom to Hope: The Catholic Church in Ireland, Twenty Years after Vatican II*, Dublin: The Columba Press, 1984; Dermot A. Lane and Brendan Leahy, eds, *Vatican II Facing the Twenty-first Century: Historical and Theological Perspectives*, Dublin: Veritas, 2006; and Sue Mulligan, ed., *Reaping the Harvest: Fifty Years after Vatican II*, Dublin: Columba Press, 2012.

remaining faithful to the mission it has received from Christ and the Holy Spirit, how does the church re-present the message of Christ in a world that is increasingly secular, multi-cultural and plural?

A twenty-first-century expression of these questions, taking account of the work of Charles Taylor in *A Secular Age* (2007), might be: Is the church relevant anymore in a world that has become self-sufficient, disenchanted socially and cosmically, and seemingly devoid of transcendence? What and where are the points of interaction between this post-modern, multi-cultural world and the Good News of Jesus Christ?

Going Back to Go Forward

A good place to start in reviewing the legacy of Vatican II for the Catholic church in the twenty-first century would be the opening address of John XXIII to the Bishops at the Council on the 11th October 1962, entitled *Gaudet Mater Ecclesiae* ("Mother church rejoices"). In that speech John XXIII stated:

- "we must disagree with the prophets of gloom who are always forecasting disaster, as though the end of the world were at hand"
- The church "must look to the present, to new conditions and new forms of life introduced into the modern world"
- "The substance of the ancient doctrine of deposit of faith is one thing, and the way in which it is presented is another"
- The exercise of the magisterium should be "predominantly pastoral in character"
- The church today "prefers to make use of the medicine of mercy rather than that of severity" in opposing errors.[7]

---

7   This address is available in Walter Abbott, ed., *The Documents of Vatican II*, London: Chapman, 1966: 710–719.

This particular speech of John XXIII was frequently quoted from the floor of the Council and has been described as "the Council's first text".[8]

In that opening speech, John XXIII was giving a deliberated direction to the Council, even at this early stage. He was inviting the church to update itself, and so reading the signs of the times became important (*GS*, a. 4; *UR*, a. 4; *PO*, a. 9; *AA*, a. 14). Likewise, he was also pointing towards a need for the church to re-present the message in a new way, and so the Council came around to acknowledging that adaptation of the perennial truth of the Gospel to "the concepts and languages of different people ... must ever be the law of all evangelisation" (*GS*, 44 and *AG*, 22). In calling for "the medicine of mercy" and a magisterium that would be pastoral in character, he was nudging the Council towards a change in style and language which became evident in several documents subsequently, especially *GS*.

According to John O'Malley, the US historian, there were three issues under the myriad of issues at the Council:[9] change, collegiality, and style. Concerning change, the question was how could the church present in a new way the message it had received from Christ and the Holy Spirit. Concerning collegiality, the issue was about the relationship between the centre and the periphery, between the papacy and the college of bishops, a recurring theme throughout the Council. In relation to style, the church in its teaching and practice had to adopt a new way of relating to the modern world.

To address these and other questions, the Council invoked a number of recurring principles: *aggiornamento*, development, *ressourcement*, dialogue, and a turn to history. *Aggiornamento*, an Italian phrase, was about updating the church and opening the windows to the world as recommended by John in his opening speech. Development was about change and this came to be seen as the unfolding of what was already implicit in the gospel and tradition. *Ressourcement*, an approach promoted especially among the French *periti* of the Council, was about going back to the sources: biblical,

---

8   Jared Wicks, *Doing Theology*, New York: Paulist Press, 2009: 22.
9   John W. O'Malley, *What Happened at Vatican II* (Cambridge, MA: Harvard University Press, 2008), 293.

patristic, and liturgical. Dialogue was brought to the floor by Paul VI: dialogue within the church, with other churches, with other cultures and religions, and with atheists became important in the course of the Council and so highlighted the pastoral character of the Council. By taking *ressourcement* seriously and entering into dialogue with others, the Council became aware of the place of history for its own self-understanding, and so historical consciousness moved to the centre, so much so that one commentator describes Vatican II as "the Council of History".[10] These three issues, and these five key principles along with others like ethics, education, ecumenism, and ecclesiology feature prominently in the essays that follow.

The Contents of this Book

In Part I, "The Memory of the Second Vatican Council in Ireland", Pádraic Conway points out that the Council was an opening up of the Catholic church to the people of Ireland. Its most immediate impact was felt through the introduction of the vernacular into the Mass and the turning around of the priest to face the congregation. He believes that the most powerful forces in disseminating the Council were the journalists.

Patrick Masterson describes the atmosphere of Irish Catholicism before the Council: high levels of sacramental practice and personal devotions. Like Pádraic Conway, he is struck by the role that Irish journalists played in mediating the Council to the public. Also significant in communicating the Council was the advent of "paperback theology" in the 1960s and 1970s, as well as a Dublin institution known as "Flannery's Harriers". He concludes that Irish Catholicism today finds itself seriously challenged.

Dermot Lane looks at reasons for keeping alive the memory of Vatican II and pays particular attention to the significance of *Gaudium et Spes* as

10   See Ormond Rush, "Toward a Comprehensive Interpretation of the Council and its Documents", *Theological Studies*, September 2012: 547–569.

the final gift of the Council to the church. He highlights solidarity, dialogue, and mutuality as first principles for reform of the church in the twenty-first century. He also outlines challenges facing the church at this time and concludes with a critique of *Gaudium et Spes*.

In Part II, "*Ressourcement* at the Council", Gabriel Flynn considers the origins of the *ressourcement* movement and argues that its leading exponents inspired a renaissance in twentieth-century Catholic theology that culminated in the reforms of Vatican II. He looks briefly at the complex question of terminology, which can only be resolved by reference to the movement's twin objectives: to effect a return to the sources and a necessary engagement with contemporary society. He assesses how the leading *ressourcement* intellectuals contributed to Vatican II and concludes with an analysis of their role in the struggle against the National Socialist German Workers' Party.

Seán Freyne reviews the genesis, development, and limitations of *Dei Verbum*. He gives an overview of trends in biblical studies since Vatican II in the life of the church. He outlines the impact the renewal in biblical studies had on the international journal *Concilium*, liberation theology, and feminist theology. He concludes by highlighting the challenge of making links between contemporary questions and the biblical data and how this can bring new life to local Christian communities.

In Part III, "Reception of the Council in the Irish Church", Jim Corkery offers an overview of the reception of Vatican II in Ireland over the past fifty years. Five areas, all inter-related, on which the Council's impact is uncontested are singled out for particular attention: liturgy; the role of the laity in the church; ecumenism and interreligious dialogue; the church's relationship with the modern world; and the nature of the church itself. He also examines the notion of reception itself and highlights the hermeneutical richness of reception. He opens up perspectives on conciliar reception that were largely absent in Ireland's receiving of the Council in the past half century but that, if attended to more fully in the future, could lead to a richer, more adequate reception of it in the twenty-first century on the part of an Irish church that is eager to reform and renew itself.

Jacinta Prunty reviews the reception of the call of Vatican II for the renewal of religious life and focuses on the Irish Federation of the Sisters of Our Lady of Charity. The process of the modernisation of High Park and Sean MacDermott Street Homes run by these Sisters, underway from 1952, was overtaken by the re-evaluation of religious life inherent in the Council's call to renewal. By 1973, the asylums had been effectively replaced by training centres, hostels, small group homes and retirement or nursing homes. The process of transformation to an active, "modern", apostolate required the Sisters to re-think the very purpose of religious life, and their own living out of it.

In Part IV, "Ethical Perspectives", Ethna Regan argues that the full acceptance, by the church, of human rights as a legitimate mode of ethical discourse was the major contribution of the Second Vatican Council to social ethics in the Catholic tradition. This full acceptance of human rights was shaped by a number of factors, especially the formal recognition of the right to religious freedom. This development enabled the church to become a full participant in the human rights movement – through intellectual engagement and front-line advocacy – in the post-conciliar period.

Linda Hogan considers some of the major developments in the evolution of Catholic moral theology since Vatican II. She notes that there has been a transformation of the discipline with a move away from the act-centred, legalistic, minimalistic and casuistic enterprise of the manuals, to more biblically-based, historically-conscious and context-sensitive theologies. This change has come about because the locations in which this theology is pursued have been transformed. Whereas previously seminaries and theological colleges were the primary fora, today theology is taught in multiple academic contexts, which may be secular, multi-religious or ecumenical in ethos. This new diversity has had a liberating effect on the discipline. She concludes by discussing how globalisation, gender politics and sexual liberation have affected the discourse of moral theology.

In Part V, "Ecclesiological Issues", Andrew Pierce shows that in framing its teaching on ecumenism, the Second Vatican Council firmly confronted some of the pivotal ways in which Roman Catholic identity had been shaped over the course of the preceding four centuries. He reviews some of the reactive dynamics that had shaped mutually exclusive narrations of where the Catholic church was to be found – both in its Western and Eastern forms. He observes how the late nineteenth and early twentieth centuries produced an anti-ecumenical Roman Catholic integralism – and notes how clericalist, anti-modernist and ultra-montane tendencies were deconstructed by the Council fathers. The Council thereby embraced the ambiguous theological context of modernity, and placed the Roman Catholic church at the heart of the contemporary ecumenical movement.

Gerry O'Hanlon holds that in Ireland the Catholic church's response to Vatican II was minimalist and that this was understandable given the apparently strong position of the church at the time, with no obvious need of change. However, we are now in a very different situation, with urgent need for change, and a papal leadership which is encouraging re-engagement with the ideas and spirit of Vatican II. The church needs to grasp the nettle of collegiality at all levels, with the transformation of culture and structures that this will involve. The convocation of a National Assembly of the church would be a good first step in that direction.

Gabriel Daly suggests there are two mentalities in the Catholic church, each exclusive of the other; but only one has recourse to power. Consensus on many theological topics is logically impossible between them. Agreement to live together in peace is the true Christian aim. The Congregation for the Doctrine of the Faith (CDF) needs radical reform; it remains to be seen whether Pope Francis, who has done so much to change the atmosphere in the church, accepts the structural implications of his attitude, and takes the CDF to task. Collegiality was a major achievement of Vatican II, but the Curia, and especially the CDF, has, up to now, successfully stymied it.

In Part VI, "Specific Questions", Declan Marmion holds that Karl Rahner had a pivotal influence on Vatican II – both during the preparatory phases, at the Council itself, and subsequent to the Council. He argues that his main influence was in the area of ecclesiology and identifies some ecclesial themes that bear the hallmark of Rahner – the church as *sacramentum mundi*, the importance of the local church, the issue of collegiality, the church of sinners, and the priority of the pastoral. He shows that Rahner's acute theological prescience in identifying issues facing the church into the future has been accurate and that his challenges to ecclesial renewal remain just as pertinent today.

Michael Drumm deals with the extremely important issue of education. Taking his cue from the title of the Declaration on Christian Education, *Gravissimum Educationis*, he writes about the grave importance of education in the life of the church and society as a whole. Following an analysis of the conciliar text three issues are studied in more detail: parental rights; holistic, integral education; and looking to the future. With regard to the future he places emphasis on inter-cultural dialogue, lay leadership, theological studies and issues arising from the digital revolution. The paper concludes with a short reflection on the relationship of Education and Eucharist.

Joseph S. O'Leary points out that with the advent of Pope Francis, there is a sharp awareness throughout the church of how the collegiality emphasised by Vatican II has failed to materialise in practice. Drawing on studies by Massimo Faggioli, Hervé Legrand, and Mary McAleese, he identifies the reasons for this failure and explores possibilities of unblocking the situation, especially through deepening a theological vision in which "communion" cannot be opposed to "collegiality" and in which both episcopal collegiality and papal primacy are rooted in the concrete life of the churches, which they serve to empower and enrich.

In Part VII, "Unfinished Business", Fainche Ryan notes that every ecumenical Council manifests or puts on display, to some extent, what the church really is. That those who gather at a Council carry lofty titles (pope, patriarch, cardinal, archbishop, bishop, religious superior, theologian) and wear somewhat unusual garb should not distract us from the fact that, at heart, they are brothers and sisters (women did play their part, however circumscribed it may have been) in the faith to all other Catholic Christians. Their deliberations represent, in a dramatic form, what the church is called to be, especially in the area of ministry.

Enda McDonagh examines the importance of style in art and architecture, poetry and politics, and then relates this to the question of style in the life of the church, especially in the area of communications. A shift in style took place at Vatican II that needs to be recovered today. Links between conversation and conversion, between communion and otherness are explored. These categories in turn are applied to gender questions. Discrimination against women in the life of the church offends against the style of community, conversation, and leadership initiated by Jesus and impoverishes the pastoral life of the church today.

Patrick Hannon argues that Irish Bishops' Conference interventions in the public square since the Council have accorded well with the Declaration on Religious Freedom but have lacked an adequate awareness of key themes of the two Constitutions on the church. He shows how attention to these themes may enrich the bishops' future contributions to debate on socio-legal issues in the changed context in which Irish Catholicism now finds itself. He maintains that public discussion of secularisation has been on the whole superficial and unhelpful, and in the light of observations by Owen Chadwick and a proposal by Charles Taylor he offers some suggestions for its improvement.

The Advent of Pope Francis

With the election of Pope Francis as Bishop of Rome, the reception and implementation of Vatican II have moved to a new phase and this new moment is primarily and distinctively about the pastoral reception of the Second Vatican Council in the twenty-first century.

There is an emerging consensus among commentators that a singular shift is currently taking place from a purely theological reception of Vatican II, promoted during the pontificates of John Paul II and Benedict XVI, to a pastoral reception of the Council. Within this new moment focussing on a pastoral reception of the Council, there is also recognition that the purpose of the doctrinal is to serve the pastoral needs and wellbeing of the pilgrim people of God. The magisterium within this new context will be not just the magisterium of Rome/the Curia, but also the magisterium of the whole people of God, made up of bishops, theologians, pastors and the *sensus fidelium*.

Any attempt to separate the doctrinal and the pastoral betrays a mis-understanding about the true nature of the doctrinal and pastoral life of the church, and goes against the teaching of Vatican II.[11] The doctrinal and the pastoral elements of the Council form a unity and, therefore, cannot be separated. The Under-Secretary of the Doctrinal Commission responsible for drafting some of the conciliar texts pointed out in 1963 in an important article:

> The pastoral perspective is not something added on to the exposition of doctrine. It is inherent to that exposition, because the truth is essentially destined to be lived, and thus cannot be confined to a theoretical knowledge. That is why a separate treatment of doctrine and practice leads to a sort of vivisection that would be the death of the message's fruitfulness.[12]

The unity between the doctrinal and the pastoral, between theological theory and *praxis*, between content and form has not always been to the fore in the reception of Vatican II in Ireland in parish life over the last fifty years. It is one of the more urgent challenges facing the Catholic church in Ireland in the twenty-first century.

It is hoped that the publication of *Vatican II in Ireland, Fifty Years On* may serve as a stimulus towards a theologically informed pastoral reception and implementation of the Council in the years ahead.

Dermot A. Lane

---

11 See for example footnote 1 of *GS* on this point.
12 Gérard Philips, "Deux Tendences dans la Théologie Contemporaine", *Nouvelle Revue Théologique*, 85, 1963: 225–238 at 237 as quoted by Catherine E. Clifford, *Decoding Vatican II: Interpretation and Ongoing Reception* (New York: Paulist Press, 2014), 41.

PART I

The Memory of the Second Vatican Council in Ireland

PÁDRAIC CONWAY

1   Ireland's Ambivalent Relationship with the Second Vatican Council

It's a daunting task to encompass in 1,000 words the content and impact of the Second Vatican Council. As I reflect on their combined efforts to convey the message from Rome – my respect for journalists has never been higher.

There can be no doubt that in 1962 the Irish church leadership was anything but ready for a Council of the kind embarked upon. A senior Maynooth professor declared that nine of the ten Commandments were grand, but that a real debate was needed on the question of servile work on Sundays.

Combine this statement with that of John Charles McQuaid after the Council, that "no change will worry the tranquility of your Christian lives", and it is difficult to avoid the conclusion that the Irish church leadership was out of touch with more than the latest trends in European theology.

Well, all that was about to change, change utterly. Whether it liked it or not, the Irish church was to have the scales removed from its eyes, like Bartimaeus, the man famously cured of blindness by Jesus.

Vatican II constituted a great opening of the Catholic church. The first manifestation of this was the arrival of the vernacular Mass: Mass would now be said in the native tongue of the congregation rather than the Latin, which had previously perpetuated a false idea of universality.

Almost as significant as this change, and one on which every architect in Ireland had an opinion, was the turning of the priest to face the people. The *ancien regime* saw the priest huddled over the bread and wine, whispering the *Te Igitur* – the predecessor of today's Eucharistic Prayers – while the people read their prayer books. This, in theory, created a heightened sense of mystery. In practice, it served to deepen the divide between clergy and laity to crevasse-like proportions.

The growing feeling among Irish people that "this will just not do!" led to the church gaining an increased sense of itself as the entire "people of God". It no longer saw itself as a caste-based system where a tiny – in numeric terms – clerical caste ruled all. The words "We, the people" suddenly became an Irish ecclesiastical reference point.

With this came a huge transformation of the ecumenical movement. In fact, you might say that with this came the ecumenical movement, as prior to Vatican II all too few were prepared to utter "that 'which' for 'who'/ And risk eternal doom", in the words of Austin Clarke in "Burial of an Irish President". The poem recounts how the Catholic members of government, obeying directions from their clergy, declined to enter St Patrick's Cathedral for the funeral of former president Douglas Hyde.

It is often a measure of the success of an idea that one finds the preceding state of affairs difficult to envisage. It is indeed difficult to imagine an Ireland where the vast majority of the population agonised over their relationship with their separated brethren, not to mention non-Christians.

Yet two documents of the Second Vatican Council changed all that or, more accurately, served to crystallise a process of change that had been ongoing. *Unitatis Redintegratio* (the Council's decree on ecumenism) and *Nostra Aetate* (on the relation of the Catholic church to non-Christian religions) marked a sea-change – for the better, especially when you consider the shameful history of anti-Semitism – in Irish Catholic attitudes towards Protestant traditions and non-Christian religions.

But perhaps the most significant change, though sadly it has not always endured, is the spirit of joy which the convenor of the Second Vatican Council brought to that role. The document Pope John XXIII used to open the Council was *Gaudet Mater Ecclesia* – "Mother Church Rejoices".

The great concluding document was *Gaudium et Spes* – "Joy and Hope". Writing almost a century earlier, John Henry Newman expressed dismay about the circumstances in which the First Vatican Council (1870) was convened: "Only a weak, fearful organisation, which has lost confidence in what it stands for, shuts down exploration and silences debate ... As Jesus warns us, it is the faithless anxious servant who keeps his master's money safe by burying it in the ground."

Finally, we should remember that Vatican II was part of the 1960s when, globally, the attitude towards authority changed: the default position became one of questioning, as opposed to deference.

It is arguable that the great failure of Vatican II was the inability of progressive forces to recognise this. Ironic too perhaps that, in hindsight, the most powerful positive forces of dissemination in Ireland were journalists such as John Horgan, Seán Mac Réamoinn and Louis McRedmond. But then again, maybe not so ironic at all.

PATRICK MASTERSON

2 Remembering Vatican II

In these brief remarks I try to recapture something of my sense of the significance of the Second Vatican Council. I try to situate it in the context and atmosphere of the Irish Catholicism of my youth which immediately preceded the Council and the changed Ireland which accompanied and followed it.

I grew up during and after the Second World War in a large typically middle class Catholic family on the north side of Dublin. It was not unusual to have a crucifix or religious picture on a bedroom wall. Family members might say their morning and night prayers privately but our mother conducted a family rosary after evening tea at which one was expected to participate. I have no recollection of my first confession but I recall my first communion as a very happy family occasion but not one on the commercial scale the ceremony has assumed today.

People seemed to go to confession more frequently in those days – even weekly. Perhaps as one got older and had more to confess one went less frequently. An element of fearfulness and scrupulosity was associated with reception of the sacraments. One could go to communion only if one was in "a state of grace" and had fasted strictly from midnight the day before. You had to go to mass on Sunday morning and no mass was later than midday – no Saturday vigil or evening mass. Your absence was obvious and noteworthy.

All major church festivals were carefully observed as holy days of obligation i.e. one was obliged to go to mass. The most joyful feast was Christmas. Before Easter you "gave up" something, e.g. sweets, for the forty days of Lent. On Holy Thursday one would pay a visit on foot to seven churches. On Good Friday there was the ceremony of the Stations of the Cross. It, together with Saint Patrick's Day, was a day on which all pubs remained closed for the whole day.

Churches had a high altar and many side altars with shrines to Our Lady and the saints alight with votive candles. There were lots of confession boxes also and a large pulpit into which the priest would ascend to deliver his sermon. Mass was in Latin with two (male) servers. You had to be fluent in the Latin responses to become a server. Everyone had a Latin missal and was adept at flicking with coloured ribbons to the right page as the mass proceeded. A popular ceremony was Benediction – a ceremony of adoration of the Eucharist – with lots of smoky incense and Latin hymns.

I attended two schools run by religious orders – Belvedere College, a day school run by Jesuits, and Castleknock College, run by Vincentian priests. Belvedere was somewhat more academic but also had good drama and sports facilities. Castleknock was a more friendly and sociable place. In both schools there were very able, dedicated, inspirational and kind priests and lay teachers. Neither I nor my friends had any experience whatsoever of the sexual abuse experienced elsewhere. However, there were a couple of people of whom we were a bit scared because they wielded the cane or strap with enthusiasm and, it seemed, perhaps even satisfaction.

A significant snapshot of the official ethos which prevailed in the Catholic church then, just prior to the Council, was provided by the promulgation of the Statutes of the Synod of Maynooth published in 1956. This document produced by an assembly of all Irish bishops enunciated over three hundred regulations governing the conduct of Catholic life in Ireland. The document was published in the form of individually numbered black books written in Latin and available only to priests who had to sign for receipt of their copy. It included regulations and recommendations on matters as diverse as the mortal sinfulness of attending Trinity College without the explicit permission of the Archbishop of Dublin, the etiquette for cycling abreast, and the superiority of traditional Irish dancing over imported foreign dances. It reflected a period in which an inward looking and very powerful local church sought to defend and protect an integral and rather narrow conception of Catholic culture against the perceived multiple threats of contemporary immorality. There was emphasis on what not to do if one wished to save one's soul – even down to detailed accounts in episcopal Lenten letters about the daily amount and kind of food one was allowed, or not allowed, to eat.

The announcement in 1959 by "good Pope John XXIII" that he intended to convene an Ecumenical Council of the church and the subsequent realisation of this decision in various sessions between 1962 and 1965 was greeted by Irish Catholics with great interest, excitement and anticipation.

At that time I had just returned from my doctorate studies in Louvain University to a position as a very junior lecturer in philosophy in UCD (Assistant Lecturer Grade 3!) – I was certainly one of the first, if not the first, laymen to teach philosophy there in recent times. I had known several prominent academics in Louvain who had contributed significantly to the preparation of the Council and I was happy to note the widespread interest it provoked in Ireland and the lively discussion generated by the various topics it debated.

I had the good fortune to visit Rome several times during various sessions of the Council. I went, as an adviser, with a talented young publisher Michael Gill. He had the innovative idea of making contemporary theology widely available in readily accessible paperback format. This idea gave birth to the highly successful "Logos Books" published by M.H Gill. This "paperback theology", readily available to a wide and interested lay readership, marked a noteworthy development within a decade from the publishing ethos of the individually numbered, exclusively clerically accessible, Statutes of the Synod of Maynooth. There were books of piety for the laity but theology was presumed to be a clerical preserve.

During our visits to Rome we had the opportunity to meet and dine most evenings with one or more of the major theologians contributing to the shape of the Council. These were people such as Karl Rahner, John Courtney Murray, Edward Schillebeeckx, Henri Bouillard, Hans Küng and Yves Congar. Their writings and those of important contemporary Irish theologians such as Enda McDonagh and Michael Hurley found their way into paperback versions of publications such as Logos Books.

The aim of the Second Vatican Council was not, as its predecessor had been, to define some particular Catholic truth. It was rather to renew the church, to bring it up to date and make it more attuned to the circumstances of the modern world. It debated crucial topics such as religious freedom, the role of the laity, ecumenism, human rights, and a more comprehensive conception of the church itself. It sought to rebut the perception of the church as modelled on the Roman Empire, a perception it was said which arose when the Roman Emperor Constantine converted to Christianity in the fourth century and made it the official State religion.

While emphasising and safeguarding the church's divinely commissioned teaching role, the case was made for a more democratic and open church. The liturgy was to be in the vernacular, not simply Latin. A more ecumenical outlook was promoted and freedom of conscience accorded greater explicit importance. Emphasis was placed on the fact that the church was not to be viewed as composed chiefly of bishops, priests and religious, conceived as its officers, with the laity conceived a merely its foot soldiers told what to do or, more likely, what not to do. Lay people were recognised as fully equal members of the church with inherent rights and responsibilities to proclaim and live the good news of the gospel.

It was a time of great hope and enthusiasm involving a much more open, innovative, exploratory, and engaged conception of the church than that of pre-Vatican II times in Ireland.

A group of people who made a huge contribution to the wide public appreciation in Ireland of the great significance of the Council were the remarkable journalists who covered it for the Irish Media. These included journalists such as Seán Mac Réamoinn (widely recognised as the doyen of international Vatican II journalists), John Horgan, Louis McRedmond, Desmond Fisher, Kevin O'Kelly, Desmond Fennell and T.P. O'Mahoney. Their dedicated and superb coverage of the events of the Council contributed enormously to the widespread awareness of and interest in them in Ireland.

After the Council had concluded its deliberations, these journalists maintained their interest in its theological issues and related concerns. I used to meet them at meetings of what became known as "Flannery's Harriers" (also sometimes as "The Plastered Saints"). These were occasional meetings of some academics, journalists, artists and religious convened by a remarkable Dominican, Fr Austin Flannery, who as editor of *Doctrine and Life* (together with Fr J.G. McGarry, editor of *The Furrow*) did so much to maintain interest in the recommendations of the Council.

The members of this varied group of "Flannery's Harriers" used to assemble, usually carrying a six-pack, in a room of the Municipal Gallery which the curator James White made available to them. It provided a locus for very lively and at times fiery debate (e.g. between Desmond Fennell of "Herder Correspondence" and Jack Dowling of "Stand Up and be Counted" RTE fame!) It also provided a platform to welcome somewhat "controversial" visitors such as Herbert McCabe, Cecil Barrett, Nicholas Lash, Adrian Cunningham and Laurence Bright.

The impetus of the Council and its widespread influence persisted throughout the country during the 1960s and 1970s. A spirit of religious renewal, fresh thinking, openness and optimism prevailed. Its recommendations were the subject of widespread publications, lectures and discussions. I had the curious experience of addressing a very large audience, which included the Taoiseach and both Archbishops of Dublin, John Charles McQuaid and George Otto Simms, on practical consequences of the Council's teaching on ecumenism. Ironically the event took place in the National Boxing Stadium!

In the Dublin Archdiocese various institutions were established partly in response to the new situation arising from the Council. These included the creation of the Radharc team which went on to produce such memorable TV documentaries and the Mater Dei Institute to teach teachers of religion in secondary schools. The Irish bishops established the Catholic Communications Centre which did valuable work in training religious and lay people alike in using modern media.

During the same period there was a vibrant movement of charismatic renewal amongst many Catholics throughout the country – an engagement which previously had been viewed as a characteristically Protestant form of enthusiasm.

Perhaps the high point of the renewal engendered by the Council was the papal visit to Ireland of Pope John Paul II. On 26th June 1979 the only show in town was the gathering of about one and a quarter million people assembled in the Phoenix Park around the huge flag-bedecked white steel cross erected in record time for the Papal mass. As the Pope descended from a large red helicopter a huge cheer of fervent welcome arose from the assembled crowd. This warm welcome was repeated with

equal fervour and comparably large numbers at the other venues of the
papal Irish visit.

In the following years and certainly throughout the nineties and the
early years of this century the heritage of Vatican II seemed to dissipate and
vanish into thin air. When I returned to Ireland in 2002 after eight years
abroad working in Florence, I was astonished at the decline of interest and
participation in the "Faith of our Fathers". Even where it persisted, interest
in and reference to the vision of the Council seemed to have slipped off the
agenda. (Symbolic of the decline was a determined attempt to remove the
cross erected in the Phoenix Park for the papal visit. It was retained only
by an intervention at the highest political level!).

More competent scholars than I will be able to analyse and explain
this remarkable decline. Certainly the impact of the sexual abuse scandals
and the manner in which they were handled played an important role,
even though the agents of the abuse represented only a small minority of
the many very dedicated priests and religious who have had to bear the
brunt of the consequent opprobrium. Candidates for the priesthood and
religious life diminished greatly in number, as did traditional attendance at
mass and the sacraments. Open criticism of church authority and operation
became commonplace. More permissive attitudes to sexual and commercial morality were readily adopted. What became acceptable commercial
practice in the ostentatious era of the Celtic tiger differed considerably
from that previously espoused, or at least proclaimed, by the Knights of
Colombanus!

However, it seems to me that certainly much more than the impact
of the sex abuse scandals is involved in this dramatic change in traditional
Irish Catholic culture.

The nineteen sixties, which witnessed the notable renewal of Catholic
faith in Ireland in the context of the Council, was also a decade of remarkable change there in many other ways. The combined impact of these
changes produced what might be called the accelerated secularisation
of Irish culture. It might be said, perhaps with some exaggeration, that
in the thirty years after the sixties Ireland underwent a process of rapid
secularisation which in other countries evolved over a period of about
three hundred years.

In the decisive decade of the sixties the country experienced what, in Marxist terminology, would be described as a major transformation of its economic infrastructure and its attendant ideological cultural superstructure. This transformation was signalled by the transition from a primarily self-contained agricultural society to an open competitive industrial society – the transition associated with the inspiration of people such as Sean Lemass and T.K. Whitaker. A significant aspect of this transformation was an enthusiastic movement of internationalisation, a determination to be no longer merely the back garden of Britain but an equal member of the European Economic Community.

During the same decade the country experienced the transformation of its channels of communication. Television channels other than RTE, mainly British, became widely available and gave eagerly welcomed access to an international culture of youthful experimentation and innovation in music, fashion, cinema, art and behaviour.

These significant developments emerging together within the same decade as the Vatican Council achieved a powerful transformation of Irish culture and Catholicism, the effects of which are widely experienced today.

Irish Catholicism today finds itself in a seriously challenged situation. It has lost the unquestioned acceptance of ecclesiastical authority of pre-Council times. But it has also lost much of the enthusiastic commitment that accompanied the Council. The evidence of decline is obvious.

However, though perhaps less obvious, there are also indications of a new more personal and convinced Catholic commitment – modest indications of a "Second Spring" to borrow Newman's felicitous phrase. These are evidenced by individuals leading truly spiritual lives of unostentatious personal holiness and dedicated service of their neighbour. There are movements, new or renewed, of Catholic involvement in issues of equality and social justice, and of caring service of the poor and the underprivileged at home and abroad. These largely lay movements correspond in a new way to the renewal effected in previous troubled ages by the creation of great religious orders such as the Dominicans, the Franciscans, and the Jesuits. Although numerically diminished, there is also the striking witness of the steadfast commitment of dedicated clergy and religious, despite their unmerited experience of indifference, disregard and even contempt.

The enthusiastic and widespread regard and admiration in which the caring and compassionate Pope Francis is held is another indication of a Catholicism seeking to recover its inspiration and its way.

Undoubtedly it is more difficult and challenging to be a Catholic in Ireland today than it was in pre-Council times. However, it is also a more interesting, provocative, and possibly a more enriching challenge. It is a challenge which would certainly be much more difficult to face were it not for the rich resources of renewal provided fifty years ago by the Vatican Council. These resources are still available for reflective rediscovery and creative development to enable a meaningful Christian life in the complex world of our time.

DERMOT A. LANE

3   Keeping the Memory Alive: Vatican II as an Enduring Legacy for Reform of the Church

The fiftieth anniversary of the conclusion of the Second Vatican Council (1965) is a significant moment in the historical consciousness of the Catholic church. For some, however, it is still too soon to assess the meaning of the Council, given the observation attributed to Chairman Mao that it was too early to determine the significance of the French Revolution. However, there are many reasons why the church in Ireland should reflect carefully on this fiftieth anniversary and treat it as a *kairos*, a moment of potential revelation, a unique opportunity for renewal and reform.

In this paper I will look at reasons for keeping alive the memory of Vatican II and in that context focus on the *Pastoral Constitution on the church in the Modern World* known as *Gaudium et Spes* (hereafter as *GS*) as the final gift of the Council to the church. Note will be taken of the principles of solidarity, dialogue and mutuality in *GS*. I will outline lessons from *GS* for a church in transition, summarise some challenges facing the church in Ireland at this time, and conclude with a critique of *GS*.

Keeping Alive the Memory of Vatican II

It is important to keep alive the memory of the Second Vatican Council since it is a memory now active only among a minority of Catholics and largely unknown to the majority of Catholics. Further, it is a memory frequently forgotten by church leadership in times of crisis when it should be a resource for addressing the various controversies confronting the church.

When I refer to the Council I include what is often called "the conciliar process" of debate and discussion, of teaching and learning, over a period of four years, the sixteen documents of the Council, the reception of the Council and its documents. Most agree that the texts are an expression of the experience and yet acknowledge they do not always capture the fullness of the actual experience.

For older Catholics, the Council was a spring-time, bringing new energy, enthusiasm and hope for the future of the church and its reform, especially in areas like the decentralisation of the church through the application of collegiality, the quest for Christian unity, dialogue with the modern world, the role of the laity, the reform of the liturgy, and the promise of a new Pentecost. Some of these hopes have been realised but many have been frustrated because of a selective and clerically controlled implementation of the vision with little regard for the *sensus fidelium*.

For a younger generation of Catholics, the Council is simply an event in a misty past which seems to have divided people into a majority and minority, "progressives" and "conservatives", bringing polarisation rather than unity. Consequently, many of this generation, especially younger clergy, are not interested in Vatican II.

In keeping the memory of Vatican II alive, it will be necessary to recover the principles of reform enunciated by the Council not as an end in itself but as a point of departure for reform in the present. We must recognise, however, that the Council took place in a world very different to the present world. One therefore cannot simply apply the teachings of Vatican II to the problems of today without a process of analysis, interpretation and application.

The world today is a different world: radically secular, global, and plural, and this is the new context in which Christian identity must be worked out in twenty-first-century Ireland. Instead of reacting against secularisation, pluralism and globalisation, the church must recognise that this is the new context in which revelation takes place, in which grace is manifested, and in which the Spirit of God is active in the world and in the church.[1]

---

1   Some of these points have been made helpfully by Anthony Godzieba in "From the Editor", *Horizons*, Spring 2012: 6.

It is an open secret that there was and still is disagreement within the Catholic church concerning the historical and theological significance of the Council and its reception over the last fifty years. Within weeks of being elected Bishop of Rome, Pope Francis, in a homily, raised the question: "The Council was a beautiful work of the Holy Spirit, but after fifty years, have we done everything the Holy Spirit in the Council asked us to do?" To his own question, he answered: "No", and then talked about "resistance" to the Spirit in the context of the Council.[2] Cardinal Walter Kasper claims that: "Many of the impulses given by the Council have so far only been implemented half-heartedly".[3]

Historians of different ideological hues are all agreed that "something significant" happened at Vatican II. For example, James Hitchcock calls Vatican II "the most important event within the last four hundred years".[4] Emile Poulat holds that "the Catholic church changed more in the ten years after Vatican II than it did in the previous hundred years".[5] Giuseppe Alberigo's five-volume *History of Vatican II* and John O'Malley's history of *What Happened at Vatican II* (2008) also emphasise that something epochal happened. It is in spelling out this "something significant" that disagreement enters. There are indeed many contending narratives and suggestions of what actually happened at Vatican II. Specific suggestions include:

- a shift from the church as institution to the church as People of God (*LG*),
- a new emphasis on decentralisation and collegiality (*LG*),

---

2   "Pope Francis says Catholics still need to enact the teachings of Vatican II", *Catholic News Service*, 16th April 2013.

3   Walter Kasper, "Renewal from the Source: Interpretation and Reception of the Second Vatican Council" in *The Theology of Cardinal Walter Kasper: Speaking the Truth in Love*, ed. by Kristin M. Colberg and Robert A. Krieg (Collegeville, MN: Liturgical Press, 2014), 285.

4   James Hitchcock, *Catholicism and Modernity: Confrontation or Capitulation* (New York: Seabury, 1979), 75.

5   Emile Poulat, *Une Eglise ébranlée: Changement, Conflit et Continuité de Pie XII a Jean-Paul II* (Paris: Casterman, 1980), 41.

- a recognition that it is the whole assembly of the baptised that celebrates the Eucharist (*SC*),
- a new focus on mutual respect for other churches and religions (*UR* and *NA*),
- the establishment of the principle of religious freedom (*DH*),
- a new appreciation of the importance of history in understanding the Gospels and Christian truth (*DV* and *GS*),
- the adoption of an experiential, personalist, and dialogical theology of revelation (*DV*),
- a new-found emphasis on the role and co-responsibility of the laity (*AA*).

While these are particular expressions of what happened at the Council, something more foundational and more fundamental took place. There are competing narratives of what this "something more foundational and fundamental" is. A summary of some of these narratives will set the context for what is to follow in the remainder of this reflection on the enduring legacy of Vatican II for reform of the church.

In 1979 Karl Rahner offered what he called a fundamental theological interpretation of Vatican II. His thesis is that the Council was the Catholic church's first official self-realisation as a world-church. Up to Vatican II, the church acted like a European export firm, offering to the rest of the world "a commodity it did not want to change".[6] Rahner situates this process of the church becoming a world-church within what he calls "theologically speaking" the "three great epochs in church history": the short period of Jewish-Christianity in the first century, the second period being the Hellenistic and European culture up to the twentieth century, and the third period is what happened at Vatican II when the church became self-consciously connected to the whole world. For Rahner, we are experiencing today a break comparable to that which took place in the transition from Jewish-Christianity to Hellenistic-Christianity.

6   Karl Rahner, "Basic Theological Interpretation of the Second Vatican Council", *Theological Investigations*, vol. 20 (New York: Crossroad, 1981), 77–89.

A second account of what happened at Vatican II is given by Pope Benedict XVI early on in his papacy in an address to the Curia on 22nd December 2005. Benedict XVI proposed, not as one might have expected and as was all too frequently reported, a hermeneutic of continuity but rather a "Hermeneutic of Reform". He describes this "Hermeneutic of Reform" as "a combination of continuity and discontinuity at various levels". Further, this "Hermeneutic of Reform" involves both "novelty in continuity" as well as "fidelity and dynamism".[7]

A third account of the meaning of the Council can be found in John O'Malley's highly acclaimed work *What Happened at Vatican II* (2008). O'Malley argues that Vatican II brought about a dramatic shift in the literary style and tone of church teaching. For O'Malley, Vatican II was "a language event".[8] A linguistic shift took place and a new vocabulary entered the Catholic lexicon: brothers/sisters, friendship, co-operation, collaboration, partnership, freedom, dialogue, pilgrim, servant ("king"), development, evolution, charism, dignity, holiness, conscience, collegiality, people of God, priesthood of all believers.[9] This change of language was not just ornamental; it carried with it a shift in values requiring a change in behaviour.[10]

A fourth description of Vatican II is presented by Peter Hünermann.[11] For Hünermann, Vatican II brought about four major breaks with the

7   On the nuance of Benedict's address, see Joseph A. Komonchak, "Benedict XVII and the interpretation of Vatican II", *The Crisis of Authority in Catholic Modernity*, ed. M. Lacey and F. Oakley (New York: OUP, 2011), 93–110.

8   John W. O'Malley, *What Happened at Vatican II* (Cambridge: Harvard University Press, 2008): 306 and 12. In a lecture in Mater Dei Institute of Education in 2005 on "*Gaudium et Spes*: The Church in the Modern World", Diarmuid Martin, Archbishop of Dublin, noted the change of style, tone and language that occurred in *GS*. The lecture was published subsequently in *Vatican II Facing the 21st Century: Historical and Theological Perspectives*, Dermot A. Lane and Brendan Leahy, eds (Dublin: Veritas, 2006), 31–48, especially 31–32.

9   O'Malley, op. cit. 306.

10 Ibid., 12 and 305.

11 Editor of *The Compendium of Creeds, Definitions and Declarations on Matters of Faith and Morals*, Latin-English (San Francisco: Ignatius Press, 2012) (sometimes known as "the English Denzinger").

past: a break with 1,500 years of Christendom; a break with 1,000 years of division between eastern and western Christianity; a break with 500 years of separation between Catholics and Protestants; a break with 100 years of Catholic lingering on the threshold of the modern.[12]

It is the thesis of this paper that these competing narratives of what happened at Vatican II are best understood in terms of a gradual dawning during the Council of a new encounter between the church and the modern world, a slow and at times reluctant but nonetheless real embrace of the modern world. It is difficult to pinpoint this outreach towards the modern world at the Council because it was incremental, graduated, and processive. It was implied in John XXIII's emphasis on *aggiornamento* in his opening address to the assembled bishops in the autumn of 1962. It was also present through the application of the fruits of *ressourcement* via the *periti* among the bishops. It also came into play through the adoption of dialogue by Pope Paul VI as a guiding principle.

Gaudium et Spes as Last Will and Final Testament of the Council

Of all the documents of the Council, it is *GS* that explicitly seeks to articulate this new relationship with the modern world. It is worth noting that *GS* came a year after the *Dogmatic Constitution on the church* (*Lumen Gentium*, 1964) which was about the mission of the church *ad intra*, whereas *GS* is mainly about the mission of the church *ad extra*.

Prior to Vatican II it would have been unthinkable for the Catholic church to be reaching out to the world. After all, the modern world was

---

12   Peter Hünermann, "Kriterien für die Rezeption des II. Vatikanischen Konzils", *Theologische Quartalschrift, 191*, 2011: 126–147 as summarised by Ormond Rush in "Towards a Comprehensive Interpretation of the Council and its Documents", *Theological Studies*, 73, 2012: 547–569 at 563.

regarded by the church with deep suspicion and resentment; it was the modern world which had produced the Enlightenment, the French Revolution, and the primacy of natural science, all of which appeared to be unsympathetic to, and unsupportive of, the church. In contrast, the church now at Vatican II is reaching out to the world, and perceiving positive things about the modern world.

It is instructive to remember that *GS* was not on the agenda at the beginning of the Council, nor was it anticipated in the preparatory documents. The need for a document of this kind came early on from Cardinal Léon-Joseph Suenens in a speech on 4th December 1962: the schema *De ecclesia ad intra* should be complemented with a schema on *De ecclesia ad extra*. *GS* represents the mature thinking of the Council and carries within itself the accumulated learning that had taken place among the bishops over four years. For some, *GS* represents the last will and final testament of Vatican II; it was passed by 2,309 votes to 75.

There can be no doubt that the encounter between the Catholic church and the modern world is a theme present throughout the Council and is found in other documents. For example, the *Decree on Religious Freedom* recognises the primacy of freedom as a distinctive value, prized by the modern world, which is now incorporated into a church-document. Further, the *Declaration on the Relationship between the church and the Non-Christian Religions* emphasises the importance of respect, appreciation and mutual understanding among the religions of the world.

However, it is in *GS* that the church explicitly embraces the modern world. There are many specific expressions of this new encounter between the church and the world within *GS* such as: a turn to history (a. 4–5), the importance of anthropology (a. 12, 22, 27), engagement with atheism (a. 19–20), an emphasis on society and the common good (a. 25–26), a critique of individualism (a. 30), a recognition of the autonomy of human affairs (a. 36), the value of human activity (a. 38), the importance of a church learning from, as well as teaching to, the world (44), a debate about economic development (a. 64, 66 and 68), the importance of public life (a. 75), a focus on peace in the world (a. 77–78), a critique of war and the arms race (a. 80–82), the discussion of international affairs and aid (a. 84, 88–90). These are modern issues discussed by *GS* in modern categories.

It is often said that the most significant thing about *GS* is its title. It is about the church *in* the world, not over or above the world, as had been the case prior to the Council, but a church now planted *in* the world. And secondly, it is about the church in the *modern* world, not the medieval world, or the counter-Reformation world, but the distinctively *modern* world. And thirdly, *GS* is about the church in the modern world *today* and not some idealised past.

Underlying this encounter between the church and the modern world is the emergence of a new and intrinsic relationship between the church and the world. This new relationship between the church and the modern world is outlined in three foundational principles: solidarity, dialogue, and mutuality. I want to suggest that these are core principles of *GS*, are essential to expressing what really happened at Vatican II, and are central to church reform.

The principle of solidarity in GS

The principle of solidarity is strong in *GS*. According to David Hollenbach, this "theme of solidarity is a *leitmotif* throughout the entire Pastoral Constitution".[13] The opening paragraph of *GS* sets the tone for this principle of solidarity in the memorable words:

> The joys and hopes, the grief and anguish, of the people of our time, especially those who are poor or afflicted, are the joys and hopes, the grief and anguish of the followers of Christ.

This is already an expression of solidarity. The same paragraph goes on to say explicitly:

> the followers of Christ cherish a deep feeling of solidarity with the human race and its history.[14]

13   David Hollenbach, *The Common Good and Christian Ethics* (Cambridge: Cambridge University Press, 2002), 149.
14   *GS*, a. 1.

This powerful and evocative opening paragraph sets the tone and style of the rest of *GS*. Although the word "solidarity" is only used four times in the document (4, 32, 57 and 90), nonetheless the spirit of solidarity suffuses the whole document in anthropological and theological terms. One commentator sums up *GS* in the following way: "Solidarity emerges in the document as a fact, a norm, and an embodied vocation".[15] As a fact, solidarity is a statement about human interdependence, suggesting "we belong to each other and are called to live with and for each other". As a norm this requires waking up to the "we-ness" of life and therefore the need to embrace a social responsibility for each other that goes beyond a merely individualistic ethic.[16] As an embodied vocation, *GS* is understandably more aspirational than specific in promoting solidarity in the institutions and structures of church and society. As the Irish theologian Donal Dorr has argued, the realisation of equality and solidarity within *GS* requires some of the insights of Liberation Theology.[17]

In article 4, *GS* notes that at no other time in history has humanity enjoyed such wealth and resources, and yet in spite of this there are extraordinary high levels of hunger, need, illiteracy, slavery, and racial antagonisms. In the midst of these paradoxes "the world is keenly aware of its unity and mutual interdependence in essential solidarity".[18] There can be no way forward out of these contradictions without attention to the fundamental solidarity of the human species.

In another section, *GS* says that in spite of the excesses of the modern world, such as claims to self-sufficiency and the neglect of higher values, nonetheless the modern world does have "a sense of international solidarity", giving it a new awareness of its responsibility to help and defend

15 Christine F. Hinze, "Straining towards Solidarity in a Suffering World", *Vatican II: Forty Years Later*, edited by William Madges, CTS Annual volume 51 (New York: Orbis, 2006), 165–195 at 173.

16 Christine F. Hinze, *art.cit.*, 173–174.

17 Donal Dorr, *Option for the Poor: A Hundred Years of Vatican Social Teaching*, Revised Edition (New York: Orbis Books, 1992), 165–166.

18 *Gaudium et Spes*, a. 4.

humanity.[19] This awareness of the place of solidarity within this new relationship between the church and the world is not something incidental
in *GS*. Instead, this emphasis on solidarity of the church with the world
is grounded explicitly in anthropological and Christological perspectives.

In terms of anthropology, the opening chapter of *GS* points out that
"God did not create men and women as solitary beings". Rather, "from the
beginning God created them male and female and so by their innermost
nature, men and women are social beings; if they do not enter into relationships with each other, they can neither love nor develop their gifts".[20]
Continuing this theme, *GS* also notes that not only are individuals social
beings, but it is only in and through a process of "sincere self-giving" that
"they can fully discover themselves".[21] It is this underlying supposition of
a deeply relational anthropology that gives an edge and urgency to the
solidarity that exists within the human family and between the church
and the world.

In relation to Christology, this new ethic of solidarity is grounded in
the doctrines of the Incarnation and the Paschal Mystery. The solidarity
of the human race is derived from the solidarity of God with every human
being. Article 22 points out that: "by his Incarnation, he, the Son of God,
has in a certain way, united himself with every individual." In addition to
this "Incarnational solidarity", the same article also notes that since "Christ
died for all and since all are in fact called to one and the same destiny, we
must hold that the Holy Spirit offers to all the possibility of being made
partners ... in the Paschal Mystery". This focus on a "Paschal solidarity"
confirms the self-giving/kenotic anthropology of article 24 noted above.
In article 32, *GS* again links solidarity with the Incarnation of God in
Jesus, and also notes that the solidarity of humanity will find fulfilment
in eternity, thus indicating an eschatological dimension to the solidarity
that exists between the church and the world.[22]

19   *GS*, a. 57.
20   *GS*, a. 12.
21   *GS*, a. 24.
22   *GS*, a. 32.

Clearly this principle of solidarity is good starting point for the reform of the church in Ireland in the twenty-first century. If this solidarity of the church with the world is to be effective, there must therefore be dialogue, and that brings us to the second principle describing the relationship between the church and the modern world.

The principle of dialogue between the church and the world

The second principle emphasised by Vatican II describing the new relationship between the church and the modern world is dialogue. If there is one word that sums up the spirit and substance of the Council, it is that of dialogue.[23] The Council called for dialogue within the church,[24] for dialogue with other Christian churches,[25] for dialogue with other religions,[26] for dialogue with other cultures, for dialogue with atheists, and for dialogue with the enemies of the church.[27]

All of this begs questions like: where did this call for dialogue come from? What is the theological basis of dialogue? Why is dialogue suddenly so important in a church that had turned its back on dialogue with the modern world in the long nineteenth century?

These questions can only be answered by recalling some of the history of Vatican II. The Council was opened in October 1962 by John XXIII. In June 1963, John XXIII died and was succeeded by Pope Paul VI. The period between the opening of the Council in autumn 1962 and the upcoming Second Session in the autumn of 1963 was a time of uncertainty. Documents were unfinished, the future was unclear, and participants were polarised on many issues.

---

23   On the dialogical imperative of Vatican II for the church today see Dermot A. Lane *Stepping Stones to Other Religions: A Christian Theology of Interreligious Dialogue* (Dublin/New York, 2011/2012): 114–128.

24   *GS*, a. 92.

25   *UR*, a. 4, 9, 19, 21, 23.

26   *NA*, a. 2 and 3.

27   *GS*, a. 44.

This was the context in which Paul VI addressed the opening of the Second Session in 1963. The theme he chose to bring calm and cohesion, direction and vision, to the Council was dialogue, especially dialogue between the church and the modern world.[28] This speech opening the Second Session of the Council was subsequently developed into an encyclical letter entitled *On the church* known as *Ecclesiam Suam* (1964). This encyclical has been described as "a programmatic encyclical" having direct influence on *GS*.[29] Further, we know that Paul VI directed, at a meeting with Pierre Hauptman in the midst of much debate about *GS*, that the "inspiring principle (of *GS*) should be dialogue and the entire document ought to be a continuum of the dialogue with the world he had begun in his encyclical, *Ecclesiam Suam*" (hereafter *ES*).[30]

Dialogue, says Paul VI in this encyclical, has its origins "in the mind of God" who initiates a "dialogue of salvation" with humanity.[31] God has entered into dialogue with the world "through Christ in the Holy Spirit".[32] The form of God's dialogue with the world, through the Incarnation, should be the model of the church's dialogue with the world: "No ... pressure was brought to bear on anyone to accept the dialogue of salvation ... it was an appeal of love".[33] Further, for Paul VI, the development of this new relationship between the church and the world in terms of dialogue is demanded by the rise of modernity and the pluralist nature of contemporary society.[34] It is this vision of dialogue, a vision based ultimately on the way God acts in the world, that informs the Council and pervades *GS*.

28   See Paul VI "Pope Paul VI to the Council", *Doctrine and Life*, December 1963: 641–654.

29   Evangelista Villanova, "The Intersession (1963–1964)", *History of Vatican II: The Mature Council, The Second Period and the Intersession, September 1963–September 1964*, volume iii, ed. by G. Alberigo and J. Komonchak (Louvain: Peeters, 2000), 448 and 456.

30   See R. Burigana and G. Turbanti, "The Intersession, Preparing the Conclusion of the Council", *History of Vatican II*, volume iv (New York: Orbis, 2005), 527.

31   *ES*, a. 70.

32   *ES*, a. 71.

33   *ES*, a. 75.

34   *ES*, a. 78.

While the actual number of references to dialogue in *Gaudium et Spes* is small, the mood music of the document is one of dialogue and this can be found in the use of synonyms for dialogue such as "address", "conversation", "communication" as well as the emphasis on reading the signs of the times.[35]

In the preface to *Gaudium et Spes*, the Council says it wishes to enter into "conversation" with the family of humanity about the problems of the world, and to shed the light of the Gospel on these problems.[36] Chapter 4, on the "Role of the Church in the World", has a significant sub-heading entitled "Mutual Relation between Church and World" which is structured around the concept of dialogue. In article 40 of this sub-section it says that: "everything discussed up to now in relation to the dignity of the person, the importance of community, and the significance of human activity provides a basis for outlining the relationship between the church and the world and the dialogue between them".

Conscious that dialogue is a two-way process, *GS* also outlines what the church can offer the world and then goes on to indicate what the church receives from the modern world in and through dialogue.

In effect, sections 40–44 of *GS* represents a kind of blueprint for reform in the 1960s and are as pertinent today as they were some fifty years ago: emphasising the call to dialogue, recognising that the church can learn from the world on many different levels, and recommending the principle of adaptation in the presentation of the Gospel message. Here is a confident and pro-active church, reaching out to the world, listening to the world, learning from the world, ready to change, and calling on its pastors and theologians to listen discerningly to the voices of the age. This church of Vatican II stands out in deep contrast to the Catholic church of the late twentieth/early twenty-first century, a church that had become

35 See James McEvoy, "Church and World at the Second Vatican Council: The Significance of *Gaudium et Spes*", *Pacifica*, 19, February 2006: 37–57 at 47 and "Proclamation as Dialogue: Transition in the Church-world relationship", *Theological Studies*, 70, 2009: 875–903.

36 *GS*, a. 3.

defensive, turned in on itself, suspicious of the world, frequently negative in its assessment of the advances of the modern world and contemporary cultures.

Lest anyone should doubt this commitment to dialogue, *GS* concludes with a rousing call to dialogue in article 92, entitled "Dialogue". In that striking article, *Gaudium et Spes* says that this dialogue should take place first of all within the church itself in a way that fosters mutual esteem, reverence and harmony, while acknowledging the existence of legitimate diversity. It notes that "the ties which unite the faithful ... are stronger than those which separate them" and that the guiding principle should be: "let there be unity in what is necessary, freedom in what is doubtful, and charity in everything". This same article also calls for dialogue with other Christians, with other religions, with non-believers. Lastly, it calls for a dialogue that "excludes nobody", not even those who oppose the church and persecute it.

In brief, the call to dialogue is one of the great gifts and challenges coming from the Council to the church which is now more urgent than ever. Reform without dialogue would be a betrayal of the teaching of Vatican II. If the church in Ireland does not learn the art of dialogue and become an agent of dialogue, it runs the risk of ending up as a sect.

The principle of mutuality between the church and the world

The third principle capturing the new relationship between the church and the world is the principle of mutuality. This principle of mutuality is of course implied in the turn to dialogue at the Council. For dialogue to be authentic and to succeed there must be a process of reciprocity, best summed up in terms of the enriching experience of mutuality. The principle of mutuality adds a further dimension to dialogue, namely the importance of empathy within human exchanges.

The Council invokes the principle of mutuality in different documents. It is found in embryonic form in the *Decree on Ecumenism* which emphasises the importance of safeguarding "mutual relations" and "mutual love" in ecumenical discussions.[37] The *Declaration on the Relationship of the church to Non-Christian Religions* encourages "mutual understanding and appreciation" among Christians and Jews, and urges "mutual understanding" between Christians and Muslims.[38]

It is in *GS* that the implications of the principle of mutuality are spelled out. Chapter 4, entitled "Role of the Church in the World", contains as noted above a sub-section called "Mutual Relationship of Church and World". This sub-section outlines what the church offers to the individual: the dignity of the individual, the inner truth about the individual, and God as the destiny of every individual. It also outlines what the church offers to society: the mission of the church in the world, especially in relation to those in need, an understanding of the church as sacrament of communion with God and the unity of the human race, and a desire to foster truth, goodness and justice (a. 42). Thirdly, *GS* outlines what the church offers to human activity through its members: a way of overcoming the dichotomy between Christian faith and daily activity, the unity between faith and professional life, the animation of the world with the spirit of Christianity, and the importance of dialogue with the world (a. 43).

It then goes on in a new section, "What the Church Receives from the Modern World", to outline what the world has offered to the church: the "experience of past ages ... the progress of the sciences, and ... the riches hidden in various cultures, through which greater light is thrown on human nature and new avenues to truth are opened up" (a. 44). It also notes that "the evolution of social life" as well "developments in family, culture, economic and social life" and "national and international politics" can also contribute to the community of the church. In addition to all of this it says: "The church recognises that it has benefitted, and is still benefitting from the opposition of its enemies and persecutors" (a. 44). A little later on in *GS*, the Council speaks about a relationship of mutual enrichment taking place between the church and different cultures (a. 58).

37   *UR.*, a. 4 and a. 5 respectively.
38   *NA.*, a. 4 and a. 3 respectively.

In these few articles in *GS* (a. 40–44) there is recognition of an underlying relationship of mutuality between the church and the world. There is also an understanding of church as a teaching and a learning community. While these references to the importance of mutuality in the church's relationship with others are scattered, they should not be regarded as casual and haphazard. Instead, these references to mutuality mirror the twin influence of *ressourcement* and *aggiornamento* at the Council which came to be seen as complementary.

Furthermore, this new principle of mutuality presupposes an appreciation of the underlying unity of Nature and Grace, one of the fruits of *la nouvelle théologie*, which permeate the proceedings of the Council, especially in *Gaudium et Spes*. In addition, the principle of mutuality is founded on the doctrine of the Incarnation which, according to *GS*, recognises that "the Son of God has, in a certain way, united himself with each individual".[39] Moreover, the principle of mutuality is also inspired by the Council's awareness of the action of the Spirit of God in other churches, in other religions, and in other cultures.[40]

This theme of mutuality is, as the Canadian theologian John Dadosky points out, "something historically unprecedented in the church's self-understanding" and as such is "unique to Vatican II" and represents "a permanent achievement of Vatican II";[41] it is also the basis for a new "reinterpretation" of Vatican II and a new self-understanding of church.[42] Mutuality is central to the reform of the church in Ireland because it recognises that every human being has something to offer to the life of the church and requires empathy on all sides.

39   *GS*, a. 22.
40   *AG*, a. 4; *GS*, a. 24 and a. 41.
41   John D. Dadosky, "Is there a Fourth Stage of Meaning?", *Heythrop Journal*, 2010: 768–780 at 775 and 777.
42   See John D. Dadosky who carefully explores the ecclesiological implications of this principle of mutuality in "Towards a Fundamental Theological *Re*-Interpretation of Vatican II", *Heythrop Journal*, XLIX, 2008: 742–763 and "Has Vatican II been *Hermeneutered*? Recovering and Developing its theological Achievements following Rahner and Lonergan", *Irish Theological Quarterly*, 2014, no. 4: 327–349.

Lessons from *Gaudium et Spes* for a Church in Transition

Looking back at *GS*, it is clear it opened new ground: it brought the Catholic church into the twentieth century, it engaged critically with the modern world, it marked a decisive end to a lingering Christendom-self-understanding of the church, and it began to take history seriously. In doing this, the church at Vatican II was embracing the values of democracy, the importance of human rights, and the place of equality within society, values that up to then had been largely resisted by the church in previous centuries.

GS represents what was best about the conciliar process: debate and discussion, teaching and learning, consensus and adaptation. It read the signs of the times, it listened to the world and learned from it (a. 44), it heard the Word of God speaking in the twentieth century, it responded to the impulses of the Spirit *ad intra* and *ad extra*. In doing this, the church embarked on a new methodology, an inductive methodology committed to critical engagement with the world in the service of the Reign of God.

The neglected principles of solidarity, dialogue and mutuality must now be urgently recovered in the life of the Catholic church in Ireland. By failing to practice these principles, the church has lost contact with the people and has ended up all too frequently talking to itself. The mission of the church *ad intra* has suffered by the absence of a mission *ad extra* and vice versa. The church must now, as Francis has repeated, move out from its self-centred interests to the peripheries and listen to the *sensus fidelium*.

These principles of solidarity, dialogue and mutuality require a church that not only teaches but also learns, a church that not only offers something to the world, but also receives from the world, a church that not only announces a message but also listens to the insights of the world at the same time. As we now know only too well from the most elementary philosophy of education, there can be no teaching without learning. When learning ceases, teaching loses its edge and becomes wooden.

One painful example of the value of this dynamic between teaching and learning is the current crisis in the church around the sexual abuse of children. It was only when the church began to listen to, and learn from, the world that progress began to take place. It is unlikely that the church would have come to grips with this crisis if it had relied solely on its own teaching and canonical procedures. It was only when the church was reminded about the criminality of paedophilia by the secular world, and when it learned about the pathology of paedophilia from psychology and psychiatry, that it began to put in place proper procedures for the protection of children.

This model of teaching and learning is found also in other documents of the Council. For example, in *Lumen Gentium* the recognition of the church as a pilgrim people assumes a process of offering to the world and also receiving something from world during the journey of faith. More explicitly, the theology of Revelation in *Dei Verbum* acknowledges a process of learning and listening in relation to the Revelation of God in Christ. *Dei Verbum* talks about "making progress", about "growth in insight", about the possibility "of advancing towards the plenitude of truth", and about leading people to the full truth (a. 8). In making these points, article 8 appeals to the role of human experience and the guidance of the Holy Spirit. However, this personalist theology of Revelation in *Dei Verbum* was all too quickly forgotten after the Council by a return to a largely propositional view of Revelation which emphasises adherence to doctrinal formulae and cat-echetical texts, at the expense of the primacy of a personal encounter with God in Christ through the action of the Spirit. Without a personal experi-ence of God, statements of faith go over the minds and hearts of people.

In looking back at the unified vision of *Gaudium et Spes*, it is startling to discover that a new series of theological disjunctions have been allowed to develop in recent times. These include disjunctions:

- between a pessimistic neo-Augustinian theology and a more holistic Thomistic theology;
- between a *Communio* ecclesiology and a *Missio* ecclesiology;
- between continuity and discontinuity in the interpretation of Vatican II;
- between *aggiornamento* and *ressourcement*;
- between the spirit of the Council and the letter of the Council;
- between the people of God and the institutional church;
- between the papacy and collegiality;
- between spiritual renewal and structural reform.

These disjunctions are contrary to the vision of the Council and especially the teaching of *GS*. Such dualisms must be transformed into a higher synthesis in the service of the pilgrim people of God under the guidance of the Holy Spirit as active within the *sensus fidelium* and the teaching church.

It is equally disturbing to note the presence of new pastoral polarisations emerging in the life of the Catholic church in Ireland that need healing and transformation. These include:

- the alienation of committed Catholic women from the institutional church (e.g. the reaction of women to the introduction of the male-only deaconate in Killaloe diocese in 2014);
- the gap between the *sensus fidelium* and the teaching of the church (e.g. as became evident at the 2014 Synod);
- declining trust between bishops and priests (e.g. the uneasy relationship between the Association of Catholic Priests and many bishops with some striking exceptions);
- the strained relationship at times between religious and the hierarchy;
- the neglect of the divorced and remarried in the pastoral outreach of the church;
- the estrangement of lesbian, gay, bisexual, and transgendered persons from the pastoral and sacramental life of the church.

If these disjunctions and polarisations are to be resolved, then the theology of solidarity, dialogue and mutuality must be invoked as first principles of reform.

New Challenges Facing the Church in the Twenty-First Century

It would be naïve to suppose or suggest that *GS* has answers to the new questions that the church faces in the twenty-first century. To be sure, *GS* has an energising Spirit-led vision and principles. That vision and the principles of solidarity, dialogue, and mutuality must become embedded in the structures, institutions, and personnel serving the life of the church. A new stage, a new moment, is required in the Irish church for the pastoral reception and implementation of the Second Vatican Council. What the next stage might look like can only be sketched here, confining ourselves to what seems most urgent at this time in the life of the church in Ireland.

The first challenge facing the church in the twenty-first century is to draw up and put in place new structures for consultation among the whole people of God: bishops, people, pastors, theologians and the magisterium. At present, there are no formal structures for listening to what the Spirit might be saying to the church at this time. In June 2014, the International Theological Commission published an important document on the "*Sensus Fidei* in the Life of the Church". This document describes the *sensus fidei* as a "spiritual instinct that enables believers to judge whether a teaching or practice is not in conformity with the Gospel and the apostolic faith.[43] The document suggests that: "those who teach in the name of the church should give full attention to the experience of believers, especially lay people".[44] Pope Francis tried with varying success to consult the people of God on marriage and the family in preparation for the Extraordinary Synod in October 2014. Another consultation for the 2015 Synod is underway. At present, such consultations are sporadic, inadequate and unaccountable. New mechanisms for listening, for receiving, and for reporting on the *sensus fidelium* are necessary, as well as for hearing back.

A second challenge for the church in the twenty-first century is to draw up guidelines for the conduct of dialogue within the church and between the church and the world. Without robust guidelines, the call for dialogue will remain at the level of empty rhetoric. The church has issued a variety of documents on the importance of dialogue: *On Dialogue* by Paul VI (1964), *Mission and Dialogue* (1984), *Dialogue and Proclamation* (1991), *Educating to Intercultural Dialogue in Catholic schools: Living in*

---

43   See *Sensus Fidei* in the Life of the Church, 2014, a. 49, available at <http://www. vatican.va/roman_curia/.../rc_cti_20140610_sensus-fidei_en.html>.
44   Ibid., a. 59.

Harmony for a Civilisation of Love (2013), *Dialogue in Truth and Charity: Pastoral Orientations for Interreligious Dialogue* (2014). These documents need to be translated into concrete proposals and user-friendly frameworks for use in local churches.

A key principle to guide dialogue in the church and between the church and the world is to recognise that pluralism is an intrinsic part of church history and, as such, can often be a source of enrichment rather than a problem to be solved. Diversity, plurality, and historicity are a necessary part of faith and belief. In an address to the International Theological Commission in December 2014, Pope Francis pointed out that: "Diversity of viewpoints should enrich Catholicity without damaging unity". He spoke of "a healthy pluralism" and suggested that various theological methods "cannot ignore each other, but in theological dialogue should enrich and correct each other".[45]

A further point to guide dialogue is the need to recognise that there are different kinds of differences. Some differences are complementary; others are conflictual; while others are genetic or historical in origin.[46]

By far the most important and urgent third challenge facing the church in the twenty-first century is to provide principles for discerning the action of the Spirit *ad intra* in the life of the church and *ad extra* in other religions and the secular world. One of the great failures in the reception of Vatican II has been the neglect of taking seriously the stirrings of the Spirit within the church and within the world.

In the early church, the Christians were advised: "Do not quench the Spirit" while at the same time encouraged to "test everything" (1 Thess. 5: 19–21). At the end of the first century a key question for the early church was: what is the Spirit saying to the churches? (Revelation 2: 2, 7, 11, 29; 3: 6, 13).

---

45   Udienza ai Membri della Commissione Teologica Internazionale, 05.12.2014/BO922. See account by Joshua J. McElwee in *National Catholic Reporter*, 5th December 2014.
46   For development of this point drawing on the work of Bernard Lonergan, see John Dadosky in footnote 41.

As noted, there was an awakening to the presence and creativity of the Spirit at the Council. This beginning of a new Pentecost was all too quickly forgotten after the Council. For example, this neglect of the Spirit is reflected in the fact that the new code of Canon Law, published in 1983, does not even mention the Spirit in the area of governance.[47] As a result, there are no principles for discerning the action and presence of the Spirit in the life of the church and the world. This neglect is acknowledged at the 1985 Extraordinary Synod of Bishops in Rome celebrating the twentieth anniversary of Vatican II: "From time to time there has also been a lack of discernment of spirits, with the failure to correctly distinguish between a legitimate openness of the Council to the world and the acceptance of a secularised world's mentality and order of values".[48] This lack of discernment of the Spirit continues right up to the present day, thirty years later. Without a prayerful discernment of the Spirit, there will be no active inner life in the church, and the external structure will remain in a lifeless standstill position.

This discernment of the Spirit will require the drawing up of clear criteria, even though there is never anything clear about the action of the Spirit. These criteria will include attention to the biblical narrative surrounding the activity of the Spirit in the Hebrew and Christian scriptures. In addition, there will be a cluster of theological criteria such as those promoting worship of the one God (Rom. 8: 14–17), bringing about a recognition of Jesus as Lord and from God (1 Cor. 12: 3 and 1 Jn. 4: 1–3), and building up the well-being of the Body of Christ (1 Cor. 12: 7–11 and Ep. 4: 4–13). A third set of criteria would embrace a recognition of the Spirit as a source of creativity in the world, bringing order out of chaos, especially in the arts

---

47   On this extraordinary neglect see Walter Kasper, "The church's Communion: Reflections on the Guiding Ecclesiological Idea of the Second Vatican Council", *Theology and Church* (New York: Crossroad, 1989), 148–165 at 153; James Coriden, "The Holy Spirit and Church Governance", *Jurist*, 66, 2006: 339–373; Ormond Rush, "Ecclesial Conversion after Vatican II: Renewing 'the Face of the Church' to Reflect 'the genuine Face of God'", *Theological Studies*, 74, 2013: 785–803 at 800–801.

48   *The Final Report*, 1985: I, 4.

and the dazzling discoveries of modern science, in a way that serves what is best in human flourishing and the healing of a planet in peril.

A fourth challenge facing the Catholic church in Ireland at this time is the following: can the church enter into a relationship of genuine solidarity, dialogue and mutuality in terms of learning what the world has to offer as proposed by *GS*? Can the church become again a learning church as it was at Vatican II? The most obvious areas where learning from the world needs to take place include gender studies, bio-medical sciences, and environmental issues. This process of learning happened not only at Vatican II with outstanding results, but also during the patristic and mediaeval periods with equally outstanding results. Can it happen again?

Acknowledging the Limits of *Gaudium et Spes*

A final point about *GS* is as follows: Lest anyone think that we are being naïve and overly optimistic about this document, let me conclude briefly by offering some criticisms. *Gaudium et Spes* at times adopts an overly optimistic view of the world and the course of history, running the risk of confusing the modern myth of progress with the content of Christian hope. Whatever hope may mean, it includes a fundamental refusal by the human spirit to succumb to closed systems of thought, whether these exist in the world, in history, or in theology.

A second criticism of *GS* is that it pays far too little attention to the presence of evil, suffering, and human tragedy in the world. *Gaudium et Spes* needs a theology of the cross to balance its one-sided emphasis on Incarnation.

A third criticism concerns the appeal to the Spirit that is present, not only in *GS*, but also in many other documents. One of the strengths of the Council was the turn to the Spirit and we do well to remember that John XXIII expressed the desire for a new Pentecost in the church. This new emphasis on the Spirit is of course to be welcomed as a counterbalance to an existing Christo-monism, but these appeals to the Spirit in the Council documents are often too vague, too elusive and too subjective to carry weight. Such appeals will succeed only if they are accompanied by an understanding of the Spirit that is philosophically more robust and theologically more grounded in the action of the Spirit in the Bible, in the Christian community, and in history.

A fourth criticism centres on the notion of the "world" in GS. Clearly, there is much about the world that is incompatible with the church. This incompatibility is found in St Paul and John's Gospel, both of whom talk about the evil and darkness of the "world".

Many of these criticisms of GS were voiced by Karl Rahner and Joseph Ratzinger during the Council. For Rahner, GS was "too euphoric in its evaluation of humanity"; it needed a theology of sin; it lacked what he called "a Christian pessimism" (meaning realism) about human existence.[49]

In a similar though somewhat different vein, Ratzinger claimed that GS was insufficiently rooted in biblical theology, tended to collapse the coming of the Reign of God into contemporary human progress, and needed to begin with Christology rather than anthropology. These reservations of Ratzinger continued to be voiced throughout his life.[50]

In conclusion, Vatican II offers a vision for the reform of the church in Ireland and GS in particular provides pastoral and theological principles for moving forward in hope. The reform of the church, initiated at the Council, must now be allowed to continue and should be guided by principles of solidarity, dialogue and mutuality; it should be attentive to the impulses from the Holy Spirit in the church and in the world; and be informed by an ongoing return to and retrieval of the Word of God for the twenty-first century. The energy, enthusiasm, and hopefulness of the Council must be communicated to the people of God if this much-needed renewal and reform is to take place.

49   Karl Rahner, "Christian Pessimism", *Theological Investigations*, Volume XXII (London: DLT, 1991), 155–162 at 157–158.
50   A more detailed and enlightening account of these reservations by Rahner and Ratzinger can be found in Brandon Peterson, "Critical Voices: The Reactions of Rahner and Ratzinger to 'Schema XIII' (*Gaudium et Spes*)", *Modern Theology*, January 2015: 1–26.

The Council does not give us a blueprint, nor does it give us answers for tomorrow. The problems of today are different. They revolve around the role of women in the church, the place of religion in the public square, the credibility of theological discourse in a radically secular world and a disenchanted universe, and the ongoing scandal of Christian disunity after fifty years of ecumenical dialogues. In all of this, Rahner was surely right in reminding us that Vatican II is only "the beginning of the beginning".

PART II

Ressourcement at the Council

GABRIEL FLYNN

4 *Ressourcement* and Vatican II: Reform and Renewal[1]

Introduction

The renowned generation of French *ressourcement* theologians, whose influence pervaded French theology and society in the period 1930 to 1960, and beyond, inspired a renaissance in twentieth-century Catholic theology and initiated a movement for renewal that made a decisive contribution to the reforms of the Second Vatican Council (1962–1965).[2] The foremost exponents of *ressourcement* were principally, though not exclusively, leading

1   This chapter is a revised and extended version of my "Introduction: The Twentieth-Century Renaissance in Catholic Theology" in Gabriel Flynn and Paul D. Murray, eds, *Ressourcement: A Movement for Renewal in Twentieth-Century Catholic Theology*, paperback edition (Oxford: Oxford University Press, 2014), 1–22. I express my appreciation to OUP for permission to use the original material and to Gary Carville for his contribution to the section on *ressourcement* in Ireland; I also thank Robert Bonfils, SJ, Director of the French Province Jesuit Archives, Vanves, Paris, and Marie-Gabrielle Lemaire, Archivist, de Lubac Archives, the University of Namur, Belgium, as well as the Jesuit community there for their generous assistance and gracious hospitality.
2   See Rosino Gibellini, *Panorama de la théologie au XXe siècle*, trans. Jacques Mignon, new edn. (Paris: Cerf, 2004), 173–289; Bernard Sesboüé, *La théologie au XXe siècle et l'avenir de la foi. Entretiens avec Marc Leboucher* (Paris: Desclée de Brouwer, 2007), 11–51; Étienne Fouilloux, "'Nouvelle théologie' et théologie nouvelle (1930–1960)" in Benoît Pellistrandi, ed., *L'histoire religieuse en France et Espagne*, Collection de la Casa Velázquez, 87 (Madrid: Casa de Velázquez, 2004), 411–425; Fouilloux, *Une Église en quête de liberté. La pensée catholique française entre modernisme et Vatican II (1914–1962)*, Anthropologiques (Paris: Declée de Brouwer, 1998); Étienne Fouilloux and Bernard Hours, eds, *Les jésuites à Lyon XVIe–XXe siècle* (Lyon: ENS Editions, 2005);

French Dominicans and Jesuits of the faculties of Le Saulchoir (Paris) and Lyon-Fourvière, respectively. They included the Dominicans Marie-Dominique Chenu (1895–1990), Yves Congar (1904–1995), Dominique Dubarle (1907–1987), and Henri-Marie Féret (1904–1992), and the Jesuits Jean Daniélou (1905–1974), Henri de Lubac (1896–1991), Henri Bouillard (1908–1981), and Hans Urs von Balthasar (1905–1988) who, under the influence of Adrienne von Speyr (1902–1967), left the Society of Jesus in 1950 in order to found a "secular institute" for lay people.[3] The movement

---

     John R.T. Lamont, "Conscience, Freedom, Rights: Idols of the Enlightenment Religion", *The Thomist* 73 (2009), 169–239 (169, 235–239).

3   Among the main texts on the *ressourcement* thinkers are the following: Claude Geffré et al., *L'hommage différé au Père Chenu* (Paris: Cerf, 1990); Jacques Duquesne ed., *Jacques Duquesne interroge le Père Chenu. "Un théologien en liberté"* (Paris: Centurion, 1975); Joseph Famerée and Gilles Routhier, *Yves Congar* (Paris: Cerf, 2008); Gabriel Flynn, *Yves Congar's Vision of the church in a World of Unbelief* (Aldershot/Burlington VT: Ashgate, 2004); Flynn, ed., *Yves Congar: Theologian of the church* (Louvain/Grand Rapids MI: Peeters/Eerdmans, 2005); Brother Emile of Taizé, *Faithful to the Future: Listening to Yves Congar* (New York: Bloomsbury Academic, 2013); Elizabeth Teresa Groppe, *Yves Congar's Theology of the Holy Spirit* (Oxford: Oxford University Press, 2004); Jean-Pierre Jossua, *Le Père Congar. La théologie au service du peuple de Dieu*, Chrétiens De Tous Les Temps, 20 (Paris: Cerf, 1967); Jacques Courcier, "Dominique Dubarle et la Géométrie Projective", *Revue des Sciences philosophiques et théologiques* 92 (2008), 623–636; Jacques Fontaine ed., *Actualité de Jean Daniélou* (Paris: Cerf, 2006); Jean Daniélou, *Carnets spirituels*, ed. Marie-Joseph Rondeau (Paris: Cerf, 2007); Hans Urs von Balthasar, *The Theology of Henri de Lubac: An Overview*, trans. Joseph Fessio, SJ, and Michael M. Waldstein (San Francisco: Ignatius Press, 1991); Jean-Pierre Wagner, *Henri de Lubac*, Initiations aux théologiens (Paris: Cerf, 2007); Wagner, *La théologie fondamentale selon Henri de Lubac*, Cogitatio Fidei, 199 (Paris: Cerf, 1997); Paul McPartlan, *The Eucharist Makes the church: Henri de Lubac and John Zizioulas in Dialogue* (Edinburgh: T&T Clark, 1993); Michel Castro, "Henri Bouillard (1908–1981): éléments de biographie intellectuelle", *Mélanges de science religieuse* 60 (2003), 43–58; *Recherches de Science Religieuse* 97/2 (2009); John O'Donnell, SJ, *Hans Urs Von Balthasar* (London: T&T Clark, 1991); Kevin Mongrain, *The Systematic Thought of Hans Urs Von Balthasar: An Irenaean Retrieval* (New York: Crossroad, 2002); Edward T. Oakes and David Moss, eds, *The Cambridge Companion to Hans Urs von Balthasar* (Cambridge: Cambridge University Press, 2004); Oakes, *Pattern of Redemption: The Theology of Hans Urs von Balthasar* (New York: Continuum, 1994).

also encompassed Belgium and Germany.[4] De Lubac's description of the methodology of *ressourcement* is apposite:

> Without claiming to open up new avenues of thought, I have sought rather, without any antiquarianism, to make known some of the great common areas of Catholic tradition. I wanted to make it loved, to show its ever-present fruitfulness. [...] So I have never been tempted by any kind of "return to the sources" that would scorn later developments and represent the history of Christian thought as a stream of decadences.[5]

Among the great precursors of *ressourcement*, Maurice Blondel (1861–1949), the acclaimed "philosopher of action", is pre-eminent. Reference must also be made to Joseph Maréchal (1878–1944), Pierre Rousselot (1878–1915), and Étienne Gilson (1884–1978).[6] Blondel's doctoral thesis published in Paris in 1893 as *L'Action. Essai d'une critique de la vie et d'une science de la pratique* was read by the leading figures of the *ressourcement* generation. As de Lubac remarks: "During my years of philosophy (1920–1923) on Jersey, I had read with enthusiasm Maurice Blondel's *Action*, *Lettre* (on apologetics) and various other studies."[7] Congar also came under the spell of Blondel through his mentors Chenu and Ambroise Gardeil (1859–1931). Although Congar began his study of Blondel relatively late, he admits that the more he read, the more he appreciated his thought.[8] Blondel's philosophy provided

4   See Jürgen Mettepenningen, *Nouvelle Théologie – New Theology: Inheritor of Modernism, Precursor of Vatican II* (London: Continuum, 2010).

5   De Lubac, *At the Service of the Church: Henri de Lubac Reflects on the Circumstances that Occasioned His Writings*, trans. Anne Elizabeth Englund (San Francisco: Ignatius Press, 1993, 143–144; ET of *Mémoire sur l'occasion de mes écrits*, ed., Georges Chantraine, *Œuvres complètes, xxxiii, Paris: Cerf, 2006), 147.

6   See Michael A. Conway, "Maurice Blondel and *Ressourcement*" in Gabriel Flynn and Paul D. Murray, eds, *Ressourcement: A Movement for Renewal in Twentieth-Century Catholic Theology*, 65–82; and in the same volume, Francesca Aran Murphy, "Gilson and the *Ressourcement*", 51–64.

7   De Lubac, *At the Service of the Church*, 18–19; ET of *Mémoire*, 15.

8   Jean Puyo, ed., *Jean Puyo interroge le Père Congar. "une vie pour la vérité"*, Les Interviews (Paris: Centurion, 1975), 72.

the basis for the dialectic of structure and life, a fundamental feature of Congar's ecclesiology.

This chapter is divided into four parts. Firstly, it examines the origins of the *ressourcement* movement, while also assessing its contribution to theological renewal and ecclesial reform in the twentieth century.[9] Second, it analyses the complex question of terminology, the interpretation of which continues to cause controversy in the analysis of *ressourcement* and *nouvelle théologie*. Third, it assesses how the leading *ressourcement* intellectuals contributed to Vatican II. Fourth, it studies the role of the most prominent French *ressourcement* theologians in the struggle against National Socialism, thus pointing to the practical dimension of *ressourcement*. It concludes by pointing to the enduring relevance of *ressourcement* for the Christian churches and modern society.

Ressourcement: A Movement for Renewal in Twentieth-Century Catholic Theology

A host of new initiatives emerged in the French church during and after the Second World War (1939–1945). This included the movement for the reform of the liturgy, *Centre de Pastorale Liturgique*, the return to the biblical and patristic sources, exemplified especially in the foundation of the *Sources chrétiennes* series, the renewal of ecclesiology, demonstrated by the establishment of the *Unam Sanctam* series, and the realisation of the church's missionary task.[10] It should be noted that *nouvelle théologie*

9   See Étienne Fouilloux, "Dialogue théologique? (1946–1948)" in Serge-Thomas Bonino ed., *Saint Thomas au XXe siècle. Actes du colloque du Centenaire de la Revue Thomiste* (Paris: Centre National de Livre-Saint Paul, 1994), 153–195.

10   As Congar remarks: "Anyone who did not live through the years 1946 and 1947 in the history of French Catholicism has missed one of the finest moments in the life of the church. In the course of a slow emergence from privation and with the wide liberty of a fidelity as profound as life, men sought to regain evangelical contact

is a complex historical movement that emerged from the wider political, cultural, and intellectual milieux of twentieth-century France. A related question concerns that movement's connection with Modernism.[11]

The *ressourcement* passed through various stages of development.[12] The biblical renewal, which began in Germany in the course of the inter-war period, spread progressively to the rest of the Catholic world and even to what may be considered the less progressive countries. The liturgical renewal is older than the biblical renewal. Although known in France from before the First World War (1914–1918), its first intense period of activity was linked with the name of Dom Lambert Beauduin (1873–1960), the Belgian liturgist and founder of Chevetogne, who was condemned by a Roman tribunal in 1930 following the publication of his view that the Anglican church should be "united to Rome, not absorbed" ("unie non absorbée"). But it was in Germany during the inter-war period that the liturgical renewal blossomed when the church was forced, especially during the Nazi era, to renounce social action and to focus instead on the lively celebration of the divine mysteries. The liturgical renewal, which was not limited to Germany and France, could count on the active goodwill of the Holy See.

with a world in which we had become involved to an extent unequalled in centuries." (See Yves M.-J. Congar, *Dialogue between Christians: Catholic Contributions to Ecumenism*, trans. Philip Loretz [London: Geoffrey Chapman, 1966], 32; ET of *Chrétiens en dialogue. Contributions catholiques à l'oecuménisme*, Unam Sanctam, 50 [Paris: Cerf, 1964], xliii). De Lubac also refers to the spirit of hope, creativity, and originality that pervaded this period in the history of the French church, with *Chantiers de Jeunesse*, the *Cahiers du Témoignage chrétien*, producing a rich harvest. As he comments: "Both in 1940–1942 and under the total occupation in 1942–1944, Lyons was quite different. Just as earlier, in the sixteenth century, it had been the 'intellectual capital' of France, it became in 1940, the 'capital of the Resistance.'" (See de Lubac, *At the Service of the Church*, 45, 48; ET of *Mémoire*, 44–45, 47).

11 See Gerard Loughlin, "*Nouvelle Théologie*: A Return to Modernism?" in Flynn and Murray, eds, *Ressourcement: A Movement for Renewal in Twentieth-Century Catholic Theology*, 36–50.

12 See Congar, "Tendances actuelles de la pensée religieuse", *Cahiers du monde nouveau* 4 (1948), 33–50; Daniélou, "Les orientations présentes de la pensée religieuse", *Études* 249 (1946), 5–21; Roger Aubert, *La Théologie Catholique au milieu du XXe siècle* (Tournai: Casterman, 1954).

The biblical renewal and the liturgical movement were completed by a
patristic rejuvenation.[13] The movement towards fuller contact with patristic
thought is perhaps the most interesting and challenging of the various currents of renewal in theology in the early part of the twentieth century, as
it provides an authentic witness to the faith in a way that is sensitive to the
ever-changing needs of humanity. There were new missionary strategies in
France, including the Young Christian Worker/Young Christian Student
movements, which developed during the inter-war period, and, during
World War II, Godin and Daniel's *La France: Pays de mission*?

In September 1946, Pope Pius XII expressed his concerns regarding the
nouvelle théologie to representatives of both the Dominicans and the Jesuits,
warning against an attack on the fundamental tenets of Roman Catholic
doctrine. Then in late November 1946, an unknown group of Jesuits published an anonymous and impassioned defence of *Sources chrétiennes* in the
Jesuit periodical *Recherches de Science Religieuse*, thereby making a difficult
situation worse.[14] In an atmosphere of suspicion and controversy, *Humani
Generis* was published on 12 August 1950.[15] As the clouds began to gather
over the church in France in the wake of the controversial encyclical, it is
hardly surprising that both Congar and de Lubac, astute political analysts,
rejected the term *nouvelle théologie*. In 1950, Congar compared *nouvelle
théologie* to the "tarasque", a legendary monster of Provence.[16] De Lubac
expressed his view vehemently: "I do not much like it when people talk of
'new theology', referring to me; I have never used the expression, and I detest

13   See Louis Bouyer, "Le Renouveau des études patristiques", *La Vie intellectuelle* 15
      (1947), 6–25; Bouyer, *Life and Liturgy*, 3rd edn. (London: Sheed & Ward, 1965).
14   "La Théologie et ses sources: résponse aux Études critiques de la Revue thomiste
      (mai–août) 1946", *Recherches de Science Religieuse* 33 (1946), 385–401.
15   Pius XII, *Humani Generis*. Encyclical Letter concerning some False Opinions
      Threatening to Undermine the Foundations of Catholic Doctrine, *Acta Apostolici
      Sedis* 42 (1950), 561–578; ET, *False Trends In Modern Teaching: Encyclical Letter
      (Humani Generis)*, trans. Ronald A. Knox, rev. edn. (London: Catholic Truth Society,
      1959). See Robert Guelluy, "Les Antécédents de l'encyclique 'Humani Generis' dans
      les sanctions Romaines de 1942: Chenu, Charlier, Draguet", *Revue d'histoire ecclési-
      astique* 81 (1986), 421–497.
16   Puyo ed., *Jean Puyo interroge le Père Congar*, 99.

the thing. I have always sought, on the contrary, to make the Tradition of the church known … 'New theology' is a polemical term … which most of the time signifies nothing."[17] De Lubac's *confrère* Henri Bouillard argued in 1947 along similar lines that "the creation of a *théologie nouvelle* was not something to which he pretended", a conviction he was to repeat forcefully some three years later.[18]

Although no names had been mentioned in *Humani Generis*, the Jesuit and Dominican superiors felt compelled to act. Congar read *Humani Generis* very attentively, having been advised by Emmanuel Suárez, OP, the then Master of the Dominican Order, that there were things in it which concerned himself. Congar denied, however, that either he or anyone in his ecumenical milieu ever practised a bad "irenicism".[19] In February 1954, he was summoned to Paris by the Master of the Dominican Order and together with his *confrères* Chenu, Féret, and Pierre Boisselot, was dismissed from his post at Le Saulchoir. At his own suggestion, Congar went into exile in Jerusalem. Then, in November 1954, he was assigned to Blackfriars, Cambridge. The fate of the leading Jesuits was no different. De Lubac was permanently removed from all lecturing duties at Fourvière. *Humani Generis* had effectively signalled the end of his academic career, while his books were withdrawn from Jesuit libraries. As he writes:

> Around the end of August 1950, the encyclical *Humani generis* appeared in *La Croix*; I read it, toward the end of the afternoon, in a dark, still-empty room, in front of an open trunk … I later wrote about it to someone asking me for information: "It seems to me to be, like many other ecclesiastical documents, unilateral: that is almost the law of the genre; but I have read nothing in it, doctrinally, that affects me

17   De Lubac, *At the Service of the Church*, 361; *Mémoire*, 362. See further de Lubac, *Entretiens autour de Vatican II. Souvenirs et Réflexions*, Théologies, 2nd edn. (Paris: France Catholique/Cerf, 2007 (1985), 12; Chantraine, *Henri de Lubac. De la naissance à la démobilisation (1896–1919)*, vol. i, Études lubaciennes, vi (Paris: Cerf, 2007); Chantraine, *Henri de Lubac. Les années de formation (1919–1929)*, vol. ii, Études lubaciennes, vii (Paris: Cerf, 2009).

18   Bouillard, *Vérité du christianisme*, Théologie (Paris: Desclée De Brouwer, 1989), 401, 406.

19   See Puyo ed., *Jean Puyo interroge le Père Congar*, 106–113.

[4:28]." ... I should also have said above that, shortly after the publication of the encyclical *Humani generis*, a new measure had been taken. The order was given to withdraw from our libraries and from the trade, among other publications, three of my books: *Surnaturel, Corpus mysticum* and *Connaissance de Dieu*.[20]

De Lubac's colleagues, Henri Bouillard (1908–1981) and Gaston Fessard (1897–1978), were temporarily exiled from the lecture theatre and were forbidden to publish, while Daniélou, with characteristic serendipity, remained active at the Institut catholique de Paris.[21] But neither war nor persecution could deflect Congar or de Lubac from their vocation to service of the church and of truth.

Congar is honoured as a pioneer of church unity and a champion of the laity. At the same time, his role as reformer is ambiguous and his theology remains obfuscated to the present day.[22] Careful study of his contribution to church reform shows him to be an architect of the contemporary church. Congar, in fact, viewed his theology as an integral part of the Second Vatican Council, a point he expressed succinctly as follows: "If there is a theology of Congar, that is where it is to be found."[23] While Congar's participation in the proceedings of that Council, notably his close association with the Belgian theologians, indicates his obvious political adroitness, we must ever bear in mind that it is primarily as a servant of truth, and of the bishops, that he perceived his role there.[24] As he explains:

20   De Lubac, *At the Service of the Church*, 71, 74; ET of *Mémoire*, 72, 75.
21   See Brian Daley, "The *Nouvelle Théologie* and the Patristic Revival: Sources, Symbols and the Science of Theology", *International Journal of Systematic Theology* 7 (2005), 362–382.
22   See Flynn, "Yves Congar and Catholic Church Reform: A Renewal of the Spirit", in Flynn, ed., *Yves Congar: Theologian of the Church* (Louvain/Grand Rapids MI: Peeters/Eerdmans, 2005), 99–133; also Paul J. Philibert, OP, "Retrieving a Masterpiece: Yves Congar's Vision of True Reform", *Doctrine and Life* 61 (2011), 10–20.
23   Congar, "Letter from Father Yves Congar, O.P.", trans. Ronald John Zawilla, *Theology Digest* 32 (1985) 213–216 (215).
24   See Flynn, "Book Essay: *Mon journal du Concile* Yves Congar and the Battle for a Renewed Ecclesiology at the Second Vatican Council", *Louvain Studies* 28 (2003), 48–70.

All the things to which I gave special attention issued in the Council: ecclesiology, ecumenism, reform of the church, the lay state, mission, ministries, collegiality, return to the sources and Tradition ... I've consecrated my life to the service of truth. I've loved it and still love it in the way one loves a person. I've been like that from my very childhood, as if by some instinct and interior need.[25]

At Vatican II, the path of church reform and renewal by way of a return to the biblical and patristic sources was pursued not only by Congar, but also by de Lubac, Daniélou, Rahner, and Ratzinger, among others.[26] Congar's most significant contribution to *ressourcement* is undoubtedly the Unam Sanctam series launched by *La Vie intellectuelle* in November 1935, which became a highly influential ecclesiological and ecumenical library of Éditions du Cerf, running to some 77 volumes. Congar acknowledges that Unam Sanctam prepared the way for Vatican II while Chenu saw in this new collection "one of the most beautiful fruits of our theology at Le Saulchoir".[27]

De Lubac, like Congar, had a dynamic view of tradition: "What I have more than once regretted in highly regarded theologians, experienced guardians, was less, as others have made out, their lack of openness to the problems and currents of contemporary thought than their lack of a truly traditional mind (the two things are moreover connected)."[28] His prodigious theological programme impacted directly on the documents of

25 Congar, "Reflections on being a Theologian", trans. Marcus Lefébure, *New Blackfriars* 62 (1981), 405–409 (405–406). That Congar considered himself a servant of the church is clear from the guiding principle he adopted to govern his work at the Council: "As a pragmatic rule, I have taken this one: to do nothing except that solicited by the bishops. IT IS THEY who are the Council. If, however, an initiative bore the mark of a call of God, I would be open to it". (See Congar, *Mon journal du Concile*, Éric Mahieu, [ed.], 2 vols. [Paris: Cerf, 2002], i. 177 [31 October 1962]).

26 See George Lindbeck, "Ecumenical Theology", in David F. Ford, ed., *The Modern Theologians: An Introduction to Christian Theology in the Twentieth Century*, 2 vols. (Oxford: Blackwell, 1989), ii. 255–273 (258).

27 See Congar, "Reflections on being a Theologian", (405); Fouilloux, "Frère Yves, Cardinal Congar, Dominicain: itinéraire d'un théologien", *Revue des Sciences philosophiques et théologiques* 79 (1995), 379–404 (386).

28 De Lubac, *At the Service of the Church*, 145; ET of *Mémoire*, 148.

Vatican II.[29] As Joseph Ratzinger (1927–), Pope Benedict XVI: (2005–2013), states: "In all its comments about the church [Vatican II] was moving precisely in the direction of de Lubac's thought".[30] De Lubac was instrumental, with others, in the foundation of the *Théologie* series, a project of the Fourvière Jesuits, dedicated to the "renewal of the church". He launched the series before the end of the Second World War with Henri Bouillard, who became the project's first secretary. Bouillard said that the twofold objective of the project was "to go to the sources of Christian doctrine, to find in it the truth of our life."[31] But it was *Sources chrétiennes*, a bilingual collection published by Éditions du Cerf, under the general editorship of de Lubac and Daniélou, which was the crowning glory of the Fourvière Jesuits, as well as their greatest and most enduring contribution to *ressourcement*.[32] De Lubac elucidated the importance of *Sources chrétiennes* for renewal as follows: "Each time, in our West, that Christian renewal has flourished, in the order of thought as in that of life (and the two are always connected), it has flourished under the sign of the Fathers."[33] This project was thought up and elaborated between 1932 and 1937 by Victor Fontoynont, SJ († 1958), who was the true founder of the collection, as de Lubac acknowledged in his *Mémoire sur l'occasion de mes écrits*.[34] Perhaps the most eloquent testimony to the relevance and success of this venture, the principal aim of which was to provide high-quality translations of the Fathers in contemporary French, is the publication to date of over 500 volumes of Greek, Latin, and occasionally Syriac and Aramaic authors.

---

29   See de Lubac, *Carnets du Concile*, Löic Figoureux, ed., 2 vols. (Paris: Cerf, 2007), i.
      421–425 (30 November 1962); de Lubac, *Entretiens autour de Vatican II. Souvenirs
      et Réflexions*, 41–69.

30   Joseph Ratzinger, *Principles of Catholic Theology: Building Stones for a Fundamental
      Theology*, trans. Mary Frances McCarthy (San Francisco: Ignatius, 1987), 50.

31   See de Lubac, *At the Service of the Church*, 31; ET of *Mémoire*, 29.

32   See Fouilloux, *La Collection "Sources chrétiennes". Éditer les Pères de l'Église au XXe
      siècle* (Paris: Cerf, 1995), 219. Fouilloux notes that one of the aims of *Sources chré-
      tiennes*, from its beginnings, was a *rapprochement* between separated Christians of
      East and West. (See further Aubert, *La Théologie Catholique*, 84–86).

33   De Lubac, *At the Service of the Church*, 95–96; ET of *Mémoire*, 96.

34   De Lubac, *At the Service of the Church*, 94; ET of *Mémoire*, 95.

Benedict XVI, one of the last surviving theologians of the pre-Vatican II era, also contributed to *ressourcement*. He viewed *ressourcement* as a hermeneutic of continuity rather than as a rupture with the church's past. Jared Wicks describes his role at Vatican II in precise terms: "He helped on the Doctrinal Commission's revisions of *De ecclesia* and *De revelatione*; he assisted the Council's Commission on Missions in its early 1965 creation of what became Ch. I of *Ad gentes*; and he proposed in October 1965 a revision leading to new material in *Gaudium et Spes* no. 10."[35]

A Question of Terminology: *Ressourcement* or *Nouvelle Théologie*?

Ressourcement engendered controversy from its inception and attracted considerable attention beyond those directly concerned with it. An inevitable part of that controversy related to the vexed question of terminology. The word *ressourcement* was coined by the poet and social critic Charles Péguy (1873–1914).[36] According to Congar, Péguy was a great influence in favour of *ressourcement*, though in his view Péguy's understanding of the Christocentric dimension of the faith was weak. The liturgical changes inaugurated by Pope Pius X (1835–1914) were also an inspiration for *ressourcement*.[37] Congar adopted *ressourcement* as the standard for church reform understood as an urgent call to move from "a less profound to a

---

35 Jared Wicks, "Six texts by Prof. Joseph Ratzinger as *peritus* before and during Vatican Council II", *Gregorianum*, 89/2 (2008), 233–311; also Lewis Ayres, Patricia Kelly, and Thomas Humphries, "Benedict XVI: A *Ressourcement* Theologian?" in Flynn and Murray, eds, *Ressourcement: A Movement for Renewal in Twentieth-Century Catholic Theology*, 423–439.

36 Congar, "Le prophète Péguy", *Témoignage Chrétien*, 26 August 1949, 1.

37 See Congar, "Autour du renouveau de l'ecclésiologie: la collection 'Unam Sanctam'", *La Vie intellectuelle* 51 (1939), 9–32 (11).

more profound tradition; a discovery of the most profound resources".[38]
Much later, Congar would restate this original emphasis in the context of
a glowing tribute to his beloved master and *confrère* Chenu:

> One day the balance will be drawn up, but already the positive quality can be sensed.
> What would a little later be called "ressourcement" was then at the heart of our efforts.
> It was not a matter either of mechanically replacing some theses by other theses or
> of creating a "revolution" but of appealing, as Péguy did, from one tradition less
> profound to another more profound.[39]

The *ressourcement* project was severely criticised by M.-Michel Labourdette,
as well as by Réginald Garrigou-Lagrange who seems to have borrowed the
phrase "*la nouvelle théologie*" to describe it.[40] The epithet *nouvelle théologie*
in fact corresponds to a theology that is concerned to know the tradition, as
opposed to a purely scholastic and repetitive theology. The view of tradition
proposed by the *nouvelle théologie*, far from being traditionalist, in the sense
of a repetition of the recent past, is concerned rather with the unity of the
ever-living tradition. As we have seen, this is precisely Congar's position.[41]

38   Congar, *Vraie et fausse réforme dans l'Église*, Unam Sanctam, 20 (Paris: Cerf, 1950),
       601–602.
39   Congar, "The Brother I have known", trans. Boniface Ramsey, OP, *The Thomist* 49
       (1985), 495–503 (499); ET of "Le frère que j'ai connu", in Geffré et al., *L'hommage
       différé au Père Chenu*, 239–245 (242).
40   Réginald Garrigou-Lagrange, "La nouvelle théologie où va-t-elle", *Angelicum* 23
       (1946), 126–145. See also M.-Michel Labourdette, "La Théologie et ses sources", *La
       Revue Thomiste* 46 (1946), 353–371; Labourdette, "La Théologie, intelligence de la
       foi", *La Revue Thomiste* 46 (1946), 5–44; Aubert, *La Théologie Catholique*, 84–86.
       The controversial term was first used by Pietro Parente, Secretary to the Holy Office,
       in an article entitled "Nuove tendenze teologiche" which appeared in *L'Osservatore
       Romano*, 9–10 February 1942, 1. Parente saw this "*nouvelle théologie*" as a crude
       attempt to demolish the by then classical system of the schools ("... tenta di demolire
       rudemente il sistema ormai classico delle nostre scuole").
41   Congar, *Tradition and the Life of the Church*, trans. A.N. Woodrow, Faith and Fact
       Books, 3 (London: Burns & Oates, 1964), 146; ET of *La tradition et la vie de l'Église*,
       2nd edn, Traditions chrétiennes, 18 (Paris: Cerf, 1984), 118–119.

De Lubac and Daniélou were the leading practitioners of *ressourcement*. Their books often seem like a rich, intricately woven tapestry of texts from the tradition. Congar and Chenu, without diminution or denial of the return to the sources, represent a strongly historical theology, what their neo-Thomist *confrères* would doubtless call a "historicist" approach to theology, including the theology of St Thomas. What distinguishes the *ressourcement* theologians from the *nouveaux théologiens* is that the former were also *nouveaux théologiens* while the latter were not always committed to *ressourcement*. Rahner's approach sets him apart from other *nouveaux théologiens*; his "supernatural existential" is an attempt to rethink the supernatural – one of the preoccupations of the *nouveaux théologiens*. In his later writings, however, he does not tend to refer explicitly to the Fathers or to cite them. What unites these overlapping elements is a certain *froideur* towards Thomism, or what they insist on calling neo-Thomism. Étienne Fouilloux contends that Congar became, with Chenu, de Lubac and Daniélou "the incarnation of a 'new theology', French-style, less concerned with conformity to Scholasticism as with the return to the sources of Christianity and to a dialogue with the great prevailing currents of thought."[42]

The Flowering of *Ressourcement* at the Second Vatican Council

Vatican II provided a historic opportunity for the *ressourcement* intellectuals to influence the Christian churches and modern society. They brought to the Council important but neglected elements of the tradition including biblical studies, the patristic and liturgical renewal, ecumenism, and the revitalisation of Thomism. Gerald O'Collins depicts the influence of *ressourcement* on the conciliar texts with acuity: "Those who scour the

42 Congar, *Journal d'un théologien (1946–1956)*, ed. with notes by Étienne Fouilloux and others, 2nd edn. (Paris: Cerf, 2001), 1–2.

sixteen documents of Vatican II for *explicit* reference to *ressourcement*, or the return to the sources, will find something to report." He points to the Decree on the Appropriate renewal of Religious Life (*Perfectatae Caritatis*, 28 October 1965) as "the clearest endorsement of *ressourcement*". In like manner, the Decree on the Training of Priests (*Optatam Totius*), promulgated on the same day as *Perfectatae Caritatis* (28 October 1965) with its provision for study of the biblical languages provided access to the sources (§13). The Dogmatic Constitution on Divine Revelation (*Dei Verbum*, 18 November 1965) called on all Christians to be "nourished and ruled by Sacred Scripture", "the pure and perennial source of spiritual life" (§§21, 25), while the Decree on the Ministry and Life of Priests (*Presbyterorum Ordinis*, 7 December 1965) exhorted clergy to read and meditate on the scriptures. The Constitution on the Sacred Liturgy (*Sacrosanctum Concilium*, 4 December 1963) and the Decree on Ecumenism (*Unitatis Redintegratio*, 21 November 1964) also contained innovative ideas for a recovery of the ancient tradition.

De Lubac and Congar at the Council

On 20 July 1960, John XXIII (Pope: 1958–1963) nominated de Lubac and Congar as consultants to the Preparatory Theological Commission. The Commission's President Cardinal Alfredo Ottaviani (1890–1979) was a veritable opponent of the *nouvelle théologie* and did not share the Pope's confidence in de Lubac while the Commission's Secretary Sebastian Tromp (1889–1975), a Jesuit, could hardly be considered a friend of de Lubac or Congar. De Lubac later commented poignantly on the historical significance of the Pope's nominees: "These were two symbolic names. John XXIII had undoubtedly wanted to make everyone understand that the difficulties that had occurred under the previous pontificate between Rome and the Jesuit and Dominican orders in France were to be forgotten."[43] Although de Lubac considered resigning from the Preparatory Theological

43   De Lubac, *At the Service of the Church*, 116; ET of *Mémoire*, 117–118.

Commission, he ultimately recorded two notable achievements. First, he successfully defended his friend Pierre Teilhard de Chardin (1881–1955) from an explicit condemnation by the Council. Second, he defended the orthodoxy and integrity of his own writings against false interpretations.

De Lubac's membership of the Preparatory Theological Commission brought him "almost automatically to the Council" and on 28 September 1962, he was appointed an expert on the Doctrinal Commission.[44] At the Council, he influenced such questions as the nature of the church and its mission, revelation, the relationship between the church and the world, and the church's response to atheistic humanism.[45] The publication of *Carnets du Concile* (2007) and *Entretien autour de Vatican II* (2007/1985) provides a clear representation of de Lubac's role at Vatican II, as well as his mature reflections on critical issues for the contemporary church.

De Lubac was "one of the best-known and most outstanding from the very beginning".[46] His influence on *Lumen gentium* and *Gaudium et spes* has been carefully delineated by scholars. The following elements of *Lumen gentium* are attributed to him: (i) the duty of the church to proclaim the gospel to all peoples as explained in *Le fondement théologique des missions*; (ii) the idea of Mary as a type of the church and (iii) the use of the term "the mystery of the church" both of which are expounded in his *Méditation sur l'Eglise*. Karl Heinz Neufeld provides a precise *résumé* of de Lubac's influence on *Lumen gentium*:

> *Lumen gentium* also shows signs of de Lubac's influence. In 1963 he had already described the church as the sacrament of Jesus Christ, just as Jesus Christ as man is for us the sacrament of God. This is the expression of one of the principles of the Council's view of the church. De Lubac developed this from his idea of the church as mystery, which he had used as a title in his *Méditation sur l'Eglise* and which he was to discuss in detail after the Council in his *Paradoxe et Mystère de l'Eglise*. But

---

44 De Lubac, *Carnets du Concile*, i. 89.
45 De Lubac, *Entretien autour de Vatican II*, chs. 2–5; see Karl Heinz Neufeld, "In the Service of the Council: Bishops and Theologians at the Second Vatican Council" in René Latourelle, ed., 3 vols. *Vatican II: Assessment and Perspectives Twenty-Five Years After (1962–1987)*, vol. i (New York: Paulist Press, 1988), 74–105 (103, note 56).
46 Neufeld, "In the Service of the Council", 88.

Catholicisme and *Corpus Mysticum* had already taken important preparatory steps in this direction. However, it was above all the *Méditation sur l'Eglise* with which the Council Fathers were familiar as a source of theological ideas and as inspiration for the spiritual life.[47]

De Lubac's influence at Vatican II was also evident on the question of the relation of the church to non-Christian religions, drawing on *Catholicisme* and his works on Buddhism. He wrote a commentary on the Preamble and first chapter of *Dei Verbum* in 1966 and again in a larger work published in 1968. He considered this text the most important of Vatican II. De Lubac was a member of the sub-commission that produced the first chapter of *Gaudium et spes* that reflects his vision of the place of the church in the modern world, as outlined in *Catholicisme*. He was also invited to write an Introduction to *Gaudium et spes*. Further, de Lubac exercised a profound influence on the treatment of atheism in the Pastoral Constitution through his work *Le Drame de l'Humanisme athée*.

Turning to the contribution of Congar, it is evident that he placed himself entirely at the disposition of the Council.[48] The success of his ecclesiological programme is nowhere more apparent than in its impact on the teaching of the church at Vatican II. The far-reaching programme of ecclesial reform executed at the Council is the *de facto* consummation of his whole previous theological œuvre. Congar describes his role in the drafting of texts in *Mon journal du Concile* where he inserted a useful note, "*Sont de moi*", to indicate precisely his part in the genesis of the Council's documents. He says that he worked on *Lumen gentium*, especially the first draft of many numbers of Chapter I, and on numbers 9, 13, 16, and 17 of Chapter II, as well as on some specific passages. In *De Revelatione*, he worked on Chapter II, and on number 21 which came from a first draft by him. In *De oecumenismo*, the preamble and the conclusion are, he says, more or less by him. Likewise, in the *Declaration on Non-Christian Religions*, the introduction and the conclusion are, he says, more or less his. In *Schema*

47 Neufeld, "In the Service of the Council", 94; also de Lubac, *Le fondement théologique des missions* (Paris: Seuil, 1946).
48 See Congar, *My Journal of the Council*, 17; ET of *Mon journal*, i. 20.

XIII ~ Gaudium et spes, he worked on Chapters I and IV. He wrote all of Chapter I of *De Missionibus*, while Ratzinger contributed to number 8. In *De libertate religiosa*, Congar says that he co-operated with the entire project, and most particularly with the numbers of the theological part, and on the preamble which was entirely his own. Congar indicates that he reworked the preamble of *De Presbyteris*, as well as numbers 2–3, while also writing the first draft of numbers 4–6, and revising numbers 7–9, 12–14 and the conclusion, of which he compiled the second paragraph.[49] Further, it is to Congar, among others, that credit must also be given for one of the most important achievements of the Council, namely, the transition from a predominantly juridical conception of the church to a more eschatological vision of the church as the People of God.[50]

In any account of the influence of *ressourcement* at Vatican II, reference should also be made to the role of Gérard Philips (1899–1972) who, with his colleagues from Louvain made an indispensable contribution to the overall success of the Council. In his capacity as the Assistant-Secretary to the Doctrinal Commission, he was pre-eminent. As Congar remarks: "The theological centre is Msgr Philips. [...] Without any doubt, Philips is the number one artisan of the theological work of the Council."[51] He enjoyed the admiration and respect of all, including Ottaviani and Tromp.[52] The Belgians occupied important positions on the Theological Commission,

49 Congar, *My Journal of the Council*, 871; ET of *Mon Journal*, ii. 511.
50 Following the Council of Trent, a juridical model of faith with a strong emphasis on orthodoxy and certitude was imposed universally throughout the Catholic church. In most seminaries and universities, theology and philosophy were taught without reference to the primary sources and gave an impression of rigidity and narrowness through excessive dependence on scholastic philosophy. In order to overcome the intransigence and aridity of the manuals, Congar, together with his colleagues Chenu and Féret, embarked on an enterprise to eliminate "baroque theology", and to initiate "the return to the sources." See Marie-Dominique Chenu, *Une école de théologie. Le Saulchoir* (Paris: Cerf, 1985), 127.
51 Congar, *My Journal of the Council*, 510; ET of *Mon Journal*, ii. 55–56.
52 See Congar, *My Journal of the Council*, 509; ET of *Mon Journal*, ii. 55.

and exercised a commanding role in the Biblical Sub-Commission, where
they effectively dominated everything.[53]

Ressourcement and Ireland

Ireland was not always peripheral to the currents of theological thought
in continental Europe from which *ressourcement* sprang so vividly in the
twentieth century. Among its forerunners in the nineteenth century were
Johann Adam Möhler (1796–1838) and John Henry Newman (1801–1890),
two of the foremost pioneers of theological renewal of the period. In 1851,
Newman was appointed first rector of the Catholic University of Ireland
(resigning in 1858) and his Dublin lectures, which caused him great anxiety, were eventually published as *The Idea of a University*. His contribution
to ecclesiology would later find expression in *Lumen gentium*, as Ian Ker
points out:

> The French *ressourcement*, or retrieval of the scriptural and patristic sources, without
> which the Council's Constitution on the church could hardly have been formulated,
> had already been pioneered by Newman and his Tractarian colleagues in the Oxford
> of the 1830s a hundred years before.[54]

Cardinal Cahal B. Daly (1917–2009), Archbishop of Armagh (1990–
1996) was a *peritus* at the Council and a friend of de Lubac's. He says that
he came into contact with *ressourcement* during graduate studies in Paris
(1952–1953), when he took courses in theology and philosophy at the *Institut
Catholique*. In his memoirs, Daly contends that a Maynooth priest of his
generation was by no means unprepared for *ressourcement* and could trace
the continuity between the Council's teaching and what he had learned
at the seminary. In this regard, he stresses the importance of situating the
definitions of the great Councils of the church in the history of their time
and in the context of the theological debates out of which they emerged.

---

53 Congar, *My Journal of the Council*, 510; ET of *Mon Journal*, ii. 56.
54 Ian Ker, "Foreword" in Avery Dulles, *John Henry Newman* (London: Continuum,
    2002), viii.

As a result, he saw his own study of theology as helping him in advance "to see the documents of the Council when they came as a development, not a rupture, and to find in them a return to deeper sources of the faith".[55] However, an examination of the seminary *Kalendarium*, the Maynooth College Calendar, for the period 1950–1970 shows only scant attention to *ressourcement* with little evidence of teaching or research in that field.[56]

National variations notwithstanding, Vatican II effected a Copernican revolution in the doctrine and teaching of the Catholic church by a retrieval of vital elements from the biblical, liturgical, and patristic sources. As O'Collins remarks: "In major ways that teaching was shaped by theologians of the *ressourcement* movement: Chenu, Congar, Daniélou, de Lubac, Philips, Rahner, Ratzinger, Smulders, and others. They left the whole Christian church a life-giving legacy in what they retrieved from the scriptures and the great tradition for the documents of Vatican II."[57] The Council represented the flowering of the *ressourcement* movement that not even the difficulties of the post-conciliar period could overshadow.

Post-conciliar concerns

Some of the leading *ressourcement* thinkers expressed concerns about the *aggiornamento* in unambiguous terms. In 1967, Congar asked: "Where are we to go from here? Where shall we be in twenty years? I, too, feel almost every day a temptation of uneasiness in the face of all that has changed

---

55 Cahal B. Daly, *Steps on my Pilgrim Journey: Memories and Reflections* (Dublin: Veritas, 1998), 91.

56 Professor John O'Flynn offered courses on Dei Verbum while Professor Gerard Mitchell expounded on comparative religions, the history of Protestantism and Anglicanism. As President of Maynooth (1959–1967), Mitchell received Michael Ramsey, Archbishop of Canterbury (1961–1974) on 25 June 1967, though the inspiration for the visit came from Enda McDonagh, a member of the Faculty of Theology at the time.

57 Gerald O'Collins, "*Ressourcement* and Vatican II" in Flynn and Murray, eds, *Ressourcement: A Movement for Renewal in Catholic Theology*, 372–391 (391).

or is being called into question."[58] For his part, de Lubac made no secret
of his concerns and criticised the fundamental misinterpretation of the
Council.[59] He believed that the crisis at the heart of the church after the
Council was a reflection of the crisis at the heart of western society, origi-
nating from a refusal to acknowledge the transcendent, a kind of modern
Gnosticism that he referred to as "a global repugnance to admitting the
idea of a divine revelation". This refusal to believe resulted inevitably in a
spiritual decline and a corresponding growth in secularisation. In 2010,
Benedict XVI alluded to the unresolved tensions concerning the Council's
reception, and called into question both the interpretation and the implementation of its programme of renewal.[60]

The twentieth-century renaissance in Catholic theology coincided
with the rise of totalitarianism.[61] It emerged that the *ressourcement* theologians were not afraid to accept responsibility and to summon others in
their respective spheres of influence to judgement and action in response
to the dark side of totalitarianism in its various expressions. Failure to
acknowledge their contribution to the French Resistance would also be a
failure to recognise that *ressourcement* is fundamentally a practical theology engaged in an open, critical, and sometimes militant fashion with the

58   Congar, "Theology's Tasks after Vatican II", in Laurence K. Shook, ed., *Renewal of
      Religious Thought*, 2 vols. (New York: Herder and Herder, 1968), i. 47–65 (50); ET
      of "Les tâches de la théologie après Vatican II", in L.K. Shook and Guy-M. Bertrand,
      eds, *La Théologie du renouveau*, 2 vols, Cogitatio Fidei, 27 (Montreal: Fides; Paris:
      Cerf, 1968), ii. 17–31, (19).
59   De Lubac, *At the Service of the Church*, 158–159; ET of *Mémoire*, 162–163; see
      Christopher J. Walsh, "De Lubac's critique of the postconciliar church", *Communio*,
      19, (1992), 404–432.
60   See Benedict XVI, "Pastoral Letter of the Holy Father Pope Benedict XVI to the
      Catholics of Ireland", 19 March 2010, par. 4, available at <http://www.vatican.va/
      holy_father/benedict_xvi/letters/2010/documents/hf_ben-xvi_let_20100319_
      church-ireland_en.html>. Accessed 13 November 2014.
61   See Stephen J. Lee, *The European Dictatorships, 1918–1945*, 3rd edn (Oxford:
      Routledge, 2008); Norman Davies, *Europe: A History* (Oxford: Oxford University
      Press, 1996), chapter xi; Hannah Arendt, *The Origins of Totalitarianism*, 9th edn.
      (New York: Schocken Books, 2004).

most pressing issues affecting contemporary society. Essentially they were religious men of ideas, driven along by the emerging currents of the times that they helped to create and in which they lived. An important part of their mission was the construction of a Christian humanism in response to the challenges of the Enlightenment, European totalitarianism, and secular modernity. The final part of this chapter assesses the contribution to the leading French *ressourcement* thinkers in the struggle against totalitarianism.

Ressourcement and Totalitarianism

Catholic and Protestant bishops, priests, and pastors, both German and French, are often accused of being either sympathetic to German National Socialism or generally tolerant of its anti-Jewish stance during the period of the Third Reich (1933–1945). Among the notable exceptions, on the Protestant side, were Dietrich Bonhoeffer (1906–1945), head of the German Confessing church's seminary near Stettin, and Max Metzger (1887–1944); both were influential religious activists, writers whose deaths are considered martyrdom. Bonhoeffer's heroic opposition to German National Socialism, a political system which he publicly condemned as corrupt and misleading, is well known because of his execution at the hands of the regime on 9 April 1945.

On the Catholic side, the anti-Nazi activists include, among others, Romano Guardini (1885–1968) and Engelbert Krebs (1881–1950), both of whom publicly criticised Hitler and were eventually dismissed from their professorships by the Minister for Education.[62] The courageous witness of Cardinal Clemens August, Count von Galen (1878–1946), Bishop of Münster, who exposed and publicly condemned the attacks of the Nazi regime against persons with intellectual disability, must also be acknowl-

---

62   See Robert A. Krieg, *Catholic Theologians in Nazi Germany* (New York: Continuum, 2004), 118–119, 148–150.

edged. The actions of von Galen and his fellow bishops Cardinal Konrad von Preysing (1880–1950), Bishop of Berlin and Johannes Baptist Sproll (1870–1949), Bishop of Rottenburg would have gained greater papal support if Pope Pius XI had lived long enough to issue his planned new encyclical *Humani Generis Unitas*, denouncing anti-Semitism much more vociferously than he had in *Mit Brennender Sorge*.[63]

Congar was an implacable enemy of National Socialism. As a prisoner-of-war in Colditz and Lübeck (1941–1945), following a brief time of combat, he demonstrated a defiant and obstinate "opposition to the enemy".[64] De Lubac's strident opposition to anti-Semitism during the Nazi occupation of France merits consideration, notably, his role as co-editor of the clandestine *Cahiers du Témoignage chrétien*.[65] De Lubac unambiguously aligned himself with Pius XI, and was deeply critical of historians who sought to minimise the significance of the encyclical *Mit Brennender Sorge*.[66] In a letter to his superiors on 25 April 1941, de Lubac described the conquests by Germany as "an anti-Christian revolution" the aim of which was "to subjugate the church" and to impose Nazi methods and ideas. As evidence of this, he pointed to the presence on French soil of concentration camps, the propagation of anti-Semitism and, at the same time, the rise in France of a wave of neo-paganism.[67]

Nothing could have prepared de Lubac, Congar, and their erstwhile colleagues for the extraordinarily difficult leadership role they were to play in the renewal of Catholic theology and liturgy, the reform of the churches,

---

63   See Georges Passelecq and Bernard Suchecky, *The Hidden Encyclical of Pius XI*, trans. Steven Rendall (New York: Harcourt Brace, 1997).

64   Congar, *Dialogue between Christians*, 30; ET of *Chrétiens en dialogue*, xli.

65   See de Lubac, "La question des évêques sous l'occupation", *Revue des Deux Mondes* (février 1992), 67–82, de Lubac Papers, Jesuit Archives, Vanves, Paris, Dossier 5, "Résistance spirituelle au nazisme, 1940–1945."

66   Pius XI, "'Mit Brennender Sorge': Encyclical of Pope Pius XI on the church and the German Reich March 14, 1937", *AAS* 29 (1937), 145–167; ET in *The Papal Encyclicals 1903–1939*, iii, ed., Claudia Carlen, 5 vols. (Raleigh: Pierian, 1990), 525–535.

67   De Lubac, "Letter to My Superiors", *Theology in History*, trans. Anne Englund Nash (San Francisco: Ignatius, 1996); ET of "Lettre à mes supérieurs", *Théologie dans l'histoire* (Paris: Desclée de Brouwer, 1990), 220–231 (221–225).

and the rejuvenation of European culture in the period after World War II. Their critical voice raised against Nazi nihilism in the wartime chaos bespeaks a deep-seated respect for humanity. Essentially they were religious men of ideas, driven along by the emerging currents of the times that they helped to create and in which they lived. An important part of their mission was the construction of a Christian humanism in response to the challenges of the Enlightenment, European totalitarianism, and secular modernity.

Conclusion

The achievement of the *ressourcement* theologians lay not so much in their rejection of an arid neo-Scholasticism as in their dual concern to engage with the contemporary world and to ensure the essential unity of theology. This reached its zenith at Vatican II, perhaps the greatest expression of the *ressourcement* movement. The responsibility of constructing a theology that is capable of responding to the ever-changing needs of the times is a perennial one. The restoration of the ancient sources of Christian theology through the *ressourcement* project, with its essential turn to history, constitutes what is perhaps that movement's greatest legacy, a legacy that has contributed since the mid-nineteen sixties to church reform, to necessary dialogue between the Christian churches and contemporary society, as well as to ecumenism and interreligious dialogue.

SEÁN FREYNE

5   *Dei Verbum*: The Bible in the Post-Conciliar Church

I have two abiding memories from Vatican II, both dealing with the Bible. One is the open book of the gospels that was in front of the main altar in St Peter's during the Council's sessions, underlining the aspiration of Pope John that the Bible would be the heart and soul of the church's life. The second memory concerns two of my professors at the Pontifical Biblical Institute, both Jesuit priests and well advanced in years. Both were suspended for their opinions on key scriptural passages, as far as the Holy Office was concerned. Maximilian Zerwick, a German scholar, had suggested that the Matthean text dealing with the Petrine Primacy (Mt 18, 17f) should be dated to the post-Resurrection appearance to Peter (1 Cor 15, 4), rather than to the life of the historical Jesus. Frenchman Stanislaus Lyonnet questioned Augustine's interpretation of Paul's notions of Adam's sin (the "in whom all sinned"/*in quo omnes peccaverunt*, of Romans 5, 12), which had given rise to a distorted notion of original sin, as this had come to be understood in the west. To say the least of it, these were mixed messages as to how one should approach the study of the Bible.

The Constitution *Dei Verbum*: Its Genesis and Limitations

The first draft of the decree *Dei Verbum*, as proposed by the Theological Commission of the Holy Office, was severely and rightly criticised by many commentators for its conservative and scholastic thinking. Frantic "behind the scenes" lobbying of bishops took place to have the document rejected.

While there was a substantial vote against it in the Council chamber, the stipulated 66 per cent negative views had not been reached. Mercifully, Pope John withdrew the proposed draft and set up a much more representative commission which produced the draft of the current document, entitled "Dogmatic Constitution on Divine Revelation." After several discussions and emendations at the general assembly, the revised document was eventually passed unanimously at the fourth and final session in November 1965.

While this document deals with the Bible, its first concern was to situate the Scriptures within a proper understanding of Revelation. Moving away from a propositional approach which understood Revelation as a body of revealed doctrines, the text adopts a much more biblical understanding of the notion, based on the idea of God's Word, symbolising God's interpersonal relationship with humanity (Heb 1, 1–4). God speaks to humans through deeds and words, climaxing in the life of Jesus of Nazareth, as God's Word incarnate. Revelation, though emanating from this single well-spring, is transmitted in two streams, namely, through Scripture and Tradition that are intimately interconnected. This formulation was directed somewhat obliquely at certain developments in post-Tridentine Catholic Theology that spoke of two *independent* sources of Revelation that were separate and distinct. The insistence that there was a single source that came to us via two separate, though related, streams was an important milestone in terms of ecumenical dialogue with the Protestant churches, for whom the principle of *Sola Scriptura* was paramount in determining God's revelation to the church.

Four further chapters in *Dei Verbum* are devoted to the Bible, namely, ch. 3, Divine Inspiration, ch. 4, The Old Testament, ch. 5 the New Testament, and ch. 6, the Bible in the life of the church. The chapter on Divine Inspiration is an uneasy effort to strike a balance between older views of Divine authorship of the books of the Bible that are contained in the Canon, and newer theories as to how the notion of inspiration might be understood within a framework in which human authorship can be taken with full seriousness. This cautious compromise becomes apparent in the fact that Par. 11 of the Constitution includes on the one hand statements from Vatican I (1870) and Leo's XIII encyclical *Providentissimus Deus* (1892), both of which stress the older, Thomistic view of God's direct authorship in the writing of the biblical books, and on the other hand, the views of Pius XII, expressed in his 1942 encyclical, *Divino Afflante Spiritu*, which insists on the freedom of the human authors of the Bible to express themselves appropriately.

This latter document had assisted the drafters of the Constitution *Dei Verbum* in presenting a more contemporary view of authorship of both the Old and New Testaments. Thus in ch. 3, par 12, already, interpreters are encouraged to seek out literary forms in deciding what the sacred writers intended in accordance with their time and culture, as Pius XII had authorised. Yet when the Decree comes to deal with the Old Testament in ch. 4, there is little sign of this openness to understanding the Hebrew Scriptures on their own terms. Rather the perspective adopted is that of the Old Testament as the preparation for the New. As such these books are "permanently valuable" (Par 14). Yet in the following paragraph we read that while they show us the divine pedagogy, "they contain some things which are incomplete and temporary," and "Christians should receive them with reverence" (par. 15), a comment that suggests understatement to me. In short, the old patristic adage that "The New Testament was hidden in the Old and the Old was made manifest in the New" is repeated. The only full and proper meaning of the Old Testament is to prepare for the coming of Christ, announce this coming in prophecy and indicate its meaning through various types. This reduces Old Testament persons and events to the role of imperfect anti-types, with no significance in their own right for Christian or human living.[1]

Similarly, in the treatment of the New Testament the authors are able to avail of a document published by the Pontifical Biblical Commission in 1964, between two sessions of the Council. Again we can see the wisdom of the Pope in having this highly controversial issue of "The historical truth of the Gospels" dealt with by Biblical scholars independently of the of the Council, but with the issue which had brought about the banning of Father

---

1   B. Kowalski, "The Relationship between the OT and the NT according to *Dei Verbum. Response to Jan Lambrecht 'The Significance of Dei Verbum for Biblical Studies Today,'"* in Kieran O'Mahony, ed. *Proceedings of the Irish Biblical Association,* 28 (2005) 21–27.

Zerwick very much in mind. In fact he and Father Lyonnet had been rein-stated by the time this document was published and I had the privilege of attending several of their courses. This statement recognised the value of Form and Redaction Criticism, methods in use in critical Protestant schol-arship of the gospels for over half a century. These approaches were now officially open to Catholic scholars also. It placed Catholic New Testament scholarship on an entirely different footing to what it had been previously. It was of course hailed at the time in the Biblical Institute where I was then preparing my dissertation, a redactional study of the first three gospels, and in the Introduction I was able to draw on it in developing an appropriate methodology.[2]

While the Decree *Dei Verbum* certainly opens the door to critical gospel studies as these were being conducted in academic institutions in the Protestant world, the Council document does not use the terms "form" and "redaction" criticism, something the 1964 instruction had done. With hind-sight one can see the cautious nature of the acceptance of critical study of the gospels that is being proposed: the four gospels were written by apostles or apostolic men, who were acting under the guidance of the Holy Spirit; there is no recognition that the evangelists may have used sources, such as the Q document, or the several Johns associated with the Fourth Gospel. Thus the issue of how to understand the notion of Inspiration in the context of multiple authorship of documents is not even foreseen.[3] Furthermore in affirming the historical character of the gospels, the Constitution goes to great pains to assert that the authors were not only witnesses of all that Jesus had said and done during his earthly life, but were also instructed by him after the Resurrection for forty days in accordance with the Lukan fiction in Acts 1, 1–2. This information is repeatedly used subsequently in the various Nag Hammadi texts, all of which adopt and build on the idea of Jesus' continuous instruction of the disciples after the Resurrection.

2   S. Freyne, *The Twelve: Disciples and Apostles, An Introduction to the Theology of the First Three Gospels*, London: Sheed and Ward, 1968, especially 1–11, discussing the new instruction on the gospels.
3   Karl Rahner had addressed this question in an important study on *Inspiration in the Bible*, Quaestiones Disputatae, 1 (London: Burns and Oates, 1961).

Incidentally, the notice in Acts does not correspond to what Luke tells us elsewhere, in the third gospel, about Jesus' Ascension which took place immediately after the Resurrection, it seems (Lk 24, 50–52).

The creative role of the evangelists is reduced to selecting, synthesising and explicating (Latin *explanantes*) some things "in view of the situation of the churches," but always in such a manner that "told us the honest truth about Jesus." The word translated as "explicating" is an unusual Latin term, and difficult to determine what precisely is meant, but it must be assumed that a certain amount of adaptation to the "Sitz im Leben der Gemeinde" is intended.[4] This raises the question of how we should understand the word "truth" in the above citation. Does it mean an accurate historical report of what really happened, the "as it really was" of those who followed the nineteenth-century Von Ranke school of history? Or is "truth" being used here in a more holistic sense of the salvific meaning of the text in the light of the whole of Scripture, as was enunciated earlier in par 12 of the document as the goal of all interpretation?

In contrast to the discussion of the gospels, *Dei Verbum* has very little to say about the Pauline or other letters in the Canon, even though there are critical questions to be raised there also, not least the issue of which are the authentic Pauline letters and which are post-Pauline. Nor is there any reference to extra-canonical texts such as those discovered in Nag Hammadi in Egypt, in 1945, which included one with the subscript "The Gospel (*euaggelion*) of Thomas."

Perhaps the most significant aspect of the discussion regarding the gospels is the way in which Jesus is presented in the text. It is noteworthy that the document cites John's Gospel repeatedly, thereby presenting a Jesus with a "high Christological awareness" from the outset. Thus the legitimate distinction between the pre- and post-Easter phases of early Christian self-understanding is blurred, or at least passed over too lightly.

The final chapter of *Dei Verbum* deals with "Sacred Scripture in the Life of the church." After repeating again its understanding of Revelation

---

4   J. Fitzmyer, "The Interpretation of the Bible in the Church Today," *ITQ* 62 (1996/97) 84–100.

as God speaking to humans in and through the Scriptures, which are said both to contain the Word of God and be the Word of God, the document goes on to deal with practical issues – translation, education of the clergy and others involved in catechesis, and above all in the liturgy. Significantly, Biblical scholars are expected to work "under the watchful eye" of the teaching magisterium of the church. Noteworthy also is the suggestion that suitable translations should be accompanied with adequate explanations and shared with non-Christians. Surprisingly, however, there is no explicit recognition of other Christian churches at this point, and no mention of Jewish interest in the Bible also.

It was quite some time since I had read *Dei Verbum*, and in re-reading it for this paper I was struck by how much the situation has changed in the interim, both in regard to Catholic Biblical Studies and the attitude of the church towards the Bible. While the decree *Dei Verbum* did indeed open the door to the academic study of the Scriptures in line with the Council's biblical emphasis generally, it is noteworthy how cautious and circumscribed the approach of this document sounds today. However, there is no denying that it has borne much fruit in terms of a Biblical awareness in the Roman Catholic church, especially in the liturgy, even when many celebrants seem to be uncomfortable or incapable in regard to the use of Scripture in their homilies. In the second part of this paper I would like to draw attention to a few noteworthy trends that have emerged and point to some of the roadblocks to a genuinely biblical understanding of our shared Christian heritage.

The Bible in the Post-Conciliar Church: Some Trends

Two writings in particular that have emerged from Rome since the Council reflect the manner in which Catholic Biblical Studies have progressed, and at the same time stood still in the post-conciliar period. The first of these was produced by the Pontifical Biblical Commission and appeared in 1992 with an enthusiastic introductory address by Pope John Paul II.

This was launched on the occasion of the publication of the document to celebrate the centenary of *Providentissimus Deus* and the jubilee *of Divino Afflante Spiritu*. It is entitled *The Interpretation of the Bible in the Church*. The second document appeared two years later in 1994, *The Catechism of the Catholic Church*, and was intended as an encylopedia, or resource book for bishops preparing local catechisms.

Inevitably the *Catechism* gives Guidelines as to how the Bible should be used in the explication of the Christian faith, following *Dei Verbum* (nos. 103, 105, 107 and 109). Yet it goes on to declare that "the Christian faith is not a religion of the book", citing Bernard of Clairvaux as the authority for this claim. At best this statement is open to misinterpretation, implying that the sacred text is not essential to the church's life, and denying the life-giving effects that elsewhere are attributed to the books of the Bible. Throughout, there are many examples of how the task of interpreting the Bible for theology can and should be approached in the view of the Catechism's authors. In general it must be said that despite citing *Dei Verbum* on the importance of the literal sense, the authors revert to the ancient typological and anagogical methods of the Patristic era in dealing with many issues. To cite American scholar Gerard Sloyan, "The clear intention of the sacred authors will time and again not be attended to, while the illustrative use of texts in another sense will be." Thus Sloyan concluded that in a volume intended as an aid to bishops, and from which they could oversee the production of materials suitable to a variety of people and cultures, the authors have resorted to a set of principles known to very few peoples today, but which were much in operation in the Patristic Age. This decision is all the more remarkable in view of the fact that that despite the blessing which the PBC document had received two years earlier by Pope John Paul II, the authors of the Catechism have reverted to modes of reading the Scripture which can indeed be fruitful, but which should play at best a secondary role in the post-Vatican II era.[5]

---

5   G. Sloyan, "The Use of the Bible in a New Resource Book. A Review of the Vatican's Catechism," *Biblical Theology Bulletin*, 25 (1995) 3–13, here p. 5f.

One is entitled to wonder whether the hand of Joseph Ratzinger was behind this deliberate move, especially in view of his own ambivalent approach to the historical critical method in his book, *Jesus of Nazareth*, (2007). Indeed in his short introduction to the PBC document, Ratzinger struck a note of caution with regard to the historical-critical method. He writes: "Everything that helps us better to understand the truth and to appropriate its representations is helpful and worthwhile for theology. It is in this sense that we must seek how to use this method in theological research. Everything that shrinks our horizons and hinders us from hearing and seeing beyond that which is merely human, must be opened up. Thus the emergence of the historical-critical method set in motion at the same time a struggle over its scope and over its proper configuration, which is by no means finished as yet."

The document produced by the Biblical Commission is an interesting contrast to all previous documents dealing with the Bible and emanating from Rome. It engages fully, and for the most part fairly, with a whole range of methodologies that have developed in Biblical Studies over the past thirty-odd years, everything from Reader Response Criticism, to Social Scientific approaches, as well as Feminist and Liberationist Hermeneutics. Patristic exegesis too, is mentioned, but with much less emphasis than that of the authors of the Catechism. The mode of procedure is to describe each of the approaches under discussion, its history and presuppositions, concluding with an evaluation of its significance.

It is somewhat ironic that what was previously regarded as a threat to Christian faith, and about which Joseph Ratzinger has his reservations, namely the historical-critical method, is here lauded "as the indispensable method for the scientific study of the meaning of ancient texts." Because the Scriptures in all their parts and sources have been written by human authors, "its proper understanding not only admits the use of this method, but actually requires it" (PBC 1A). A brief historical overview shows that the method is not just an innovation of the Enlightenment but was practised to a limited degree in Patristic times, and formed an important element of the return to the sources of *Ressourcement*. However, it was the development of the Documentary Hypothesis regarding the sources of the Pentateuch and the Quest for the Historical Jesus in the nineteenth century that really gave the impetus for this method in modern Biblical Studies.

Nevertheless, despite this ringing endorsement, the Document goes on to speak of the over-emphasis in some quarters on seeking to discover sources behind the texts, a process that lead to their being dismantled, thereby running the risk of destroying the texts entirely, as it puts it. It also criticises the use of what it describes as philosophical presuppositions that expressed highly negative judgements on the Bible, referring to the de-mythologisation of the gospels by Rudolph Bultmann and his students.

Despite these reservations with regard to various practitioners' uses of the method, the Document goes on to emphasise that the method itself is both *historical* in the strict sense of seeking to uncover as far as possible the diachronic processes that were operative in the production of the text, and *critical* in that it applies scientific criteria that seek to be as objective as possible. In order to overcome the earlier criticism of the over-emphasis on the search for sources, the Commission insisted that the synchronic aspect of texts should also be included in the final step of the historical analysis. There is a pragmatic aspect to the completed work with regard to the actions and life-style that it enjoins, and this must not be lost sight of.

Even this brief discussion of the two documents shows the ambivalence with regard to the proper way to appropriate the Biblical message in contemporary Theology. While the Catechism is an official document for the Magisterium, the Commission Document is not, as Cardinal Ratzinger makes clear in his preface to the Document. He writes as follows: "The Pontifical Biblical Commission in its new form after the Second Vatican Council, is not an organ of the teaching office, but rather a commission of scholars, who, in their scientific and ecclesial responsibility as believing exegetes, take positions on important problems of scriptural interpretation, and know that for this task they enjoy the confidence of the teaching office."

Thus the reception and development of the insights of Vatican II's *Dei Verbum* in the post-conciliar official documents, is ambivalent at best. However, this is not by any means the whole story, and there are many indications that the Bible plays an important role in the lives of many Catholics today. Scripture study groups, Pilgrimages to the Holy Land, the Lectionary, as well as popular publications such as *The Bible Today* and *Biblical Theology Bulletin* in the US, and here at home, *Scripture in church*, were and are offshoots of the intention of the Council's document. At the more scholarly level, it is often difficult to distinguish in terms of content and approach between a Catholic and a Protestant scholar in the pages of the *Catholic Biblical Quarterly* and the *Journal of Biblical Literature* both coming from America. The same is true of SNTS, which was initially founded to bridge the divide between continental and British NT scholarship in the immediate post war years. Today its membership is truly international with well over 1,000 scholars on its list. Recently it has established an International Secretariat, whose special brief is to foster the academic study of the Bible in Asia, Africa and South America. Here at home The Irish Biblical Association has been steadfast in it ecumenical outlook, and resisted all attempts by certain bishops to have it called the Catholic Biblical Association at its inception in the 1960s. Indeed the continued publication of the annual Proceedings of the Irish Biblical Association (Number 35 has just appeared) provides a forum for young Irish Biblical scholars to present their research to a wider scholarly public.

Between 1988 and 2004 I had the privilege of being on the editorial board of the journal *Concilium*, a journal that took its inspiration from the Council and continued to develop its insights in several directions, especially in the areas of Liberation Theology and Feminist theology. It is interesting that the PBC document singles out these two areas also for comment under the heading of contextual approaches, in its comprehensive list of other different ways of interpreting the Scripture, following on from the treatment of the historical-critical method. The policy of the *Concilium* board in those years was to address topics that were deemed to be relevant and of general interest, and deal with them in the spirit of the Council documents. Instead of having numbers that followed the old seminary model of covering the various theological disciplines (Dogma, Moral, Spirituality etc.), the idea was to treat the particular topic from various angles, historical, ethical, theological and scriptural. Issues as diverse as Ageing and Sport are examples of this approach. In addition feminist, and liberationist topics were assigned a separate number every second year, because these were deemed to be very important issues that the Council had not mentioned, yet became burning and controversial topics in the post-conciliar church and world, and both had good lobbyist in Elizabeth Schussler Fiorenza and Gustavo Gutierrez. By adopting this approach to diverse topics a kind of Concilium template was developed, one that was pluralist in its outlook and sought to take full cognisance of multi-cultural context of Christian witness today.

In addition to contributing articles to several of these topical numbers, I also shared with Wim Beuken SJ of Leuven, editorial responsibility for specifically Biblical numbers, one every two years approximately. The challenge was to invite articles that were up-to-date in terms of the methodological changes that were occurring in the broader field of Biblical studies, while also maintaining the focus on the important issues of the day, e.g. Jewish-Christian dialogue, Eschatology, and of course feminist and liberationist themes also. This demanding but rewarding work put me in touch with the development of Catholic Biblical scholarship in a more global context, and underlined the variety of perspectives that the different continents gave rise to in the study and use of the Bible in theological and pastoral circles.

Here I can mention just one number that compares in interesting ways with the PBC's approach, namely *The Bible and its Readers* (1991). The suggestion for this title was based on the so-called literary turn in NT studies at the time, one that favoured the synchronic over the diachronic approach, and often drew on studies of the modern novel, with the emphasis on plot, characterisation, point of view etc. The popularity of this approach arose from the fact that it did not make undue demands on those who were unfamiliar with biblical history. It also made the reader central to the enterprise of interpretation, thereby doing away with the illusion that the text was a container of meaning that the reader takes in passively. However, as Ben Meyer points out in a hard-hitting methodological essay, the danger is that readers may not "measure up" to the text, by failing to recognise its layered potential to challenge their deepest assumptions and prejudices. At the same time he is equally critical of a certain type of historico-critical approach to texts that ends up being banal because of its positivistic bent, one that excludes the possibility that the author may be saying "more" than a consideration of time, place, cultural influences etc. can tell us about his/her intention. While Meyer's article is couched in philosophical language, his conclusion is not that far removed from that of the PBC document, as discussed earlier.

This same number carries two articles dealing with feminists and lib-erationist issues. In her article "The Magisterium and the Bible: North American Experience," Christine Gudorf, a Christian ethicist, casts a criti-cal eye on various documents emanating from the Congregation for the Doctrine of the Faith (CDF), highlighting the ways in which the Bible is made to agree with tradition in some of its declarations, thereby precluding the possibility of new understandings of the tradition to emerge, such as the possibility of same sex relations. She is particularly critical of the US bishops' various pronouncements such as that on Christian marriage where texts such as Eph 5, 22–33 are proposed as resources where Christian couples can draw a sense of their mutual love. The bishops' statement ignores com-pletely the subordination of women that the text presupposes, and Gudorf is indignant that such a text would be seen as the basis for a Christian mar-riage of equals in today's world.

In his contribution to this number of *Concilium*, liberation theologian Carlos Mesters presents a lively picture of how the Bible came to be more important in Brazil. It was partly due to the success of the Protestant mis-sionaries among the ordinary people and partly because of the shortage of priests, giving rise for the need to develop other ways of nurturing faith communities. Initially it was a middle-class phenomenon, but gradually the poor were also included. Mesters writes: "Without money or ability to read books about the Bible, the poor read the Bible by the only criterion they possess, their faith lived in community, and their lives of suffering as an oppressed people." Reading the Bible in this way the poor discover within it the obvious truths that they did not know or which were hidden from them for centuries, namely: 1. A history of oppression like their own today, with the same conflicts; and 2. a liberation struggle for the same values that they pursue today here in Brazil: land, justice, sharing, fraternity, a decent life.

This practice of finding parallels between various biblical situations and ones that obtain in Brazil today, has been criticised as too simplistic in that ignores the huge differences between ancient societies and all modern ones, even those of the poorest of the poor. Furthermore, it limits the Biblical message to certain passages only and narrows the Jesus story to one aspect only. Mesters is well aware of these criticisms, yet he insists that once the people are aware of the need to become involved in community through service of the poor, it challenges them to know the Bible better and to create and strengthen communities of faith, and increase their active service of the less well off. He freely admits that the Bible can become a reactionary influence, legitimating various injustices in terms of social engagement when it is presented as some miraculous instrument, as happens in the Pentecostal communities. It is for this reason that he insists that practice makes it imperative to have a better foundation in the world of the Bible, something the South American scholars are doing by producing their own books and pamphlets, or by translating books by Europeans and Americans that stress the social and culturally historical dimension of the text, but without excluding the spiritual and mystical dimensions also.

Conclusion

These examples of the insights of Vatican II with regard to the importance of the Bible for the Christian life make it clear that there is still a deep ambivalence about how this can be done, and for what purpose. Clearly people need guidance, but they must also be encouraged to find their own meanings and have these challenged within a living and loving community. Perhaps the present serious crisis in Irish Catholicism will give rise to such faith communities as emerged in Brazil. The fact that we are still without a national pastoral Council for the laity tells its own story as to how far behind the leadership of the Irish church is in developing structures that will enable the faithful to express, to explore and to act.

PART III

Reception of the Council in the Irish Church

JIM CORKERY

6   The Reception of Vatican II in Ireland Over Fifty Years

Introduction

So much has been and continues to be written about the reception of the Second Vatican Council that it is important to mention at the outset how little of it can be dealt with in this chapter, which is limited to examining the reception of Vatican II in Ireland. The writings I have in mind, of theologians and historians, deal mostly with the reception of Vatican II more widely than in particular contexts or local churches, even if these are, of course, at times also considered in them. I will draw less on such work than on *Irish* reflection on the reception of Vatican II, which is extensive at present due to two important contextual elements: the fiftieth anniversary of the Council itself (1962–1965) and the contemporary crisis in the Irish church that reached its most acute level following the revelations, beginning in the early 1990s, of the sexual (and physical) abuse of children by religious and clergy that led to the publication, in 2009, of the Ryan and Murphy Reports concerning these abuses. Earlier anniversaries of the Council have given rise to published reflections also such as, in Ireland ten years ago, Dermot A. Lane's article on the Irish experience of Vatican II, in which a specific section is devoted to "The reception of Vatican II in Ireland."[1] I will avail of and build upon what Lane has said, as well as reflecting on what reception is, on how it has been carried out in Ireland,

---

1   See Dermot A. Lane, "Vatican II: The Irish Experience," *The Furrow* 55:2 (February 2004), 67–81, 69–72 in particular.

and on how it could, in the future, bear greater fruit if dimensions of it that have hitherto been sidelined were given more adequate attention.

Reception Itself

"Reception" is a word that refers to a much richer process than is indicated by terms such as "implementation," "application," or "following the directives of." "The very category 'reception' has only recently been retrieved," writes Ormond Rush, recalling Jean-Marie Tillard's reference to it as "certainly one of the most important theological re-discoveries of our century."[2] Since Vatican II, there has been a great deal of writing about "reception," but it is only in more recent times that the rich levels of meaning of this term have begun to break through more fully, such that the receiving process itself is now seen to involve not only texts (the documents of Vatican II) and the world behind them (what flowed into them, the discussions and debates around them, the intentions of the authors framing them), but also the world in front of them: the new contexts, and the diverse receivers, that give particularity and specificity to how richly Vatican II can be understood and made effective.[3] This inclusion of "receivers" is crucial:

> Councils do not have an effect or impact on church life independently of the interpretative and applicative work of receivers who make the potentiality of the Council a reality.[4]

2   Tillard, writing in 1992, was referring to the twentieth century. See his "Reception-Communion" in *One in Christ* 28 (1992), 307–322, at 307, quoted by Rush in his book *Still Interpreting Vatican II: Some Hermeneutical Principles* (New York/Mahwah, NJ: Paulist Press, 2004), 53 (Tillard reference, 108).
3   See Ormond Rush, *Still Interpreting Vatican II*, xi. Note also that chapters 1–3 deal with a hermeneutics of the authors, the texts and the receivers respectively.
4   Ormond Rush, *Still Interpreting Vatican II*, ix.

In Ireland, the Council was not immediately followed by reception of the kind of which Rush speaks. The bishops acted as the Council's main receivers and – in some cases, such as in the founding of educational institutes of various kinds – were assisted by religious-sponsored initiatives. The bishops set up a number of Commissions that sought to implement the Council's various decrees but, while these did much to make the Council a reality in Ireland, they operated largely independently of one another, not coming together to share a vision,[5] and remained to a large extent under the bishops' exclusive control. The hierarchical church in Ireland, but not the whole people of God in Ireland, acted as the receivers of the Council, so that the very ecclesiology of the Council about the mutual ordering to one another of the priesthood of the faithful and the ministerial priesthood (*Lumen Gentium* 10, also *Sacrosanctum Concilium* 14) was lost from view. The idea that the whole people of God is the main receiver of Vatican II[6] achieved little traction in practice, with the result that the reception of the Council in Ireland was rather "top down" and one-sided.

The verb "to receive," while perhaps appearing at first glance to suggest passivity, in reality connotes relationship because each side involved contributes something to the process, which then becomes more like a conversation or even a dialogue rather than simply "putting to use" or "directing towards an effect." This kind of process, through expressing ownership, by the whole people, of the Council, has a much greater likelihood of bearing fruit; it is also consistent with a number of Vatican II documents, which emphasise relationship and with *Gaudium et spes* in particular, which works with a dialogical framework.[7] The notion of "reception," retrieved

5   See Dermot A. Lane, "Vatican II: the Irish Experience," 72.
6   See Rush, *Still Interpreting Vatican II*, 31, 39–40, 50–51, 53f., 78, 82, 84 and 115. The entire People of God is the primary receiver; the hierarchy are not the primary receivers.
7   See Suzanne Mulligan, "The Church in the World: A Light for the Nations?" in: Suzanne Mulligan, ed., *Reaping the Harvest: Fifty Years After Vatican II* (Dublin: Columba Press, 2012), 39–62, at 42. Mulligan is drawing here on R. Gaillardetz and C. Clifford, *Keys to the Council: Unlocking the Teaching of Vatican II* (Collegeville, MN: Liturgical Press, 2012), 89.

around the time of Vatican II from ecumenical research into the principle of "conciliarity" in the early church, was recognised as something that had marked ecclesial life in the first millennium. Following studies carried out in the early 1970s by Alois Grillmeier and Yves Congar, "reception" was recognised, in the case of a Council, to be "significant in judging its effectiveness, and therefore its meaning, as a historical event."[8] It was seen that reception and conciliarity belonged together and that to lose sight of one was to lose sight of the other also.

Once the whole people of God as "receiver" comes into the picture, the character of the Council as an event, a reality, of "world-church" (Rahner) comes to the fore, bringing to awareness that receiving is worldwide, not just local (Irish), and that there must therefore be "receivings" by the church in different places giving rise to – although it is the one church – diverse discoveries of the various riches of the Council as these come to light in diverse contexts. Such *contexts* are necessarily part of the picture because Councils are always received in particular circumstances. Contexts and receivers are indeed inseparable, with receiving being necessarily selective because it is always carried out in specific *loci* that require particular emphases in the receiving.[9] This is no bad thing; it is how a rich, dynamic, ongoing process must be if it is to bear continued fruit and to plumb the Council's depths.[10] Rush states:

---

8   Ormond Rush, *Still Interpreting Vatican II*, 53–54, drawing on Rush's own summary of the writings of A. Grillmeier and Y. Congar concerning the reception of Councils in his book, *The Reception of Doctrine* (Rome: Gregorian University Press, 1977), 125–161.

9   See Ormond Rush, *Still Interpreting Vatican II*, 33; also 55f.

10   See Dennis M. Doyle, "An Interpretative Introduction to Vatican II," in William Madges and Michael J. Daley, eds, *Vatican II: Fifty Personal Stories*. Revised and expanded edition (Maryknoll, NY: Orbis Books, 2012), xv–xix, at xviii: "The history of the Council includes not only what led up to it and what happened in the proceedings and the discussions and in the drama of events, but also what has been happening since the Council in terms of how it has been received and lived out. From an historically conscious viewpoint, the meaning of Vatican II is still being worked out in the life of the church."

The questions historians pose to the text change in the light of new contexts; these new questions are not necessarily illegitimate, despite the fact that they might not have been in the minds of the Council members.[11]

Receiving, adequately, an event such as the Second Vatican Council is, then, a process that occurs in a variety of contexts that all affect the receiving and make it a "conversational" event that is not passive but is interactive in nature and exceeds the mere giving of new "data" on one side and the passive acceptance of these data on the other. This dynamic, interactive, mutual character of reception is often overlooked. When used as a noun, the word "reception" can fall victim to a reduction to one dimension: the kerygmatic – acceptance or rejection of official teaching.[12] This sort of reduction goes hand in hand with a *propositional* notion of revelation, static and ahistorical, and, consequently, with an *epistemology* that is out of kilter with Vatican II's *Dei Verbum* and, indeed, with the epistemological thrust of the Council as a whole.[13] Bearing this, and *Dei Verbum's* episte-mology, specifically, in mind,[14] it becomes clear that reception cannot be as passive a thing as reduction to its first dimension seems to suggest. If one emphasises the *process* of receiving, paying attention to its contexts and to the various receivers, then one comes to see that it is "alive," involving the interplay of God and humanity in history, creative, ever-unfinished, and Spirit-guided but not Spirit-dominated.[15] This very last point may seem shocking, but in fact the Creator invites and also respects the human contribution – and receivers are *contributors*, not passive entities. Much of this was lost in Ireland, as I have already indicated, because there was not that full hermeneutical reception of the Council of which Ormond Rush speaks.[16] One can say that Vatican II was not *conversed* about because there is no receiving of the Council's texts until the receivers enter into dialogue

---

11   Ormond Rush, *Still Interpreting Vatican II*, 33.
12   Ibid., see p. 54.
13   Ibid., see p. 66.
14   Ibid., see pp. 65–67.
15   Ibid., see chapter 4 (pp. 76f. in particular).
16   Ibid., see p. 55, indeed pp. 54–58.

with these, *making* sense *of* them as well as *finding* sense (meaning) *in* them.[17] The process is both creative and receptive.

Reception of Vatican II in Ireland

Anyone who was an active Catholic in Ireland before Vatican II, and then after it, could not possibly deny that the Council had a huge impact, changing, in many ways, the church's self-understanding as well as Catholics' own view of themselves. It will not be possible here to do justice to all the areas upon which the Council had an effect, but I will examine five on which its impact was keenly felt: the liturgy; the role of the laity in the life of the church; ecumenism and relationships with people of other faiths; the relationship between the church and the secular world; and the nature, the inner constitution, of the church itself.

The liturgy

The first document of the Council to be voted on and passed was its document on the liturgy, *Sacrosanctum Concilium* (December 1963). The bishops were quick to act in response to this text, which "gave rise to a Liturgy Commission in 1964 and a Commission on Art and Architecture in 1965."[18] Very soon after the completion of Vatican II the impact of its Constitution on the Liturgy was evident everywhere, most vividly in vernacular celebration and in celebration *versus populum*. The text's principle of "fully conscious, and active participation in liturgical celebrations which is demanded by the very nature of the liturgy" (*SC* 14) came visibly to life, with many laypersons, men and women, becoming increasingly evident in the exercise

17   Ibid., see p. 55.
18   Dermot A. Lane, "Vatican II: the Irish Experience," 70–71.

of liturgical ministries. There was increased participation, on the part of everyone, in the assembly, due not least to the shared language that was now permitted. A number of the liturgical changes occurred rather quickly after the Council, not always accompanied by the kind of dialogue and reflection that a true receiving process would require. Complaints were even aired occasionally about excesses – liturgical, ecumenical and in regard to the church-world relationship – on the part of a Fr Joseph Ratzinger, for example, writing in *The Furrow* in 1967.[19] Also, the Irish journalist, John Horgan, who covered the last session of the Council, recalled, when writing forty years later, how the leader of the Irish hierarchy prodded his brother bishops into taking on the changes while cautioning younger clergy and laity who wanted everything all at once.[20]

These last imperfections notwithstanding, the effects of the Council's Constitution on the Liturgy were rapid and, on the whole, positive and the experience of Sunday Mass became a changed one that, for the most part – and even for those who were older and had been brought up with something very different – was well, if not always enthusiastically, received. The bishops "managed" the liturgical changes well; and most Catholics who are old enough to remember that time would spontaneously list those changes as among the most memorable innovations of the immediate post-Conciliar era.

Other initiatives in regard to liturgy occurred also in the wake of the Council and remain ongoing in the Irish church today. The Bishops' first National Secretary for Liturgy, Father Seán Swayne, was appointed in 1973 and he set up, in the same year, an institute of pastoral liturgy to house his secretariat and also to reach out to parishes and communities. Today's National Centre for Liturgy, located at St Patrick's College, Maynooth, continues the work that began with him. There is also a Council for Liturgy composed of three bishops, eight priests, one religious sister

19   Joseph Ratzinger, "Catholicism after the Council," *The Furrow* (1967), 3–23, at 3–5.
20   See Dermot A. Lane, "Vatican II: the Irish Experience," 70, where he refers to John Horgan's "Remembering How Once We Were," a review-article on Louise Fuller's book, in *Doctrine & Life* (April 2003), 231.

and six lay women; and it comes under the Episcopal Commission for Worship, Pastoral Renewal and Faith Development.[21] The existence of these bodies testifies to the ongoing influence and "presence" of Vatican II's Constitution on the Liturgy in the life of the Irish church. But it does not mean, however, that certain matters from the Council, such as the competencies accorded to local – and especially to same-language regional – conferences of bishops to approve liturgical texts for use in their own geographical regions (see *SC* 22 and 36), have been given their due weight. Rather there has been a one-sided "re-balancing" of these competencies with the powers of the Holy See to permit the latter the kind of undue influence manifested recently in the production of the new liturgical texts for the English-speaking world.

An expected fruit of the perspective of *Sacrosanctum Concilium* on the active participation of all the people in the liturgy should surely have been a recognition of their baptismal right to participation in various other dimensions of the church's life and, particularly when they possess the relevant competencies, in its decision-making processes. But this has not been realised in Ireland due to a "receiving" of the Council that was weighted in favour of the hierarchy over the whole people of God.

The role of the laity

The Dogmatic Constitution on the church, *Lumen Gentium* (1964) brought to light how all God's people were called to holiness of life and also how the priesthood of all the faithful (*LG* 10) made for an equality of, and a union among, the entire people of God, making everyone, in a sense, a bearer of the church to the world and a preacher of the Gospel (a point that Pope Francis repeatedly returned to in his apostolic exhortation,

---

21   For more information on the National Centre for Liturgy, see <www.liturgy-ireland.ie>. On the Council for Liturgy, see <www.liturgy-ireland.ie/council-for-liturgy.html> and for the Episcopal Commission for Worship, Pastoral Renewal and Faith Development, see <www.catholicbishops.ie/faith/>.

Evangelii Gaudium). In the wake of Vatican II, greater numbers of lay-people became teachers of religion and training became available for this. Mater Dei Institute of Education opened in 1966, having as its purpose the academic and professional formation of religious educators and teachers for post-primary schools in Ireland. From 1969, at Mount Oliver, near Dundalk, training in catechetics was available through a variety of programmes and courses. Catholics became more active in their parishes – in liturgical ministries, as we already saw – and in other ways too, but always, and far too much, at the discretion of the priest.

It is clear that it would be incorrect to say that nothing happened after Vatican II with regard to the greater inclusion of lay people in the life and activity of the church. Yet lay involvement never reached the point whereby it was provided for at a structural level, in terms of vocational pathways for participation in the pastoral ministry of the church. Dermot Lane writes:

> No formal mechanisms exist in the church for a genuine spirit of co-responsibility between priests and people or for the participation of lay people in the decision-making processes of the church.[22]

Thus the Council's vision for the active participation of *all* the church's members in its life has been, and remains, largely unrealised. Already in the mid-1980s this was evident in such events as the founding of *Pobal Dé*, a committed group of Catholics who were concerned at the failure (or lack of desire?) on the part of the leadership of the church to empower them for service in the church and to the world. *Pobal's* submission to the Synod of Bishops on the Laity, published in *Doctrine & Life* in May-June 1987, reads as a *cri de coeur* and is an indictment, really, of a church that acknowledges the centrality of lay people by virtue of their baptism, yet denies them structural inclusion. That *Pobal* continues today, along with organisations that have since come on the scene such as *We are church Ireland* (1997), *Voice of the Faithful Ireland* (mid 2000s) and, most recently, the *Association of Catholics of Ireland* (2012) indicates that, with regard to

---

22   Dermot A. Lane, "Vatican II: the Irish Experience," 75.

lay participation, there remains a great urgency if the church's future in Ireland is to be guaranteed.

A brighter light has been the inclusion of lay writers in theological and pastoral journals, the latter more, with lay men and women penning many articles, in *The Furrow* above all other journals, as the years have passed.[23] This has been related to the gradually increasing presence of lay people in the study of theology, something that had been encouraged, in fact, in *Gaudium et spes*,[24] and, from the 1980s (which saw also the 1966-founded Irish Theological Association flourishing with lay, as well as clerical, members), lay persons had begun teaching theology. Jobs have remained a problem, however, since the lion's share of positions on theology faculties, for institutional/structural reasons, go to priests and religious.

Lane says: "the most serious neglect by the Catholic church in Ireland since Vatican II has been the failure to activate the priesthood of the laity as outlined in the documents of the Council."[25] Here Lane is close to Rush's hermeneutical key that sees the "active participation" of all in the liturgy (*SC* 14) as expressing what the Council desired in all its undertakings for all the members of the one, baptised people of God: active participation, according to their competencies, in every area of the church's life. Until the laity gain their rightful place, rightful because they too are baptised, reception of the Council will be manifestly one-sided and incomplete. Furthermore, it is increasingly argued that, because of the absence of lay persons from the church's decision-making processes, something like

23   See James Corkery SJ, "Cultural Change and Theology in Ireland" in *Studies* 352:88 (Winter 1999), 371–380, at 372.

24   See Suzanne Mulligan, "The church in the World: A Light for the Nations?" 48–50.

25   Dermot A. Lane, "Vatican II: the Irish Experience," 74. Lane's observation remains correct today, ten years later. A point to note, however, is that in 2008 the Dublin diocese introduced a programme of formation for Lay Parish Pastoral Workers on a pilot basis for three years. Each year around ten Parish Pastoral Workers at the end of their formation were appointed by the Archbishop of Dublin to parishes, with the result that around thirty Parish Pastoral Workers are now in full time ministry in parishes. Alas, the programme was discontinued after the three year pilot for financial reasons. This initiative was an important step towards implementing the vision of Vatican II; it is surely a disappointment that it is not continued.

a myopic clericalism has allowed things to happen – the worst of these being the institutional covering up of the abuse of children by clerics and religious – that would not have occurred if lay persons, especially women, had been party to the decisions also.[26]

Ecumenism and interreligious relations

In the recent past, I have written about John XXIII's ecumenical and inter-religious experiences in Bulgaria, Greece and Turkey prior to the Council that shed light on his desire for a truly ecumenical event, as well as about the encyclicals of Pius XII on Scripture, church and Liturgy that benefited from the influence of ecumenical scholarship before the Council and without which Vatican II's teaching in *Dei Verbum*, *Lumen Gentium* and *Sacrosanctum Concilium* would have been much less ecumenically significant.[27] In the same article, I sought to trace the reception of Vatican II in Ireland with regard to ecumenism,[28] highlighting what Dermot Lane had referred to as "theological landmarks" in the Council's teaching about the church – how the church of Christ "subsisted" in the Catholic church as distinct from being identical with it – and about the presence of "elements of truth and grace," and "seeds of the word," in other religions.[29]

Vatican II's Decree on Ecumenism, *Unitatis Redintegratio* (November 1964) gave rapid rise to various initiatives in Ireland: "the establishment of the Episcopal Commission of Ecumenism 1965, the Greenhills Conference in 1966, the Ballymascanlon (Inter-church) meetings from 1973 onwards and a *Directory on Ecumenism for Ireland* in 1976."[30] The Decree on

26 Ibid., see p. 75.
27 See Jim Corkery SJ, "Vatican II and its Reception in Ireland," *Doctrine & Life* 63:6 (July–August 2013), 32–45, at 33–34 especially.
28 Ibid., see pp. 34–36.
29 Ibid., see p. 34, drawing on Lane's "Vatican II: the Irish Experience," 69. Conciliar texts giving expression to Lane's "landmarks" are: *Lumen Gentium* 8, *Unitatis Redintegratio* 11, *Nostra Aetate* 2 and *Ad gentes* 9, 11, 15.
30 Dermot A. Lane, "Vatican II: the Irish Experience," 71.

Ecumenism, like the one on the Liturgy, had on-the-ground effects also because of the changes it permitted:

> I think here of the more open and reciprocal manner in which inter-church marriages could be celebrated: of the attendance (hitherto forbidden) by Roman Catholics at the weddings and funerals of their Protestant neighbours and friends; of participation in ecumenical study groups; and the setting up of the first Irish Inter-church Meeting, in Ballymascanlon, County Louth, in 1973.[31]

Many ecumenical initiatives undertaken in the wake of the Council continue. The Irish School of Ecumenics, founded in 1971, flourishes today in a university setting, seeking to be faithful to its original inspiration and sensitive to the context of religious plurality in Ireland today. The Irish Inter-church Meeting continues its work; my recent reflections on Vatican II's reception in Ireland in relation to ecumenism were developed for one of its gatherings. Within the Irish Bishops' Conference's Commission for Catholic Education and Formation is found the Council for Ecumenism (and Dialogue), which services various ecumenical bodies, both national and international.

Yet it cannot be said that fostering relations between the churches has received the attention it is due and for which Vatican II called. Catholic clergy report not having been able to prioritise ecumenical activity as much as they would have wished.[32] In Ireland, especially in Northern Ireland, inter-church initiatives are vital, yet in recent years these have become harder to achieve, and inter-confessional study of theology harder to attract people to, due to a variety of social, cultural and ecclesial factors that require further research if we are to understand them properly. There is no room for complacency about the reception of *Unitatis Redintegratio*, *Nostra Aetate* and *Ad Gentes* in Ireland's confessionally plural and religiously plural context. Initiatives of Rome have affected reception too. To know that there have been important issues at stake here, one only has to remember the document of the Congregation for the Doctrine of the Faith in 2000, *Dominus*

---

31   Jim Corkery, "Vatican II and its Reception in Ireland," 34.
32   See Jim Corkery, "Vatican II and its Reception in Ireland," 41.

Jesus, which (addressed to Catholics) sought to "re-centre" ecumenical and interreligious discussion, drawing it back from its post-conciliar openness into an expression that – fearing religious and ecclesiological relativism – favoured proclamation over dialogue as the way forward for Catholics. Thus balance was lost between these two approaches, with the very fruitful tension between them being collapsed into one side. It was another example of one-sided receiving of Vatican II.

The church's relationship with the world

Pope John XXIII, from the moment that he called the Council, made it clear that he wanted it to be *pastoral* in character, no less than it was to be ecumenical. By "pastoral" he had in mind that the church would seek to enter into a positive relationship with the modern world rather than (continue to) adopt an admonishing, even rejecting, stance. The Council document that came closest to achieving what Pope John had in mind was the Pastoral Constitution on the Church in the Modern World, *Gaudium et spes*, with its reference to the church as having "the duty of scrutinising the signs of the times and of interpreting them in the light of the Gospel" (*GS* 4). This document on the church was focused *ad extra*, inspired by a speech of Leo Cardinal Suenens, in December 1963, in which he distinguished between the church *ad intra* and *ad extra* and underscored the importance of both. What eventually emerged as the document, *Gaudium et spes*, finally passed just the day before the Council ended, was this church *ad extra* document and it had an extraordinary effect on Catholic life in the years that followed the Council. It was revolutionary in its inductive methodology, its emphasis on dialogue – and even on learning from the world (see *GS* 44, also 42), its inclusiveness, its "more sensitive and person-friendly understanding of conscience,"[33] its encouragement of lay people to study theology and of theology to engage with other academic disciplines,

---

33   Suzanne Mulligan, "The church in the World: A Light for the Nations?," 45.

its attention to human rights and social development and its focus on the family, on the political community, and on issues of peace and war.[34]

For many Catholics, after the Council (and still!), *Gaudium et spes* proved to be almost too much; yet for others it expressed the realisation of an unhoped-for dream that the church, which for so long had resisted the world, was now willing to reach out and embrace it. Attitudes to it came to serve as a kind of touchstone for where one stood in relation to the Council as a whole. The document had a considerable impact in Ireland. For one thing, the theological academics took it up – the religious in particular – in founding, and in the particular directions given to, new Institutes of Theology such as, for example, the Milltown Institute of Theology and Philosophy (1968) – and also in their various journals, fostering theological treatments based on a reading of the "signs of the times." The journals that were pastoral achieved this with more immediate success, the Dominican *Doctrine & Life* above all.[35] The Irish Theological Association showed fidelity, in its concerns and development, to the thrust and themes of *Gaudium et spes* and it continues to do so today. The bishops, in their writings, addressed issues of social justice, most notably in their fine Pastoral Letter, *The Work of Justice* (1977). The religious orders promoted and engaged in justice work in a myriad of ways. Many, for example the Jesuits in 1975, made the service of faith and the promotion of justice integral to their vision; and this led to the establishment in Dublin of the Jesuit Centre for Faith and Justice in 1978. It was *Gaudium et spes*, with its methodology of "scrutinising the signs of the times and of interpreting them in the light of the Gospel," that gave the impetus for many of these initiatives.

In the 1970s and 1980s in Ireland, the focus of the *ad extra* thinking that characterised *Gaudium et spes* was frequently the economy, particularly work and unemployment, due to Ireland's high rates of unemployment during those years. Peace, due to the ongoing conflict in Northern

---

34   Ibid., see pp. 44–61 (for this impressive list indicating the scope of *Gaudium et spes*).
35   See Jim Corkery SJ, "Cultural Change and Theology in Ireland," 375. Also, specifically on the attentiveness of *Doctrine & Life* especially to social-political issues, p. 373.

Ireland, was also a focus.[36] Many religious communities, religious sisters in particular, began to live and work among the poor, following the "preferential option for the poor" that emerged from the Medellín meeting of the Conference of Latin American Bishops in 1968, three years after the promulgation of *Gaudium et spes*, in a courageous episcopal exercise of that document's "signs of the times" methodology. I was a student of theology in the Milltown Institute in Dublin in the early 1980s and our studies and pastoral activities were enriched by these perspectives. All in all, there was, in Ireland, a positive and enthusiastic reception of *Gaudium et spes*, even if, as Sue Mulligan has written, this "shining light" from the Council continues to ask more of us.[37]

The church itself

The Dogmatic Constitution on the church, *Lumen Gentium*, in its highlighting of the call of all to holiness and in its recognition that, through the sacrament of baptism, all share in the priesthood of the faithful and are members of the one People of God, enabled a more "egalitarian" and mutual self-understanding of the church to emerge, even while its hierarchical structuring still remained firmly in view. In 2012, Gerry O'Hanlon, drawing on his book, *A New Vision for the Catholic Church: A View from Ireland* (2011), offered this encouraging statement of what the Second Vatican Council achieved by way of a vision of the church:

> The Second Vatican Council outlined a renewed, biblically inspired, vision of Church as People of God, with hierarchy in service of the people and due rights afforded to local churches, in a re-balancing of the power between the periphery and the centre.[38]

---

36 See E. McDonagh, T. McCaughey, M. Hurley, et al., *Northern Ireland – A Challenge to Theology*. Occasional Paper no. 12 (Edinburgh: Centre for Theology and Public Issues, University of Edinburgh, 1987).

37 See Suzanne Mulligan, "The church in the World: A Light for the Nations?" 61–62.

38 Gerry O'Hanlon SJ, "The People of God: Towards a Renewed church?" in *Reaping the Harvest: Fifty Years after Vatican II*, 63–87, at 63.

This vision offered the possibility for all members of the church to secure
a place in its life and activities and, as noted earlier, not a little was done to
involve them in liturgical ministries and to bring them more visibly into
the life of the parish, and even the wider church, in various ways. Thus, on
the basis of the vision of the church of Vatican II, real changes came about
for both laity and clergy that saw them working together better as members of the one Body of Christ and as sharers in the life and mission of the
church. And yet, as was seen earlier when discussing the role of the laity,
the Council's vision for them has never really been realised. O'Hanlon had
this to say, following his statement of the vision achieved by the Council
for the church:

> However, while this vision won the theological battle, it was not victorious in the
> war of implementation which followed. A substantially unreformed Roman Curia
> had no stomach for radical change, the Synod of Bishops, as established unilaterally
> by Paul VI, acquired no effective independence, and the revised canon law of 1983
> was regressive in terms of implementing the notion of collegiality and in reference
> to the decision making powers of laity in particular.[39]

So all is not well; and the "balances" achieved in the Council's texts
between, for example, the priesthood of the faithful and the priesthood
of the ordained, the primacy of the pope and the collegiality of the bishops,
the primacy of conscience and the teaching of the magisterium, the church
teaching (*docens*) and learning (*discens*), the church as collaborating with
the world rather than seeking to control it,[40] were not carried through.
O'Hanlon, drawing on Ladislas Örsy,[41] has, in his recent writings, been

---

39   Gerry O'Hanlon, "The People of God: Towards a Renewed church?," 63.
40   See Suzanne Mulligan, "The church in the World: A Light for the Nations?," 58;
     here M. draws on David Hollenbach's "Commentary on *Gaudium et Spes (Pastoral
     Constitution on the Church in the Modern World)*" in: Kenneth Himes, ed., *Modern
     Catholic Social Teaching: Commentaries and Interpretations* (Washington DC:
     Georgetown University Press, 2005), 275.
41   See Gerry O'Hanlon, *A New Vision for the Catholic Church: A View from Ireland*
     (Dublin: Columba Press, 2011), 12 and 65–67; see his essay, "The People of God:
     Towards a Renewed Church?" 70 (also 76–77); and see Ladislas Örsy, *Receiving the
     Council* (Collegeville, MN: Liturgical Press, 2009), 12.

calling for a re-balancing of dimensions of the church's life such as these. So have I; and so have others.

We emphasise such re-balancing because we see the situation that exists now as the product of inadequate reception, reception that favours one set of receivers and that manifests a self-understanding of the church that falls far short of that "communion with God and with one another" that marks the ecclesiology of the Council. In other words, the vision achieved in the Council's "balancings" (just recalled) has not carried through into the church's life; and we have returned to the "defaults" of an older theology that forgets historical consciousness, is cautious about dialogue, untrusting of humanity, unsure about the epistemology embedded in such texts as *Dei Verbum* and unable to envision the receiving of the Council as an act, first and foremost, of the whole church. For this reason, in a final section, I will attempt to highlight, based on the ground that has been travelled so far, some *perspectives* on receiving the Council that (we already noticed!) have not been to the fore in Ireland but that would, if attended to in the future, help to broaden and enrich the self-understanding of the Irish church and aid it in its reform and renewal in the twenty-first century.

Towards a More Adequate Reception of Vatican II in Ireland

My reflections in the opening section, "Reception Itself," revealed, with the help of Ormond Rush, a host of matters that belong to rich and full reception but that were not prominent as the Council was received in Ireland. Here I wish to highlight just three. The first is that the *primary receiver* of the Council is the People of God as a whole. The second is that the one church, the "world-church" (Karl Rahner), exists in and receives the Council in many *contexts*, each of which contributes to the articulation of its meaning and of the possibilities that flow from it. The third is that *conciliarity*, "a being together of the church that represents it in its entirety and that occurs most fully when an ecumenical Council is gathered"[42] is the companion of receiving and is the facilitator of its fullest expression.

(1) The process of receiving the Council must include *the entire People of God* and not just those in positions of authority in the church. This means that, in Ireland, the primary receiver of the Council is the People of God assembled here, but not out of relationship, of course, with the People of God everywhere else. However, this has not been the case, operatively, in the Irish church's reception of Vatican II. Even when I found it possible, in the previous section, to speak of a positive reception of the Council, it had to be admitted that much of this was "top down" in character, with the bishops seeking to manage or control the process of reception and the rest of the members of the church in Ireland more or less allowing this to happen. This is one-sided receiving; it fails to do justice to the mutuality between the priesthood of the faithful and the ordained priesthood to which the Council gave expression (see *LG* 10). It has kept the laity from finding their included place in the life of the Irish church and has permitted clericalism to continue. The years ahead can be different.

Because receiving belongs primarily to the people of God as a whole, it relates to the entirety of their Christian life and "sense of the faith" and it cannot be reduced to its kerygmatic dimension only: acceptance or rejection of official teaching. This leaves every dialogical element out of the process and it ignores the fact that there are theological and spiritual dimensions to receiving also.[43] Such a reduction is arid, even static: it causes revelation, and doctrine, to re-assume the kind of propositional character that they manifested at Vatican I but that was developed, in Vatican II's *Dei Verbum*,

---

42   Jim Corkery SJ, "Whither Catholicism in Ireland?" in *Studies* 101:404 (Winter 2012), 387–396, at 394, where he is drawing on Yves Congar, cited by Richard R. Gaillardetz in the latter's article "Conversation Starters: Dialogue and Deliberation during Vatican II" in: *America* (February 13, 2012), 1–4, at 1.

43   See Ormond Rush, *Still Interpreting Vatican II*, 54–55 (Rush is drawing on Alois Grillmeier here).

along more historical, relational, dynamic lines. Roman reception of the Council – in particular the emphasis of (then) Cardinal Ratzinger on the *letter*, the texts (to a fearful inclusion of any talk of the Council's *spirit*) – tended to move in this reductive direction where receiving was concerned, thus eclipsing its more relational, "conversational" character and confining it, in the main, to a merely passive reception of what the Council taught. This represented a "clawback" not only of the epistemology of *Dei Verbum* but also of the dialogical character of many of the Council documents and even, indeed, of the dialogical emphases in Ratzinger's own theology. It made receiving passive; the main body of receivers was required simply to "swallow" what they were told the Council taught rather than – as one can now hope for the future – becoming actively involved in determining its meaning and realising its possibilities in their own circumstances. Did such an approach to reception represent the kind of loss of nerve at the centre of the church that I have written about before[44] and that led to the publication of the *Catechism of the Catholic Church* in 1992, although the Council itself had not intended (or thought necessary) such an act of reception (it *was* a key Roman act of reception of the Council on the thirtieth anniversary of its opening)?

(2) Reception is *contextual* in character. This means that it is necessarily selective, showing rich and varied possibilities for how the Council can be realised in different places. The Extraordinary Synod of Bishops in 1985 acknowledged this somewhat, but its norms for interpreting the Council ran, for the most part, in a direction counter to it. Ormond Rush reminds us that contextual receiving, while necessarily selective, is not necessarily myopic. Indeed, once it is realised that the whole People of God is the primary receiver of the Council, then different receptions will be both expected and welcomed and the rich possibilities envisaged in the documents of the Council will find creative and diverse

44   See Jim Corkery SJ, "'Our Own Hope Had Been ...' (Luke 24:21), The Promise of Vatican II: Reality or Illusion?" in *Reaping the Harves: Fifty Years after Vatican II*, 13–37, at 30–32.

expression throughout the world and will foster a mutual enrichment between the various local churches. Contextual receiving is not isolated receiving. Much depends on the receivers, of course; they can be narrowly selective and belong to particular groups or "camps," as has been seen in the wake of Synod 1985 and in the battles over interpretation that have raged since then. What remains clear, however, is that the Council's being received in different contexts – Latin America, Africa, Asia – of a world-church is, rather than being a problem, both an enrichment and a necessity.

There is another sense in which a Council is never received in isolation. The dominant "receiving posture" of the church in Rome, at any given time, affects the receiving of the Council in all local contexts. As an example, I have in mind here Ireland in the wake of the publication of the Ryan and Murphy Reports in 2009. At that time, the impact of Rome was great, through the Apostolic Visitations of Irish seminaries and religious communities and the Reports that followed these. It was clear that the perspective of the Visitations, especially that of the seminaries, reflected a concern about priestly identity and "separateness," moral theology and canon law, and orthodoxy in matters to do with ministry and on moral questions, and that these areas – more or less beforehand – were considered the principal "slippery slopes" that underlay the clerical child-abuse crisis. Pope Benedict XVI's Pastoral Letter to the Catholics of Ireland, in the wake of the Ryan and Murphy Reports, was compassionate in its dialogical paragraphs but, as regards solutions, totally impervious to the need to examine ecclesial structures and, consequently, able only to provide traditional-spiritual, indeed spiritualising, solutions to the problems that had arisen. Its impact was therefore demoralising; but in the absence of the fuller approach to reception that I have been highlighting there was no real way to dialogue about this because the local context was *not* seen as a place where the Spirit might be working and where traces of Spirit-inspired responses might be discernible in the very location in which the scandals themselves had occurred. The context, in other words, instead of being a *locus* in which ways could be found, based on the theology of

Vatican II, to move the People of God to a better place, was eliminated from the picture. This amounts to an ignoring of this same People of God in Ireland as active receivers.

Ireland has had a range of its own interpretation-affecting *contexts* over the years also: increased separation between church and state; growing secularisation, cultural-postmodern changes, economic realities (most recently the recession that began in 2008) and, of course, the clerical sex abuse scandals. Furthermore, our contexts continue to change all the time, as Bishop Donal Murray has pointed out[45] and as Ormond Rush has also, referring to class, gender, race, culture, geography and local history as just a few of the factors that "come to bear on the reception process of making new meaning."[46] This last is a salutary phrase, indicating that receivers are creative; they are *contributors*. "Macro-contexts" other than Rome that affected Ireland also were related to large-scale contextual receptions of the Council in other places, for example, in Latin America's liberation theology and in the feminist theologies that developed in North America and Europe in particular. These inter-contextual receivings of the Council gave breadth to Ireland's own attempts to receive it and caused discussions to arise that brought the Christian community here into rich conversation and even into energetic, robust dialogue. This is a development to be maintained.

(3) The mention of conversation brings me to my final point: conciliarity. Receiving and conciliarity go together; in its full richness, the nature of reception is that it is "conversational," for receivers are also *contributors*. To emphasise conciliarity, as I and others have done many times recently when trying to envision the way forward for the church in

45   See Bishop Donal Murray, *Keeping Open the Door of Faith: The Legacy of Vatican II* (Dublin: Veritas, 2012), 58–60.
46   Ormond Rush, *Still Interpreting Vatican II*, 55.

Ireland,[47] is to think about the whole church meeting, with voice given to all. By the mid-1980s the church in Rome was pulling away from this and growing more centralised. There began a gradual letting go of those things from Vatican II that fostered *trust* in the people of God, the whole People, and the Spirit working in all. Sight was lost of the perspective that *Gaudium et spes* opened up with regard to the church collaborating with the world rather than seeking to control it.[48] Sight was lost of a church that could trace the Spirit in the world and learn from the same Spirit's creative presence in it. Thus the possibilities afforded by the kind of reception-pneumatology that Ormond Rush puts forward as a reforming reception model involving what he calls "'constant re-reception,' effected in the Spirit" are put aside, even as such a model "highlights the creative involvement with God on the part of the receivers of revelation."[49]

What Rush is talking about here is the People of God, in communion with God and one another, acting together in history under the ever-fresh guidance of the Holy Spirit, to bring about the renewed future that, in being God's discerned plan, will no less be the result of the actions of actively participating receivers of revelation and grace. Rush calls it a model of reform; I note that it is essentially *conciliar*, involving God and all God's people in creative conversation about how best to go forward. It is the perfect picture with which to close these reflections, promising, as it does, a church in search of renewal.

47   See Jim Corkery SJ, "Whither Catholicism in Ireland?", 393–394. On "conciliarity"
      – one can speak also of "synodality" and of "collegiality" (thinking of the bishops)
      – I am influenced much by the work of Gerry O'Hanlon and supportive of his
      suggestion that there be a "National Consultation of the Faithful" in Ireland (see
      "Appendix" in O'Hanlon's *A New Vision for the Catholic church*, 107–114, also p. 57
      and note 3 – quoting Brendan Leahy).
48   Recall Suzanne Mulligan, drawing on David Hollenbach, in "The Church in the
      World: A Light for the Nations?" 58 (and note 40 above).
49   Ormond Rush, *Still Interpreting Vatican II*, 75 (see 75–78 here).

Conclusion

By examining "reception" as a notion, and then as a historical reality in Ireland, it became possible to glimpse what goes wrong when reception is short-changed and – from observing this – to see what *could* be possible if reception were given that full scope which takes the Spirit-guided, ongoing, discerning activity of the whole community of believers fully into account. The International Theological Commission's recent (June 2014) document on the *sensus fidei* is a step in the direction of taking all believers seriously. Might its publication at this time when we are celebrating the fiftieth anniversary of Vatican II be a "sign," a sign *of* and *for* our time, suggesting that any future reception of the Council must be something that engages *all* believers spread throughout the world, yet gathered together, too, into the one, holy people of God?

JACINTA PRUNTY

7   Reception of the Call of Vatican II for
     Renewal of Religious Life: Case Study
     of the Irish Federation of the Sisters of
     Our Lady of Charity

Two American sisters of Our Lady of Charity (OLC), then studying in
Regina Mundi in Rome, provided their sisters in the Dublin convents
with eye-witness accounts of the preparations afoot for the opening of the
Second Vatican Council. The young Americans reported on how radio and
television stations set up the most modern equipment in the colonnade of
St Peter's Square "to give the world the best possible 'on the spot' information and pictures of the Council in action".[1] The sense of expectation that
gripped these young sisters and which they tried to communicate to those
not privileged to be so near the excitement is palpable: "you can see the
acceleration and the crescendo coming... so many ardent hopes are awaiting
this Council and so many important issues are at stake".[2] The young sisters
go on to explain something of the content of a course they are taking in
moral theology and its relevance to "some of the most modern problems

---

1   Sister Mary of St Francis (Rochester) and Sister Mary of the Holy Spirit (Wheeling),
     OLC Monastery, 10 Via Della Sagrestia, Vatican City, circular letter, 14 Jan. 1962
     (OLC1/03/3 no. 45). Items with the prefix OLC (Our Lady of Charity) are held
     in the archives of the Sisters of Our Lady of Charity (Irish Region), Beechlawn,
     Grace Park Road, Dublin 9. The collections are as follows: OLC1 High Park; OLC2
     Gloucester Street/Sean MacDermott Street; OLC3 St Anne's Kilmacud; OLC4 The
     Grange, Kill o' the Grange; OLC5 Central administration.
2   Sister Mary of St Francis (Rochester) and Sister Mary of the Holy Spirit (Wheeling),
     preamble dated 9 Oct. 1962 to "Travelogue, Summer of 1962", from OLC Monastery,
     10 Via Della Sagrestia, Vatican City, 21 pp (OLC1/3/3 no. 46).

that face the church".[3] That the church, and by extension their much-loved religious order, is in a whirlwind of change, is the message communicated, as is their own sense of energy and optimism in being part of it.

Back in Dublin, the Sisters of Our Lady of Charity received these eye-witness accounts and followed the media coverage with avid interest. The Council had been announced on 25th January 1959, opened on 11th October 1962, meeting over four separate Autumn periods of roughly ten weeks each, and concluded 8th December 1965. Commissions were appointed to prepare norms for the carrying out of the decrees of the Council producing their rules or guidelines over the following months and years.[4] The momentum of the Council was thus carried over several years, with intense drafting and rewriting of documents undertaken during the inter-sessional periods, and a succession of post-conciliar documents and locally produced statements, exhortations and guidelines stretching the immediate reach of the Council well into a second decade.

The High Park circular letter of December 1962 is a reminder of how at that point in time nobody could predict the direction the Council would take or even how long it would continue:

> Wholeheartedly we are united in a spirit of prayer and sacrifice, with His Holiness, Pope John XXIII, presiding over the second Vatican Council, and we pray that his efforts to restore the church to her pristine fervour may be successful, and that our separated brethren, attracted by her beauty and solidity, may seek security in her maternal outstretched arms.[5]

As the drama unfolded over the next three years, and John XXIII was succeeded by Paul VI, the Dublin OLC sisters continued to voice their

---

3   Quoting from the students' letter of 14 Jan. 1962, "Moral theology is minutely pin-pointing for us some of the most modern problems that face the church: psychology, psychiatry, narcoanalysis, hypnotism, psychoanalysis, all kinds of problems that arise condemning the life of the unborn child, the problem of mutilation, the morality of the new drugs, some not even perfected yet, which control or impede conception").

4   Ambrose McNicholl, "Why the Council was needed", *Doctrine and Life*, vol. 16, no. 2 (Feb. 1966), pp. 87–102 at 101–102, quoting *AAS*, LI (1959), 70.

5   High Park, circular letter, 12 Dec. 1962 (NDC Caen, copy in OLC1/3/1).

prayerful support for the Council fathers and their loyalty to the church, though what exactly this would entail, for them as for others, was all rather uncertain. The one point on which there was agreement was that change in the church was imminent. Profound changes were already underway in Irish society, as they were across much of the globe, and there was an obvious need for the church to move with the times.

The selection of Our Lady of Charity as a case study is due firstly to the author's knowledge of the archival record covering this period and the access that has been allowed for research purposes – a full-length history of the institute, from 1853 to the 1970s is with the publisher (Four Courts Press) at the time of writing. The volume, quality and good organisation of the materials is a testimony in itself to the seriousness with which the Council was taken by this small and unremarkable group of sisters. The above-mentioned series of letters from Rome are extant, as are community letters or circulars. There are marked-up and heavily annotated copies of the various conciliar and post-conciliar documents along with references to the setting up of study groups and attendance at outside lectures. Subscriptions were taken out to the journal *Doctrine and Life* and its supplement on religious life (published from 1964), and commentaries made. The *aggiornamento* or renewal chapter ordered by the Council for the revision of constitutions generated a wealth of paperwork, including questionnaire surveys, reports and study papers. The various drafts and revisions of constitutions, minutes of the ordinary federal and house Council meetings, manuscript reports on the apostolate and oral interviews are also extant. This large and richly varied body of research materials makes it possible to track the engagement of this group with the calls of Vatican II from 1962 to the mid 1970s, and in particular, the reception given to the call for the renewal of religious life.

But there are other reasons also for the use of Our Lady of Charity as a case-study and for the case-study approach in itself. Founded by St John Eudes in 1641, its constitutions modelled on those of the Visitation Sisters (founded by St Frances de Sales and St Jane Frances de Chantal), its core ministry was the "rescue" of girls and women in moral danger, manifest practically always in the provision of a refuge or magdalen asylum within the convent enclosure, the first house of the order, in Caen, going by the name of Notre-dame de Charité du Refuge. The sisters took a fourth vow, the salvation of souls, to underline what John Eudes had set down as their distinctive vocation. The term "magdalen laundries" has been more recently used in public discourse to describe these residential homes; the two run by the Sisters of Our Lady of Charity, alongside those of the Good Shepherd, the Sisters of Charity and the Mercy sisters, have been the subject of a major Department of Justice inquiry under the chairmanship of Dr Martin McAleese published in February 2013.[6] The movement away from the penitential aspect of their refuges and the speeding up of their modernisation (underway since 1952) and their effective replacement by 1973 by training centres, hostels and retirement or nursing homes, is an important aspect of the renewal of ministry that was inherent in the call of Vatican II to the renewal of religious life.

The Sisters of Our Lady of Charity had a long-established and closely regulated form of religious life and a highly structured core apostolate rooted in seventeenth-century France. And rather than casting off outmoded practices, the accretion of customs ever since made for an exceptionally unwieldy body of prescriptions that by the early 1960s was difficult if not impossible to challenge. The call of Vatican II for the renewal of religious life might therefore be seen in this case to be particularly disruptive of what had gone before. The long tradition of enclosure ensured that the lives of the sisters and of the women residents, however short their stay, had always been constructed as "apart from" the world. The high walls and time-honoured daily routines of what was called the monastery ensured that even on a congested city-centre site OLC saw itself as providing an oasis of peace and healing apart from the world. In addition, the two principal OLC monasteries in the Dublin archdiocese had a long tradition of autonomy, namely, High Park in the suburbs to the north east of the city, founded 1858 from an earlier asylum on Drumcondra Road, and Gloucester Street/Seán MacDermott Street, in the north inner city, founded 1888 from

6   *Final report of the Inter-Departmental Committee set up to establish the facts of State involvement with the Magdalen Laundries* (Dublin, 2013). Online at <www.justice.ie>.

High Park. The two smaller and more recent foundations, both in the south city suburbs, St Anne's Kilmacud (founded 1948) and Kill o' the Grange (1957) were also operating in a largely self-contained fashion by the 1960s. Although the superior general had visitation and some other rights since the imposition of a federation in 1948 by Dr John Charles McQuaid, in practice these houses operated independently with little communication or knowledge of each other, so that an investigation into how these sisters handled the requirement for dialogue that came with Vatican II will be illuminating. In the case of the Sisters of Our Lady of Charity, this dialogue had to extend internationally, at least, to the Continent, to England and to North and South America, where the creation of local federations of traditionally autonomous houses was already underway though in a partial, piecemeal fashion. They had no experience of general chapters or general assemblies and few traditions or routines to draw upon – there had been three such meetings only in the history of the institute, in 1734, 1909 and 1931, all held in Caen, the first to approve the constitutions of the founder, the later meetings to deal expressly with the threat of centralised government to the "primitive tradition" of the order. Communication with other houses of the order internationally had been faithfully maintained by some of the houses through circular letters, at three-yearly intervals, but the kind of sharing envisaged by the Council was of a much more demanding character. The transformation from an essentially monastic lifestyle with strict enclosure to one more suited to an active, "modern" apostolate would require the sisters to re-think the very purpose of religious life and to participate in the remodelling of countless aspects of their personal and communal lives. The obligation to attend the community mass and to sing in choir the daytime canonical hours, the public prayer of the church, was a "sacred duty" that underpinned their vocation as religious and gave shape to daily life.[7] They were hugely attached to their own choir ceremonial, which

7   The sisters were obliged to say "the Little Office of Our Lady as reformed by the holy Council of Trent and by Pope Urban VIII". *The book of customs for the religious of Our Lady of Charity of the order of St Augustine, containing the directory and the ceremonial of the divine office, the ritual for administering the last sacraments, and for burying the dead, according to the Roman rite; together with the customs and usages*

though based on the Roman missal, breviary and ritual had many details that were specific to them. The "good father and founder" himself, John Eudes, named the ceremonial, along with the constitutions, directory and book of customs, as "the foundation, soul and heart" of the congregation, and though unfinished at his death, the later compilation carried the full weight of his authority.[8] It is therefore self-evident that changes in liturgical matters would be immediately and profoundly felt by the Sisters of Our Lady of Charity. In contrast, the institute to which the author belongs, the Congregation of the Sisters of the Holy Faith, a far younger congregation of lay origins which operated in the same diocese of Dublin for many decades without an approved rule of life or constitutions and without the divine office, carried a much lighter weight of tradition. By taking an institute that put great store on monastic enclosure, regularity and autonomy and that was still committed in the early 1960s, despite some new projects, to a model of care that critics inside and outside condemned as outdated, it is expected that the call of Vatican II for the renewal of religious life would come to light with greater vividness.

However, while the case for "exceptionalism" might be made of Our Lady of Charity in some respects, its response might be explored as an example of how the call by Vatican II for the renewal of religious life was received by women's institutes at least in Ireland. The relevant documents and decrees were addressed to all religious, not to named institutions, and the requirements or stages to be followed were set out for all by Rome, including the revision of constitutions and the calling of a special *aggior-namento* general chapter. The full-length case study by Louise O'Reilly on the Union of Irish Presentation Sisters demonstrates how these steps were followed in the case of a much larger religious institute, paralleling the process undertaken by OLC and with some remarkably similar outcomes.[9] The

---

     of their congregation, and the directories of the offices of the house, trans. Peter Lewis (Aberdeen, 1888), iv, 3. Hereafter, *Customs, directory and ceremonial.*

8   Dedicatory letter, undated, of St John Eudes, died 1680, reprinted in the preamble to *Customs, directory and ceremonial,* xi–xiii.

9   Louise O'Reilly, *The impact of Vatican II on religious women: case study of the Union of Irish Presentation Sisters* (Newcastle Upon Tyne: Cambridge Scholars, 2013).

steps taken and the difficulties encountered en route by the Sisters of Our Lady of Charity as set out in this paper are specific to that institute, but by focusing on this particularly rich case study, it is argued, new insights may be gained into how Vatican II was received by women's religious orders more generally. The construction of further case studies, using the full range of documentary and oral evidence, is an obvious requirement for a fuller assessment.

The Vatican Documents: At the Core

While media coverage of the Council brought the gathering of so many bishops at Rome into the community rooms of religious institutes, it was the published documents of the Council and associated bodies that were to be the focus of common study and reflection in an unprecedented way. The way was led by the Constitution on the church, *Lumen gentium*, published 21 November 1964, regarded as one of the four key documents which provided the orientation according to which the remaining documents were to be interpreted.[10] In its theology of church as the baptised people of God where, "in the various classes and differing duties of life, one and the same holiness is cultivated by all", all the faithful, of whatever rank or station, are called "to the fullness of the Christian life and to the perfection of charity", all sharing in the universal call to holiness.[11] *Lumen gentium* presents religious life as a particular expression of a common baptism, characterised by an explicit profession of the evangelical counsels (the vows of chastity dedicated to God, poverty and obedience), positioned within the church and devoted to the welfare of the whole church.[12] It is

---

10 John W. O'Malley, *What happened at Vatican II* (Cambridge, MA, 2008), 2.

11 *Lumen gentium, The constitution on the church of Vatican Council II*, English translation, Missionary Society of St Paul the Apostle/Darton, Longman and Todd (London, 1965), nos. 40–41.

12 *Lumen gentium*, nos. 43–44.

this common baptism that constitutes the church a single people, brothers and sisters in the one Christ, each called to bear witness to him "especially by means of a life of faith and charity".[13]

The young American OLC sister students wrote of their astonishment at discovering, for the first time, that encyclical letters were addressed "to all the Clergy and Faithful of the Catholic world", not just to the bishops, and realising that they personally had an obligation to be well-informed "dynamic Catholics", not just "static Catholics": "the church has no need of Holy Sleepers in our needs of today".[14] The same realisation was dawning on their sisters in Ireland, as indeed elsewhere. As one Dublin sister worded it, the challenge was to stimulate within themselves the outward-looking spirit of the Council, *l'oecuménisme*.[15] Placing to one side the concrete characteristics and detailed rules of religious life, chapter 6 of *Lumen gentium* "treats exclusively of what is essential, immutable, of what transcends circumstances of space and time, of what therefore must be found in any authentic form of religious dedication".[16] This treatment on the nature of religious life, stripped of canonical prescriptions or rules, teaches that the gift of religious life to the church is so that "each in one's own way, may be of some advantage to the salvific mission of the church", with the duty to work "to implant and strengthen the kingdom of Christ in souls and to extend that kingdom to every land".[17] What was asked of the church in *Lumen gentium* was asked of religious life: deep reflection on its nature and limits, its functions, its meaning and mission in the world. The challenge was to see what religious life might look like when its countless small regulations, observances, mortifications, customs, devotions and rules on precedence – as exemplified for the Sisters of Our Lady of Charity in its four-part Book of Customs – were put to one side. The long-entrenched view of the church as somehow a closed society "confronting" the world

13   *Lumen gentium*, nos. 10, 12.
14   Sister Mary Francis and Sister Mary of the Holy Spirit, circular letter, 14 Jan. 1962.
15   Sainte Anne, *circulaire*, janvier 1966 (OLC 3/3/1 no. 11).
16   Gilbert Volery, "Renewal and adaptation", *Supplement to Doctrine and Life*, vol. 4 no. 2 (Summer 1966), 59–75 at 59.
17   *Lumen gentium*, no. 44.

was paralleled in religious life in its self-understanding as "apart from" the world or "flight from" the world; in OLC the enclosure was regarded as "the very basis of the religious state" and its infraction a matter of punishment.[18] The new understandings of church – as a leaven in human society, the keeper of the gospel conscience of the world, a people on pilgrimage, all of whom, without exception, are called to holiness – would destabilise the old certainties in religious life. Far from being cut off from the world, *Lumen gentium* taught, "Let no one think that religious have become strangers to their fellowmen or useless citizens of this earthly city by their consecration".[19]

It is in final major constitution of the Council, *Gaudium et spes* (7 December 1965) that the modern world as the theatre within which holiness is to be lived, is taken up more forcefully. It sets out the call to "continually examine the signs of the times and interpret them in the light of the gospel" and to get to know and understand this world, "its expectations, its aspirations, its often dramatic character".[20] The overall orientation or spirit of the Council is articulated in the much quoted phrase from the preamble to *Gaudium et spes*, namely, a wholehearted engagement with "the joy and hope, the sorrow and anxiety of the men of our time".[21] For the Sisters of Our Lady of Charity, who prided themselves on their enclosure, apartness and self-sufficiency, on their unswerving loyalty to the immutable rule of the founder and to the refuge tradition he created, the new direction taken by the church would require much more than the shedding of practices and customs that were self-evidently outdated.

The Vatican II document concerned expressly with religious life and with implementing in concrete ways its teaching is *Perfectae caritatis* (28th October 1965). The pursuit of perfect love, *perfectae caritatis prosecutio*, following the teaching and example of Jesus Christ and by means of the evangelical counsels (chastity dedicated to God, poverty and obedience),

18   *Customs, directory and ceremonial*, Article xx, Enclosure, 234.
19   *Lumen gentium*, no. 46.
20   *Gaudium et spes, Pastoral constitution on the church in the modern world*, Rome, 7 Dec. 1965, English translation, Catholic Truth Society (London, 1966), no. 4.
21   *Gaudium et spes*, preamble, para. 1.

is presented as a universal call, not at all the preserve of religious. As a distinctive way of life, which developed in different forms over the centuries, the church accepts religious life as a gift; but one which will become ever more fruitful in so far as religious more fervently "join themselves to Christ by this gift of their whole life" and involve themselves in the life and mission and of the church.[22] The decree *Perfectae caritatis* places the following of Christ, *sequela Christi*, as put before mankind in the gospel, as the supreme rule of life for all institutes,[23] allows for the special character and functions of each institute (its charism)[24] and relates religious life closely to the general pattern of the church:

> All institutes should share in the life of the church. They should make their own and should foster to the best of their ability, in a manner consonant with their own natures, her initiatives and plans in biblical, liturgical, dogmatic, pastoral, ecumenical, missionary and social matters.[25]

Institutes were called to ensure that their members have "a proper understanding" of humankind, of present-day conditions, and of the needs of the church – a theme that was taken up even more forcefully in *Gaudium et spes*, and left no room for misreading.[26]

Not only was the "the manner of life, prayer and of work" but also "the manner of governing" in religious institutes were to be re-examined to bring them into line with the "present-day physical and psychological circumstances of the members" and also with the demands of culture, and social and economic circumstances:

> For this reason, constitutions, directories, books of customs, of prayers, of ceremonies and suchlike should be properly revised, obsolete prescriptions being suppressed, and should be brought into line with conciliar documents.[27]

---

22   *Perfectae caritatis, The decree on the renewal of religious life*, promulgated 28 Oct. 1965, trans. Austin Flannery, commentary by Gregory Baum, New York: Paulist Press, 1966), no. 1.
23   *Perfectae caritatis*, "General principles of renewal", no. 2(a).
24   *Perfectae caritatis*, "General principles of renewal", no. 2(b).
25   *Perfectae caritatis*, "General principles of renewal", no. 2(c).
26   *Perfectae caritatis*, "General principles of renewal", no. 2(d).
27   *Perfectae caritatis*, "Criteria of renewal", no. 3.

Key themes in *Perfectae caritatis* had been foreshadowed in a number of addresses by prominent church leaders.[28] Cardinal John Baptist Montini, later Paul VI, as archbishop of Milan addressed an assembly of nuns on 11th February 1961, calling on them to take their place in the world today, to become active collaborators in the church "which seeks to sanctify and save the world", to live in small groups, in direct contact with "modern humanity", and to "prepare well, to become qualified so that you will be able to influence, to educate, to Christianise the world".[29] As Paul VI his address to sisters in the diocese of Albano, delivered on 8th September 1964 and widely reprinted, set out in unequivocal terms what the new pope thought of those religious who remained "on the outskirts of the church constructing for oneself a spirituality which is cut off from the circulation of word, of grace and charity in the Catholic community of brothers in Christ".[30] His call for "a more direct and fuller participation in the life of the church, in the liturgy especially, and in social charity, in the modern apostolate, in the service of one's brothers" was in line with what the Council was working towards in the long-drawn-out compilation of what was to be *Perfectae caritatis*, promulgated a year later (28th October 1965).[31]

Only the general principles of the up-to-date renewal of the life and discipline of religious institutes were dealt with in *Perfectae caritatis*; the norms for implementing the decree were issued in *Ecclesiae Sanctae II* (6 August 1966), coming into effect on 11th October 1966, marking the fourth anniversary of the inaugural session of the Vatican Council under John XXIII. The programme of *aggiornamento* as set out in *Ecclesiae Sanctae II* placed the onus for renewal on the sisters themselves. This was unprecedented for the Sisters of Our Lady of Charity, as indeed it was for many other religious congregations; their most recent experience of significant

28   George Andrew Beck, "The schema on religious", *Doctrine and Life*, vol. 15, no. 8 (Aug. 1965), pp. 419–429.

29   John Baptist Montini, "Apostolic involvement", *Supplement to Doctrine and Life*, no. 8 (Winter 1964), pp. 171–180, at pp. 177, 179.

30   Paul VI, "Nuns and the church", trans. Austin Flannery, *Supplement to Doctrine and Life*, vol. 3 no. 3 (Autumn 1965), 145–147, at 146.

31   Paul VI, "Nuns and the church", 147.

change, the OLC Irish federation of 1948, had been masterminded from start to finish by the archbishop, Dr McQuaid, with only their *fiat* required.[32]

Several areas of Council teaching seem to have been received with particular enthusiasm by the Sisters of Our Lady of Charity in Ireland. Its teaching that up-to-date renewal involved "a constant return to the sources of the whole of the Christian life", engendered a surge of interest in scripture studies and in the liturgy of the church.[33] The call "to strive to achieve a true understanding of the spirit of their foundation" led the sisters to reflect on how John Eudes' response to need was circumscribed by time and place.[34] By moving beyond the four-part book of customs (with directories, ceremonials, rituals) which (they believed) had come directly from the founder's hand, they were caught up in the Council's wish that "their religious life may be purified from elements alien to it and freed from matters that have become obsolete".[35] The modernisation of ministry, informed by new insights into the charism of the founder and tied up with the revision of the constitutions, generated much discussion and experimentation. It is important to note that the founding apostolate of Our Lady of Charity, the refuge or magdalen asylum, was already in process of modernisation in Dublin before the Council commenced; an early effort was the introduction in 1954 of "curtained cubicles" in place of the large dormitories and reported as progress made "towards modernising our penitentiaries".[36] Other incremental improvements were the ending of uniform dress, replacing the long refectory tables with small tables, dropping the "house names" (given to preserve anonymity), allocating "pocket money", and the inauguration of classes in domestic economy for

32   See Jacinta Prunty, *From Magdalen asylums to small group homes: the Sisters of Our Lady of Charity in Ireland, 1853–1973* (Dublin: Fours Courts Press, 2015), chapter 7.
33   *Perfectae caritatis*, "General principles of renewal", no. 2.
34   *Ecclesiae Sanctae II*, 6 August 1966, "Rules for the execution of the decree *Perfectae caritatis* of the Second Vatican Council" in *Vatican Council: applying the decrees*, trans. by J.G. McGarry (Dublin: Catholic Truth Society of Ireland, 1966), no. 16.3.
35   *Ecclesiae Sanctae II*, no. 16.3.
36   High Park local Council, minutes, 14 Sept. 1954, 2 Oct. 1954 (OLC1/5/2 no. 1); Report on the second general chapter of the Irish federation, 24 Nov. 1954 (OLC1/5/2).

the younger women, "with a view to their re-establishment in the world".[37] The earliest extant "home movie" records a day trip to the beach in July 1961, the women wearing skirts and dresses of every colour and design.[38] The implementation of the "group system", namely, smaller numbers in a more homely setting with greater personal autonomy and independence became official High Park policy in 1967 for all residents,[39] requiring the reconstruction of an enormous institutional building to give each group its own sleeping accommodation, recreation room and dining area, a craft room or workroom, with its own allotted "house mother", its own schedule of outings, celebrations and holidays, and managing – in a small way – its own purchases of clothing, shoes, other necessities and small treats. Change in the refuges or laundries, well documented in the archival record, speeded up in the later 1960s though Vatican II was not the only factor forcing modernisation – Diarmaid Ferriter points out how in that decade television came into Irish homes, foreign investment and international trade opened up, involuntary emigration slowed, the opportunity of second-level education was greatly extended, married women began to form a significant segment of the paid labour force, and there were new fora for thoughtful, critical analyses of the status quo.[40] Margaret MacCurtain draws attention to the efforts made in the 1950s by sisters, urged on by Rome, to bring themselves up to date in terms of professional qualifications and how the isolation of communities was broken somewhat by the emergence of confederations and opportunities to meet with other sisters.[41] While these factors certainly contributed to the momentum building up towards change, there can be no doubting the significance of Vatican II thinking

---

37   Irish federation general chapter 1954 record.
38   "Outing to Rush, July 1961", 16mm cine film (OLC1/12/5 no. 1).
39   High Park, circular letter, 8 Dec. 1967 (NDC Caen, copy in OLC1/3/1).
40   Diarmaid Ferriter, *The transformation of Ireland 1900–2000* (London, 2004), pp. 536–622.
41   Margaret MacCurtain, "Godly burden: Catholic sisterhoods in twentieth-century Ireland", reprinted in Margaret MacCurtain, *Ariadne's thread, writing women into Irish history* (Galway: Arlen House, 2008), pp. 321–322.

on the direction the sisters' traditional concern with women and girls "on the margins" would now take.

Another major issue for Our Lady of Charity, though progress was to stall for some decades more, was the creation of an effective central government for what had always been autonomous houses. In offering himself as director of the process of *aggiornamento* among the OLC sisters internationally, the French-Canadian Eudist priest Fernand Lacroix stated the need for a "quickening pace to canalise all efforts" lest the deviations become too great "and a final synthesis near impossible".[42] Though he did not have success on this front, he did oversee tangible and substantial progress in other overlapping and inter-related areas – charism, the role or purpose of the order, revision of the constitutions, and modernisation of ministry, which have been selected here for discussion as exemplifying the reception of the call of Vatican II for the renewal of religious life in this particular case study.

Preparations for the 1969 *Aggiornamento* General Chapter and the Irish Federal Chapter of 1973

It was the promulgation on 11th October 1966 of the norms for implementing the decree on the renewal of religious life that put the business of adaptation and renewal into action; *Ecclesiae Sanctae II* forced an immediate engagement through its ruling that "to promote adaptation and renewal" each institute must convoke a special general chapter within two, or at most three, years.[43] The International Union of Superioresses General (UISG) teased out the norms with its own summaries and studies, most

---

42   Fernand Lacroix, Rome to all the Sisters of Our Lady of Charity of the Refuge, 7 Oct. 1966, copy letter, 2pp (OLC5/3/1).
43   *Ecclesiae Sanctae II*, no. 3.

usefully in *Revision of the constitutions* (August 1967).[44] Responsibility lay with the institutes themselves and would require the co-operation of every superior and of every member at each stage of the process; this was not a task that could be subcontracted or "bought in" from another institute and there were no short cuts. The steps taken towards renewal across all four federations of Our Lady of Charity followed much the same pattern as those taken by other institutes though that did not lessen their novelty for the sisters involved.

It is the Irish federal *aggiornamento* chapter of October 1973, held in Our Lady's Retreat House, Finglas, Dublin that must be the focus of this paper as that was the meeting at which the renewal called for by the Second Vatican Council took shape at the local level through the decisions made about how to implement the revised constitutions. It was only when the revised constitutions were in their hands that the sisters knew for sure what they were working with. Work in advance of that date, directed by Fr Lacroix, required several pre-chapter meetings at local, federation and international level. A "first contact" or consultative meeting, of representatives of all the federations and of the independent houses, was held in Rome in September 1967 to agree the plan of preparatory work.[45] A further purpose of the September 1967 meeting though it did not make progress was "to study the possibilities of the unification of the whole Order, the necessity of which is felt more and more each day".[46] This meeting did however agree on the creation and funding of a central "Commission for the *aggiornamento* of the Order" composed of sixteen members and chaired by Sister Mary of St Bernard Scanlon (England) who was based in Rome "in order to be impartial to the federations". The chairman and two assistants formed the "central bureau" with the task of working closely with the delegate, Fr Lacroix, to co-ordinate and simulate the work of preparation.[47]

---

44 International Union of Superioresses Generals (U.I.S.G.), *Revision of the constitutions*, bulletin no. 5 (Rome, August 1967), 24.

45 Order of Our Lady of Charity, Rome meeting, minutes, Sept. 10–20, 1967, no. 1 (OLC5/3/1).

46 OLC, Rome meeting, minutes, Sept. 10–20, 1967, no. 1.

47 OLC, Rome meeting, minutes, Sept. 10–20, 1967, no. 18.

Once the general chapter was formally convoked and the election of delegates was completed,[48] the central bureau in Rome took responsibility for the logistics of the chapter, circulated questionnaires and guidelines for discussion groups, and sent out syntheses of the material collated to date, what amounted to a "preliminary draft" of the text of constitutions but "as a basis only for discussion".[49]

In the returns from Ireland to the questionnaire survey of 1967, dissatisfaction with a large number of domestic arrangements came to light: the lack of hot water, the bulk purchase of shoes and the false economy of over-repairing, the asking of "petty permissions" within the house to lend or borrow small items, the barrack-like community room, which "ought to have the appearance of a home, even to have arm chairs is recommended".[50] The day's timetable left little if any choice to the individual, with repeated appeals to lift the obligation to sew during recreation time, to be "allowed to go out walking in groups and not in procession", even perhaps to walk in the locality "with choice of companion or perhaps with some of the girls".[51] Norm no. 26 was quoted verbatim and underscored: "In all cases the order of the day must be arranged in such a way as to provide for the religious, besides the time given to spiritual exercises and apostolic activities, a little time for themselves and sufficient time also for legitimate recreation".[52] There are demands for further updating in all that relates to the sisters' ministry and a concern about equity, justice and greater respect for the individual girl or woman resident: "Opportunities, equipment and time

48   The general chapter was formally convoked on 25 Nov. 1968 to open on 5 Oct. 1969;
       for a lengthy discussion on why there was need for an indult of the Holy See to hold
       it and the structure of the electoral colleges, see Fernand Lacroix to Dear Reverend
       Mothers and very dear Sisters, 25 Nov. 1968, copy letter (OLC5/3/1).
49   Central bureau, Rome, "Preliminary project of a text of constitutions to form a basis
       for discussion now and the general chapter in October", 16 June 1969 (OLC5/3/1).
50   Compilation of the results of the discussions held by the Sisters of the Irish Federation
       on the response to the questionnaire which was sent out in January 1967, nos. 8, 10,
       13, 34, 47, 49, 160 (OLC5/3/1). Hereafter, Questionnaire.
51   Questionnaire, nos. 155, 159, 162, 174, 180, 184.
52   *Ecclesiae Sanctae II*, no. 26 as quoted in Questionnaire, no. 162.

for developing gifts of intellect and nature should be available to all, according to their capabilities; at present, only a select few are benefiting by such openings".[53] The conciliar teaching on obedience, traditionally at the heart of religious life, had a strong appeal: "we agree that the sisters be treated as mature, responsible adult women, like our sisters in the world and be given scope to use our initiative in our employments".[54] The superior's right to decide was not at issue, but the right to submit views and to be heard, to have "regular discussions and staff meetings where opinions could be freely given and problems sorted out" was pressed, also that letters might come and go without being opened by the superior.[55]

The *aggiornamento* general chapter of the Order of Our Lady of Charity opened on 5th October 1969 under the direction of Fr Fernand Lacroix, apostolic delegate, at the Institute of St John Eudes in Rome. The forty-five capitulants or chapter members, representing all four federations and practically all non-federated monasteries, were drawn from houses in France, Ireland, US, England, Portugal, Italy, Canada, Spain, Mexico, and Nairobi.[56] Lacroix must be credited with knowing his audience well.[57] He urged great objectivity among the chapter delegates, "which means in practice great elasticity and suppleness", warning against giving what happens in any country "an absolute value": "if you feel you cannot accept another country's views and values as being of use, it is better that you leave immediately as otherwise we will do no good".[58]

---

53 Questionnaire no. 66, see also nos. 6, 56, 114.
54 Questionnaire, no. 81.
55 Questionnaire, nos. 2, 76, 83, 85, 81, 145, 165, 188.
56 The chapter sent a formal letter to Mother M. Clare Huriek, superior, Carrolton, Ohio, insisting on the necessity of her presence or that of a delegate; she replied, giving as the reason for non-involvement that no sister could be spared from their exceptionally busy work. General chapter, detailed minutes, seventh session, 10 Oct. 1969 and twenty-sixth session, 31 Oct. 1969.
57 Père Lacroix was involved in numerous federation, inter-federation and individual house meetings in North America and in Europe over at least a decade, including the meetings in Rome in 1960 and 1967.
58 Sister Lucy to Dear Mother and Sisters, 9 Oct. 1969.

Of all the matters that were to concern the delegates over the seven weeks of the chapter, the need to identify the end of the order, to be clear about what it is, and what it is not, was paramount.[59] The "free exchange of views" set out for the first few days of the chapter and undertaken initially in language groups centred on the theme: "Our Lady of Charity in the church and in the world of today; what it was, what it is and what it should become"; it resulted in a storm of requests for clarification, no doubt the intention of its skilled facilitator. "The end of the Order is important, we must have a very precise idea of it, and the best opportunity to do this is when all the countries are meeting here together".[60] Five commissions or teams were set to work on different sections of the pre-chapter submissions; the work of Commission no. 1 was titled "The apostolate", its subject matter "the end of the order – the fourth vow – zeal for the salvation of souls – the missions".[61]

Pre-chapter submissions from Ireland were crystal clear on the vocation of the order: "we have been founded for the fallen and delinquent girl, we should not depart from our vocation in this important matter". Underlying this was a concern that the institute in Ireland was being used as a home for mentally retarded girls, for whom the sisters could do very little in terms of training and for whom the concept of rehabilitation had no relevance, a concern for OLC communities elsewhere also.[62] Another shared concern was of elderly women remaining in the house, "because in the past, it was more our policy to protect them than to rehabilitate the younger ones into society. We believe now that we must keep those with us, but that it is it not the aim of our Order to accept or receive any others".[63] Group discussion revealed an alarmingly wide range of activities across all countries; it was already self-evident that unless the institute knew what its work was, and was not, it could not refuse anything at all that might

59   *Perfectae caritatis*, "General principles of renewal", no. 2(b).
60   General chapter, general minutes, fourth session, 8 Oct. 1969.
61   General chapter, general minutes, third session, 8 Oct. 1969.
62   Questionnaire, nos. 99, 116–117. See also General chapter 1969, general minutes, fourth session, 8 Oct. 1969.
63   General chapter, general minutes, fourth session, 8 Oct. 1969.

be asked of it by bishop or state authority. The first constitution as finally approved by the chapter after numerous drafts and animated discussion opens with the following:

> Art. 1. The Order of Our Lady of Charity, founded by St John Eudes in 1641, is an apostolic religious institute of pontifical right.

> Art. 2. It is especially for the service of socially and morally maladjusted girls and women who voluntarily ask for their help or who are confided to their care.

> Art. 3. As religious of Our Lady of Charity we ought to help those persons to recover confidence in life, to acquire or regain the sense of their human dignity and their personal value as children of God.

The church's missionary thrust is acknowledged, as is the need for courageous witness regarding the human dignity of the individual, while the charism of John Eudes is set out in simple language:

> Art. 6. It is in the Heart of Jesus that we discover those who are confided to us. We learn to see them through his eyes, to love them with His heart. We wish Christ to continue through us and by us his work of mercy and love.

The first constitution concludes with a restatement of the institute's traditional devotion to Mary, whom God has associated in the salvation of the world and in whom the Holy Spirit has formed Jesus.

Implementing the 1969 *Aggiornamento* Chapter: The OLC Federal Chapter, October 1973, Dublin

Only eight sisters – seven capitulants and one secretary – from the Irish Federation were present at the *aggiornamento* general chapter in Rome 5th October to 29th November 1969. The long letters composed each week on behalf of the "Irish Contingent" by a young secretary, Sister Lucy Bruton, brought to those left at home some sense of the unfolding drama of the chapter as well as more homely matters – there were outings on Sundays, new foods and mad motorists. The chapter itself was a "veritable tower of Babel at the outset", with mass "a polyglot affair".[64] Rome itself was a wonder; there were tours of the catacombs of St Callixtus, a visit to San Clemente by kindness of the Irish Dominicans, and an audience with Paul VI at which he extended his apostolic blessing.[65] In St Peter's, "the statue of St John [Eudes] is looking down as you come in to the basilica and you would think he was peeping out to see us".[66] The principal work, the revision of the constitutions, had been accomplished, and nobody could accuse the capitulants of rushing them through.

A short federal chapter was held in March 1970 at which typescripts of the "experimental" constitutions were available but much was left on hold until these were formally presented to Rome.[67] The next federal chapter was held, as scheduled, in January 1971, at which a new federal superior, Mother Nativity Kennedy, was elected. The matter of simplifying the habit and veil of the sisters, the dress of future novices, and when lay dress might be worn were among the maters aired.[68] But the chapter that mattered was the federal chapter of October 1973. It followed much the same pattern as the *aggiornamento* general chapter of 1969; composed of *ex officio* and elected delegates (twenty-two sisters in all), it voted its own rules and procedures, appointed secretaries and scrutineers, and elected four moderators who, with the chapter secretary and one other nominee, would form the central co-ordinating committee.[69] It voted to allow observers from the different communities attend the plenary sessions, an invitation that was taken up most days, and there was also one outside observer, Sister Mary Coyne of

64   Lucy Bruton, Rome to Dear Mother and Sisters, 9 Oct. 1969 (OLC5/3/1).
65   Lucy Bruton, Rome to Dear Mother and Sisters, 20 Oct., 7 Nov., 14 Nov. 1969 (OLC5/3/1).
66   Lucy Bruton, Rome to Dear Mother and Sisters, 20 Oct. 1969 (OLC5/3/1).
67   This was a continuation of the August 1969 federal chapter which had been adjourned not closed.
68   Memo, Chapter 1971, Matters to be decided by the superior general and her Council (OLC5/1/1 no. 6).
69   Federal chapter, minutes, 5 Oct. 1973, preliminary session, p. 2.

the English Federation, present on behalf of the Council of the Order. The preliminary or preparatory commissions were constituted by the federal chapter to be chapter commissions; each had prepared a draft document to be presented, discussed and voted on in plenary session. The task was to produce a local directory, and the headings, as finally agreed, were religious apostolic life (prayer, community life, community regulation), apostolate, missions, formation, government, temporal administration. The challenge was to be faithful to the spirit of *aggiornamento* as articulated in the conciliar documents and in the order's new constitutions, and in a way that could be embraced by four essentially autonomous communities.

The federal superior's summary report covering 1970–1973 is an update on the move to small group care and what this involved in terms of reorganisation of the residential work already being done and the reconstruction of houses into self-contained units. It is an audit of their apostolic work within the Dublin diocese at that particular date, and how far the sisters had moved from the "magdalen laundry" and reformatory/industrial school models of institutional care with which they had been associated since the 1850s. There were units or "small group homes" for teenagers (High Park, Drumcondra and Sean MacDermott Street in the north inner city), for children (two units in High Park, one in the Grange, Kill o' the Grange), an after-care unit for former residents (The Grange), and groups for older women (three in High Park, three in Sean MacDermott Street). But there were also "new works", involving the reconstruction or re-allocation of existing buildings: a project with women working in prostitution (bungalow at High Park), a transition hostel (Sean MacDermott Street) and casual unit (Sean MacDermott Street), also Girlsville transition unit at St Anne's Kilmacud and two new "family group homes", accommodating twelve each, at The Grange.[70] Martanna House Hostel, in the grounds of High Park, for girls in transition, was supplemented by 124 Grace Park Road (seven girls), while a very small number of girls on remand, no more than four in total at a given time, could be received in Grianan (High Park),

---

70   For young people "small group" meant ten to fifteen maximum; for the women the
      groups were thirty-five to forty persons maximum.

the Casual Unit (Sean MacDermott Street) and St Anne's (Kilmacud), "for a temporary period pending the building of a new state prison for women".[71] Residential care for "persons of low intellectual ability, likely to be exploited and for whom no other provision is made" would continue for those already in OLC care, but the chapter resolved that no other persons in this class were to be admitted, even for short-term care, without careful prior investigation and with full consultation with the health board and with organisations "directly involved with mentally handicapped".[72] Accommodation for "lady boarders", the guest houses at High Park (St Michael's) and Kilmacud (Kilmacud House), would be "retained but not developed", with a note that in the long term this work might be entrusted to another body.[73] These changes were to realign with what the new constitutions specified as the purpose of the order, "for the service of socially and morally maladjusted girls and women who voluntarily ask for their help or are confided to their care".[74] Emphasis was to be placed on rehabilitation and on "open settings"[75] with aftercare to be factored in, with each unit to make explicit provision for this "with regard to visits, holidays, training in use of leisure time, giving help when out of work, etc.".[76] In what was traditionally called the field of "preventive work", those children "deprived of a normal home life" (in addition to "young persons endangered by the irregularities or immorality of their families"), could be cared for, but "we aim at giving them a home in keeping with today's standard of living and at preparing them to meet life according to their ability and background".[77]

The 1973 federal chapter reported on non-residential care, still a very new field for OLC in Ireland, and made possible further experiments

71   Report on the state of the Irish federation 1970–1973, federal chapter, minutes, 5 Oct. 1973, preliminary session, pp. 1–8a (OLC5/1/7).

72   Statutes, regulations and recommendations of the federal chapter, minutes, 7–13 Oct. 1973, no. 15. Hereafter, Statutes, regulations and recommendations.

73   Statutes, regulations and recommendations, no. 17.

74   Constitutions of Our Lady of Charity, 1973, art. 2 (OLC5/3/1).

75   Statutes, regulations and recommendations, no. 18.

76   Statutes, regulations and recommendations, no. 21.

77   Statutes, regulations and recommendations, no. 16.

through clubs "or any other acceptable forms of rehabilitation that may present themselves".[78] There was co-operation with the Legion of Mary in its "picket work", and in its future plans to provide an emergency service for women working in prostitution; the involvement of legionaries with the Sisters of Our Lady of Charity dates from the very foundation of the Legion in the 1920s but for the sisters in Ireland to get personally involved in street rescue work was unprecedented.[79] Of broader appeal was the "foyer project" or Contact Advisory Service set up at federation level as an "experimental project" in October 1972.[80] This advertised itself as a free, confidential and non-denominational advisory service that aimed "to offer to young people a preventative and supportive service that will help short-term wanderers avoid becoming long-term drifters, and to inform them of existing services".[81] It had drop-in offices in the centre of the city, 13 Westmoreland Street, and involved three qualified social workers (two sisters and a young lay woman); it offered a six-day service with a telephone number for further out-of-hours contact, and in its first nine months of operation it reported 416 persons assisted with 1,129 visits.[82] Another development was the presence of two sisters teaching catechetics part-time in local schools.[83]

The willingness to at least try and read "the signs of the time", to collaborate with others, and to experiment with new ways of assisting what had always been the target group – women and girls on the margins of society – was grounded in the new church teaching. At least some of the sisters made valiant efforts to become "knowledgeable and involved", as the general chapter had called them to be. There is a scrapbook collection titled "1973: news

---

78   Statutes, regulations and recommendations, no. 18.
79   Report on the state of the Irish Federation 1970–1973, p. 6; High Park local Council, minutes, 8 Jan., 25 June, 9 July, 8 Aug., 16 Aug., 20 Aug., 3 Sept., 1 Oct., 22 Oct. 1973.
80   High Park local Council, minutes, 13, 19 June, 12 Sept. 1972, 29 May 1973.
81   "Youth advisory service", *Irish Press*, 6 Feb. 1973. See also "Contact for the needy", *Irish Independent*, 8 Feb. 1973; "Helping the young who are at risk", *Sunday Press*, 11 Feb. 1973.
82   Report on the state of the Irish Federation 1970–1973, p. 6.
83   Report on the state of the Irish Federation 1970–1973, p. 6.

cuttings re the Apostolate".[84] A student research paper, on adolescent girls "in need of care and protection in Dublin", had as preamble an extract from the Constitution on the church in the modern world (*Gaudium et spes*), which warns against being content with an "individualistic morality" in this time of "profound and rapid change".[85] There was reflection and much discussion; there was some experimentation and action also.

The creation of a new federal structure which would oversee both the ongoing modernisation of residential care and the new initiatives was perhaps the most significant post-Vatican II structural change to the institute in Ireland. The "Apostolate Team" was appointed by the federal leadership to operate across all houses and works, "to be a co-ordinating centre for information and communication on matters relating to the apostolate within the Federation".[86] It had its origins in the apostolate committee created in February 1971,[87] and reconstituted by the federal chapter of 1973 as the apostolate team of four members, each with her area of special responsibility: older women, adolescents, children, special projects (Contact, Bungalow and others).[88] For near-autonomous houses, where the other communities barely knew their business and certainly did not proffer advice on how they might better conduct it, this was a departure that would have real, long-term effects: "At stated intervals each member will hold meetings with the sisters working in the field she represents, and at least once a year a general meeting of all involved in all fields".[89] There was also a gesture towards collaboration with outside projects, though in

---

84   Scrapbook of news cuttings (OLC1/12/4).
85   *Constitution on the church in the modern world*, chapter II, no. 30, as quoted in preamble to "Report on adolescent girls between the ages of 14 to 18 years in need of care and protection in Dublin", working team Sister Mary Wall OLC, Colette Murphy, Bernadette Ryan, Francis Barrington, Brendan Jackson, Mark Mulvin, Dublin Institute of Adult Education, 62 Eccles Street, Dublin 7, April 1973 (OLC archives library).
86   Statutes, regulations and recommendations, no. 22.
87   General Council, minutes, 17 Feb. 1971 also a local apostolate committee established within High Park, see High Park local Council, minutes, 16 Oct. 1972, 13 Nov. 1972.
88   Statutes, regulations and recommendations, no. 22.
89   Statutes, regulations and recommendations, no. 22.

the form of a recommendation not a regulation: "in work pertaining to our apostolate, we should co-operate with whatever diocesan efforts are made in that area".[90]

The federal superior's report of 1973 hints at the struggle to manage upheaval under so many headings, over such a short span: "Many questions in the areas of unity, diversity, communal prayer, pluralism of lifestyle, interior renewal, emphasis on the person, mutual trust and understanding, etc. remain to be answered".[91] It was the sharing in the church's liturgical life through daily mass and office, as well as the opportunities for personal prayer, spiritual reading, retreats and recollection, that was credited with supporting and strengthening the life of the federation.[92] The chapel timetable had been simplified, with morning and evening prayer said in common, and compline (night prayer) to be said in groups or in private.[93] One of many challenges was to protect the divine office from having trimmings added.[94] In terms of community regulation, small changes helped draw daily life more into accord with the spirit of *Perfectae caritatis* and with the new constitutions.[95] The 1973 statutes set out that "the order of the day shall be arranged in such a way that each sister has time also for relaxation" and formalised one half-day free per week, either morning or afternoon.[96] The new statutes allowed each sister to "assume personal responsibility for correspondence and phone calls"[97] and also made provision for an annual holiday.[98] The constitutions and statutes were to be studied and discussed in small group settings, no longer read aloud in the refectory.[99]

90   Statutes, regulations and recommendations, p. 10.
91   Report on the state of the Irish Federation 1970–1973, p. 7.
92   Report on the state of the Irish Federation 1970–1973, p. 6.
93   Statutes, regulations and recommendations, no. 7.
94   Federal chapter, minutes, 12 Oct. 1973, fifteenth session, p. 58.
95   *Perfectae caritatis*, no. 3.
96   Statutes, regulations and recommendations, no. 13, p. 6.
97   Statutes, regulations and recommendations, p. 4.
98   Statutes, regulations and recommendations, p. 6.
99   Statutes, regulations and recommendations, p. 4.

In the area of formation or training to be offered to new entrants, measurable progress was made between the general chapter of 1969 and the federal chapter of 1973. An enthusiastic five-strong formation team, appointed early in 1971,[100] took on as its first task the organising of "live in" weekends and open days for girls interested in the OLC apostolate and also drew up an advertising brochure.[101] Members of the team attended lectures and workshops on the topic held in Bellinter, County Meath, with formation personnel from other congregations, both men and women.[102] Given due credit for their efforts at studying and trying to implement "the recommendations of recent decrees, documents etc. on novitiate formation", there were calls at the chapter to give the new formation programme and personnel a chance to develop.[103]

What the formation team proposed was derived largely from *Renovationis causam*, on the renewal of religious formation, issued by the Sacred Congregation for Religious and for Secular Institutes (6th January 1969); this instruction broadened the canons or regulations governing formation, to allow each congregation "to make a better adaptation of the entire formation cycle to the mentality of younger generations and modern living conditions, as also to the present demands of the apostolate, while remaining faithful to the nature and special aim of each institute".[104] The innovative OLC programme included apostolic formation periods outside the novitiate and a scholasticate after first vows which would include twelve months "complete integration in the community and apostolate of a house of the federation".[105] The two-month programme of preparation before final vows was to be tailor-made to suit the individual candidate.[106]

---

100   General Council, minutes, 17 Feb. 1971.
101   High Park local Council, minutes, 15 June, 4 Sept., 9 Oct. 1970.
102   High Park local Council, minutes, 20 April 1971.
103   Federal chapter, minutes, 9 Oct. 1973, eighth session, p. 38.
104   Introduction, Sacred Congregation for Religious and for Secular Institutes, *Renovationis causam*, Instruction on the renewal of religious formation, 6 Jan. 1969, English translation from *L'Osservatore Romano*, CTS edition (London, 1969), p. 7.
105   Statutes, regulations and recommendations, nos. 32–33.
106   General Council, minutes, 17 Feb. 1971.

At the time of the federal chapter, the two novices with the congregation had just enrolled on the formation programme in Mater Dei Institute of Education, Clonliffe College, Dublin.[107] The concept of ongoing renewal, promoted in *Ecclesiae sanctae II*, was built into the remit of the formation team,[108] and a period of renewal, every ten years or so, was legislated for in the federal statutes.[109]

The ending of the obligation to maintain enclosure had been fully grasped by 1973, at least, if the numbers of sisters able to drive is any indicator.[110] Though the group photo of delegates at the November 1969 general chapter meeting shows Mother Eithne O'Neill, superior general of the Irish federation, as the only sister (among about fifty) still dressed in the "Sister Perpetua" version of the habit that had been set down by Caen in the mid-eighteenth century,[111] the Irish sisters had caught up by the early summer of 1970, when arrangements for remodelling the habits were made: "Miss Pat Coyle is being employed part-time for measuring and cutting-out and Charlotte will come from the work-room to do machining".[112] Legislating on the length of the dress was an issue but the statute as approved simply states that the habit shall be cream with a scapular and the veil shall be black.[113] An engagement with "the world" and an anxiety to keep abreast of developments was evident in the report on recent and ongoing training of the sisters: in arts, nursing, child care, religious education, commercial subjects, at courses both full-time (eleven sisters) and part-time (twenty-five sisters). At the time of the chapter there were four sisters in full-time

---

107　Report on the state of the Irish federation 1970–1973, p. 8.

108　*Ecclesiae Sanctae II*, no. 19; federal chapter, minutes, 11 Oct. 1973, fourteenth session, p. 56.

109　Statutes, regulations and recommendations, no. 4.

110　About twelve sisters passed the driving test between 1970 and 1973 (there were 87 sisters in the federation. Report on the state of the Irish federation 1970–1973, p. 7; High Park local Council, minutes, 30 May, 6 June 1972.

111　"Soeur Perpetué" is in fact a mannequin dressed *c.* 1740 in the habit of the order and preserved to this day in the Archives of Notre Dame de Charité, Cormelles-le-Royal, Caen. See also photo, 1969 General Chapter Rome (OLC5/3/1).

112　High Park local Council, minutes, 13 May 1970.

113　Statutes, regulations and recommendations, p. 7.

training: two in residential child care, one preparing for her master's degree in psychology and one in career guidance.[114]

On obedience, the conciliar teaching on the relationship that ought to subsist between superior and subjects, and the right of each sister to have a voice in what pertains to the life of the community, and to her own life and work, was taking concrete form. The small discussion groups created in preparation for the general chapter of 1969 sowed the seeds for a more inclusive local government at the largest monastery of High Park, where the sisters numbered forty-six in October 1973.[115] The leaders of the four discussion groups became the first "councillors" for High Park, each bringing her group's suggestions and findings to a larger "Council meeting" which included the superior and her assistant; in due course the federal chapter decreed that "the community as a whole is the local Council", but if a need is felt for a more restricted Council, "the community shall decide on the number of councillors and their method of election".[116] The new statutes legislated for two kinds of community meetings: a meeting at which spiritual matters are discussed, and an administrative meeting, the form to be left to a local decision, but always to be with agenda, advance notification and minutes taken.[117]

The change in habit and the greater visibility of the sisters were but small elements of a much larger, more complex and unfinished, international story. The desire expressed by the federal superior, Sister Mary of St Aloysius Pilkington, at the opening of the chapter in 1973 is a succinct summary of the challenge of *aggiornamento* as experienced in mid-stream: she hopes that with prayer and dialogue they might continue the attempt "to reconcile the best of the old and the new as we search for a community life that is truly based on the spirit of the Gospel and the charism of St John Eudes".[118] This recalls the teaching of *Perfectae caritatis*, that the

114   Report on the state of the Irish federation 1970–1973, p. 7.
115   Report on the state of the Irish federation 1970–1973, p. 7.
116   High Park local Council, minutes, 28 April 1970; Statutes, regulations and recommendations, no. 111.
117   Statutes, regulations and recommendations, no. 12.
118   Report on the state of the Irish Federation 1970–1973, p. 7.

gospel be taken as the supreme rule of all religious institutes,[119] and that the spirit and aims of the founder be faithfully accepted and retained.[120] And this was far easier said than done, with important issues at stake. How the founding charism might be understood was central to the deliberations of the OLC general chapter in Rome in November 1969 and resulted in the publication of the "experimental constitutions" at the start of 1973. But it was the follow-up federal or house *aggiornamento* chapters that were concerned with its interpretation in real, local circumstances. The February 1973 chapter of the Irish federation of Our Lady of Charity held in the north city suburb of Finglas followed on almost a decade of discussion, reflection, preparation and tentative "new efforts". It was at this assembly that the call to the renewal of religious life issued by the Second Vatican Council was formally taken on board by the Irish sisters of Our Lady of Charity. Some elements of this renewal would involve "loosening up" a tradition that critics outside and inside judged to be out of touch with the modern world. After all, the modernisation of the apostolate was underway, albeit in increments, since the early 1950s. But the renewal called for by Vatican II involved the transformation of religious life over a short period such that no OLC sister could stay standing outside it. They were fortunate in having some wise advice and skilful facilitation or direction along the way – the role of Père Fernand Lacroix must be noted – but ultimately there was no course but to wrestle with what was asked of them, for the first time ever. That other institutes faced similar difficulties was consoling but little more; the process of renewal still had to be worked through on the basis of the personal maturity, good will and professional experience of their own small numbers. The archival evidence points to a genuine desire among very many sisters to engage with the excitement and to embrace "the new", though as yet no-one could tell what shape it would take or what of the old would prove most valuable. It is no exaggeration to claim that the institute was "refounded" in the early 1970s in Ireland at least; what happens in the aftermath of Vatican II is a new and as yet unwritten story.

119   *Perfectae caritatis*, no. 2a.
120   *Perfectae caritatis*, no. 2b.

PART IV

Ethical Perspectives

ETHNA REGAN

8   Vatican II and Human Rights: From Religious Freedom to Frontline Advocacy

The full acceptance, by the Roman Catholic church, of human rights as a legitimate mode of ethical discourse was the major contribution of the Second Vatican Council to social ethics in the Catholic tradition. This full acceptance was shaped by a number of factors, the most significant of which was the formal recognition of the right to religious freedom. This development enabled the church to become a full participant in the human rights movement in the post-conciliar period. This essay will examine the movement from initial hostility to gradual acceptance of human rights, the key role played by the issue of the right to religious freedom, and subsequent developments in intellectual and practical engagement with human rights in the last fifty years.

Hostility to Human Rights

Belief in the inherent dignity of the human person is the foundation of Catholic social teaching. The development of this social teaching constitutes an attempt to discover and articulate – in terms of foundational justification, norms, and praxis – the concrete implications of human dignity in interpersonal, social, structural, and international terms. The acceptance of the notion of human rights by the church and the incorporation of that discourse into its social teaching was a slow and complicated process. The relationship between the Christian churches and human rights has been characterised as a movement from reluctance and hostility to acceptance:

"reluctance" was the general response of Protestantism and "hostility" the general Catholic response.[1] The hostility of Catholicism to democracy and human rights since the French Revolution is exemplified in Gregory XVI's 1832 encyclical *Mirari Vos*. This issued condemnations of liberties which Gregory viewed as perilous: liberalism, individualism, democracy, the insanity (*deliramentum*) of the view "according to which freedom of conscience must be asserted and vindicated for everyone whatsoever", freedom of opinion, press freedom, and the separation of Church and State.[2] This condemnation of the "insanity" of freedom of conscience and worship was repeated by Pius IX in his encyclical *Quanta Cura* (1864). The defensive position of the Catholic church in the nineteenth century resisted attempts to engage positively with the new intellectual milieu of the period. It was was hostile to the conception of liberties associated with the Enlightenment, perceiving therein an idea of freedom lacking any normative framework that would maintain a proper relationship between freedom, justice and order. J. Bryan Hehir contends that historically the "neuralgic point of conflict between Catholic teaching and democracy was the idea of religious freedom."[3] It is only at Vatican II that this neuralgic point of conflict is finally resolved.

The Catholic transition to full acceptance of human rights was influenced by a number of factors, including the ground laid by Pope Leo XIII (1878–1903). Leo, a man whose hierarchical view of civil society made him fearful of modern notions of freedom and equality, became the founder of modern Catholic social teaching, setting that teaching in a direction that would eventually lead to wholehearted acceptance of religious freedom, human rights, and democracy. Leo's 1891 encyclical, *Rerum Novarum* (On Capital and Labour), taught that "the human being is prior to the State

1   See Charles E. Curran, "Churches and Human Rights: From Hostility/Reluctance to Acceptability", *Milltown Studies* 42 (1998), 30–58.
2   Gregory XVI, *Mirari Vos: On Liberalism and Religious Indifferentism* (Kansas City, MO: Angelus Press, 1998).
3   J. Bryan Hehir, "Catholicism and Democracy: Conflict, Change, and Collaboration", in Charles E. Curran, ed., *Change in Official Catholic Moral Teachings: Readings in Moral Theology No. 13* (New York/Mahwah, NJ: Paulist Press, 2003) 20–37, at 22.

and has natural rights that do not depend on the State".[4] It established the basic right to a living wage, not just a minimum wage, but one that would enable a family to be properly provided for. Leo also vindicated, albeit cautiously and in a limited way, the rights of workers to unionise.[5] While his position may be described as paternalistic and defensive about socialism, Leo moved the church in the direction of social and economic rights, and structured the sufferings of the poor, especially the exploited industrial workers, into the concerns of official church teaching.

In the face of twentieth-century totalitarianism, the complex and controversial Pope Pius XII (1939–1958), addressed the question of civil and political rights, particularly in his Christmas Messages of 1941–1945.[6] Pius stressed the distinction between society and the state as an essential bulwark against totalitarianism, accepting what would have been unthinkable to Leo XIII, a juridical or limited constitutional state. This more positive assessment of rights was not developed due to the continued influence of nineteenth-century anti-liberalism.

Both Leo XIII and Pius XII, in different ways, contributed to the Catholic transition from hostility to acceptance of human rights discourse. In the time between the end of World War II and the Second Vatican Council there was considerable Catholic intellectual engagement with the

4   *Rerum Novarum*, no. 7, available online at <http://www.vatican.va/holy_father/leo_xiii/encyclicals/documents/hf_l-xiii_enc_15051891_rerum-novarum_en.html>. Accessed 2 October 2014.

5   See *Rerum Novarum*, nos. 49–61.

6   In his 1942 Christmas broadcast, Pius spoke of the unspeakable horror of "the hundreds of thousands who, through no fault of their own, and solely because of their nation or race, have been condemned to death or progressive extinction" (Rome: *Acta Apostolicae Sedis*, 35, 9–24, 1943) 9–24. However, it is his failure to more explicitly denounce the persecution and extermination of the Jews that is ultimately the legacy of Pius XII. While a thorough analysis of this complex and contested question is not possible here, it could be suggested that Pius' failure had less to do with anti-Semitism and moral cowardice, than with his concentration on diplomacy, the intense fear of communism, fear of reprisals, and an ecclesiology that saw the church as essential for salvation therefore needing to be protected in order to facilitate access to the sacraments.

themes of democracy, human rights and religious freedom, engagement which laid the groundwork for the first systematic treatment of human rights in official Catholic social teaching, the encyclical of Pope John XXIII (1958–1963), *Pacem in Terris*.

Pacem in Terris: "A Decisive Move away from the Right"

Pacem in Terris (1963) was issued by John XXIII between the first and second sessions of Vatican II. It reflects his desire that *aggiornamento* would involve new reflection on themes such as democracy, freedom of religion, and human rights.[7] When John XXIII – then Angelo Roncalli – was Papal Nuncio in Paris in the 1940s, he participated, with René Cassin, in discussions about the drafting of the Universal Declaration of Human Rights (UDHR). This was the time of the establishment of UNESCO in Paris and Roncalli was influential in ensuring that the Catholic church would make connections with the United Nations (UN) and its organisations. *Pacem in Terris* recognises the role of the UN, and makes special reference to the UDHR, seeing therein a profound recognition of the dignity of every person.

Due to the reference to economic rights in *Rerum Novarum* and other influences – including the work of the American social reformer, John A. Ryan – the Catholic tradition did not have the same difficulty with socioeconomic rights as it did with civil and political rights.[8] *Pacem in Terris* is a major development because of its endorsement of civil and political rights. The document's distance from the older Catholic preference for the union of church and state also led to the endorsement, by the Council, of

7   The first session lasted from October 11–December 8, 1962. *Pacem in Terris* was promulgated on April 11, 1963. John XXIII died on June 3, 1963. The second session opened on September 29, 1963.

8   Inspired by *Rerum Novarum*, John A. Ryan wrote an influential book entitled *A Living Wage: Its Ethical and Economic Aspects* (New York: Macmillan, 1906).

democracy and pluralism. Furthermore, there is a change in the perception of state authority, a shift from a paternalistic role of directing its subjects in the ways of truth, justice and religion, to an understanding of its function in terms of the protection of human rights. All states are considered equal in dignity and each state has the right to play the leading part in its own development.[9] *Pacem in Terris* also upholds a more positive and comprehensive view of the constitutional state than was normal in natural rights theories. Rights are discussed in the context of some issues of the time: racism, the arms race, industrial progress, social welfare, economic sharing, and political participation. While the document's broad canvas of rights does not clarify how these rights are to be prioritised, it marks an important contribution to Catholic discussion of human rights and links it with the debate within the UN, at that time, about the primacy of particular rights.

Pacem in Terris stresses the relational character of rights and the reciprocity of rights and duties. "Hence, to claim one's rights and ignore one's duties, or only half fulfil them, is like building a house with one hand and tearing it down with the other."[10] While the document does not clarify how rights and duties are adjudicated when they are in conflict, the focus on the relationship between rights and duties places the discussion about human rights in a framework of sociality and responsibility. John XXIII issues a subtle challenge to those who make ideological use of Catholic social teaching in order to prevent greater social justice, e.g., where the appeal to the right to private property is being claimed without any sense of social responsibility. He had in mind the neglected rights of the poor in situations of injustice and landlessness. In his encyclical *Mater et Magistra* (1961), John XXIII made another significant contribution to the development of Catholic social teaching by shifting from the traditional Catholic opposition to State intervention and the "Welfare State" and, in combination with

---

9   *Pacem in Terris*, nos. 86, 89, 92, 120, available online at <http://www.vatican.va/
     holy_father/john_xxiii/encyclicals/documents/hf_j-xxiii_enc_11041963_pacem_
     en.html>. Accessed 2 October 2014.
10   *Pacem in Terris*, no. 30.

his treatment of human rights in *Pacem in Terris*, he contributed to what
Donal Dorr describes as a "decisive move away from the right" in Catholic
social teaching.[11] The political philosopher Maurice Cranston described
Pacem in Terris as an appeal "to the Christian conscience, and beyond that
to the conscience of mankind", with an intellectual force comparable to
that of Kant's *Zum ewigen Frieden*.[12] *Pacem in Terris* influenced the position of Vatican II on human rights and on the relationship between the
church and democracy.

Gaudium et Spes: Grounding the Promotion of Human Rights Theologically

Gaudium et Spes (1965) introduces a historically conscious and inductive
methodology in an attempt to ground natural law specifically in the human
person, not in an abstract conception of human nature, seeking to hold
in tension the commonality of natural law and the specifics of historicity.
Nature is not viewed as consisting of fixed and changeless essences, nor is
ethics presented as the deduction of decisions from unchanging principles.
It is a watershed in the movement from an emphasis on human *nature* in

11   Donal Dorr, *Option for the Poor and for the Earth: Catholic Social Teaching* (Maryknoll,
      NY: Orbis Books, 2012) Chapter 5: "Pope John XXIII – A New Direction?" 89–123,
      at 118.
12   "Pope John XXIII on Peace and The Rights of Man", *The Political Quarterly*, Vol. 34
      (1963) 380–390, at 390. Cranston was critical of the weak treatment of the "common
      good" in the document, the lack of awareness of the dangerous use of the notion of
      the common good by totalitarian regimes, and the failure to analyse more carefully
      the relation between the common good and the specific human rights that it men-
      tions. However he admired the document for its fresh appeal to natural law, seeing
      the papal approach as grounded in the Stoic tradition – rather than what he perceived
      as the orthodox Catholic approach – with its reference to the order of the universe,
      and its appeal to something discernible by the eye of reason alone and pertaining to
      humanity as a whole.

official Catholic documents to an emphasis on the human *person*. It marks what Bernard Lonergan describes as a shift from a classicist, deductive natural law approach to a historically conscious, inductive, personalist approach to ethics.[13] This was a fecund approach for later developments of more specific forms of ethical personalism and theological anthropology, and for facilitating a dialogue between theological ethics and human rights.

A historically conscious approach seeks to take history seriously, without reducing to historical or cultural relativism. The responsibility the church carries is that of "reading the signs of the times and of interpreting them in the light of the Gospel".[14] The call to be readers of the signs of the times is a reminder that the specific demands of human dignity cannot be defined *a priori*. The promotion of human rights is one of the ways in which the church carries out her role as "champion" of the dignity of the human vocation: through proclaiming and fostering human rights, building up the human community, and the initiation of action for service of all people, especially the poor.[15]

There is an insistence on the right of the poor to their share of the Earth's resources and – evoking the Fathers of the church – on the responsibility of the rich that goes beyond the giving of charity out of superfluous wealth.[16] We see here the influence, albeit faint, of a group at Vatican II called the church of the Poor Group, constituted by bishops and theologians mainly from Latin America, Africa and India, with Cardinal Lercaro of Bologna as spokesman. This group advocated for greater attention to the poor of the world, to hunger and to colonialism in the Council's treatment of the signs of the times. Supported by theologians like Bernard *Häring* and Marie-Dominique Chenu, the group discussed not only a church for the

---

13   Bernard Lonergan, "Theology in its New Context", in *Theology of Renewal, Vol. 1: Renewal of Religious Thought*, ed. L.K. Shook (New York: Herder and Herder, 1968), 34–36.

14   *Gaudium et Spes*, no. 4, available online at <http://www.vatican.va/archive/hist_councils/ii_vatican_council/documents/vat-ii_cons_19651207_gaudium-et-spes_en.html>. Accessed 22 August 2014.

15   *Gaudium et Spes*, no. 21; nos. 40–42.

16   *Gaudium et Spes*, nos. 69, 88.

poor but also the idea of a poor church. It is acknowledged by historians that ultimately their influence at the Council was limited and marginal. While they played "a significant role in the first two sessions of the Council and created in many fathers a new sensitivity to the issues of poverty", a report on the work of this group is described by Norman Tanner as having "disappeared into the sands of time".[17] It is interesting to see emerging in the ecclesiology and the ethics of Pope Francis, this focus not just on a church for the poor but also on a poor church.

One of the most significant contributions of *Gaudium et Spes* was to ground the protection and promotion of human rights theologically, thus placing Catholic involvement in the struggle for human rights at the heart of the mission and ministry of the church, with evangelical and eschatological dimensions.

Dignitatis Humanae: The Right to Religious Freedom

The expressed intention at the beginning of *Dignitatis Humanae* (A Declaration on Religious Freedom, 1965) is that of developing "the teaching of recent popes on the inviolable rights of the human person and on the constitutional order of society".[18] This Declaration marks the church's acceptance of a basic principle of human rights, a right that had already been recognised in civil law. *Dignitatis Humanae* had a major impact on the self-understanding of the church and on the understanding of the nature

---

17   See Giuseppe Alberigo, ed., *History of Vatican II, Vol. IV* (Maryknoll, NY/Leuven: Orbis/Peeters), 289–290, 382–386, 289, 385. This group included Juan Landázuri Ricketts of Peru, Raymond-Maria Tchidimbo of Guinea, Helder Camara of Brazil and Soares de Resende of Mozambique.

18   *A Declaration on Religious Freedom: on the right of the person and of communities to social and civil freedom in matters religious* (1965), no. 1, available online at <http://www.vatican.va/archive/hist_councils/ii_vatican_council/documents/vat-ii_decl_19651207_dignitatis-humanae_en.html>. Accessed 7 September 2014.

of doctrine in history. While it may not be a milestone in philosophical debate about rights, the significance of *Dignitatis Humanae* is acknowledged by John Rawls in one of his last essays, "The Idea of Public Reason Revisited". Rawls noted that with this document the Catholic church committed itself to the principle of religious freedom as found in a constitutional democratic regime.[19]

Interest in religious freedom arose particularly in contexts where Catholics were in a minority, but as the church began to develop its own social teaching in a more historical direction, to see value in the documents of the UN, and to struggle for the rights of those living under communist regimes, it became obvious that it was self-contradictory to continue to oppose religious freedom. *Dignitatis Humanae* was the document that brought out the struggle, at the Council, between traditional Catholic views of freedom and more "liberal" views, for the rejection of the confessional state was anathema to those who defined freedom in terms of possession of the truth. There were difficulties in the drafting of the document with the distinction between the objective right of persons with regard to religious liberty and the traditional argument regarding the right to the existence of the one true religion. The Council had to stress that a person may have duties to the truth, but the truth has no rights. The subject of rights is the human person, in truth or error, based on the dignity of that human person in their discernment and decision-making. Its starting point is thus the modern consciousness of the dignity of the human person, manifested in the gifts of rationality and freedom.

The methodology of *Dignitatis Humanae* reflects the shift from the concept of human nature to the human person and this shift enables the right to religious freedom to be grounded in the dignity of the person.[20] It uses the language of "protection and promotion of human rights", language which echoes that of the UN documents. Within *Dignitatis Humanae*, the dynamic of freedom is one of movement from personal freedom to

---

19 *The Law of Peoples with "The Idea of Public Reason Revisited"* (Cambridge, MA: Harvard University Press, 2001) 131–180, at 166–167.
20 *Dignitatis Humanae*, nos. 2, 6.

the freedom of the church. The primary emphasis is the issue of religious freedom on formally juridical grounds, i.e. religious freedom as freedom from coercion, or as an immunity. This civil right rests on the dignity of the human person who bears the responsibility to search for the truth. This search for truth transcends the authority of the State and the human person is bound to follow their conscience faithfully. Religious freedom concerns the safeguarding of that which is most precious in the human person, the capacity for transcendence, for living out the orientation to God which is the human vocation, even in the sincere search which expresses itself in agnosticism towards that transcendentality. Even if a particular religious community is given special recognition, the rights of all must be recognised, for personal freedom is constitutive of the common good. The right to religious freedom moves from personal freedom to the freedom of the church, not vice versa.

The foundation of religious freedom is the dignity of the human person and this freedom is owed to the person in justice. Religious freedom, that "neuralgic point" in the relationship between the Catholic church and Enlightenment liberty, is now held to be the primary freedom which secures other human and civil freedoms. John Witte, Jr., in his study of the Calvinist contribution to the human rights tradition, shows how the early reformers discovered the relationship between religious freedom and other rights. They saw that the proper protection of religious rights required protection of several attendant rights for both the individual and for the religious group: the right to assemble, speak, worship, educate, parent and the right to legal personality, corporate property, freedom of association and freedom of press.[21]

John Courtney Murray, the theologian who had most influence on *Dignitatis Humanae*, held that "the issue of religious freedom was in itself minor", maintaining that the hidden agenda of the document was the issue of doctrinal development and that the right to religious freedom

---

21   See John Witte, Jr., *The Reformation of Rights: Law, Religion, and Human Rights in Early Modern Calvinism* (Cambridge: Cambridge University Press, 2007).

was "simply juridical".[22] *Dignitatis Humanae* marks the first official rec-ognition of doctrinal development within the tradition of Catholic social teaching, a corpus that normally emphasises continuity. The acknowledge-ment, at the highest level, that the doctrine of the Catholic church can change is extremely significant, marking what Murray calls "progress in understanding of the truth".[23] However, it is clear that the issue of religious freedom was not "minor" in comparison with the issue of doctrinal devel-opment. Each issue, in its own way, marked progress in understanding of the truth.

Murray also argues that the right to religious freedom is a "self-denying ordinance" on the part of both the state and the church. The state denies itself the right to interfere with the free exercise of religion, except where a civil offence against public order arises, and the church denies itself any secular arm. "In ratifying the principle of religious freedom, the church accepts the full burden of freedom, which is the single claim she is entitled to make on the secular world."[24] This document cleared up what Murray calls "a long-standing ambiguity", indeed, a double standard, that is: "free-dom for the church when Catholics are in the minority, privilege for the church and intolerance for others when Catholics are a majority".[25] John Rawls summarises the trifold ethical, political and theological significance of *Dignitatis Humanae*:

> It declared the ethical doctrine of religious freedom resting on the dignity of the human person; a political doctrine with respect to the limits of government in reli-gious matters; a theological doctrine of the freedom of the church in its relations

22 John Courtney Murray, "Introduction to the 'Declaration on Religious Freedom'", in Walter M. Abbott, ed., *The Documents of Vatican II* (New York: Guild Press, 1966) 674.

23 Ibid., 677, no. 4.

24 John Courtney Murray, "The Declaration on Religious Freedom", in Curran, ed., *Change in Official Catholic Moral Teachings*, 3–12, at 7.

25 John Courtney Murray, "Religious Freedom" in Abbott, ed., *Documents of Vatican II*, 672, 673.

to the political and social world. All persons, whatever their faith, have the right of religious liberty on the same terms.[26]

Without the promulgation of *Dignitatis Humanae*, human rights would not have become integrated into the social teaching of the church. This conciliar document thus cleared the way for the Catholic church to become an active defender of human rights.

Impact of the Conciliar Legitimation

The impact of the conciliar legitimation of the right to religious freedom is seen in the fecundity of Catholic intellectual and practical engagement with human rights after Vatican II. The political scientist Samuel P. Huntington identifies three waves of democratisation experienced by the modern world, the third of which he argues was influenced by Vatican II.[27] The first, a century-long wave beginning in 1820, rooted in the American and French revolutions, occurring mainly in dominantly Protestant countries in North American and Europe. The second, beginning after the Second World War and continuing until the mid-1960s, during which countries like West Germany, Italy, Austria, Japan and Korea established democratic governments and steps towards democracy were taken in Greece, Turkey, and many countries in Latin America, with decolonisation beginning in Africa, and new democracies emerging in Asia. A diversity of religions was involved in this second wave. There was a period after each of the first two waves when some of the countries that had embraced democracy reverted to former undemocratic patterns of government. Huntington points to

26   *The Law of Peoples with "The Idea of Public Reason Revisited"*, 131–180, at 166–167, n. 75.

27   Samuel P. Huntington, *The Third Wave: Democratization in the Late Twentieth Century* (Oklahoma City: University of Oklahoma Press, 1991) 72–85.

the fall of the Portuguese dictatorship in 1974 as the beginning of "the third wave" which, at least in the first fifteen years, was overwhelmingly Catholic (in countries in Europe, Latin America, and Asia). He argues that after 1970, Catholicism was a force for democracy due to the Vatican II change in official teaching regarding democracy and human rights, and the subsequent increased local involvement of clergy and laity in social justice. He argues that "Catholicism was second only to economic development as a force for democratisation particularly in the two decades after Vatican II".[28] Huntington specifically mentions the following: Pope John XXIII; the CELAM (*Consejo Episcopal Latinoamericano*) meetings at Medellín (1968) and Puebla (1979); the growth of grass roots movements such as the *Comunidades Eclesiales de Base* in Latin America; and the popular mobilisation for democracy in Poland. The conciliar recognition of human rights as a legitimate mode of ethical discourse and the formation of national episcopal conferences after Vatican II meant that in some countries, e.g. the Philippines, Poland, and Brazil, these episcopal conferences played a key role in the struggle for human rights and democracy. Huntington's thesis is that if it were not for changes within the Catholic church and the consequent stance of the church against political authoritarianism, "fewer third wave transitions to democracy would have occurred and many that did occur would have occurred later".[29]

Huntington's thesis on the role of post-conciliar Catholicism as a force for democracy in Latin America finds support in Jeffrey Klaiber's comparative analysis of the efforts of the church in eleven different countries to defend human rights and support democracy. Without either triumphalism or censoring of failures, Klaiber's analysis shows that the church – in different ways and to varying degrees – contributed to the redemocratisation of many countries, through denouncing dictatorships, protecting the persecuted, documenting the violations of human rights, legitimising

28 Huntington, *The Third Wave*, 85.
29 Huntington, *The Third Wave*, 85.

opposition, and creating "participatory spaces" for religious groups or other groups associated in some way with the mission of the church.[30]

In Ireland, the Irish Episcopal Conference for Justice and Peace was founded in 1971 and its initial human rights engagement was shaped by the violence in Northern Ireland. Its 1971 statement *Violence in Ireland* condemned what might be described as the institutional violence of "the forces of law and order" and the reactive violence of the oppressed. While there is just one reference to "respect for the rights of our neighbour", the entire statement gives evidence of a move towards an implicit rights-based approach to social justice.[31] In 1973, the year following the most violent year of the Troubles, talks began between the Catholic church and the Irish Council of Churches in Ballymascanlon, which over the course of time became formalised as the Irish Inter church Meeting (IICM), addressing matters of ecumenical concern from doctrinal to pastoral, including human rights and social justice. In 1971, the Conference of European Justice and Peace Commissions (*Justitia et Pax Europa*) was established by eleven national Justice and Peace Commissions, including the Irish commission, and today this is a network of thirty Justice and Peace commissions mandated by their respective episcopal conferences to speak out on human rights, poverty, violence, reconciliation and development.[32] Since 2001, *Justitia et Pax Europa* has been recognised by the Council of Europe as an international non-governmental organisation (INGO) and has a "participatory status" at the Council of Europe, participating in the work of the Human Rights Committee of the INGOs. Since Vatican II, human rights emerged as one of the six major themes dealt with in the social documents of the episcopal conferences worldwide.[33] Across differences of culture and

---

30   Jeffrey Klaiber, *The church, Dictatorships, and Democracy in Latin America* (Maryknoll, NY: Orbis Books, 1998) 269–270.

31   Irish Commission for Justice and Peace, "Violence in Ireland", *The Furrow*, Vol. 22, No. 12, (Dec., 1971) 796–798.

32   The founding countries were Belgium (Fr.), England & Wales, France, Germany, Ireland, Luxembourg, Malta, the Netherlands, Poland, Spain and Switzerland.

33   Terence McGoldrick, "Episcopal Conferences Worldwide on Catholic Social Teaching", *Theological Studies* 59 (1998) 22–50.

politics, the theme of human rights – either explicitly or implicitly – has become a key motif in modern Catholic social thought.

Pope John Paul II and Human Rights: Commitment and Critique

John Paul II showed a consistent concern for human rights throughout his pontificate (1978–2005, the longest since Vatican II) using the language of human rights to ground the discussion of justice in his social teaching. John Paul had a generally positive view of the secular human rights movement, seeing therein evidence both of a universal human nature and also of a humanism that speaks to all people of goodwill. He described the UDHR as "one of the highest expressions of the human conscience of our time".[34] He advocated for a culture of human rights – which is accommodating of legitimate cultural and political differences – to become "an integral part of humanity's moral patrimony".[35]

John Paul viewed the hunger for justice and peace as evidence of a hunger for the Spirit of God.[36] He identified the growing awareness among human beings of their inherent dignity, expressed in the concern for human rights, as "the first positive sign of the time".[37] However, this pneumatological perspective on social ethics, and positive assessment of the potential of

---

34 *Address to the United Nations General Assembly*, no. 2, 5 October 1995, available online at <http://www.vatican.va/holy_father/john_paul_ii/>. Accessed 2 October 2014.

35 Address for *World Day of Peace, 1999*, available online at <http://www.vatican.va/holy_father/john_paul_ii/messages/peace/>. Accessed 11 October 2014.

36 "Our time – a time particularly hungry for the Spirit, because it is hungry for justice, peace, love, goodness, fortitude and possibility." *Redemptor Hominis*, no. 18, available online at <http://www.vatican.va/holy_father/john_paul_ii/>. Accessed 2 October 2014.

37 *Solicitudo Rei Socialis*, no. 26, available online at <http://www.vatican.va/holy_father/john_paul_ii/>. Accessed 31 August 2014.

the UN and the global human rights movement, coexist with an increasingly oppositional view of modernity, especially evident in his later writings.

During his pontificate, John Paul endorsed the broad range of political, social and economic rights found in the UN documents, "thickening" the notion of human rights in the Catholic tradition.[38] The language of human rights becomes more nuanced than in *Pacem in Terris*, with greater emphasis on the relationship between rights, duties and truth. Rights are understood not simply as immunities, but as indicators of the obligations of human persons toward one another. He deepens the notion of obligation, grounding it in his personalistic interpretation of the commandment of love, a commandment which he presents as an affirmative deepening of the Kantian imperative which is "negative in character and does not exhaust the entire content of the commandment of love".[39] In this context, John Paul offers a view of human freedom as oriented toward being a gift for others. "If we cannot accept the prospect of giving ourselves as a gift, then the danger of a selfish freedom will always be present."[40] Thus John Paul not only "thickens" the notion of human rights within the Catholic tradition, but he also deepens the understanding of human freedom that rights are protective of.

For John Paul, religious freedom, as per *Dignitatis Humanae*, constitutes the very heart of human rights; it is the cornerstone and safeguard of all other rights. During his pontificate, there was a shift in John Paul's reception of *Dignitatis Humanae*. For many years, he placed the question of religious freedom in the context of the struggle against atheistic communism; however, in later years, while not denying that religious persecution still existed in many parts of the world, he saw religious freedom as under assault from the forces of secularism and relativism.[41] John Paul

---

38   This "thickening" is especially evident in *Centesimus Annus. Solicitudo Rei Socialis*, no. 15, had already outlined the "right to economic initiative".

39   See John Paul II, *Crossing the Threshold of Hope* (London: Jonathan Cape, 1994) 200–201.

40   Ibid., 202.

41   Herminio Rico identifies three moments for *Dignitatis Humanae*: (i) Religious Freedom replaces Established Catholicism: Vatican II and the past to which it brought

appeals for the rights of conscience because of the persistence of old forms of totalitarianism in parts of the world, the increasing influence of utilitarian values in the developed world, and the threat posed by new forms of religious fundamentalism in other countries.[42]

John Paul's reading of the secular became increasingly negative and oppositional with time. In *Centesimus Annus* (1991), he posits that the root of social problems lies in the turn of modernity to secularism, a concern that is augmented in *Veritatis Splendor* (1993) and *Evangelium Vitae* (1995). The only solution to social problems, he holds, lies in a return to religious values, for secular humanism cannot provide the answers. This view is a significant contrast with his earlier positive view of the secular human rights movement, of the moral significance of the UDHR, and the perception of pneumatological presence in the modern striving for justice and peace. Within his vision of the conflict between a "Culture of Life" and a "Culture of Death", there is increasing emphasis on the right to life, particularly in a society where "everything is negotiable ... even the right to life".[43]

John Paul offers a valuable critique of the "surprising contradiction" in human rights discourse between a growing moral sensitivity to the dignity of all human persons without distinction, on the one hand, and the undermining of that dignity "especially at the more significant moments of existence: the moment of birth and the moment of death", on the other.[44] He suggests that this contradiction is rooted, firstly, in an extreme and distorted form of subjectivity and, secondly, in a "mentality which tends to equate personal dignity with the capacity for verbal and

---

closure; (ii) Freedom of the church against Atheistic Communism; (iii) The present situation, now unfolding: new encounters of Catholicism with an evolved liberalism. See *John Paul II and the legacy of "Dignitatis Humanae"* (Washington, DC: Georgetown University Press, 2002).

42 See *Centesimus Annus*, no. 29, available online at <http://www.vatican.va/holy_father/john_paul_ii/>. Accessed 2 October 2014.

43 *Evangelium Vitae*, no. 20, available online at <http://www.vatican.va/holy_father/john_paul_ii/>. Accessed 2 October 2014.

44 Ibid., no. 18.

explicit, or at least perceptible communication".[45] This contradiction forges an individualistic understanding of human freedom that risks becoming "the freedom of 'the strong' against the weak who have no choice but to submit".[46] Notwithstanding the complexity of the issues, and the often polarised discussions surrounding the ethical questions at the beginning and end of human life, John Paul issues an important challenge to the human rights movement to recognise this contradiction and the implications of the contradiction for our understanding of human dignity, freedom and vulnerability.

The difficulty with John Paul's vision of a conflict of cultures is that it tends to overlook the elements in secular culture that are compatible with the Christian vision of the flourishing of the human person and the justice of human community. This vision also tends to inflate the previous contribution of the church to the development of human rights, an inflation that is not consistent with the historical record of the hostility of the Catholic church to democracy and human rights. The recent record of the church's responses to the crimes of child abuse does not witness to this culture of life. It must be noted, too, that John Paul himself gave inadequate leadership in the face of these violations of the rights of children.

In spite of the failures and an increasingly oppositional view of the secular, John Paul II made the defense of human rights the primary mode of engagement of the church with politics. He consolidated the relationship between the Catholic church and democracy, in a way that both facilitated the challenging of inhumane authoritarian rule and offered a critique to democracy itself, pointing to an authentic democracy grounded in explicit recognition of human rights and decision-making focused on the common good.[47]

45   Ibid., no. 19.
46   Ibid., no. 19.
47   See, e.g., *Centesimus Annus*, nos. 46–47.

Pope Benedict XVI: Justice Overshadowed by Charity

In his address to the UN General Assembly on the sixtieth anniversary of the UDHR in 2008, Benedict XVI (2005–2013) spoke of human rights as "the common language and the ethical substratum of international relations". He reflected on the global significance of human rights and the accompanying responsibilities. He specifically addressed the emerging norm in international human rights discourse, the "responsibility to protect" (RtoP). Benedict upheld the importance of the UN's role in the defense of human rights, the promotion of which are "the most effective strategy for eliminating inequalities between countries and social groups, and for increasing security".[48] He stated that it is not intervention that is a limitation on sovereignty – provided it is consistent with international law – but rather "it is indifference or failure to intervene that does the real damage".[49]

His UN speech, while continuing the church's support of the modern human rights project, also issues a caution against human rights becoming a "relativistic conception" that denies their universalism. He expresses concerns about a legal positivism which risks allowing rights to become "weak propositions divorced from the ethical and rational dimension which is their foundation and their goal". In this brief speech, Benedict addresses a number of dimensions of human rights including their foundations, selective application, unlimited expansion, and the privileging of an individualistic approach to rights. The right to religious freedom, he reminds us, is not limited to freedom of worship but includes the public dimension of religion and hence "the possibility of believers playing their part in building the social order". Benedict's speech to the UN deepens

---

48   Address to the Members of the General Assembly of the United Nations Organisation, 18 April 2008. Available online at <http://www.vatican.va/holy_father/benedict_xvi/>. Accessed 25 October 2014.

49   Here Benedict is building on the principle established in *Pacem in Terris* (no. 61) that the legitimacy of a government is based on its respect for the rights of its people.

Catholic engagement with the discourse of human rights, an engagement characterised by both commitment and critique.

It could be argued that Benedict demonstrated greater fluency in human rights discourse when speaking to secular agencies than in his encyclicals. His first encyclical *Deus Caritas Est* (2005) contains only two references to human rights, the first refers to the nineteenth-century suppression of the rights of the working class and the second cites John Paul II on "respect for the rights and needs of everyone, especially the poor, the lowly and the defenceless".[50] The purpose of Benedict's encyclical is to offer a reflection on God's love and does not, as such, necessitate an extensive discussion of human rights. The second part of *Deus Caritas Est*, however, focuses on Catholic "charitable" organisations and offers a reflection on "the distinctiveness of the church's charitable activity".[51] Thus the theme of human rights is not extraneous to the document, as it is a key dimension of the work of such Catholic organisations.

Benedict begins this second part by looking at the relationship between charity and justice, reminding the faithful that the just ordering of society is the central responsibility of politics.[52] He refers to the Marxist elimination of charity in the struggle for justice. The danger in using the Marxist critique of charity and advocacy of justice as foil for the argument about charity is that rather than achieving proper equilibrium in terms of the relationship between charity and justice, justice becomes overshadowed by charity in the Christian vocabulary, an overshadowing that is not helpful to the work of Catholic justice and human rights organisations.

Benedict reminds such organisations about the relationship between love and bearing credible witness, of the insufficiency of action without love, of the reciprocal relationship between those who work in these organisations and those who are served by them, of the temptation to forget that the work of justice is ultimately God's work, and of the "formation of the

---

50   *Deus Caritas Est*, nos. 26, 30. Available online at <http://www.vatican.va/holy_father/
      benedict_xvi/encyclicals/documents/hf_ben-xvi_enc_20051225_deus-caritas-est_
      en.html>. Accessed 25 October 2014.
51   *Deus Caritas Est*, no. 31.
52   *Deus Caritas Est*, nos. 26–30.

heart" that must accompany professional training. These are important reminders for persons and organisations who profess to work for justice and human rights within a Catholic framework. They are cautions at a time when funding can be tied to conditions that may not fit with the aims of Catholic organisations or when the theological foundations may seem remote from the language and practice of an organisation. It is my experience of a number of Catholic agencies engaged in development and human rights work, in different parts of the world, that they strive for an integrity that keeps them both grounded in their faith community and professionally credible in the wider non-governmental sphere. Benedict's caveats and challenges are helpful in this regard.

The Catholic "charitable organisation" that is specifically mentioned in the encyclical is Caritas Internationalis,[53] a confederation of over 160 members – in almost every country of the world – working in relief aid, social and human development, and the promotion of global and economic rights.[54] It must be noted that most organisations in the Caritas confederation would identify themselves as justice, human rights or development organisations and would rarely use the term "charitable", while not eschewing the primacy of love that *Deus Caritas Est* highlights as central to the mission of the church. There were growing concerns, from the later years of the pontificate of John Paul II, about the increasing lay control of Caritas and the consequent erosion of clerical control. In 2004, the year before the publication of *Deus Caritas Est*, the relationship of Caritas with the Holy See was formalised and the organisation was recognised as a "public juridical person" under church law, subject to the direction of the Pontifical Council Cor Unum. Its president and secretary-general require a *nihil obstat* before their appointment. In 2011, its secretary-general, Lesley Anne Knight, was denied a *nihil obstat* for a second four-year term by the Vatican. In 2012, Caritas accepted revised statutes and rules that increased the oversight of the organisation by the Vatican. This is a complex situation, born of concerns alluded to in *Deus Caritas Est*, concerns about the status,

53   *Deus Caritas Est*, no. 31.
54   Caritas Internationalis, henceforth Caritas.

staffing, and perceived secularisation of these "charitable organisations".[55]
The professionalisation of Catholic agencies has increased public credibility,
but a focus on professionalisation, to the perceived neglect of "formation
of the heart", has also caused some ecclesiastical unease.

It could be argued that one issue that contributes to the tension
between such organisations and the Vatican is, in fact, the foundation of
Catholic development and justice work since Vatican II on a human rights
basis. A human rights approach to development work and rights-centred
policies in social justice agencies have become the norm. Church agencies ground this human rights approach on the fundamental theological
principle of the human person as *imago Dei*. A human rights approach
allows Catholic agencies to work professionally and collaboratively with
other secular and religious agencies, and to make funding applications
that meet criteria recognised in a variety of contexts. A rights approach,
for example, to gender issues – an approach which is consistent with the
principles of Catholic social teaching – raises concerns within church
leadership about what "limits" will be set on this approach in neuralgic
areas such as reproductive rights. In general, Catholic agencies negotiate
this contested territory with integrity and authenticity. The organisations
that make up Caritas, and other Catholic justice and human rights organisations, should be accountable to and open to critique by the church they
represent; but such accountability and critique should take place in a spirit
of dialogue and collegiality. It must also be recognised that the majority of
these organisations offer a positive representation of the Catholic church
at a time of a crisis of authenticity and are exemplars of what John Paul II
called an "apostolate of human rights".[56]

55   For a detailed examination of the issues, see Donal Dorr, *Option for the Poor and for
     the Earth*, Chapter 15: "*Deus caritas est* and Catholic Charitable and Development
     Agencies", 340–367.
56   See reference to this in *Human Rights and the Catholic Church* (Catholic Bishops'
     Conference of England and Wales, Catholic Media Office, London, 1998) no. 10.
     This reference to an "apostolate of human rights" gives a pastoral-theological dimen-
     sion to the promotion of human rights.

Caritas in veritate (2009), Benedict's major social encyclical, has a number of references to human rights, but the focus of this document is on gratuitousness and an "economy of communion", an economic paradigm which brings Gospel values to bear on market structures, combining profit-making with social benefits. Benedict's Post-Synodal Apostolic Exhortation, *Africae Munus* (2011), mentions a wide range of human rights including the rights of prisoners, the right of victims of injustice to truth and reconciliation, women's dignity and rights, and the right to freedom of conscience.[57]

Benedict's engagement with the ethical discourse of human rights is not as extensive as his predecessor, but his approach is marked by both acceptance and critique of this discourse. However, it is possible to interpret his approach to Catholic "charitable organisations" in *Deus Caritas Est*, and the new juridical status conferred on Caritas Internationalis, as evidence of a lessening of enthusiasm for the Catholic adoption of human rights discourse that emerged from Vatican II. This is shaped by John Paul II's increasingly oppositional view of the secular during his pontificate and by Benedict's own pessimism, not so much about human rights discourse *per se*, but about the very significance of the Council itself, the "real reception" of which, he holds, "has not yet even begun".[58]

Conclusion

Pope John XXIII and the Second Vatican Council, through the full acceptance of human rights – including, most significantly, the right to religious freedom – cleared the way for the Catholic church to become a full

---

57   *Africae Munus*, nos. 83, 21, 56, 94; Available online at <http://www.vatican.va/holy_father/benedict_xvi/apost_exhortations/documents/hf_ben-xvi_exh_20111119_africae-munus_en.html>. Accessed 25 October 2014.

58   Joseph Cardinal Ratzinger, *Principles of Catholic Theology: Building Stones for a Fundamental Theology* (San Francisco: Ignatius Press, 1987) 390.

participant in the human rights movement, through intellectual engagement and front-line advocacy. The impact of the conciliar legitimation is seen in the contribution of the church to the protection of human rights and the promotion of democracy in a number of countries. It is often said that the contribution of the church to democracy and human rights in the civil realm is not matched by respect for human rights in its own internal governance. The tension between Catholic teaching about the equality of men and women and domestic ecclesial practice regarding the role of women in the church is often cited, as is the contradiction between participation as a principle of Catholic social teaching and the actual ecclesial decision-making structures. The assessment of the impact and enduring relevance of the Council, after half a century, no longer focuses solely on these issues but also on the crimes and scandals of child abuse highlighted in recent years. The failure to protect human dignity, respect human rights, and respond justly to victims remains as a scar on the church's ongoing involvement in the promotion of human rights. Despite our failures, the contemporary challenges of social, global and ecological justice make the Catholic church's continued intellectual and front-line promotion of human rights an urgent imperative. We can add to those challenges a new challenge, that of forging an ecclesiological ethic that matches *ad intra* what the church seeks to be *ad extra* in terms of human dignity and human rights.

LINDA HOGAN

9 Catholic Theological Ethics since Vatican II

Catholic moral theology changed significantly over the course of the twentieth century. Indeed it is widely acknowledged that the transformation of the discipline has been a radical one, with a move away from the act-centred, legalistic, minimalistic and casuistic enterprise of the manuals, to the more biblically based, historically conscious and context-sensitive theologies of today. Between the Council of Trent and the Second Vatican Council the manuals of moral theology reigned supreme. They were the primary mode through which moral theology was taught and the context was almost entirely seminary-based. Moreover when we examine the history of the composition of particular manuals, especially in the last decades of the nineteenth century and the first decades of the twentieth, we can see that deference that was a constant feature of the relationship between the manualists and the Roman Curia. The experience of the manualist Aloysius Sabetti as he was involved in articulating the church's "settled position" on abortion, craniotomy and ectopic pregnancy is very illuminating. Not only does it exemplify how the church's teaching on these difficult issues evolved, developed and changed over time, but even more interestingly it also illustrates how, in this period, the curial congregations became ever more involved in authoritatively deciding concrete moral dilemmas.[1]

However in the years immediately preceding and immediately following the Council there was a significant change in the way in which moral theology was done. Much of the initial impetus came from the

---

1   Charles Curran, *Catholic Moral Theology in the United States: A History* (Washington: Georgetown University Press, 2008), 17–21.

work of certain key theologians, including Odon Lottin,[2] Herbert Doms,[3] and Klaus Demmer,[4] who recast the way in which the fundamental questions about the nature of morality began to be asked and answered. Thus through the 1940s and 50s, but especially in the 1960s, moral theology became more theological, more biblically based, and in some senses more speculative. And so began what has come to be known as the personalist strand in moral theology – namely a moral theology that is committed to the idea that the truth about the human person must constitute the basis of the understanding of morality. Moral theology was thus no longer to be focused primarily on parsing acts, but rather on understanding the person and her context, on character, on virtue and the virtues. Many will be familiar with the names of the individuals who shaped and embodied this transformation, including Bernard Häring,[5] Louis Janssens,[6] Josef Fuchs,[7] Charles Curran,[8] Margaret Farley[9] and Enda McDonagh.[10] Indeed the

2   Odon Lottin, *Morale Fondamentale* (Paris: Desclee & Cie, 1954).
3   Herbert Doms, *The Meaning of Marriage* (New York: Sheed & Ward, 1939).
4   The most recent English-language articulation of his theology is found in Klaus Demmer, *Living the Truth: A Theory of Action* (Washington: Georgetown University Press, 2010).
5   Bernard Häring, *Free and Faithful in Christ: Moral Theology for Priests and Laity* (Slough: St Paul's Publications, 1978–1979, 1981).
6   Louis Janssens, *Personalisme en democratisering* (Bruxelles: Arbeiderspers, 1957).
7   Fuchs, Josef, *Personal Responsibility and Christian Morality* (Washington: Georgetown University Press/Gill and MacMillan, 1983).
8   Curran's works are manifold. Recent works include *The Moral Theology of Pope John Paul II* (Washington: Georgetown University Press, 2005), *Loyal Dissent Memoir of a Catholic Theologian* (Washington: Georgetown University Press, 2006), *Catholic Moral Theology in the United States: A History* (Washington: Georgetown University Press, 2008) and *The Social Mission of the U.S. Catholic church* (Washington: Georgetown University Press, 2011).
9   Farley, Margaret *Personal Commitments: Beginning, Changing, Keeping* (New York: Harper & Row, 1990) and *Just Love: A Framework for Christian Sexual Ethics* (New York: Continuum, 2006).
10   See for example, Enda McDonagh *Gift and Call, Towards a Christian Theology of Morality* (Dublin: Gill & MacMillan 1975) and *Theology in Winter Light* (Dublin: Columba, 2010).

long-term impact of their work can be seen in the fact that, although the field of moral theology today is deeply contested, nonetheless, the entire field of moral theology looks very different today from the theology that pertained in the decades before Vatican II.

The Impact of the Ecclesiology of Vatican II

Although the Second Vatican Council had a major impact on the field of moral theology, it actually said very little specifically about moral theology. Rather the impact of the Council lay primarily in how the ecclesiology of Vatican II affected the shape of the discipline. There is no doubt that the ecclesial landscape has changed radically in the century since Pius X's char-acterisation of the relationship between clergy and laity in his now infamous 1906 encyclical on the French Law of Separation, *Vehementer nos*. In that encyclical Pius X confidently declared that "so distinct are these categories [of pastors and flock] that with the pastoral body only rests the necessary right and authority for promoting the end of the society and directing all its members toward that end; the only duty of the multitude is to allow themselves to be led, and, like a docile flock, to follow the pastors."[11]

To the modern ear the "docile flock" metaphor has pejorative conno-tations that, in so far as one can judge, it did not have in 1906. Moreover the starkly hierarchical model of church finds little resonance in the post-Vatican II ecclesiologies of today. The ecclesiology of *Vehementer nos* was no doubt shaped by its proximity to Vatican I, part of whose legacy was an exaggerated sense of the distinctive (and unequal) roles of laity, clergy, bishops and pope. Moreover the impact of such an ecclesiology was felt in all aspects of the church's life, and particularly in how the moral life was understood. Much of the moral theology that flowed from this hierarchical

11   Pius X, *Vehementer nos* (Encyclical on the French Law of Separation), February 11
      1906, #8.

conceptualisation of church was conducted through the idiom of law, which emphasised the objective character of morality (at the expense of the subjective dimension), and stressed the absoluteness of moral norms, including of material norms. In fact the "docile flock" was especially expected to allow itself to be led in matters of moral concern, with the "necessary right and authority" to teach on moral matters residing with "the pastors".

However Vatican II marked a critical turning-point. By introducing the metaphors of pilgrimage and communion, it shaped a new ecclesiology, and by extension a new moral theology. As a result, not only has the role of the formal teaching offices of the church been rearticulated, but there has also been a comparable transformation in how the relationship between individual moral discernment and the moral tradition of the church is conceived. Nonetheless the picture is a complicated one since the legacy of Vatican II has itself become the object of debate within Catholicism, with what might be termed rival versions of that legacy constantly in view. Nor can these conflicting interpretations of the theological and ecclesiological legacy of Vatican II be resolved simply by appealing to the conciliar texts themselves since within these texts are the traces of the conflicting paradigms of "law" and "person", "hierarchy and communion".[12]

It is widely acknowledged that these ecclesiological developments have utterly transformed the internal landscape of Catholicism and have allowed questions about the nature of moral discernment, authority and tradition to emerge in a different register. The communion ecclesiology promoted by the Council envisions a church whose self-understanding is premised on mutual and reciprocal relationships. Authority is thus no longer conceived in autocratic terms, but rather is based on collegiality and consultation. Indeed some of the conciliar texts themselves already reflect this more collegial model of ecclesial authority.

Moreover, Vatican II's constant reiteration of the fact that it is the whole people of God who have been addressed by the word of God has, in turn, occasioned the retrieval of a more nuanced account of the means by

---

12   I discuss this in detail in my *Confronting the Truth: Conscience and the Catholic Tradition* (New York: Paulist Press, 2000).

which people learn the art of moral discernment. There is no doubt that this renewed ecclesiology engendered great hope and promise amongst Catholics. In particular it created a sense of expectation that they not only had the permission, but also the duty to discuss and debate the morality of the new questions which they were encountering. This expectation has been especially pronounced in the field of sexual ethics since it was here that the dissonance was strongest.

Of course the church has long-since recognised the complex nature of moral authority, even if it has at certain times in its history, presented a more truncated and simplistic view of the issue. Pastors, bishops, pope, theologians and laity each have distinctive responsibilities and duties as both learners and teachers, a point that has been very explicitly developed in the post-Vatican II era, with much of the discussion focussed on the issue of dissent. Key here has also been the re-affirmation of the significance of the *sensus fidelium* particularly in the articulation of the church's moral teaching. In this context Richard Gaillardetz's work on the *sensus fidelium* has been particularly significant since he nuances the traditional concept, so that the *sensus fidelium* is understood in terms of being "a process of articulation, which leads to pedagogy, which leads to reception, which in turn engenders a new articulation". It is effectively "a spiral like movement in the church's traditioning process", that can help dispel the tendency to work with "a linear conception of church teaching, which ... starts with the deposit of faith, which first resides in the hierarchy and then is being dispensed to the faithful."[13] In effect it forms the bedrock for a moral theology that can cope with the dynamism that is at the heart of the church's moral tradition.

Much of the moral theology that has developed in the shadow of Vatican II reflects and embodies an ecclesiology of pilgrimage and participation, acknowledging that all Catholics, lay and ordained, are partners in the process of moral discernment. The church is thus understood as a community of learning and teaching, of discernment and dialogue, with the

---

13 Richard Gaillardetz, *Teaching with Authority, A Theology of the Magisterium in the church* (Collegeville, MN: The Liturgical Press, 1997), 232.

magisterium and faithful each playing a role in all aspects. It is clear that the laity have embraced a form of participation in community life, including in church life, which draws on and celebrates the depth and variety of the human experience. As a result the relationship with teachers and teaching has changed. The laity now think of themselves as partners in a complex process of teaching and reception. When a teaching resonates with lived experience, when it is developed in a collaborative manner or when it is refined in a dialogical process, its reception is likely to be successful. Where there is dissonance however, it is unlikely to be received.

The Changed Contexts of Moral Theology

Over the last century, but particularly since Vatican II, moral theologians have become increasingly aware of the defining role that context has played in the composition and development of the discipline. Moral theology as a field of study emerged within a particular historical, ecclesial and theological world-view, with many of the discipline's fundamental assumptions formed in this post-Tridentine context. This post-Tridentine context was the frame of reference in which the norms of rationality and argumentation were established, and in which the broad shape of its subject matter was delineated, and to a certain degree settled. Indeed John Mahoney's *The Making of Moral Theology*[14] continues to provide one of the most compelling accounts of the manner in which particular theological and cultural features of that post-Tridentine world-view shaped the discipline. More recently James Keenan's *History of Catholic Moral Theology in the Twentieth Century*[15] has further clarified the formative role that particular

---

14   John Mahoney, *The Making of Moral Theology: A Study of the Roman Catholic Tradition* (Oxford: Oxford University Press, 1987).
15   James Keenan, *A History of Catholic Moral Theology in the Twentieth Century: From Confessing Sins to Liberating Consciences* (New York: Continuum, 2010).

historical contexts have had on the subsequent development of the field. The importance of post-Tridentine Catholicism in the development of the discipline is, therefore, well understood. Moreover, as moral theologians have reflected on the changing shape of the discipline in recent decades, they have acknowledged that the field has been radically reshaped in response to what John O'Malley unapologetically calls "the spirit of Vatican II".[16] In the earlier section of this essay I discussed how the ecclesiology of Vatican II has shaped the discourse of moral theology. Of equal significance, however, is how the changed contexts of moral theology have altered, in a fundamental way, the nature of the discipline.

There is no doubt that both the norms of the discipline and its preoccupations have been transformed through the encounter with non-western cultural values and traditions, and with the increasing voices of non-western theologians, both male and female. Not only have they demonstrated that the presumed universality of certain fundamental disciplinary assumptions is illusory, but through their particular, culturally embedded elaborations of the discipline, they have radically disrupted the traditional paradigm of moral theology, and re-shaped its content. Indeed the works of Benezet Bujo[17] (Zaire), Agnes Brazal[18] (Philippines) and Shaji George Kochuthara[19] (India) to mention just a few, reveal the dynamism inherent in this interculturation of moral theology worldwide.

Much of this change has come about because the locations in which this theology is pursued have been transformed. Whereas previously seminaries and theological colleges were the primary fora, today theology is taught in multiple academic contexts, which may be secular, multi-religious or ecumenical in ethos. In addition the complexion of the traditionally Catholic

16 John O'Malley, *What Happened at Vatican II* (Cambridge, MA: Harvard University Press, 2010).

17 Benezet Bujo, *Foundations of an African Ethic: Beyond the Universal Claims of Western Morality* (New York: Crossroad, 2001).

18 Agnes Brazal, ed. *Body and Sexuality: Theological-Pastoral Perspectives of Women in Asia* (Quezon City: Ateneo de Manila University Press, 2007).

19 Shaji George Kochuthara, *The Concept of Sexual Pleasure in the Catholic Moral Tradition* (Rome: Pontificia Università Gregoriana, 2007).

contexts has also changed, so that the seminaries, theological colleges and Catholic universities are no longer predominantly clerical and male. This new diversity within these traditional institutional settings has had a liberating effect on the discipline. It has been one of the most significant drivers of change, and has enabled theologians to engage more deeply with the ethical pluralism that characterises contemporary life.

However, perhaps its greatest effect can be seen in how and by whom the discipline is now populated. The second international gathering of Catholic theological ethicists in Trento, Italy in 2011 has been perhaps the most visible expression of this change thus far. Entitled "In the Currents of History: From Trent to the Future"[20] the conference attracted 600 Catholics, all working in the field of theological ethics, primarily in the academy, but also in NGOs, as well as in policy development and advocacy. The conference graphically captured the revolution that has occurred in Catholic theological ethics, particularly in terms of the heterogeneity of those writing and teaching in the field. While overall, it may still be predominantly clerical and lay, in some regions including Europe, the USA and parts of South East Asia, the balance is quickly shifting, so that one can certainly envisage the field being equally composed of lay persons and of women within a generation or two. In other regions, including in Africa and Latin America the change is not as pronounced, but it is happening nonetheless.

Moral Theology Today: Globalisation as a Context

The effects of these changes can especially be seen in the changed nature of the substantive questions with which moral theology is concerned. In particular one can see that, in the last two decades, moral theology

---

20   The proceedings of this conference have been published as James Keenan, ed., *Catholic Theological Ethics, Past, Present, and Future: The Trento Conference* (New York: Orbis, 2011 and Bangalore: Theological Publications in India, 2012).

has begun to reckon with the contexts in which millions world-wide live and work, namely, in the midst of chronic poverty, deep-seated structural inequalities, violence and environmental destruction. In this regard moral theologians have engaged vigorously with the debate about the nature and effects of globalisation. Many have been to the fore in highlighting that the contemporary experience of globalisation is a paradoxical, and often a negative one. Thus although globalisation through trade, technology and tourism has created an unprecedented interdependence, it has also set in train a trajectory of fragmentation, seen in the forces of nationalism, identity politics and religious fundamentalism. Moreover, although globalisation has made available to many an experience of economic opportunity, it also has its shadow-side of emiseration and violence. Zigmunt Bauman explains the paradox in terms of what he calls "glocalisation", that is "globalisation for some, localisation for others."[21] Thus "globalisation reinforces already existing patterns of domination, while glocalisation indicates trends to dispersal and conflict on neo-traditional grounds. The privileged walk, or fly, away: the others take revenge upon each other."[22] This scenario, in which the economic, cultural and political forces of globalisation create contradictory processes of integration and fragmentation, and of opportunity and emiseration, is at the heart of the challenge that it poses for individuals and communities, and has been a central preoccupation of moral theology in the last two decades. Moreover in this regard moral theologians have made a significant contribution particularly in terms of being the voice of those for whom globalisation is less an opportunity than a threat.

The ever-increasing economic disparity between North and South as well as the shameful impoverishment of the African continent are of particular concern to moral theologians. Theologians from developed and developing countries are acutely aware of the negative effects of globalisation, namely chronic poverty, increasing inequality between and within states, and environmental destruction. And while the countries of the South

---

21   Bauman, Zigmunt, "On Glocalization: Globalization for Some, Localization for Others" in *Thesis Eleven*, 54, 1998, 37–49.

22   Ibid., 37.

are affected disproportionately by these problems, there are also emerging difficulties in advanced economies so that although wealth is increasing, inequality is also growing, with minority groups and migrants experiencing new levels of poverty, threat, and social exclusion.[23]

Indeed moral theologians from around the world have provided detailed and persuasive analyses of the impact that unregulated and unfairly regulated trade has on the lives of the poor, with the language of the option for the poor and of liberation evoked in order to convey their conviction that there is a fundamental incompatibility between neo-liberal economics and Christian values.[24] Moreover they, along with others concerned with social justice, have had a major impact on the global debate about globalisation, in particular by being a voice for those whose experiences are rarely audible in boardrooms in New York, Geneva, or Beijing.

Moral Theology Today: Gender as a Context

A concern for ethical forms of globalisation, based upon respect for human dignity and social justice also features prominently in the work of post-Vatican II feminist theologians. We know that women are disproportionately affected by poverty, and this of course is a major concern for feminist moral theologians. However in addition to this problem of the feminisation

23   See Tadeusz Budinski and Dariusz Dobrzanski, ed., *Eastern Europe and the Challenges of Globalization* (Washington: Council for Research in Values and Philosophy, 2005) and Marianne Heimbach-Steins's contribution to "The European Continental Panel," in James Keenan, *Catholic Theological Ethics in the World Church: The Plenary Papers from the First Cross-cultural Conference on Catholic Theological Ethics* (New York: Continuum, 2007).

24   See for example the essays of Humberto Miguel Yánez (Argentina) Alejandro Llorente (Argentina) John Chathanatt (India) and Aquiline Tarimo (Kenya) in Linda Hogan, ed., *Applied Ethics in a World church*, New York: Orbis Press, 2008. See also the significant body of work by David Hollenbach, Kenneth Himes, Tina Beattie, and Julie Clague in this context.

of poverty, feminist moral theologians have also been concerned with how Catholic theology exacerbates the exclusion of women world-wide because of its traditional approach to gender and sexuality.

The publication, in 1968, of Mary Daly's *The Church and the Second Sex* marked a sea change in how the theological discussion about gender, and particularly about the female body was conducted. Prior to Daly's searing critique of Catholicism on account of its endemic misogyny, little attention was given to the ongoing impact of this patriarchal heritage. Subsequent to Daly's initial intervention, feminist theologians began to analyse the scale and depth of the misogyny inherent in the traditions and practices of Christianity, including Catholicism, and, as a result, today we are more clear-sighted about the nature and extent of the problem. Throughout the 1960s and 1970s, feminist scholars excavated the biblical and theological canon, unearthing the ideologies of subordination that were embedded in the tradition. Half a century on, the significance of the feminist critique of Christian theology, including of theological ethics, is undisputed and the cumulative impact of this work is that we can now see how thoroughly and energetically ideologies of subordination were adopted, developed, and promoted within the Christian tradition more generally, and Roman Catholicism in particular.

In the post-Vatican II period the significance of gender has come to the fore in an unparalleled way. In relation to the field of theological ethics this work has emphasised how, running through all of the different historical periods of Western theo-politics, there has been a deep-seated ambivalence, not only towards the body, but especially towards the female body. As the carrier of new life or as mother, she is to be revered and respected, but as carnal woman, as a sexual being, she evokes anxiety and dread. Within the theological traditions of Western Christianity, and especially within Roman Catholicism, these tensions are highly visible. On the one hand, there is the "fear and loathing" of bodies, particularly of women's bodies. Moreover, the fear and loathing is exaggerated because of the tradition's tendency to view the meaning and significance of bodiliness exclusively, or at least primarily, through the lens of sexuality. Indeed, many of the more infamous misogynistic theological statements about women's nature exemplify this and regard women's bodies, paradoxically, as both the cause and consequence of their inferior status.

Much of the post-Vatican II theology has been highly critical of what it regards as the reductive and punitive character of the church's traditional approach to the body, and of its pathologically dysfunctional attitude to sexuality. In this context feminist theologians in particular have raised fundamental questions about the validity of a sexual ethic that has emerged from an institution that has so systematically excluded women's voices. The ethical challenges associated with the HIV/AIDS pandemic have made addressing these issues even more important than ever, and over the last fifteen years, beginning with the seminal Keenan collection, Catholic ethicists have placed a major focus on this critical global challenge.[25] We know that poverty, deprivation, gender inequality and the denial of human rights all figure in the creation of a vulnerability to HIV and that the pandemic is deeply destructive of the protective social fabric of societies. Even more worryingly however, we can see that existing layers of inequality and of inequitable power relations (including inequitable gender relations) tend to be reinscribed locally and globally as a result of the pandemic. Catholic ethicists from the developing world have taken a lead role in this global ethical debate. Agbonkhianmeghe Orobator,[26] Teresia Hinga,[27] Lillian Dube[28] and Philomena Mwaura[29] each have argued

25 James Keenan, Jon Fuller, Lisa Sowle Cahill & Kevin Kelly, eds *Catholic Ethicists on HIV/AIDS Prevention* (New York: Continuum, 2002).

26 See Agbonkhianmeghe Orobator, *Theology Brewed in an African Pot* (New York: Orbis 2008) and *From Crisis to Kairos: A Critical Theology of the Mission of the church in the Time of HIV/AIDS, Refugees and Poverty* (Nairobi: Paulines Publications, 2005).

27 Teresia Hinga, "AIDS, Religion and Women in Africa: Theo-Ethical Challenges and Imperatives" In *AIDS, Religion and Women In Africa: Theological and Ethical Challenge*, ed. The Circle Of Concerned African Women Theologians, Cluster Publishers, 2005.

28 Lillian Dube, with Tabona Shoko & Stephen Hayes, *African Initiatives in Healing Ministry*, University of South Africa (UNISA) Publications, 2011, and with Philomena Mwaura eds *Theology in the Context of Globalization: African Women's Response*, Nairobi: EATWOT Women's Commission 2005.

29 Philomena Mwaura and Lilian Dube Chirairo, eds *Theology in the Context of Globalization: African Women's Response*, Nairobi: EATWOT Women's Commission, 2005.

for the need to develop and support new paradigms that take seriously the complex synergy of deprivation and disenfranchisement that is at the heart of the trajectory of this pandemic. Each is highly critical of the role that gender inequality and misogyny play in the church's inability to grapple fully with the ethical issues associated with the pandemic. The work of Lisa Sowle Cahill,[30] Margaret Farley[31] and Mary Jo Iozzio[32] has also been tremendously influential in recalibrating the debate about how the combined effect of theologically based misogynistic views of the female body, gender inequality and economic deprivation create a perfect storm that affects millions of women in the developing world, and in marginalised communities in the developed world. Moreover their work highlights how crucial it is that theologians continue to frame the discourse of moral theology in response to diverse cultural, economic and ecclesial contexts, and in a manner in which the concrete ethical issues with which people are grappling are to the fore.

Moral Theology Today: Sexual Liberation as a Context

The post-Vatican II period was also a period of profound social change, particularly in relation to sexual norms. Technological developments raised new moral questions and rearticulated the old ones in a different register, and this, combined with the renewed ecclesiology created an expectation among Catholics that they would participate in the construction of a theology that recognised this changing landscape. It is neither possible nor necessary to rehearse these debates. Suffice it to say, however, that underlying many of the most contentious disagreements, especially disagreements

---

30 Lisa Sowle Cahill, "AIDS, Women and Empowerment", in *Calling for Justice Throughout the World*, ed. Mary Jo Iozzio, with Mary Doyle Roche & Elise M. Miranda (New York: Continuum, 2008).

31 See note 9.

32 Op. cit. note 30.

about reproductive rights and same-sex relationships, one can discern fundamentally different theological understandings of the nature of the human body, the relationships between the sexes, and the malleability of sexuality. In this context there is a concern that the still-dominant strand of Catholic ethics tends to essentialise sexual difference and sacralise complementarity, notwithstanding the fact that in contemporary society these long-dominant assumptions are currently undergoing interrogation. Inevitably theologies of complementarity are especially under the spotlight, and are the subject of ongoing contestation, including by moral theologians.[33] The church's failure to incorporate new insights from the human and social sciences in its teaching can also be seen, for example, in the way it persists in its condemnation of homosexual sex despite significant scientific advances in our understanding of human sexuality. Of course many Catholics still accept and defend the church's positions on sexual matters, and in recent years catechetical and other initiatives have been introduced to explain and promote these teachings. However, whether the focus is on reproductive rights or on the rights of same-sex couples, the divergence of views on sexual ethics is now as intense and intractable within the church as it is in the wider society. Those who are committed to implementing the reforms envisaged by Vatican II insist that the church's moral tradition must evolve in line with changes in scientific understanding and in light of the experience of those whose voices are now audible but which were previously ignored.

Conclusion

Although the language of tradition tends to evoke thoughts of something that is static and unitary, in fact the church's moral tradition is dynamic and internally diverse. Indeed, as the historian John Noonan has demonstrated,

33   Todd A. Salzman, and Michael G. Lawler, *The Sexual Person: Towards a Renewed Catholic Anthropology* (Washington: Georgetown University Press, 2008).

this idea of a fixed and unchanging moral tradition is a fiction. Noonan summarises the ways in which the church's moral tradition has changed thus: "what was forbidden became lawful (the cases of usury and marriage); what was permissible became unlawful (the case of slavery); what was required became forbidden (the persecution of heretics)."[34] So whether one examines the Catholic church's tradition on marriage, divorce, abortion, slavery, human rights, conscientious objection to war or religious freedom, one encounters an always evolving, often inconsistent, and occasionally contradictory body of thought. Previously unquestioned positions have been abandoned, and substantial innovations have occurred. Moreover, not only have the conclusions about the morality of certain practices changed, but the ethical frame within which many practices are evaluated has also been transformed. Of course it would be wrong to overstate the trajectory of change, since it is precisely as *tradition* that it has evolved. Nonetheless it is important to emphasise that the church's moral tradition is a discursive tradition, forged through a dynamic of continuity and change.

Understood in this way it is clear to see why the stakes are so high in the debates about the legacy of Vatican II. The issue comes down to whether the church will continue to pursue the inclusive vision of Vatican II or whether it will retreat into the privileged and increasingly remote world of unaccountable power. On the fiftieth anniversary of the opening of the Council much of the theological and journalistic commentary focused on the fact that the gulf between those who are committed to the implementation of "the spirit of Vatican II" and those who were pursuing a different theological model, was as wide as ever. Since the election of Pope Francis however the discourse has undergone further change. Although there has been no significant shift in the substantive positions on which the church is divided, nonetheless there has been a change in tone and approach. The contentious issues of gender equality and sexuality have been debated

---

34 John T. Noonan Jr., "Development in Moral Doctrine" in James F. Keenan and Thomas A. Shannon eds, *The Context of Casuistry* (Washington: Georgetown University Press, 1995), 194.

in a more open and participatory environment, and with a recognition that earlier church discussions had been conducted through a harsh and judgmental tone. There is no doubt however that doctrinal change, if it is to come, will come slowly, and not without rancour and difficulty. In the interim, however, the importance of the change in style and tone should not be underestimated.

PART V

Ecclesiological Issues

ANDREW PIERCE

10   The Ecumenical Church of Vatican II[1]

Introduction

For many of us who, like our lamented friend Pádraic Conway, were born either in the years of the Council or shortly afterwards, the land described by older friends and family members under the legend "pre-conciliar" seems a remarkably alien environment. In the mid 1960s, to borrow a phrase from the philosopher Charles Taylor, nothing less than the theological, political, ethical – in short – the entire "social imaginary" of the Roman Catholic church altered as Pope John opened windows that had long been kept firmly closed. That such an alteration in the experience of Roman Catholic Christians – and, consequently, in the experience of non-Roman Catholic Christians – could be effected in the course of a mere half century is truly remarkable. Tranquilities have been, and remain, disturbed; *et ad Deo gratias*.

In order to investigate the emergence of the ecumenical church of Vatican II, this chapter reflects on some of the ways in which Catholic identity had been shaped, particularly in the century or so before the Council. An initial stance of official hostility to the modern world and its liberal ways began to yield to a less reactionary and, initially, more deeply ambivalent experience of Catholic modernity. This ambivalence left a profound impact on the Conciliar experience of contending with both tradition and modernity, as well as on the continuing reception of Conciliar teaching.

---

1   Earlier versions of this paper were delivered at events marking the fiftieth anniversary of the start of Vatican II. I am grateful to the editors of *Milltown Studies* and *Search* for their kind invitations to reflect on the Council's legacy.

Fraught discussions over the degree of continuity to be affirmed between the teachings of Vaticans I and II continue both to attract interest and to betray a wider range of interests than those of the hermeneutics of doctrine: historical change retains its capacity to offer a theological challenge to historically embedded institutions. Indeed, one of the key themes where interpretative discontinuity between the Councils is evident is that of historiography. As Gerald A. McCool has demonstrated, the ascendent neo-scholasticism of late nineteenth-century Catholicism may well have safeguarded the freedom of the act of faith to the satisfaction of Joseph Kleutgen – the theologian nicknamed "Thomas *redivivus*" – but it exposed a soft underbelly of generous proportions in its inability to deal with the theological significance of historical change.[2] Vatican II would embody a less uniform theological methodology than its predecessor, partly as a result of its indebtedness to a more historically nuanced understanding of tradition and its development.

Before turning to the immediate background to Vatican II, three broad brush-strokes frame the interpretation of the Council that follows: these concern an historical imbalance between theologies of creation and of redemption, the ecclesiological disputing of authority within and between churches, and the extent to which the experience of dialogue may be received *via* its textual legacies.

First, an observation from the field of historical theology, presenting legacy issues for East-West relations, as well as for relations within the Western churches. The post-Reformation Western churches witnessed almost the eclipse of the theology of creation in favour of a theology of redemption; pneumatology became marginalised and soteriology monopolised theological agendas. Sixteenth-century debates over the dynamics of nature and grace in justification, and, in particular, on the capacity – or otherwise – of sinful nature to receive divine grace, positioned thoroughly

2   Gerald A. McCool, *Catholic Theology in the Nineteenth Century: The Search for a Unitary Method*, New York: Seabury Press, 1977. McCool identifies Kleutgen (1811–1883) as a key architect of the neo-Thomistic revival, particularly through his drafting of Vatican I's constitution *Dei Filius*, and Pope Leo XIII's encyclical *Aeterni Patris*.

anthropo- and indeed profoundly andro-centric notions of "fall" and "fall-enness" in unqualified positions of theological pre-eminence. The ensuing neglect of the theology of creation in an era of scientific and technological revolution was pregnant with a range of important philosophical, ethical and theological consequences. This is something for which the West continues to be chided by its Orthodox sisters and brothers: a shared fixation on a sometime Bishop of Hippo – it is alleged – on the part of both Catholic and Protestant theologies, has led to the neglect and disregard of a theological legacy that had been established to resist gnostic despair in the face of both history and matter – although whether this deficit is best addressed by means of a corrective enthusiasm for the thought of St Gregory Nazianzus may be left to one side for now.

At least two consequences follow from this first point. First, the sheer weight attached to the theology of redemption in the life of the sixteenth-century church enabled a scholarly dispute amongst Augustinians to grow like Topsy into the issue on which the contemporary Western church stood and fell. Subsequently, intra-Christian polemic – and "polemic" is an unduly sanitising term – helped to secure the redemption paradigm of Christianity as Christianity's normative expression. In returning *ad fontes* (and in undertaking this journey along with Orthodox, Protestant and Anglican Christians), Vatican II has assisted in an ongoing re-framing of the paradigm in which Christian disunities had become (and largely remain) heavily invested.

A second consequence draws on the implicit Gnosticism of any theological interpretation that overplays redemption at the expense of creation. Post-Reformation ecclesiologies – Catholic and Protestant – have tended to emphasise a church-world distinction in unhealthy ways. Roman Catholic ecclesiologies traditionally emphasised the continued institutional visibility of the Catholic church to the extent of playing down, if not denying, an "eschatological proviso:" church and kingdom merge. The church – as visible as the Kingdom of France – is seen as the perfect society in a sinful world. Protestant theology was no less problematic; there, the true church became invisible, floating into history betimes in fidelity to the Word of God, but just as capable of floating away, lest weaker souls be tempted to trust in the work of belonging to the fallen, institutional means of grace. Richard and Anthony Hanson nicely parodied Karl Barth's ecclesiology by draw-ing attention to the similarities between Barth's "true church" and Lewis Carroll's Cheshire Cat. Significantly, in the pre-Conciliar period, Barth and Pius XI shared similar views on ecumenism: Pius wanted the Protestants to return; Barth considered that the only appropriate response to Catholicism was evangelism. Post-Reformation and pre-Conciliar ecclesiologies thus seemed reasonably content that Providence had ensured that the church of Christ coincided helpfully with the boundaries of their own habitations.

The second interpretative point is that the disputes over justification broke out in a church that possessed an impressive track record for energetic and divisive debate over the vexed issue of authority. East and West had struggled with one another over this issue, resulting in schism and mutual condemnation. In the Western church, the medieval variation on this very old conflict took the form of a debate between Conciliarists and Papalists: in blunt terms, where did supreme authority lie in the church? In a General Council? In Pope and Council acting in concert? Or, in Pope alone?[3] This struggle between Conciliarists and Papalists is woven into the very fabric of the later Reformation debates, with many of the Reformers echoing the claims and concerns that had characterised the Conciliarist tradition.[4] The decisions made at the reforming Council of Trent (1545–1563) represented not only a firm refusal of Protestant claims (though some Protestants were present until the second session), but also the triumph of the Papalist party in the contemporary church.

3   A blurring of meanings between the historical position of those who had advocated a Conciliar approach to authority in the pre-Tridentine church, and the adjective relating to the work of the Second Vatican Council allowed later interpreters to catch threatening or hopeful echoes from the past. On historical conciliarism, see Francis Oakley, *The Conciliarist Tradition: Constitutionalism in the Catholic Church 1300–1870* (Oxford: Oxford University Press, 2003). Oakley places the death of Conciliarism at Vatican I, rather than at Trent.

4   For a recent Anglican reconsideration of these debates, see Paul Avis, *Beyond the Reformation? Authority, Primacy and Unity in the Conciliar Tradition* (London and New York: T & T Clark, 2006).

From the latter years of the nineteenth century onwards, an increasing number of Catholic writers (including John Henry Newman's nervously apologetic biographer, Wilfred Ward) expressed a concern that the teaching of the Tridentine fathers had overly identified Catholicism with anti-Protestantism, and that a less-reactive, positive statement of Catholic identity was becoming increasingly necessary. The reputation of Tridentine teaching has suffered more than it merits as a result of its association with an ascendant anti-Protestant Papalism. Immediately after the Council of Trent, the Tridentine documentation underwent a Papalist hermeneutical makeover courtesy of Pius IV and his nephew, St Charles Borromeo, who together synthesised the complexities of the Council's teaching into the significantly less-complex texts *The Catechism of the Council of Trent* and *The Tridentine Confession*. Thus was post-Reformation Catholicism set on a Papalist trajectory that, arguably, reached its zenith at the next Council of the church, Vatican I, between 1869 and 1870. Almost a century later, and exactly four centuries after Trent, Vatican II attempted to restore balance in a church whose official self-understanding had swung too far in a reactionary direction.

Third, the texts themselves bear witness to the passions that they produced in the *Aula*. An appropriate interpretation of Conciliar texts needs to attend to the sounds of compromise and to the presence of deliberate ambiguity, and, at times, of ambivalence. Massive works of scholarship, including those of Giuseppe Alberigo, and before him Caprile and Vorgrimler, as well as the Council diaries of participants (recently and notably the Council diary of Yves Congar), bring alive the energetic interplay of theology and politics in the emergence of Conciliar teaching.[5]

---

5   Giuseppe Alberigo ed., *The History of Vatican II*, 5 vols. (Maryknoll: Orbis; Leuven: Peeters, 1996–2006); Yves Congar, *My Journal of the Council*, 2002; Translated from the French by Mary John Ronayne OP and Mary Cecily Boulding OP, English translation editor Denis Minns OP (Dublin: Dominican Publications, 2012).

Modern Ecumenism and Anti-Modernism

Shaped by a variety of distinctively modern factors – including factors as diverse as nineteenth-century historicism and missionary experience – and, from the start, struggling to deal with its inevitably compromised context of origin (characterised by other no-less modern notions such as eurocentrism and colonial expansion), Christian ecumenism understands itself to be concerned with articulating and sustaining the intrinsically interconnected realities of unity and diversity in Christian identities.

Since the sixteenth century in the West, prevailing notions of unity had been definitively shaped through conflict with other traditions: others were vilified and selves were defined, resulting in an inevitable impoverishment of how ecclesial expressions of both unity and diversity were to be understood (*ad intra et ad extra*). In the nineteenth century, the deconstruction of what we might call notions of a cheap unity owes much to biblical and historical scholarship for having drawn attention to the significant plurality and diversity in the very sources claimed as authoritative by the competing Christian traditions – scriptural, institutional, dogmatic. And, in the twentieth century, in dialogue with social science, H. Richard Niebuhr charted the disturbing elective affinities between class and denomination in the United States.[6] Race and class, rather than doctrine and ethics, according to Niebuhr, exercised power in shaping the lived realities of believing and belonging – and not only in the USA. Hence the ecumenical significance of Niebuhr's claim that denominationalism – which is satisfied with a *status quo* in which inter-institutional mobility is taken as the meaning of diversity and in which, consequently, the transcending of existing corporate identities garners neither interest nor support – represented nothing less than a moral failure of Christianity.

Nascent ecumenical theology drew on these kinds of analyses of both past and present experience, as it set about articulating normative claims

6   H. Richard Niebuhr, *The Social Sources of Denominationalism* (New York: Henry Holt & Co., 1929).

about a situation characterised by the theologically painful and unsatis-factory willingness of far too many churches to remain content with their existing, unevangelically limited expressions of unity and diversity. And, as ecumenical relationships developed and strengthened, it became increas-ingly apparent that ecumenics was concerned with more than interchurch diplomacy. New configurations of how theology deals with unity and diversity cannot rest content with critically reconciled expositions of ethics and doctrine; ecumenics seeks more partners in dialogue than traditionally constituted the ranks of separated brethren. As Niebuhr had demonstrated, churches and religious communities – whether they understand themselves this way or not – are profoundly shaped by non-doctrinal factors that need to be engaged by a theology in a new key.

In the 1980s both Konrad Raiser and John D'Arcy May theorised these new ecumenical configurations in term of a new paradigm of ecumenical, political and interreligious engagement.[7] Yet, rather than a shift in paradigm, the 1980s witnessed resurgent religiosity and psycho-social retrenchment on a global scale: the Religious Right and the culture wars in the USA, Khomeini in Iran, Thatcher in Britain, the pontificate of John Paul II, the bloody conflict over identity in the former Yugoslavia – all, to some extent, symbolise a popular cultural option for identity over relevance, to use Jürgen Moltmann's helpful distinction. And not only have the energies of ecumen-ics been drained by the experience of swimming against neo-conservative currents – the post-modern preference for particularity and difference over against an allegedly modern tyranny of the universal and the common, has also contributed to the emergence of a challenging atmosphere in which to re-engage the ecumenical imagination. Karl Rahner's cutting phrase, "the winter time", described the ecumenical climate at the end of his life; it stands in marked contrast with the energetic ecumenical engagement undertaken by the Council at which he was a *peritus* in the 1960s.

7   John D'Arcy May, "Integral Ecumenism", *Journal of Ecumenical Studies* 25/4 (Fall 1988), 573–591; Konrad Raiser, *Ecumenism in Tradition: A Paradigm Shift in the Ecumenical Movement?* 1989; English translation by Tony Coates (Geneva: WCC, 1991).

To receive Conciliar teaching into the life of the church and into the experience of the churches is a complex matter. Another former Conciliar *peritus*, Josef Ratzinger, is keen to acknowledge continuities between Vaticans I and II – and undoubtedly these ought not be ignored – but, given the extent to which John XXIII and Paul VI insisted on the ecumenical character of Vatican II, and bearing in mind that this ecumenical Council sought to synchronise its deliberations with a growing ecumenical convergence *extra ecclesiam* – it is vital that due attention be given to a distinctively new and ecumenical orientation in Catholic self-understanding. Not only did ecumenical engagement characterise Vatican II; it also repudiated the integralism and anti-modernism of the late nineteenth- and early twentieth-century church. Archbishop Diarmuid Martin has said of *Gaudium et spes* that it "envisaged a new style for the life of the church", and this raises questions concerning why and how Vatican II undertook a step back from the old style of the pre-Conciliar church.[8]

To grasp the specifically *ecumenical* significance of Vatican II, one need only recall the ecclesial and political atmosphere in which Vatican I had taken place. After a brief flirtation with liberalism, Pius IX had swung to the opposite extreme, and there he remained for the duration of his remarkably long pontificate. His *Syllabus Errorem* (1864), provided a list of ideologies and developments that the Pope condemned; but there is something philosophically unsatisfactory in the *ad hoc* nature of the syllabus of errors. The real significance of the *Syllabus* was symbolic, with popular *and* ethical ramifications that are well captured by Owen Chadwick:

> Europe ... saw the Pope condemn liberalism – whatever that was, the Pope condemned it. And without precisely defining liberalism, or defining it in diverse ways, Europe saw that this was the irresistible force of the age. The Pope sat on his throne like Canute amid the incoming tide. But the Pope looked not merely ridiculous. Ethical ideals were associated with the slogans of liberalism, words like liberty and fraternity, freedom of conscience, tolerance, justice in the way of equality before the

8   Archbishop Diarmuid Martin, "*Gaudium et spes*: the Church in the Modern World," in Dermot A. Lane and Brendan Leahy, eds, *Vatican II Facing the 21st Century: Historical and Theological Perspectives* (Dublin, Veritas, 2006), 31–48; 31.

law. Many western Christians had the sensation, not just that the Pope was wrong, but that he was morally wrong.[9]

The *Syllabus* caused scandal; and the deliberations of Vatican I were viewed, contemporaneously, in the light of the *Syllabus*: rather than concerning the relationship of faith and reason, or the infallibility of the papal magisterium, the key question faced by Vatican I was whether the Roman Catholic church could interpret itself as belonging companionably in the context of an emerging, self-consciously "liberal" Europe. Symbolically, in the *Syllabus* and at the Council, the church was seen to have repudiated liberalism – whatever that was.

The *Syllabus* was, however, merely a menagerie of the unacceptable. Only with the enforcement of neo-Thomism, under Pius' successor Leo XIII in 1879, could there develop the kind of theoretically comprehensive rationale for the earlier papal condemnation of a wide range of modern ideas and beliefs. When Pius X condemned the heresy of modernism in 1907, he was consolidating the reactionary nature of the ultramontane papacy of the nineteenth century, with an ideological coherence drawn from the Thomistic revival enforced by his immediate predecessor, Leo. A key difficulty faced by this development was that by identifying Catholicism with neo-Thomism, those Catholics who – philosophically – were not fully persuaded by neo-scholasticism, now found their credentials as Catholics under severe scrutiny. Pius X's anti-modernist encyclical *Pascendi* offered a detailed description and analysis of the various manifestations of modernism, but the theory was largely superfluous. The modernist's defining crime was that he or she was not a neo-scholastic in a church where neo-scholasticism had been declared to be the Catholic means of answering modernity. Aside from the non-scholastics condemned as modernists, this strategy would have awkward consequences for noteworthy non-neo-scholastics: John Henry Newman's *Essay on the Development of Christian Doctrine* had brought its author perilously close to doctrinally hot water on two occasions in his lifetime; the modernist crisis ensured that Newman's

9 Owen Chadwick, *The Secularization of the European Mind in the Nineteenth Century*, 1975 (Cambridge: Cambridge University Press, 1995), 111–112.

legacy was in trouble – or, at best, in a state of official neglect – where it largely remained until Vatican II.

This tightly defined and officially promulgated Catholic identity was profoundly ultramontane; its mandatory neo-scholasticism fostered deep hostility towards historical consciousness; and its public pronouncements were anti-modern, anti-liberal, and anti-Protestant. This reactionary combination of philosophical cohesion with a traditionalist imaginary produced the "integral catholicism" or "integralism" that characterised official self-presentations of Catholicism from the pontificate of Pius X to the Council. Catholicism was to be seen, not as an integrated and complex whole, but as an undifferentiated totality; to call into question any one part of that whole (famously, for example, the authenticity of the Johannine comma – 1 John 5: 7–8), would bring the whole edifice tumbling down.

Charting the path between the two Vatican Councils highlights the problematic nature of ecumenism when Catholicism sees itself in integralistic terms. The *unam sanctam*, by definition, has no need of the other *soi-disant* churches. Individuals outside might have some mysterious connection with those inside, "by desire," but that was it. Hence, the rug was pulled from under the Malines conversations in 1928: the proposal that Anglicans might be "reunited" with Roman Catholics, rather than "absorbed" (the terms from a famous paper given by Dom Lambert Beaudouin in 1925), was definitively scotched by the encyclical *Mortalium Animos*: unity was understood as the denial of diversity; those outside needed to return to their rightful place, on the inside.

The historical coincidence of a modern ecumenical movement with a regnant anti-modern paradigm of Catholic self-understanding is the context of Pius XII's encyclical *Mystici Corporis* (1943). A budding biblical scholar at the time of the modernist crisis, the young Eugenio Pacelli re-orientated his energies towards diplomacy; as Pope, however, his encyclical *Divino Afflante Spiritu* (issued in 1943 – the same year as *Mystici Corporis*), created space for Catholic biblical scholars to focus on the challenges and opportunities offered by a gentle embrace of historical-critical methods of exegesis. These encyclicals embody a significant ambivalence in magisterial teaching. Although it was intended to redirect ecclesiology towards more mystical, and less juridical understandings of the church as the body of Christ, *Mystici Corporis* presented an historically naïve account of the descent into history of the spotless bride of Christ, and it clearly identified the mystical *unam sanctam* with the somewhat less mystical denominational reality of the contemporary Roman Catholic church. *Divino Afflante Spiritu*, by contrast, opens onto the more uncertain and liminal space of modern historiography, and into territory that had proven dangerous for scholars. The danger remained. Pius clearly considered that undue advantage had been taken of his historiographical openness; seven years later, his encyclical *Humani Generis* took aim at evolutionism (the *bête noire* of the anti-modernist campaign), existentialism and historicism.

Aside from its echoes of anti-modernism, the period between 1943 and *Humani Generis* in 1950 keenly anticipates some of the issues that came before the Council. In terms of the personnel involved, the 1943 encyclicals reflect a tension between the neo-scholastic curial establishment on the one hand and non-neo-scholastic voices on the other. The principal draftsman of *Mystici Corporis* was the Jesuit theologian, Sebastian Tromp (1889–1975), who would later become secretary to the preparatory theological commission for Vatican II, and whose draft of *De Ecclesia* would be severely deconstructed by the Council fathers. *Divino Afflante Spiritu* was drafted by another Jesuit, the then-Rector of the Biblicum, Augustin Bea (1881–1968), who was amongst the most influential of *De Ecclesia's* critics. Although *Humani Generis* did not identify specific theologians for censure, the spotlight fell on a number of French theologians whose work took seriously the historical context of their subject matter.[10] These included Henri de Lubac (1896–1991), Yves Congar (1904–1995) and Marie-Dominique Chenu (1895–1990), who were dismissed from their teaching positions; yet, in just over a decade, their work and presence would be pivotal in resourcing the deliberations of the Council.

10   See the comprehensive assessment offered in Gabriel Flynn and Paul D. Murray, eds, *Ressourcement: A Movement for Renewal in Twentieth Century Catholic Theology* (Oxford: Oxford University Press, 2011).

Conciliar Contestings of Ecumenicity

Debate continues over the central theological achievements of Vatican II.[11] Conciliar teaching on ecumenism – which pervades the Conciliar corpus and is not confined to *Unitatis Redintegratio* – suggests that the Council's significance lay at least as much in what it learnt with difficulty to un-say, as in what it promulgated positively.

It is significant that the textual origins of Conciliar teaching on ecclesiology, ecumenism, revelation and religious freedom were enmeshed, with important implications both for their emergence at the Council – and for their ongoing reception in the lives of the churches. In the beginning, a single ecclesiological document – *De Ecclesia* – had been envisaged by the preparatory commission. *De Ecclesia* also furnished the origins of the Decree on Ecumenism, *Unitatis Redintegratio*, and of the Declaration on Religious Freedom, *Dignitatis Humanae*. Concern for how best to address the Jewish people, and the proper location of conciliar teaching on Mary were also addressed in the context of re-thinking ecclesiology.

Concerning ecumenism, it initially appeared as though the Fathers would consider ecumenical teaching in detail in three different texts – in chapter 11 of *De Ecclesia*, in a text from the commission on the Eastern churches, and in a text devoted solely to ecumenism to be produced by the Secretariat for Promoting Christian Unity. The conciliar decision to centralise its ecumenical teaching, with the Secretariat for Promoting Christian Unity given responsibility for drafting *Unitatis Redintegratio*, should not be taken as limiting the Council's fundamentally ecumenical orientation – a point underscored by Paul VI's opening address to the second session of the Council, and, especially, in his speech at the solemn promulgation of the decree.

Redefining the church without re-inscribing integralism would, however, prove intensely challenging. Integralism offered no ecumenical

---

11   See, for example, Massimo Faggioli, *Vatican II: The Battle for Meaning* (New York/ Mahwah, NJ: Paulist Press, 2012).

possibilities beyond a monistic "return;" and it is arguable that the key ecumenical achievement of Vatican II was its public and institutionalised *coup de grace* to integral Catholicism. The fatal blow came in Pope John's opening address to the Council address – characteristically entitled "Mother church rejoices" – the "speech of his life," according to John's biographer, Peter Hebblethwaite.[12]

In its first, Italian, draft, the key sentence states: "For the substance of the ancient deposit of faith is one thing, and the way in which it is presented is another." This sense is reflected in the Latin text as delivered by John and included in most critical editions of the conciliar texts. By the time an official, Latin text was published in *Acta Apostolicae Sedis*, however, the curial spin-doctors had struck. The term "substance" had been entirely omitted; the new sentence reads: "For the deposit of faith itself, or the truths which are contained in our venerable doctrine, is one thing, and the way in which they are expressed is another, retaining however the same sense and meaning." Fans of the anti-modernist oath will undoubtedly recognise the last clause inserted into the pope's address. Angelo Roncalli, however, knew only too well how the curia operated (indeed, he alludes to them in unflattering terms in that opening address), and, once aware of his censored condition, he took great care to quote the key passages from his uncensored self on public occasions. In *Unitatis Redintegratio*, the Council developed a nuanced theoretical backing for John's distinction between substance and its presentation in its delineation of a hierarchy of truths: not every teaching carries equal dogmatic weight.

Moreover, according to *Unitatis Redintegratio*, division is a matter of scandal, and historically no side is blameless. In spite of lamentable divisions, there remains a unity that is real, though imperfect. To address this imperfect communion, Christians are called into a life of dialogue with one another, sharing in worship where appropriate. Officially, therefore, Ecumenism is no longer the lamentable hobby of doctrinally suspect

12   The following account of John's speech, and its immediate consequences, relies on Peter Hebblethwaite, *John XXIII: Pope of the Council* (London: Geoffrey Chapman, 1984).

ecclesiastics and less-controllable, eccentric lay fifth columnists; henceforth, Catholic theology is to be ecumenical. As the *Decree on Ecumenism* 10 states:

> Instruction in sacred theology and other branches of knowledge, especially those of a historical nature, must also be presented from an ecumenical point of view, so that at every point they may more accurately correspond with the facts of the case.
>
> For it is highly important that future bishops and priests should have mastered a theology carefully worked out in this way and not polemically, especially in what concerns the relations of separated brethren with the Catholic church. For it is upon the formation which priests receive that the necessary instruction and spiritual formation of the faithful and of religious depend so very greatly.
>
> Moreover, Catholics engaged in missionary work, in the same territories as other Christians, ought to know, particularly in these times, the problems and benefits which affect their apostolate because of the ecumenical movement.

Commenting on the impact of *Unitatis Redintegratio*, Tom Stransky has remarked that "Ecumenism deals not with foreign relations, but with domestic ones." This unsettling vision of ecumenicity continues to challenge church structures that all-too-frequently treat ecumenism as though it were merely concerned with inter-church diplomacy. Stransky further observes that *Unitatis Redintegratio* calls, not for "a return to the past but a common search for future reconciliation."[13] This is a welcome orientation away from retentive reiterations of conflicts – although too great an emphasis on the future place of reconciliation may downplay the reconciliatory significance of the present "common search".

Conciliar engagement with ecclesiology began by considering a first draft of *De Ecclesia*, which represented Cardinal Alfredo Ottaviani's (1890–1979) curialist restatement of a highly defensive and reactionary position. To Ottaviani and his colleagues, *De Ecclesia* stated what the church needed to know about itself: viewed from a post-Conciliar standpoint, however, *De Ecclesia* appears as an incoherent jumble of themes, an intrinsically

---

13   Tom Stransky, "Ecumenism (*Unitatis Redintegratio*)," in Adrian Hastings, ed., *Modern Catholicism: Vatican II and After* (London: SPCK; New York: Oxford University Press, 1991), 113–117; 114.

reactionary product of a prolonged post-Reformation and anti-modernist hangover. The proposed chapter headings offer a flavour of the draft:

1. The nature of the church militant
2. The members of the church and the necessity of the church for salvation
3. The episcopate as the highest grade of the sacrament of orders; the priesthood
4. Residential bishops
5. The State of evangelical perfection
6. The Laity
7. The teaching office of the church
8. Authority and Obedience in the church
9. Relationships between church and state and religious tolerance
10. The necessity of proclaiming the gospel to all peoples and in the whole world
11. Ecumenism

The Fathers considered this draft at the end of the Council's first session in December 1962. Their earlier deliberations had been concerned with the liturgy; and, as a result, from the start of the Council, the specifically ecumenical implications of revising liturgical teaching had drawn attention to the inherently ecumenical dimension of the Council's work in its totality. Some of the bishops, it is true, responded positively to *De Ecclesia*; observers of the Council noted that the first speakers often spoke firmly in favour of the curial draft or *schema*, but as more critical voices began to be raised, it was clear that first drafts were often in grave difficulties.

Cardinal Leo Josef Suenens (1904–1996) proposed radical surgery for *De Ecclesia*. Rather than starting with the church militant, Suenens argued that the text's proper point of departure involved attending to the mysterious gift of the church's inner life; only then could the text move towards addressing how that life is lived in the world. This proposal found favour with the Council; *De Ecclesia* was quarried for 2 long texts, the Dogmatic Constitution on the church, *Lumen Gentium* (for which Suenens supplied the title) and the – until recently somewhat neglected – Pastoral Constitution on the Church in the Modern World, *Gaudium et Spes*.

Suenens was not alone in voicing strong criticisms of the hitherto prevailing paradigm. In more abstract terms, Bishop Emiel Jozef de Smedt (1909–1995) of Bruges claimed that the text exuded "triumphalism," "clericalism," and "juridicism." Cardinal Montini, the future Paul VI, was bothered by its treatment of the laity as a kind of unduly sheep-like after-thought in an otherwise shepherd-dominated church. Similarly, he found the document grudging and minimalist in its acknowledgement of the reality and integrity of the state. He lamented the draft's inattention to the Greek Fathers, and especially its failure to draw on the riches of biblical images of the church, singling out the image of the church as "people of God" for favourable comment. By contrast, Montini's enthusiasm for this image would fail to convince his successor John Paul II, who considered that a pilgrim "people of God" effectively compromised the idea of the church as a perfect society – in their disagreement we catch a re-contesting of the ecclesiological vision of *Mystici Corporis*, which would re-echo under John Paul II in the Congregation for the Doctrine of the Faith's statement, *Dominus Iesus* (2000).

The first draft was sent back to the drawing board, and after a 9 month recess, draft number 2 came before the bishops in September 1963. Four chapters had survived the first cull:

1. The mystery of the church
2. The hierarchical constitution of the church and the episcopate in particular
3. The people of God and the laity in particular
4. The call to holiness in the church

In the discussion of the second draft, a difficulty with a bright future made its first appearance. Chapter II spoke of the collegiality of bishops, thereby raising the spectre of conciliarism *redivivus* by compromising the ultramontane Petrine monopoly that had followed in the wake of Trent and Vatican I. A majority of the bishops – and Pope Paul himself – did not see matters this way, but collegiality and its allegedly harmful potential for the creative interplay of episcopal autonomy and papal authority, would become and would remain a key element in the paradigmatic clash between the majority and the minority at the Council. Despite securing the support of 80 per cent of the Council fathers, the conservative minority and its curial supporters continued to press the case that collegiality had not received precise definition in the *schema*, and therefore could not be said to have received the Council's support.

During the deliberations of the second draft, there was an important public clash over the Holy Office and the extent to which it was aligned with the papacy. This altercation was between Cardinal Frings (1887–1978) of Cologne and Cardinal Ottaviani: the Irish Dominican Cardinal Michael Browne (1887–1971) – Ottaviani's vice-chairman on the Theological Commission – had disputed the significance of the vote for collegiality, and had claimed that the Theological Commission, rather than the Council fathers, would decide whether such a doctrine was true or not. The Theological Commission, insisted Frings, did not sit in judgement on conciliar teaching, but existed only to do the bidding of the Council. Moving, significantly, from Theological Commission to the Holy Office, Frings criticised it as no longer fit for purpose: it harmed the faithful, and was a source of scandal throughout the world. The fathers interrupted Frings with sustained applause. Ottaviani's angry response drew a strong connection between the papacy and the Holy Office – to criticise the latter, he claimed, was to attack the former. Full authority was given to Peter and to his successors, not to the other disciples – supporters of collegiality overlooked these facts. Following Ottaviani to the microphone, Browne reminded the fathers that collegiality compromised papal power and contradicted the solemn teaching of Vatican I: "*Venerabiles patres*", he concluded, "*caveamus, caveamus!*" As Robert McAfee Brown reported at the time, the eruption of this conflict into the *Aula* was seen by some as serving the hygienic purpose of positioning the Conciliar conflict between conservatives and progressives in open view.[14]

14   Robert McAfee Brown, *Observer in Rome: A Protestant Report on the Vatican Council* (Garden City, NY: Doubleday, 1964), 151–152. Brown attended the second session of the Council (September–December 1963) as an observer from the World Alliance of Reformed and Presbyterian churches.

A third draft was presented to the Council in its third session, which began in September 1964. The shift away from the first draft continued: church was explicitly subordinated to kingdom; the church of Christ and its relationship with the Roman Catholic church was explained in a manner that did not monopolise the *unam sanctam* – the former is held to "subsist in" the latter; and Paul VI's much-loved image of the people of God was developed with historical sensitivity.

Once again, episcopal collegiality provoked unease amongst the minority, which had, by this stage in the life of the Council, settled at approximately one third of the bishops. That proportion of opposition would have resonated unpleasantly with the Pope; the conclave at which he had been elected had concluded with somewhere between 22 and 25 of the cardinals unwilling to bring themselves to vote for him, even though their votes could not halt a Montini papacy. This level of potential dissent in high places may also have helped to animate Paul's concern with securing the greatest possible level of support for Conciliar decisions, even though his activities to mollify the minority clearly antagonised many amongst the Council majority. By the end of the third session of the Council, in November 1964, the minority had become organised into the *Coetus Patrum Internationalis*, and it could look back on the session with no little satisfaction.

"November 1964 was Paul's cruellest month" according to Peter Hebblethwaite.[15] Three ecumenically pivotal documents were on the verge of being finalised and promulgated – *Lumen Gentium*, *Unitatis Redintegratio* and *Orientalium Ecclesiarum*. The cruellest month culminated in what has come to be known as the "Black Week" – a tag deriving from the Dutch bishop Msgr Beckers, who dubbed it the "*sombre semaine*", and which was in turn rendered into Italian by Giovanni Caprile SJ as "*settimana nera*".

Four sets of events combined to render the week "*sombre*". First, the text on religious liberty was postponed to the following session. In retrospect, its advocates acknowledged that this was fair, as the text had altered

15   Peter Hebblethwaite, *Paul VI: The First Modern Pope* (London: HarperCollins, 1993), 398.

radically and it deserved to be treated as a new text. The suspicion remained, however, that it had been withdrawn under pressure from the minority who could not stomach any shift from affirming that "error has no rights" to a position that went beyond tolerance to an affirmation of religious freedom. Second, a prefatory explanatory note appeared "from a higher authority", i.e., from Paul himself, to govern the correct sense of collegiality in *Lumen Gentium*. Third, the Pope provided a total of nineteen modifications to the text of *Unitatis Redintegratio* – a text that had already been finalised by the Council, and therefore these modifications would have to be accepted without discussion. And, fourth, during the closing ceremonies and solemn promulgation of the Council's teaching, Paul acted unilaterally to confer on the Virgin Mary the title *Mater Ecclesiae*, Mother of the church. Internal Conciliar opinion had been wary of such a move, as had the Theological Commission. Ecumenically, this was badly received – particularly by the Orthodox – in a context where Pope and Council were working together, a papal solo run was apt to confirm the worst fears of those most nervous of a petrine ministry.

Pope Paul is sometimes portrayed as indecisive, or, worse, as selectively decisive. That verdict is altogether too harsh for a helmsman at the centre of a storm in which the barque of Peter took stock of itself and opted for what appeared, to many, as a fundamental change in direction. At least a third of his fellow bishops were dubious if not openly hostile. Chadwick described Paul as the most open-minded Pope in two centuries; but there are limits to what even a pope can achieve, especially a pope supportive of episcopal collegiality. The key point, and one with which Anglicans reaping the whirlwind of Lambeth 1998 can readily sympathise, was that Paul was acutely sensitive to the theological inadequacies of reaching a simple majority on questions affecting identity and unity; as far as possible, his target was consensus. He was, after all, a reader of John Henry Newman; and Newman's angriest comment – directed at some of the Fathers at Vatican I – referred to an "aggressive, insolent faction" – and the term of greatest abuse is "faction."

Together, the final texts promulgated by Paul and the Council Fathers in November 1964 embodied an extraordinary development of doctrine (both in form and in content) from the curial texts of 1962. The a-historical ecclesiology of *Mystici Corporis* yielded before a more dynamic, historically informed theology of church that drew on biblical and patristic resources. But paradigm shifts take time, and the time of "shifting" is characterised by ignorant armies clashing by night; the move to a more thoroughgoing historical theology may be underway, but it is far from accomplished.[16]

Ironically, the promulgation of the texts was carried out in a politically tense atmosphere; the Council majority felt betrayed by the Pope and the ecumenical observers were clearly uneasy with the outcome of the Black Week – Congar feared that trust had been lost. Yet, amidst the gloom of November, one hopeful sign passed almost unnoticed. In his address to the Council Fathers and observers, Paul explained how he saw the connection between the Decree on Ecumenism and the Dogmatic Constitution on the church – the former explains and completes the latter: "ea doctrina, explicationibus completa in Schemata "De Oecumenismo" comprehensis." Becoming church is now an ecumenical matter.

Conclusion

Great ideas, according to John Henry Newman, take time. Hence, the ecumenical movement takes time to give serious thought to how Christian churches and traditions may best resist the perpetual ecclesiastical temptations of imperial pretence and parochial retreat. Vatican II signalled the arrival of the Roman Catholic church as a committed member of the modern ecumenical movement. The church's journey, from Trent to Vatican II *via* Vatican I, entailed a deeply painful and protracted restructuring of

16   That, at any rate, is the view of René Girault, in his assessment of an important debate sparked by Joseph Ratzinger's personal appraisal of the *Final Report* of ARCIC I in 1981, and the responses of two Roman Catholic members of ARCIC, Edward Yarnold and Marie-Jean Tillard. See René Girault, "The Reception of Ecumenism", in Giuseppe Alberigo, Jean-Pierre Jossua and Joseph A Komonchak, eds, *The Reception of Vatican II*, 1985 (Washington: Catholic University Press of America, 1987), 137–167; 158.

relationships with those in other churches and traditions, and of relationships within the Roman Catholic tradition itself. The recovery of an appreciation for internal diversity and pluralism – across all of the ecumenically engaged Christian denominations – has been a source of joy and stimulation to post-Conciliar ecumenism.

The Catholic experience of transforming identity was distinctive, but the experience of ecumenical transformation *per se* was not unique to the Roman Catholic church. When the World Council of Churches held its first assembly, at Amsterdam in 1948, it observed bluntly that the western world had fallen into two totalising and self-contained traditions of ethno-religious identity – Catholic and Protestant – and that, through mutually exclusive systems of deeply entrenched beliefs and practices, neither seemed to know or need the other. Yet, within a period of two decades, the situation was changing, as churches began to confront themselves – and to confront themselves together.

Paul Tillich famously distinguished between "Catholic substance" and "Protestant principle", and he lamented those ecclesial developments in Europe's history that had seen these housed separately, their symbiotic possibilities frustrated. The growth in ecumenicity across the churches has enabled traditions to receive – as gifts from one another – aspects of what was rightfully a part of their own identity, but which had been denied and repressed. This is not an easy process. The conciliar minority saw an alien agenda pressing for married deacons, for ecumenism, for positive relations with the Jewish people, for religious freedom. If there is to be an alternative to spiritualities of nostalgia and strategies of retrenchment, then the churches must acknowledge their continuing need of appropriate resources to assist in addressing and engaging the tendency, present in all Christian traditions and further afield, to identify one particular strand in tradition with the ambiguous complexities of tradition itself.

In part these resources are theological. The texts examined in this chapter provided a deeply theological reflection on the nature of the church, drawing critically on history and tradition. This raises the issue of the place of theology in the life of the churches: what kind of theological education and formation will help the churches to negotiate the reality – and not just the imperfections – of their communion with one another? It also raises a question about the critical and self-critical nature of ecclesiology, and of its place in society and in the academy. Churches think theologically about themselves, or else they will, inevitably, conduct their self-reflections in some kind of sanctified quasi-managerialism. Ecclesiology, if it is a genuinely critical and self-critical theology, is not simply an account of how "we" do what "we" do in "our" church.

A further dimension of the significance of theology comes from the remark – attributed to Yves Congar – that the theology of Vatican II, and especially of Paul VI was an *emergent* theology. It was incomplete in the 1960s, and to a significant extent it remains so. Paul was sometimes criticised for lacking a theology that would have supported and enhanced some of his remarkable gestures – disposing of the papal tiara, the gift of his ring to Archbishop Michael Ramsey and his reference to Anglicanism as an "ever-beloved sister," his relations with the Oecumenical Patriarch, Athenagoras. Perhaps that is true; but as well as simply noting the not-fully-formed character of both Paul's and the Council's theology, their example should help to stimulate the development of a theology that anchors such gestures and explores the sound theological instincts that lay behind them.

Intimately connected with its ecclesiological teaching, Vatican II is also ecumenically significant for what it says about dialogue in the context of a theology of revelation. In its teaching on divine revelation, Vatican II shifted decisively away from the hitherto prevailing understanding that revelation essentially entailed the transfer of information from God to human beings. Revelation was thus seen as taking the form of propositions, with faith taking the form of a cognitive assent – and there are important ecclesiological consequences to this presupposition, as the church then needed to find ways in which both to safeguard and dispense its divinely sourced data by means of a clerical caste and a clearly defined catechism.

At Vatican II, however, revelation is increasingly understood in experiential terms as dialogue. The mystery of God does not present creation with nuggets of information; divine mystery initiates a dialogue in which the participants grow in mutual understanding of one another. Dialogue is thus not primarily concerned with the transfer of information (which might be obtained elsewhere without the troublesome business of encounter); it is, rather, a transformative process of encounter, and in dialogue with one another we share in the structure by which we come to relate intentionally with the mystery that surrounds us.

A final point draws on one of the striking features of Yves Congar's Council diary. Congar repeatedly expressed his own frustration, and the frustration of the Fathers, at the lack of space and time to reflect on important issues raised within the life of the Council. And that, truly, is an ecumenical matter; how might we integrate the Conciliar experience of taking counsel together into the life of the churches? The Council's experience of itself led not only to promulgation of texts; it also embodied a practice of encounter (albeit limited encounter) that goes towards the heart of what it is to be in communion with one another.

Finding the space and time in which to act together in dialogue gained an urgency at Vatican II that cries out to be rediscovered as an ecumenical imperative in our own time. The Council proved to be ecumenical in more than its technical designation: to be an *ecclesia semper reformanda* is an ecumenical undertaking; we travel together now, or not at all.

11 Vatican II as a Resource for the Renewal of the Church in Ireland in the Twenty-First Century

Commemorative anniversaries may be used predominantly to recall and celebrate a past event or to explore its meaning for today. The 2014 celebration of the Battle of Clontarf seems to have fallen largely into the former category, while the centenary of the Easter Rising, not least due to the proposal to invite a member of the British royal family to attend, seems set to include a strong dimension of the latter. As the title of this piece indicates, and as a Christian theology of the Word and Spirit of God as "alive and active" would invite, the celebration of the fiftieth anniversary of Vatican II involves an opportunity, even a demand, that what happened then might be a resource for what is needed now.

In what follows I want, with the hindsight of fifty years, to assess the reception and implementation of Vatican II in Ireland, in particular as pertaining to the church itself, and then try to indicate resources for ecclesial renewal and reform based on this assessment and on the historical and theological significance of the Council. The church in question is the Catholic church – this focus does not by any means preclude the essential learning which Catholics need to imbibe from other Christian communions.

Part One: The Reception of Vatican II by the Irish Catholic Church

As in the church in general, it would seem that little new was expected or indeed desired of Vatican II in Irish church circles. The preparatory input from Ireland (thirty episcopal submissions very much "in the spirit of the pre-conciliar church"[1]) was undistinguished, as indeed was the contribution within the Council itself. This was not surprising – the Irish church went into the Council in a state of apparent rude good health, with a complacency and almost triumphalism that left it ill-prepared for the changes that were to come. This was the context in which the oft-quoted remark of Archbishop Charles McQuaid of Dublin, on his return from Rome, may be understood: "You may have been worried by much talk of changes to come. Allow me to reassure you. No change will worry the tranquillity of your Christian lives".[2]

The nineteenth-century closeness of the church to an oppressed people, followed by the mutual legitimisation process of church and State that developed in the first half of the twentieth century, had left the Republic of Ireland at least with a seemingly all-pervasive culture of Catholicism. Besides high rates of practice, there was strong religious influence on politics, education, health, sports and leisure, the arts (not least due to strict censorship)-in short, on seemingly every aspect of life. The religion in question was marked by an unquestioning, un- and even anti-intellectual quality, with an emphasis on rule-keeping and fear of sin, and characterised by a deep popular devotion featuring the likes of the rosary, benediction, sodalities, indulgences and processions. There was a strong ethos of sacrifice and delayed gratification, a familiarity with austerity, a hope for fulfilment in the after-life. This was a religion in which the voice of the priest, the bishop, and the pope could rely on its formal authority to get a serious hearing, not just from the faithful, but also from politicians. A paternalistic ethos reigned and was accepted almost universally.

This was the background context to the Irish church experience of Vatican II. But in fact things had already begun to change in Ireland itself. One can trace the beginnings of this change back to 1959 when, seemingly for the first time, the Government of the day faced down church opposition to a legislative change. This was in the matter of more liberal Sunday

1   Louise Fuller, *Irish Catholicism since 1950: The Undoing of a Culture* (Dublin: Gill & Macmillan, 2002), 106.
2   *The Irish Times*, 10 December 1965.

opening times for pubs, in which the economic logic of publicans won the day.[3] This was also around the time of the Lemass-Whitaker *Programme for Economic Expansion 1958* – now it became apparent that values other than austerity would compete with the dominant Christian ethos. Then there was the influence of media, television in particular, first the BBC and then RTE itself, opening Irish society out to a wider world in which our insular certainties were exposed to an uncensorable other view and critique.

This was the changing context to which Archbishop McQuaid and his fellow bishops returned after Vatican II. In truth, they had some Good News from the Council in terms of the evolving situation at home – the centrality of our loving, saving and life-giving relationship with Jesus Christ, rather than any more propositional or rule-keeping approach (the Decree on Revelation); the new focus on the "joys and griefs" of all human beings in this life, the values of socio-economic justice and well-being, of peace (The Church in the Modern World); the recognition of the equal dignity of all the baptised, and the collegial re-shaping of the church, more in tune with the democratic ethos of the age (The Dogmatic Constitution on the Church); the embrace of ecumenism; the distinction between church and state, the recognition of the value of conscience, religious freedom, and, by implication, other human rights (Declaration on Religious Freedom); the liturgical changes, with eucharist in the vernacular and a sense of more active participation by the faithful; and, perhaps more important than all that, a new style, a new sense of being church in which there appeared an openness to the world, a willingness to learn from as well as teach the world, a sense that the church could really be "a light for the world", could, in the words of Pope John XXIII, dispense the medicine of mercy rather than of severity.[4]

And at first it seemed that this was working in Ireland, that, despite some confusion and even disruption, people were taking to the changes with enthusiasm. This was most visible liturgically – active participation in the

3   Fuller, 58–60.
4   See John W. O'Malley, *What Happened at Vatican II* (Cambridge, MA: Harvard University Press, 2008), 95.

vernacular eucharist, redesigned sanctuaries to image a greater sense of the
church as the People of God, and, over time, the introduction of Readers,
Eucharistic Ministers, more lay participation – even, in admittedly too few
places then, parish Councils. The Bishops – and, to be fair, Archbishop
McQuaid in particular – showed a real leadership in engaging with media
(the training of priest, the Radharc initiative, the Catholic Communications
Institute of Ireland), while many Episcopal Commissions were set up, with
often expert lay involvement, to service the Episcopal Conference. There
was also a real energy around issues of social justice, at home and abroad,
as evidenced not least in the establishment of Trocaire.[5]

However, events were also moving fast in the secular world. The introduction of "Free Education" in the late 1960s, Ireland's entry to the then
EEC, the ongoing focus on economic development, the accelerated pace of
urbanisation, the "gentle revolution" of third-level students in the late 1960s,
increased travel opportunities – all these meant a more open and critical
public forum in which a pluralism of ideas and world-views emerged with
force to challenge the previously dominant Catholic hegemony in Ireland.
From their 1973 statement of principle about church – state relations in
which they admitted the possibility that state law need not always mirror
church law or values the Bishops seemed to have found a workable principle by means of which to negotiate a *modus vivendi* with the State.[6] But
as the constitutional reform agenda of Garrett Fitzgerald gathered pace it
seemed that particularly in areas to do with sexuality and gender the stance
of the bishops became increasingly at odds with that of the population
in general. This situation, already apparent *in nuce* in the 1970s and then
developing more significantly in the 1980s and 1990s, was exacerbated to
a fatal degree by the emergence of the various clerical scandals in the 1990s
and the first decade of the new millennium and the initially poor handling
of these scandals by those in authority. I say to a fatal degree because in this
context it became apparent that formal, juridical authority on its own had

---

5   For a fuller account of the reception of Vatican II in Ireland, see Dermot A. Lane,
     "Vatican II: The Irish Experience", in Liam Bergin, ed, *Faith, Word and Culture*
     (Dublin: Columba Press, 2004), 54–70.
6   Fuller, ch 14, especially 208–209.

lost its moral credibility, that paternalism was no longer possible: people simply would not listen, unless what was being said made sense to them.

And, in truth, in hindsight we can see that in fact, perhaps for understandable reasons given the previous recent history of the Irish Catholic church, too little was done to implement the letter and spirit of Vatican II. Perhaps, at heart, the Irish Bishops in particular were not convinced of the need to change, and perhaps the Irish faithful presumed that, given our strong Catholic tradition, that God would "always be with us", we did not need to claim the rights and duties implied by Vatican II. And so, despite a growth in the number of laity studying and now teaching theology, the Catholic ethos in Ireland remained un- and even anti-intellectual, unprepared to deal with a rapidly changing culture. Moreover it quickly became apparent to a discerning laity that their participation in a predominantly clericalised church was to remain at the level of discretionary cooperation – they had no real say in decision making. This became particularly irksome to women, who, despite making such a strong contribution to church life, understood that the ban on ordination – given the effective restriction of "sacred power" to the ordained – meant that their "say" in church life was limited, in contrast to the emerging situation in civil life and in some other Christian communions.

This focus on Ireland needs to recognise other explanatory factors at play. There is in our Western world in particular a general culture of secularisation which easily verges on secularism: God is either "missing or not missed" or is presumed to be dead or anti-Modern. This goes side-by-side with the increasing globalisation of a neo-liberal model of economic development which has a hard time accommodating values other than economic ones, and within those, what is perceived as the rightful freedom of markets.

There was, in addition and very crucially, in the ecclesial world at large – and not just in Ireland – what theologian Jim Corkery has referred to as a "loss of nerve", even a "loss of faith", with regard to the teachings of Vatican II.[7] Massimo Faggioli has noted that some historians distinguish

---

7   Jim Corkery SJ, "Our Own Hope Had Been ..." (Luke 24:21), The Promise of Vatican II – Reality or Illusion?, in Sue Mulligan, ed, *Reaping the Harvest: Fifty Years after Vatican II* (Dublin: Columba Press, 2012), 13–37; 32.

the age of "euphoria" in the reception of Vatican II as lasting about ten years up to 1975, followed by a decade of "contestations" up to 1985, and then concluded by what he refers to in 2012 as the "current period of 'restauration' that had begun well before 2005".[8] He goes on to observe that from an intra-Catholic perspective "it can be argued that the honeymoon between the Council, the pope, and mainstream culture lasted even less than ten years".[9] He is referring here to the watershed promulgation of *Humanae Vitae* in 1967, "symbol of the first crisis in the renewed relationship between church and modern world".[10]

What Corkery and Faggioli are referring to is also articulated in historian John O'Malley's judgement that the Synod of Bishops (as constituted unilaterally by Paul VI) failed to offer institutional grounding to the principle of collegiality espoused by Vatican II– it was as if the bishops imagined that ideas on their own were enough to bring about change, without realising that appropriate institutional and structural, not to mention cultural, change was needed as well – and this was left to the Curia, "the centre", predominantly peopled by the Council "minority" who had been opposed to change, to implement.[11] Ladislas Orsy notes also the need to implement legal change, to enshrine the values taught by Vatican II, and notes how in several key instances this failed to happen – the lack of proper autonomy of the Synod of Bishops (as already noted), the limitation to affective and not effective collegiality of the role of Episcopal Conferences, the restriction of "sacred power" to the ordained and hence the untraditional limitation of serious decision making powers by laity in Canon 129,[12] the lack of justice

---

8   Massimo Faggioli, "The Future of Vatican II", in Anthony Ciorra and Michael W. Higgins, eds, *Vatican II, A Universal Call to Holiness*, New York: Paulist Press, 2012, 7–26; 8.

9   Faggioli, 8.

10   Faggioli, 8–9. For his fuller account of the reception of Vatican II, see Massimo Faggioli, *Vatican II, The Battle for Meaning* (New York: Paulist Press, 2012).

11   O'Malley, op. cit, 292, 311–313.

12   I note here the reference by Pope Francis, in the context of remarks on the restriction of ordination to men only, of the divisiveness this causes especially "if sacramental power is too closely identified with power in general" – *Evangelii Gaudium*, 104.

in procedures governing contentious theological opinions and the lack of a culture of more open theological debate in the church.[13]

Among the casualties of conciliar restorationism was a certain lack of vigour around ecumenical progress, in particular with respect to Roman Catholic relationships with Anglicans and Protestants. This meant that in Ireland, despite ongoing cordial contacts among church leaders and many prophetic acts by church members, the Christian contribution to a resolution of conflict in Northern Ireland was not as radical and imaginative as it might otherwise have been.

Archbishop Diarmuid Martin has spoken of the challenge to ensure that Catholicism in Ireland does not become "an irrelevant minority culture".[14] One could see traces of this already in the 1970s, not least in the rapturous reception given to the charismatic figure of John Paul II on his visit to Ireland but the less than whole-hearted acceptance of his message. Even then it was apparent that a fundamentally changed Irish society "is now influencing Irish Catholicism whereas formerly the position was reversed – Catholicism was influencing Irish society".[15]

This rather brief historical overview will serve as a back-drop to our central concern, the exploration of resources from Vatican II which can help church renewal and reform in Ireland. This exploration takes place in the space afforded by the renewed affirmation of the Council by Pope Francis.

13   Ladislas Orsy, *Receiving the Council* (Collegeville, MN: Liturgical Press, 2009), especially chs. 1–3 and 7.
14   Speaking notes of Archbishop Diarmuid Martin: "'Keeping the Show on the Road': Is This the Future of the Irish Catholic church?", address to the Cambridge Group for Irish Studies at Magdalene College, Cambridge on 22 February 2011, available at <http://www.dublindiocese.ie/content/22022011-cambridge-group-irish-studies>. Accessed 17 November 2011, 2.
15   Fuller, 238.

Part Two: Resources for Renewal from Vatican II

One of the great gifts that Pope Francis has bestowed on the church is his seemingly effortless ability to circumvent the tired debates about a herme-neutic of continuity/discontinuity surrounding the reception of Vatican II by focussing on what is central to Christianity and indicating in a very simple way how this is faithful to the Council's teaching. This central focus similarly circumvents the tedious efforts to separate personal from structural renewal. So, Francis again and again points to the mercy and love of God for all, in particular the poor and those in need, as the Good News which Jesus Christ embodied and which he announced in his preaching of the Kingdom. The church is called to be a sign, a sacrament of this Kingdom, not something that is self-referential.

With this kind of outward looking, missionary focus Francis is clear that to be an effective sign the church needs to be renewed and reformed. It was obvious in the meetings leading up to his election that the College of Cardinals shared the more widespread view that in recent years, sadly, the church had functioned more as an anti-sign. The symptoms of this crisis may be variously described – the sexual and financial scandals; excessive centralisation and a deficit of collegiality at all levels; the unconscionable attitude to women; the lack of open debate; teaching on sexuality and gender that increasingly was honoured more in the breach than in the observance all pointed to a situation of discontent and even gloom. In taking his joined-up approach (the first chapter of his extremely missionary-oriented 2013 Apostolic Exhortation *Evangelii Gaudium* concerns "the reform of the church in her missionary outreach" (EG, 17) Francis is very effectively re-uniting the concerns expressed by the two distinct Conciliar documents (originally conceived as one) – The Dogmatic Constitution on the church (*Lumen Gentium*) and The Pastoral Constitution on the church in the Modern World (*Gaudium et Spes*). And so, writing about Francis and Catholic Social Teaching, Donal Dorr can say:

> When historians look back on the pontificate of Francis they may well conclude that the area in which his contribution to Catholic social teaching was most effective in

practice was in his commitment to applying that teaching to the church itself. This is evident most notably in the way in which he is putting into practice the fundamental principle of subsidiarity by implementing the Council's teaching on collegiality.[16]

What might collegiality look like in the Irish church? How might the Irish church benefit from a more collegial approach? Would it enable it to be more culturally relevant?[17]

Collegiality in the Irish Church

The Irish Episcopal Conference issued a very interesting statement in the aftermath of the response by "thousands of people" to the questionnaire from the Synod of Bishops on the family.[18] They noted that "many of those who responded to the questionnaire expressed particular difficulties with the teaching on extra marital sex and cohabitation by unmarried couple, divorce and remarriage, family planning, assisted reproduction, homosexuality. The church's teaching in these sensitive areas is often not experienced as realistic, compassionate or life-enhancing. Some see it as disconnected from real-life experience, leaving them feeling guilty and excluded. We recognise our responsibility as bishops to present faithfully the church's teaching on marriage and the family in a positive and engaging way, whilst showing compassion and mercy towards those who are finding difficulty in accepting or living it".

16 Donal Dorr, "Pope Francis and Catholic Social Teaching", *Doctrine and Life*, 64, February 2014, 3 (2–15).

17 For what follows, see also O'Hanlon, "The Future of the Catholic Church – a view from Ireland", *Studies*, 99, Autumn 2010, 289–301; "Irish Catholicism at a Crossroads", *Studies*, 101, Winter 2012, 375–386; "The Church of the Future", *The Furrow*, 64, June 2013, 332–341; and "Re-Building Trust: The Role of the Catholic Church in Ireland", in Patrick Claffey, Joe Egan and Marie Keenan, eds, *Broken Faith* (Oxford: Peter Lang, 2013), 259–276.

18 Statement of the Irish Catholic Bishops' Conference regarding the questionnaire from the Synod on the Family, Thursday 13 March 2014.

This statement is interesting because it indicates a welcome realism and compassion towards those who find church teaching in these areas difficult, but also a restricted understanding of their own role as bishops with regard to this teaching. Might not a more vigorous embrace of collegiality allow for the possibility that the bishops might take seriously the difficulty the faithful have in receiving the teaching, having regard to their own responsibility as bishops to be in touch with "the sense of faith" of their own faithful, and might use this as a resource in the authentic expression of their teaching office? It seems that too often – in the Irish church but more universally as well – there has developed a kind of lazy habit of interpreting the injunction on bishops to "teach faithfully" as being simply identical with teaching what Rome says, without sufficient regard to listening carefully to what people in good faith experience in their lives. A more collegial approach would take more account of "the sense of the faithful", while being careful to test and discern this in the light of Scripture, the tradition, theological opinion and being in communion with other local churches and the universal church.[19]

The late Seán Freyne, writing in 1993, saw the Irish Episcopal Conference "as having a serious image problem, perceived more as a collective of Vatican civil servants than as pastors with a genuinely independent concern for the real needs of their flocks".[20] A more collegial approach requires a change not just in theological understanding but also in imagination: bishops, theologically, are not simply papal delegates, they have an independent authority, but they need too to begin to imagine how to exercise this independence in a way that is respectful of the need for unity, for communion. The unity in question needs to respect diversity more than hitherto – this is what Cardinal Lehmann of Mainz seems to be suggesting when he is

---

19   See Richard R. Gaillardetz, *When the Magisterium Intervenes* (Collegeville, MN: Liturgical Press, 2012), and, in particular, the article by Ormond Rush, "The Prophetic Office in the church: Pneumatological Perspective on the *Sensus Fidelium*–Theology–Magisterium Relationship", 89–112. Also Gaillardetz, *By What Authority?* (Collegeville, MN: Liturgical Press, 2003).

20   Seán Freyne, "What Crisis? Some Thoughts on Irish Catholicism", *The Furrow*, 44/10, October 1993, 538.

reported as saying: "We need to be more courageous in dialogue within the church. We complain that Rome is over-powerful but that is because we are too weak".[21] And this seems also to be the direction in which Pope Francis himself is pointing when he speaks again and again of the need for a more collegial, less centralised church, in which consultation must be real and not just token, in which "thinking with the church" involves not just obeying the Magisterium but listening to the "sense of faith" of the People of God.[22] And, in line with this collegial approach, it is clear that he wants the Synod of Bishops to claim its proper authority, to consult with all the faithful in its deliberations, and it would seem that he wishes contentious issues (the admission of divorced and remarried faithful to communion) to be tackled at synodal level rather being a matter of Roman judgement alone.

This emerged again recently in the reported interview[23] with the Austrian-born Bishop Erwin Krautler of Xingu in the Brazilian rain forest who spoke with Francis about the problem created by the desperate short-age of priests in his huge diocese: "The Pope explained that he could not take everything in hand personally from Rome. We local bishops, who are best acquainted with the needs of our faithful, should be *corajudos*, that is 'courageous' in Spanish, and make concrete suggestions ... regional and national bishops' conferences should seek and find consensus on reform and we should then bring up our suggestions for reform in Rome". Bishop Krautler was then asked whether it now depended on bishops' conferences as to whether church reforms proceeded or not – "Yes", he replied. "After my personal discussion with the Pope I am absolutely convinced of this". Both the general principle (initiatives for change to come from local, regional and national contexts) and the particular issue of shortage of priests (the debate about parish "clusters") are of relevance in our Irish context.

Given this more universal changing ecclesial context why do the Irish Bishops not take the lead in considering the structures and institutions suitable and necessary for a more collegial church in Ireland, in which the

---

21　*The Tablet*, 15 March 2014, 33.
22　Interview with Jesuit journals, 2013; *Evangelii Gaudium*, 2013, 102, 119, 126, 198.
23　*The Tablet*, 12 April 2014, 28, 31.

People of God would have more say in decision making and the formation of teaching? Might a well-prepared National Assembly (building on all assemblies which have gathered in several dioceses over the recent years) be a significant and hopeful step in that direction? The words of Cardinal Lehmann, again, are instructive in this respect: "I get very annoyed when we expect everything from the Pope as far as church renewal is concerned but do nothing ourselves. That is absolutely unCatholic".[24] Might not there be useful learning obtainable from the ecclesial polity of other Christian communions in this context?

Collegiality and culture[25]

Already back in the 1960s Paul VI had written that "the split between the Gospel and culture is without doubt *the tragedy of our time*".[26] In our Modern and Post-Modern western world in particular, characterised by a scientific and relativist rationality, the core value of moral autonomy and a deep-seated preference for personal authenticity over institutional belonging, the Catholic church needs to discern how it might engage in a more fruitful conversation with our culture. Citizens in liberal democracies are used to the exercise of authority which does not depend solely on the formal, juridical status of the speaker but which draws also on the persuasiveness of what is said. And so the grounds of authoritative statements are "prepared and referenced, rulings are accompanied by reasons and assurances that relevant matters have been investigated, appropriate bodies of knowledge have been tapped, interested parties have been canvassed, and the likely consequences of the rules are understood to have been prepared for. These are now among the customary duties of rule in civil societies,

---

24   *The Tablet*, 15 March 2014, 33.
25   For what follows, see also O'Hanlon, "Voices of Hope: Echoes of the Divine", *Doctrine and Life*, 64, January 2014, 38–52; "A Dream Fulfilled?", *The Furrow*, 65, March 2014, 169–178.
26   Paul VI, Apostolic Exhortation, *Evangelii Nuntiandi*, n. 20, 1975.

and the need for something more closely comparable to them within the church is becomingly increasingly evident".[27]

It is against this cultural background that collegiality, with its attendant implications of participative subsidiarity, becomes so crucial. An educated laity, immersed in a culture which takes for granted the value of freedom (so cherished by the Declaration on Religious Freedom of Vatican II),[28] will not be able to receive teaching which is not persuasive and does not take into account their own faith experience of life – think, for example, of the reception of *Humanae Vitae* or the teaching on the role of women in the church. At best what happens is "that a spirit of reciprocal pretence seems to prevail: 'you pretend to teach me, and I'll pretend to learn'".[29] More likely what happens, however, is a shrug of the shoulders and a walking away–among many young people in particular it is indifference rather than hostility that characterises their attitude to a church that they sense is so far out of step with the contemporary *Zeitgeist*.

And of course it is not the church's mission to simply say "yes" to everything that is modern. What is required is a careful discernment so that we may distinguish "the signs of the times" from what is merely the "spirit of the age", the kind of discernment which Christians have engaged in from the very beginning (think of Paul on the Areopagus with the Athenians) as they intuitively understood that the logic of the Incarnation demanded that the gospel be always and everywhere inculturated anew. And so one sees Pope Francis excoriating the contemporary "globalisation of indifference" that is also part of the spirit of our age, the neo-liberal economic model that dominates our world, and yet able to reject a monarchical form of ecclesial government and to encourage collegiality at all levels of the church. Above all one sees him engaging in conversation, in dialogue,

---

27   Michael J. Lacey, "The Problem of Authority and its Limits", in Michael J. Lacey and Francis Oakley, eds, *The Crisis of Authority in Catholic Modernity* (Oxford: Oxford University Press, 2011), 6 (1–25).

28   See Ladislas Orsy, "The Divine Dignity of Human Persons in *Dignitatis humanae*", *Theological Studies*, 75, 2014, 8–22 for the Council's appreciation of the value of human freedom, human rights and the human capacity to know the truth.

29   Lacey, op. cit., 6.

listening and speaking, teaching (often by simply witnessing) and learning, radiating the joy of the gospel – and the world intuitively understands this, is attracted, opens its heart in response. In this sense Francis represents a counter-point to the remark attributed to Seamus Heaney: "Christian myth is so contentious and exhausted".[30]

I have focussed on the issue of collegiality from Vatican II because in itself and in what it implies it sums up the major resource coming from the Council as support for our call to renew and reform the Irish church. Our pre-Vatican II church, with all its genuine piety, lived its faith under a paternalistic model of church which is no longer culturally possible.[31] An educated laity is ready to embrace a different model. They would be helped by leadership from our bishops. They – and Irish society in general – would also be helped by a more sympathetically critical engagement with and framing of these issues by Irish media, which by and large remains either indifferent or hostile to anything other than the superficial with regard to the Catholic church and indeed religious comment in general.[32]

Questions that remain

Political scientist Scott Tarrow notes that the "political opportunity"[33] afforded by a new leader, sympathetic to reform, needs to be perceived and acted upon for results to follow. Otherwise what can happen is that reform groups, paradoxically, are demotivated by the advent of the leader, imagining that the leader can effect reform alone. He notes further that a

---

30   *The Irish Times*, September 3, 2013. See also O'Hanlon, "Voices of Hope: Echoes of the Divine", *Doctrine and Life*, 64, January 2014, 38–52.
31   For a perceptive outline of the changed cultural context in Ireland, see Michael A. Conway, "Ministry in Transition", *The Furrow*, 65, March 2014, 131–149.
32   For the crucial role of media in "framing" situations of conflict, see Sidney G. Tarrow, *Power in Movement, Social Movements and Contentious Politics* (Cambridge: Cambridge University Press, 2011), 141–156.
33   Tarrow, op. cit, 32–33; 159–169 – see also O'Hanlon, "Voices of Hope", 48–52 and "A Dream Fulfilled?", *The Furrow*, 65, March 2014, 169–178.

good way for reform to happen is that greater access to decision-making is achieved, rather than by obtaining more concrete single-issue gains on their own.

One can sense a lightening of the mood within the Catholic church as the faithful, including the bishops, bask in the reflected glow of the popularity and celebrity-status of Francis. It would be a serious mistake, however, to imagine that the serious issues of governance and doctrine which have become so recently apparent and which led to such harm, can be solved simply by a feel-good factor that, of its nature, can only be temporary – "political opportunities are fickle friends".[34] Francis himself is so clear about this: we need reform, it must include and even begin with the papacy itself. In this context it is important to resist the notion that something like a papal visit to Ireland would be a sufficient response to our church crisis.

It is true, as noted earlier, that structural reform on its own is also insufficient: we require deep personal and collective conversion, a change of attitude and culture, as embodied in Francis himself and as expressed theologically by the Second Vatican Council. But – and this is the lesson O'Malley and Orsy clearly teach from the post Conciliar experience – we need more than just this kind of conversion, theological insight, even the invaluable "feel-good" factor. We also need the structures, institutions and law capable of carrying the new vision in a way that is independent of particular personalities.

This will mean finding a way beyond the letter of Vatican II, yet very much in its spirit.[35] The unresolved question of the relationship between primacy and collegiality – and the implementation of collegiality at all levels of the church – needs to be tackled head-on. One way of doing this would be the convening of an Ecumenical Council – and there are many other good reasons to do this also. But another is for the Pope himself to

---

34   Tarrow, 169.
35   Gerry O'Hanlon, *A New Vision for the Catholic Church*, Dublin: Columba Press, 2011, 57–62; 84–93 and "The People of God: Towards a Renewed Church?", in Sue Mulligan, ed, *Reaping the Harvest: Fifty Years after Vatican II* (Dublin: Columba Press), 2012, 63–87.

govern more collegially and to give legal effect to this practice.[36] This in fact
is the direction Francis seems to be moving in – the eight-man Council of
Cardinals and the clear intention of making the Synod of Bishops a more
dynamic and autonomous body are clear straws in the wind in this direction.

The question will then gradually crystallise as to how more precisely
this collegiality is to be understood. Will it be a matter of real, and not
just token, consultation (already something to be welcomed), but with
the pope (and the Roman Curia) making the final decision, or will there
will be shared decision-making? The former is what Francis himself will
have been familiar with, at least juridically and theoretically, in his role as
Jesuit Provincial. But practically even the Jesuits have gone a long way in
the direction of more shared governance and it is only this that can yield
the synodical way of proceeding which Francis himself has professed to
be desirable. One way to achieve this has been teased by Mary McAleese,
among others: the designation of "the Synod of Bishops as a standing
decision-making body representative of the College of Bishops (whether
by partial or full delegation). The Synod's powers would be those delegated
by the College of Bishops and not those delegated by the Pope".[37] This is
similar to the "standing Synod" who would govern the church with the
pope, as advocated by Nicholas Lash.[38]

There are interesting further implications of this new approach. If
collegiality is to occur at all levels of the church so that a way needs to
be found to bring laity into governance and lift the restriction on "sacred
power", and consultation is to be real and not token or ceremonial, so that

36   I simply note here the argument by Karl Rahner that in principle at least it cannot be
      said that the issue of how collegiality is to be exercised is a matter for papal decision
      alone – see Rahner, "Structural Change in the Church of the Future", *Theological
      Investigations*, vol. 20 (London: DLT, 1981), 115–132 at 119 –also in O'Hanlon, *New
      Vision*, 57–62; 88–89.
37   Mary McAleese, "The centre cannot hold", *The Tablet*, 8 March 2014, 11–13. See also
      McAleese, *Quo Vadis? Collegiality in the Code of Canon Law* (Dublin: Columba
      Press, 2012).
38   Nicholas Lash, *Theology for Pilgrims* (London: DLT, 2008), 239.

the "sense of the faithful" (in particular those who are poor) becomes a real *locus theologicus*, then how will the church handle situations where the "sense of faith", carefully discerned, is at odds with current teaching and practice? One gets a sense that on issues like the plight of the divorced and remarried, even of married priests, the current pope is relaxed and may be prepared to let the process of collegiality play itself out – in other words it seems unlikely he will take any unilateral decisions himself but will rely on the Synod of Bishops (*cum et sub Petro*), with input from national and regional Episcopal Conferences. But what about an issue like the ordination of women, which as "a son of the church" he deems to have been already decided and not up for discussion? I simply note here his own words that a bishop should listen to everyone "and not simply to those who would tell him what he would like to hear" (*Evangelii Gaudium*, 31). The genie is out of the bottle with a more collegial church and we need to learn from our post-conciliar "loss of faith" to have more confidence and trust in the process of discernment, aided by the Holy Spirit, a process which while far from a populist adherence to the demands of the loudest voice will, nonetheless, lead the church into uncomfortable places.

Conclusion

Pope Francis radiates a personal authenticity that resonates with and also challenges the spirit of our age on so many levels – a faithful intelligence, shot through with a gift for symbolic witness and expression, which appeal to that inchoate desire for "re-enchantment" apparent in post modernity; an ability to operate at the level of desire and imagination, of freedom; a faith which focuses on what is central and gives hope – God's love and mercy – and sees life as a mysterious search and journey within love and not as some mechanical adherence to pre-packaged truths of very different degrees of certainty and importance. He is passionate about justice, about the plight and yet the gift of the poor, and sees the connection between this and the need to create a more just situation within the church in terms of financial transparency and also, it would seem, with regard to the proper role of the Congregation of the Doctrine of the Faith.

However, Francis is also "astute". He realises that it is not in his personal gift to right all wrongs, in short to live our lives for us. And so he has shown that he understands and affirms the teaching of Vatican II, above all on collegiality, and, as Donal Dorr has said, his most lasting accomplishment may well be the structural, institutional, cultural and legal grounding of this teaching in the church, fifty years after Vatican II expressed it. This can only happen if others – we too – are prepared to do our bit in accepting co-responsibility for our church. Francis is sometimes portrayed as conservative/traditional and so in some respects he may well be. But there is no mistaking the radical change that underlies this traditional presentation: and perhaps the biggest changes in society or in a group can be made by those who succeed in presenting them as hardly new at all but as a return to the charism of the founder and who succeed in maintaining the unity of the group as a result?

The implementation of the teaching on ecclesial collegiality could be transformative of the Irish church. As noted, the days of an exclusively clerical, formal and paternalistic paradigm of church are long gone. People want to experience freedom and inclusivity in their church, and an educated laity are waiting to be invited in. It is the only possible way to envisage the interest of young people being sparked. Already this new paradigm is taking shape, albeit somewhat slowly and haphazardly. The pace will be accelerated as the universal church takes further steps in that direction. One would love to see a more courageous reading of these "signs of the times" by the Irish Episcopal Conference.

12 The Church: *Semper Reformanda*

The atmosphere in the Catholic church has changed since the arrival of Pope Francis. It is clear that he is showing a very different face from that of his immediate predecessors; but it is too soon to say that he is instigating the sort of radical reform that is needed in today's church. It seems certain that many in his curia are less than happy with the face he is showing to the church and to the world. The curia is still exercising a power over the church that has centuries of precedent behind it, and, as we saw after the death of Pope John XXIII, there is the unhappy precedent of how the curia regained its power after the death of John XXIII and the closure of the Second Vatican Council. The Roman Curia has a propensity for reasserting its authority in spite of the desire of many faithful Catholics to see a less patriarchal and aggressive leadership.

I have been greatly impressed by something which Yves Congar wrote during the Second Vatican Council:

> Experience and history have taught me that one must ALWAYS protest when one feels in conscience or by conviction that there are grounds for doing so.[1]

This, it seems to me, applies not merely to distinguished theologians like Congar, but also to all who work, however modestly, in the same field as he did.

We have grown so accustomed to the regal image projected by popes down the ages, that Francis' attitude comes across as fresh and endearing; but we have seen no significant structural changes in the bureaucracies that

---

1   Yves Congar, *My Journal of the Council* (Dublin: Dominican Publications, 2012), 12. Congar has put "ALWAYS" in upper case – his usual method of emphasis.

surround him, most notably that of the Congregation for the Doctrine of
the Faith (CDF), which continues to insist on imposing its own unreformed
values on men and women who clearly do not share them. It is there to
promote and defend the views of one party in the church. How can there be
reform when any attempts to bring it about can be attacked and probably
defeated by it, because it has power and they do not? The Roman Catholic
church, like any large gathering, contains a variety of opinions and ideals
within the compass of its essential beliefs. I shall reduce them to the two
that are large enough to call for special attention.

It is not easy to find labels on which all can agree. During the meeting of the Second Vatican Council, the world's media divided the Council
members into "conservatives" and "progressives". By and large, these labels
were widely accepted as an adequate description of the field of contention –
and it *was* a field of contention, in spite of conservative attempts to gloss
over the adversarial character of what was going on. Today, fifty years later,
the terms "conservative" and "liberal" appear to be more common.

Although I am well aware of occasional protests against "labels" such
as "conservative" and "liberal", we must employ something like them to
describe where we stand on the controversial issues under discussion in the
contemporary church and world. Condemnation of labels can be an indo-
lent and convenient way of avoiding an issue by refusing to give it a name.
It is often an attempt to rise above unavoidable debate by taking refuge in
flight from difficult questions; and it patronises those Catholics who see
the urgent need for discussion, debate and willingness to live peacefully
together. Those of us who are looking for reform are not troublemakers in
the vineyard of the Lord. We are trying to clear away weeds that we believe
are interfering with the health and growth of the vines, and we are doing
so from inside the church, which can prompt anger in traditionalists who
regard as unacceptable any challenge to *their* understanding of Catholic
faith, authority and practice. Legitimate diversity is not a phrase in their
vocabulary.

It is obvious that there are two conflicting mentalities in the church that
resist any effort to conflate them. Why try to seek a consensus between conservatives and liberals? It is easily assumed that this is a laudably Christian
aim; but it is in fact aiming at an impossible goal. Consensus between two

mutually contradictory mindsets is logically impossible. The goal needs to be an agreement to live tolerantly and peacefully together in spite of their different attitudes and convictions. Why not let each abound in their own sense, and be free to discuss and dispute the issues that divide them? Pretending that a consensus is possible amounts to dissembling the truth for a well-intentioned but logically impossible reason. Discrepant attitudes are inevitable in a body as large as the Catholic church. There are no good reasons for the suppression of views with which we cannot agree. What we need is the freedom to discuss and argue the case for what we believe to be true, but to do so in a manner that befits disciples of Christ (I Pet. 3: 15). Unity does not imply unanimity.

If one party exercises control over the entire church by taking its own opinions as the only permitted orthodoxy; and if they invoke the authority of their office to attack those who legitimately disagree with them, the result is injustice and the destruction of healthy diversity. Traditionalists sometimes accuse their more liberal brothers and sisters of "heresy" in an unjust attempt to overpower them, not by argument but by prejudicial name-calling.

Diversity of opinion in matters that do not belong to the essence of the faith enriches the church. If a pope could publically recognise the importance of this legitimate diversity to the health of the church; if he discouraged his curia from elevating their opinions to the status of immutable doctrines; and, above all, if he were to prohibit the CDF from penalising those who express theologically lawful views that differ from theirs, it would be a crucial and heartening step towards reform. There is no reason why a conservative pope could not do this. He could have conservative views without using his authority to impose them on the entire people of God, and he could admit the legitimate existence of contrary views. To do so would, of course, come as a shock to many of his curial servants. Traditionalists, after all, do not have to impose their views, unless they regard such imposition as inseparable from their conservatism.

Does Francis accept the structural implications of his attitudes? He has made a very favourable impression on his church and on the world at large; but we may wonder whether he will be able and willing to take effective action against the Vatican bureaucrats who act in his name and with his presumed authority. He will continue to be faced by the problem of effecting reform within the present structures. He has committed himself to accepting what has been tendentiously described as "the teaching of the church" in matters which do not belong to the essence of Christian faith. He will have to challenge the view that former papal teaching on such controversial matters as contraception, the ordination of women and the "radical evil" of homosexuality are unchangeable. This will be difficult for him, because he is doctrinally cautious and knows that if he takes issue with some of the most intolerant of curial attitudes he will be unfairly charged with being unfaithful to "church teaching" and papal precedent.

Pope Francis has to face up to the structural implications of his preferential option for the poor; and this will entail extending his understanding of "poor" to include faithful Catholics who are being harassed for their legitimate beliefs and practices. At the moment, Francis is trying to bring about justice and peace through structures that are antithetical to his attitude and projects. The truth is that if he wishes to implement his vision, he cannot avoid confrontation with the Vatican forces that are opposed to his vision and his aims.

Here in Newman House it is appropriate to remember something that Newman wrote to his friend Bishop William Ullathorne in January 1870, during the First Vatican Council:

> Rome ought to be a name to lighten the heart at all times, and a Council's proper office is, when some great heresy or other evil impends, to inspire the faithful with hope and confidence; but now we have the greatest meeting which ever has been, and that at Rome, infusing into us ... little else than fear and dismay.

Later in the same letter he continued:

> Why should an aggressive insolent faction be allowed to "make the heart of the just to mourne, whom the Lord hath not made sorrowful?" Why can't we be left alone, when we have pursued peace, and thought no evil?[2]

2   The letter is printed in J. Sugg, ed., *A Packet of Letters: A Selection from the Correspondence of John Henry Newman* (Oxford: Clarendon, 1983), 180–182.

Ian Ker, in his book on Newman, describes this letter as "perhaps the most indignant he ever wrote".[3]

Newman is in some respects a bridge between the conservative and liberal wings of the Catholic church. He is unquestionably orthodox in his loyalty to the papacy and acceptance of papal infallibility; yet he can be critical of Roman authority, as we see in this letter, which is a perfect exemplar of faithful criticism from a man, incidentally, on the way to being canonised. He was indeed opposed to the religious liberalism of his age; but that was because the liberalism of his age tended to impugn essential Christian doctrines. As an Anglican he disapproved of Broad church attitudes to Christian doctrine. As a Roman Catholic, however, he was not at ease with the neo-scholasticism that prevailed as orthodox Catholic theology. From his letter to Ullathorne it is clear that he already believes what the First Vatican Council is thrusting unnecessarily upon the whole church, and he sees no reason for this gratuitous display of power, which can only alienate faithful Catholics who are uneasy about what is happening in Rome. He blames "an aggressive insolent faction" in the church for prompting Rome to brandish its authority in so demonstrative and unnecessary a fashion. It is worth remembering that many of the opponents of the definition of papal infallibility, owing to the pressure exerted on them, chose to slip quietly away from Rome before the definition. The conservative minority at Vatican II were treated much more gently and tolerantly.

Roman Catholics have allowed themselves to be in practice defined almost exclusively by reference to the Bishop of Rome; and thereby they have acquiesced in a self-definition that has not alone been distorted into a taboo, but has diverted attention away from the real meaning of Catholic truth, life and values. As a recent document of the World Council of Churches has put it:

> legitimate diversity is not accidental to the life of the Christian community but is rather an aspect of its catholicity, a quality that reflects the fact that it is part of the

---

3   Ian T. Ker, *John Henry Newman: A Biography* (Oxford: OUP, 2009).

Father's design that salvation in Christ be incarnational and thus "take flesh" among the various peoples to whom the gospel is proclaimed.[4]

In the church at large, the clash of different opinions should be regarded as a healthy manifestation of its life and intellectual vigour, which can contribute to making it an effective organ of evangelisation. Rome has not been accustomed to listening to the views of those whom it formerly regarded as "the learning church"; it sees itself as "the teaching church" with the authority simply to declare what it believes to be true and right and to impose it on all church members. Pope Francis is showing some encouraging signs of wishing to consult those who for long have been excluded from a hearing in the church. The Congregation for the Doctrine of the Faith (CDF) seeks uniformity rather than promoting the more difficult practice of a unity that is the result of the balance – not a consensus – between different viewpoints. Autocratic conservatives have no right to claim permanent residence in the seats of power. The CDF is the main curial candidate for radical reform. Its behaviour is often so extravagantly harsh that one wonders how even conservative popes could allow it to act as it has been doing. The tactics it has used have been unjust and sometimes cruel to good men and women who are genuinely concerned with making Christ present to the world. One Irish priest was instructed by the CDF to "cease criticising the Vatican". It said nothing to justify this absurdly dictatorial injunction!

The assertion *ecclesia semper reformanda (est)*, began its life in the seventeenth-century Dutch Reformed Church and was enthusiastically adopted by the Catholic church at the Second Vatican Council. As a result of Martin Luther's condemnation of much that was going on in the church of his time, Western Christianity, as we know only too well, became radically divided. Protestants increasingly recognised the danger of thinking that the Reformation was a once-off event, producing a reformed church that had thrown away the superstitious trappings of Roman Catholicism and, that, as a result, could now relax into its new status as a reformed

4   WCC, *The church: Towards a Common Vision*, Faith and Order Paper No. 214.

church. The full original version of the phrase is *Ecclesia reformata semper reformanda est*.

In short, many Protestants came to recognise that even a church that described itself as "reformed" remained in need of continuing reform. No reform is ever final and complete in a church that sees itself as being comprehensively under God's judgement, and is consequently aware of its continuing need for divine mercy and forgiveness, at a structural as well as at a personal level. Rome remains apparently unaffected by the growing case against its despotic methods of government. It is all too willing to speak of "renewal", understanding it to mean activity carried out within an unreformed system. Pope Benedict disliked the word "reform" and took refuge in a mystical understanding of the church. There is, of course, a proper place for a mystical interpretation of the church, but it should never be invoked to conceal structural defects; to do so is to set up a theocracy that places itself beyond all criticism.

The Second Vatican Council is impressive in its recognition of the need for reform. In article 6 of its Decree on Ecumenism it has this to say:

> Christ summons the church, as she goes on her pilgrim way, to that continual reformation of which she always has need, insofar as she is a human institution here on earth. Therefore, if the influence of events or of the times has led to deficiencies in conduct, in church discipline, or even in the formulation of doctrine (which must be carefully distinguished from the deposit itself of faith), these should be appropriately rectified at the proper moment.

You can't be clearer than that. This forthright conciliar teaching marks a radical break with the past. Without the conviction that the church is always in need of reform, the other achievements of the Council would have remained purely notional. Vatican II challenged, albeit cautiously, the hegemony of the pope, and it put forward a doctrine of collegiality that gave the world's bishops a proper role in church teaching and government. This horrified many members of the Roman Curia. Collegiality implies a radical change of attitude and governance unacceptable to them. Reform would inevitably entail changing the preconciliar understanding of Catholic authority. In traditionalist eyes this would mean destruction of the very structures that give them their power. To bring it about, Rome will have to devolve authority to the different dioceses scattered throughout the world, and it will have to sanction the local election of bishops.

Such a heartening reform, it must be conceded, remains very clerical; nevertheless, it opens the way to greater lay involvement as a further reform, if the doctrine of collegiality is to be developed in a manner that includes the laity. Much time and study have been spent on the precise meaning of collegiality. One of the best recent attempts to do so is Mary McAleese, *Quo Vadis: Collegiality in the Code of Canon Law*.[5]

At Vatican II the concept of collegiality was too weak and undefined to make untroubled progress against the ingrained autocracy and absolutism of the papal entourage. The weight of the First Vatican Council lay heavily upon theology and practice in the Catholic church, until the Second Vatican Council partially lifted it. In an age of increasing democracy in the world at large, the papacy has been imprisoned in the spirit of the old monarchism and in its absolutist approach to governance. It had come to identify papacy with monarchy until Pope Francis has begun to show that the papal office can function in a non-monarchical fashion. There is no upstairs/downstairs in the church of Christ. If those at present in power in the Roman Curia succeed in their repressive tactics, it will be impossible to achieve what Vatican II envisaged – a non-monarchical interpretation of the papacy.

McAleese quotes with approval from the 2005 report of the Faith and Order Commission of the World Council of Churches: "Speaking collegially can mean reflecting back to the community the legitimate diversity that exists within the life of the Church."[6] That is precisely the point of a concern for contemporary reform. We need to hear a great deal more from the Vatican about "legitimate diversity" in church life; for we have been living under regimes that rejected or willfully ignored it. Struggling for official recognition of that legitimate diversity will entail a long battle that will not be for the faint-hearted.

5   Dublin, 2012.
6   Ibid., 35.

McAleese claims that Vatican II never really defined the term "collegiality" with any clarity. Arguably the Council was unable to do so, because it was tackling the thorniest problem in Catholic theology. A clear definition might have looked like a defiance of all that Catholicism was taken to stand for, namely, papal supremacy and rejection of the conciliar movement. The matter at issue was whether papal monarchical power should be reduced by greater attention to the collegial status of the bishops. This is admittedly a decidedly clerical preoccupation, but it is at least a step in the right direction.

While LG acknowledges the centrality of the People of God and states that the entire faithful share in "the one priesthood of Christ" (LG 10) the words associated with "collegiality" fade from the text of LG once it has finished talking about the episcopacy. By the time it moves on to the priests, deacons, religious and the laity such words are entirely absent.[7]

This is precisely the problem with the word "collegiality". It was intended by Vatican II to perform a task that was too weighty for it. People had a general idea of what it stood for, but the pope wanted it expressed in canon law; and this transference from Council to canon law forced it to become more precise than the Council documents had been. The Council, by its redefinition of the church as the People of God, had raised hopes of giving the laity, especially women, a greater say in how the church is to be governed. However, canon law focused attention on the relationship between pope and bishops, and this said nothing about lower clergy, and still less about the laity. As McAleese points out perceptively, even *Lumen Gentium* itself failed to do this.

The weight of history lay against it, especially the defeat of conciliarism in the sixteenth century. The Council of Constance (1414–1418) proclaimed that a Council was superior to the pope. The Great Western Schism had occasioned the conciliar movement, when there were three claimants to the papacy, all of whom fiercely proclaimed their legitimacy. The Council deposed the three claimants and elected Martin V as the new pope. Since

7   Ibid., 65.

the papacy had proved unable to remedy the situation, it appeared clear that only a Council could do so. The Schism inevitably raised the question of the relationship between Councils and popes; and the Council of Constance was forthright in its declaration that a Council had its authority immediately from Christ. It was emphatic that its declarations were not limited to the ending of the Schism, but were intended to apply to all future Councils. It remains a valid but disregarded official church teaching.

There was intense conservative opposition to conciliarism, and the Fifth Lateran Council (1512–1517), on the eve of the Reformation, reaffirmed papal supremacy over Councils and condemned the conciliar movement. In the nineteenth century the First Vatican Council, by its definition of papal primacy and infallibility, completed the doctrinal restoration of papal authority and power. The comprehensive defeat of conciliarism posed an onerous challenge for Vatican II's progressives in their struggle for collegiality, and it continues to do so for their successors. The reestablishing of papal supremacy had entailed the condemnation of one Council by another – which constitutes rather serious historical evidence against the much-asserted Roman claim to continuity of magisterial teaching.

The Council of Constance had insisted that the reigning pope should call Councils regularly. However, it proved all too easy for popes to be tardy in doing so, thereby demonstrating the weakness of any reform of the institution in which the initiative lies exclusively with the pope. The blunt fact is that any successful reform of the governmental system in the Catholic church will depend on two changes: First, canon law will have to lay down precise times for the meeting of Councils, or properly representative synods that are free of papal control and have their own autonomy. Second, bishops will have to be elected locally rather than being appointed by the pope and his curia. Rome will retain the right to approve or object to an elected candidate, but it will not initiate the procedure.

This second point is the only way in which legitimate diversity can be achieved at governmental levels in the church. The present system of papal appointment practically ensures that only bishops with views similar to those of the Roman Curia will be appointed. It seems certain that Rome will fight pertinaciously to retain its prerogative of appointing bishops, since merely approving their appointment would amount to serious curtailment of its present hegemonic powers, which lie at the heart of what needs to be reformed.

Perhaps the lack of precision in Vatican II's understanding of collegiality could be beneficial for contemporary reform. The Council, in drawing attention to the church as the people of God, clearly intended its reforms to extend to more than merely the relationship between the pope and the bishops. If the idea of collegiality were tightly defined as bearing upon only the pope and the bishops, clericalism would prevail, and there would be a failure of the ideal of giving God's people a real say in how their church is to be run. This matter has become clearer and more insistent today than it was in the 1960s.

Vatican II took a momentous step forward when it espoused the notion of collegiality and the notion of reform. Giovanni Montini, the future Pope Paul VI, remarked perceptively to a friend about Pope John XXIII: "this holy old boy doesn't realise what a hornet's nest he's stirring up" by calling a Council. It was indeed a hornets' nest, and it badly needed to be stirred up. One of the most important achievements of the Council was its teaching on collegiality; and it was the doctrine of collegiality that Paul VI was most worried about.

In the light of the Council's teaching on the need for continuing reform, it is, to put it at its mildest, difficult to understand Pope Benedict's reluctance to speak of reform of the church. He prefers to speak of renewal. Today we hear a great deal about renewal and very little about reform. "Renewal" is a safe, structurally unthreatening word that conveniently evades the real problems currently facing the church; it also has the great advantage of sounding pious – or perhaps I should say "spiritual", since that is the fashionable word today, when so many are fleeing from the word "religion" to the more nebulous and non-committal idea of "spirituality". It is easy to understand why they are doing this, but their objections could be met by recognising that religion can be good, bad, or indifferent, and that we don't need to escape from "religion", just because we don't like what's going on in the church at the moment.

"Renewal" normally puts emphasis on the personal as distinct from the structural. It does not presuppose a change in the ways in which the church is being run, so, when it is used with no hint of the need for structural change, the Vatican curialists can all breathe freely and continue their oppressive practices. Structural reform is implicitly declared to be off-limits for Catholics, who have been told that because God willed the church, and Christ instituted it, it is consequently beyond reproach. The logic of this is as bad as its theology.

When, in 1968, Paul VI issued his encyclical, *Humanae Vitae*, Cardinal Suenens was unafraid to voice his misgivings. Suenens made the point that moral theology was not taking sufficient note of scientific progress which could help to determine what is according to nature (taken in a physical rather than a metaphysical sense). In a strikingly courageous remark he warned against the danger of the encyclical becoming "another Galileo affair. One is enough for the church".[8] Suenens saw the ecclesiological implications of what the Pope had done, and he pointed out that *Humanae Vitae* offended against the collegiality that had been proclaimed by the recent Council.[9] This was a crucial contribution to the debate, by a cardinal no less, though the Vatican has subsequently managed to ignore it with impunity.

When Pope Paul chose to reject the advice of the group he had set up to counsel him on marriage, sexuality and the family, and opted instead for a reiteration of the ban on contraception, he did so less because of substantive moral thinking about contraception than because of previous papal pronouncements on it. Thus, papal obsession with the immutability of former pronouncements made by the central institutional authority has prevailed over all other moral and doctrinal considerations. Opinions in the rest of the church have been dismissed – which showed that Roman opinions have been considered to be the only ones that mattered or could be described as doctrinally sound.

During Vatican II, there was much appreciation of the fact that the Council gave edifying preferential treatment to liturgy. This sounded impressive at the time, but it was, in some respects, a rather rarefied response to more pressing needs of the church. It did indeed make welcome changes, like the introduction of the vernacular into the Mass and other sacraments;

8   Peter Hebblethwaite, *Paul VI* (New York: Paulist Press, 1993), 394.
9   Op. cit. 533.

but it gave little thought to the fact that the significance and relevance of liturgy, together with an appreciation of symbol, is a fairly sophisticated matter, and is one that is wide open to preciousness and affectation. In practice, to give it meaning and pastoral vitality, liturgy needs to be adapted to the understanding and cultural experience of those who are participating in it. Aesthetic considerations have their place in any discussion of the liturgy, for example in cathedral worship, but in most other settings they need to yield to pastoral considerations.

The context of liturgical celebration determines its character and direction. The Eucharist is rightfully a constant in Christian life. It was given to the immediate associates of Jesus to be a memorial to his life, teaching, passion, death and resurrection. Its origin was a simple memorial meal, but it developed over the centuries into a ceremony often adapted to the circumstances of its celebration. There is, for example, a crucial difference of context between the celebration of the Eucharist in a great cathedral, on the one hand, and, on the other, in a domestic setting with only a family and some neighbours present. It is the same sacrament, but its resonance and function are different. It takes a baptised imagination to see in a solemn papal Mass, with a choir singing "Tu Es Petrus", a representation of the meal that took place in the upper room on the last evening of Jesus' earthly life.

There is a different resonance in a Mass celebrated on a battlefield and one celebrated in a monastery. In short, the pastoral function of the Eucharist is determined by the circumstances of its setting and the local culture of the people who are participating in it. Centralisation and uniformity may rob the Eucharist of its malleability and capability of speaking to different cultures and contexts.

For centuries it was celebrated in a language that most people did not understand. For a long time its formal structure was considered untouchable, until Pope John XXIII introduced the name of St Joseph into the canon of the Mass, thus showing that a change could indeed be made. John did a great deal more than that in calling a Council into being and enabling far-reaching changes, notably allowing the vernacular to be used. At long last, Catholics could pray the liturgy in their own language.

There were serious misgivings in some conservative minds: the abandonment of Latin might open the possibility of doctrinal innovation, as they saw it. In the event, a decent workable English text was introduced; and people were just growing accustomed to it, when the Vatican decided to impose a new translation which is inept and pseudo-orthodox. The curial mind knew that there could be no mandatory return to Latin; so it decided on a Latinised version of the new English text. (I am not competent to comment on what happened in other languages, but I imagine the result was something similar.) Widespread dissatisfaction has been expressed by clergy and laity. It is not just a case of linguistic infelicities; it is all too clear that deeply conservative minds have seized on the idea that their convictions are best conveyed by Latinising the vernacular language of the Mass and substituting such words as "chalice" for "cup" and "consubstantial" for "one in being with", to take two typical examples. This imposes a traditionalist theology indirectly through the liturgy – an imposition that counted on the subservience and lack of independence of local bishops. It is a sad example of what ultra-conservatives so often do, when they refuse to consult and discuss, and instead do by command what they might hesitate simply to commend.

Inveterate traditionalists lay the blame for what they don't like in the contemporary church on the "excesses" that they see as coming from a false interpretation of the Second Vatican Council. This ploy needs to be seen for what it is – the only way that hard-line traditionalists can challenge the changes that have taken place, without seeming to reject the authority of Vatican II, as the followers of Marcel Lefebvre have done. Unhappily, Pope Benedict seemed to take this view; and owing to the power and prestige of his office, he was able to impose it on the entire institution of which he was head. Simply by virtue of being pope, his opinions, attitudes and his theology became, in practice, immune to challenge. This taboo needs to be challenged. Behaviour at the top sets the pattern to be followed down the chain of command. There are bishops, clergy and members of religious orders who are constrained by fear that their superiors will react unfavourably, and perhaps even punitively, to any genuinely reforming initiative.

In 1968 Joseph Ratzinger published a book entitled in its English translation a year later, *An Introduction to Christianity*. It is the work of someone who is still plainly under the influence of the Second Vatican Council, though with some faint adumbrations of his later more sombre attitude to church and world. One passage in his book is striking in its directness.

> And so for many people today the church has become the main obstacle to belief. They can no longer see in it anything but the human struggle for power, the petty spectacle of those who, with their claim to administer official Christianity, seem to stand most in the way of the true spirit of Christianity.[10]

He is careful not to say whether he agrees with this observation, but he presents it as an objection demanding a response. At the very least, he shows an awareness of the impression made on some people by the institutional church and its preoccupation with power and management, which they see as an obstacle to true Christianity. It would be interesting to ask him what he now, after many years as Prefect of the Congregation for the Doctrine of the Faith, thinks of the observation. Pope Francis has warned the clerical church that an attitude of managerialism must be exchanged for one of pastoral service.

Traditionally the young have always reacted against their elders; and it is normally an honourable tradition that allows fresh ideas to enter society. What seems to be happening among young priests today, however, is a curious and disturbing reversal of the normal sequence of events.

Some young priests were recently interviewed in two national Irish newspapers. What they told their interviewers was disturbing. They could not see the significance of Vatican II or the Association of Catholic Priests, and they thought that those priests who did were out of touch with everyday reality.

It gives me no pleasure to comment adversely on the self-satisfaction of fellow priests; but I do so only to show how necessary a body like the Association of Catholic Priests is in Ireland. Other countries have their own similar associations. The Vatican dislikes all of them. One can only hope that the Association will be listened to, so that people may know that there is more to pastoral life than the short-sighted sacramental managerialism that seems to have been adopted by some young priests, one of whom

10   J. Ratzinger, *An Introduction to Christianity* (London: Ignatius, 1969), 262–263.

spoke of the silencing of fellow priests as "something I only read about in
the paper. I still have to get into school for the confirmation children, I
still have to talk to the family about the funeral tomorrow."[11]

An interviewer gave a description of another young priest:

> He is representative of a new breed of cleric who is proud to be seen in his collar, has
> no hang-ups with the Vatican, and believes the future of the Catholic church in Ireland
> is rosy. Nor has he any desire to see Rome change its stance on clerical celibacy.[12]

In other words, he is placidly incurious about the reality of his surround-
ings. He is quoted as saying: "There is a certain vintage of priest who seems
a little disgruntled, perhaps, with the church and discipline. That is not the
same attitude the younger generation have." As one of the "disgruntled"
vintage, I am happy to wish him every success in his ministry, and I hope
that he will not be discouraged when he is ejected from his Garden of Eden
and has to encounter the real world in a few years' time, only to discover
that the future of the church is rather less rosy than he expected. Although
these young men say that their attitude is to be found generally among their
contemporaries, I cannot believe that all their contemporaries think this
way. These worrying examples, however, raise the question of how well
the Council was "received", when we find some clerically educated priests
displaying such a passive acceptance of how things are in our church, and
who appear supine in their acceptance of the status quo.

Thankfully there are many other priests who are very different from
these young men. The Association of Catholic Priests is an example of pastorally engaged priests who appreciate the problems that face us all, and who
give encouragement to those who are struggling pastorally, intellectually
and psychologically with life in the contemporary church.

Many of us who lived through the exhilarating experience of the
Second Vatican Council will look back to that time wistfully, especially
in view of what has been happening in recent times. As Enda McDonagh
has pointed out, an appeal to the Council as an inspiration for today will

11   *The Irish Times*, 4 June 2012, p. 6.
12   *The Irish Independent*, 7 July 2012.

probably mean little to the under-fifties; but to those of us who lived in the church through the pontificate of Pius XII, the experience of Vatican II was exhilarating and liberating; and we are right to remember it with gratitude and joy, and to regard it as a symbol of all that is best in the church.

For four years in the 1960s we rejoiced and grew in the experience of a church-in-Council that was occupying itself with badly needed reform and change. It is important to recognise that the Council was an experience before it became a set of documents. It was called into existence by a pope who, though moderately conservative in his beliefs and spirituality, had no time for the authoritarianism and the impulse to censure that had marked earlier church Councils and papal statements. John XXIII was a model of unaggressive conservatism. His warmth was refracted into his office, and it showed how that office might be exercised, if its occupant could take a joyful, inclusive and non-condemnatory view of the church and the world.

Institutional setbacks, such as the decrease in the numbers of church-goers and the decline in the numbers of priests in the Western church, may be opportunities for reconsidering our theology of ministry, instead of trying to convert disciplinary nostrums into infallible doctrines, as Pope John Paul II tried to do in the matter of the ordination of women. (If he had had his way, he would have done irreparable damage to the doctrine of papal infallibility, if, as many Catholics believe, the ordination of women will inevitably happen.)

I would like, here, to suggest a line of thought that I think deserves serious theological attention. What was happening in the institutional Catholic church during the last two pontificates amounted to serious pastoral neglect of a significant number of its members. That there is an absence of elementary good will towards "liberals" and "dissenters" is bound up with the identification of the church-as-institution with the kingdom of God proclaimed by Jesus, and also with a rigid and rule-driven interpretation of obedience. Institutional reform is not merely an administrative convenience making the church more comfortable for its members; it is first and foremost a spiritual and evangelical matter. It is an attempt to let the Gospel shine within a body that has become rigid and rule-driven. The Catholic church needs to embrace the enriching possibilities of genuine and legitimate diversity, if it is to live up to the meaning of the term "catholic".

The leaders of the Catholic church are showing all the signs of not knowing how to respond constructively to the new situation that the church finds itself in, and so they fall back on the old ways which may have worked in the past, but which today may alienate rather than inspire. Draconian methods of government may actually become obstructions to the message of the Christian Gospel. Since bishops have to wear the straightjacket prescribed for them by Roman authority, they may not feel able to adopt the measures that are necessary to meet today's problems.

The worst effect of enforced conformity is that it weakens conscience, with the result that we may no longer convey the impression that we really believe what we proclaim, as distinct from repeating received orthodoxies and indulging in career prudence. Pope Francis has spoken emphatically about the sort of clericalism that takes over from true pastoral concern, treats the church as being there for its own sake and allows legal prescription to take the place of stimulating the exercise of conscience.

Here in Newman House it is worth remembering that it was Newman's remarks on conscience and the importance of listening to all the faithful that were arguably his most significant contribution to Vatican II. Authoritarians dislike the appeal to conscience and are quick to add that it must be an "informed conscience", by which they actually mean, not a conscience that has given careful thought to all the relevant evidence, but one that complies with official teaching out of prudential obedience. It would be more honest, however regrettable, to claim that obedience takes precedence over conscience, as the curial actions of Rome would seem to suggest. In the light of the Gospel, mere obedience to authority, without inner conviction, is spiritually dead. Blind obedience without conviction offers people a stone when they ask for bread (Mt. 7:9).

From being deeply conservative only a few years ago, many members of the Irish Roman Catholic church have become much more questioning in their approach to religion and the church. They no longer accept doctrinal and moral directions based exclusively on the word of authority, which is what they have often been given as "the teaching of the church". Many modern Catholics no longer have the unthinking respect for authority that was habitual in an earlier age – and this is surely a good thing, as long as we respond to the change positively and use the opportunity to approach faith in a deeper way that takes account of freedom and conscience.

There comes a moment in the life of a child when the answer to "why" can no longer be "because I say so". Something analogous happens in the church. Nevertheless, we are being obliged by Rome not even to discuss such questions as the ordination of women and the rights of homosexuals, even though these are questions that arise in everyday life and demand honest answers that are free from the constraints of a threatening authority. One can only regret that the Fathers of Vatican II allowed Pope Paul to withdraw certain moral questions from the floor of the conciliar aula. The Vatican has proved to be intransigent on all these questions and has turned them into unchangeable doctrines, thus putting an intolerable burden on many faithful members of the church. How can Christians witness to their faith convincingly under these restrictions? Fidelity to conscience is the lynchpin that binds together all the reforms of the Second Vatican Council. Respect for conscience, however, seems to play a negligible part in the practice of the papal bureaucracies that cling onto the old essentialist view of the world.

The election of Pope Francis has changed the scene immeasurably, and it offers serious hope of reform. He delights in informal comment and sometimes gives interviews in which he speaks in everyday language rather than in the polished language of courtly utterances. The traditional Roman attitude has been closely bound up with absolute monarchical power; and that is simply not Francis' style. He is showing an acute distaste for the grandeur of princely postures. I may be accused of reading too much into what is no more than a matter of style. However, I do not think that his is a merely idiosyncratic style of behaviour. In his case I am convinced that the style is the substance, though it will take time to see whether it will prevail over the style of the more formal pronouncements normally issued by the Vatican.

However, we should not underrate the power of the bureaucracy that surrounds the Pope. It has a long history of a hegemony that popes tacitly supported and even encouraged. The Vatican Curia will not lightly surrender the powers it has accumulated over the centuries, and it will realise that genuine reform means a significant loss of its power. Its notion of church is of a self-sufficient entity in which its authority is unquestioned, even by bishops. Rome has seen the folly of trying to command a return to the Latin liturgy, hence it has done the next best thing, namely, to Latinise the vernacular. The German bishops have resisted the effort to have a defective and ideologically inspired translation foisted on them, thereby demonstrating where legitimate authority lies in matters such as this, and incidentally giving good example to other hierarchies who normally behave in a notably subservient fashion to Rome. No Roman bureaucracy has the power to command local bishops to conform to an ideologically inspired tactic such as the newly imposed translation of the missal. We really need our bishops to demonstrate courage in the face of Vatican dictatorship, and show a leadership that the Second Vatican Council made possible, mainly by its doctrine of collegiality.

Perhaps because he is conscious of his lack of conformity with previous papal attitudes, Pope Francis has shown a desire to emphasise the link between himself and his predecessor. Curiously, he has chosen to issue in his own name an encyclical, *Lumen Fidei*, that he himself openly states to have been written mainly by Benedict, whose attitude to the world seems very different from his own. It is intriguing to note that the encyclical is not as rebarbative about the post-Enlightenment world as we had come to expect from Benedict. It would be interesting to know if Francis has quietly edited out Benedict's gloomy view of the modern secular world while retaining his predecessor's learned theological treatment of the light of faith.

Nevertheless, his eagerness to emphasise the continuity between his pontificate and Benedict's seems to gloss over the difference between the two. The word "continuity" here could be deceptive: temporal succession should not imply similarity of mindset. The traditional Roman instinct has been to accentuate the continuity between pontificates, while ignoring or playing down the significance of evident discontinuities. For many, however, it is the differences that inspire hope of change. Francis is attempting to reconcile his desire for continuity with his predecessor, together with his commitment to previous papal teaching, on the one hand, with his instinctive inclusiveness, his informality, pastoral compassion and concern for the poor, on the other.

The emphasis that Rome places on continuity is ideologically inspired and historically unconvincing. Catholic authority seems to hate admitting change in spite of clear evidence to the contrary. Benedict XVI has written a passage that is alarmingly defiant of historical evidence and displays much less sympathy for objections to the institutional church than he did in 1968:

> There is no "pre-" or "post-" conciliar church: there is but one, unique church that walks the path toward the Lord ... There are no leaps in this history, there are no fractures, and there is no break in continuity. In no wise did the Council with [Vatican II] intend to introduce a temporal dichotomy in the church.[13]

Benedict is here making use of the convenient ambiguity of the word "continuity", allowing it to mean not only temporal continuity but continuity of attitude. Furthermore he is allowing a mystical view of the church to obscure the need for structural reform. There is certainly a place for a mystical interpretation of the church, but it must co-exist with constant structural reform. It is astonishing to find a theologian of Ratzinger's repute flying in the face of plain historical evidence to the contrary of his confident assertion. Such a claim seems to ignore the effects of the passage of time and it makes hope of reform a delusion. Matters of strict Christian faith may be said to be permanent; the theologies and politics that are associated with them are always changeable, and in point of fact have manifestly changed. In this world we are pilgrims, not settlers; and with Newman we believe that to be perfect is to have changed often.

---

13   *The Ratzinger Report*, p. 35. I am indebted to Jim Corkery SJ for quoting this passage in *Doctrine & Life*, July–August, 2013, 37.

PART VI

Specific Questions

13 The Influence of Karl Rahner at Vatican II

Introduction: Rahner before the Council

Karl Rahner has come to be regarded as a key player in the theological preparations and discussions before and during the Second Vatican Council. He was also pivotal in trying subsequently to promote what he saw as important orientations of the Council, particularly in the area of ecclesiology. However, regarding Rahner's "influence" at the Council, we should be wary of treating him in isolation. One looks in vain for a specific theological draft or *schema* drawn up solely by Rahner.[1] Rather, he was part of a network of theologians, one of hundreds of *periti* or theological advisers to the bishops at the Council. But what was to Rahner's advantage was that, firstly, he had become well known in the theological world through his numerous publications even prior to the Council [five volumes of his *Schriften zur Theologie* (1954–1962) had already been published]; secondly, he had a great ability for teamwork[2] and theological collaboration, evident, for example, in the many theological encyclopaedias, dictionaries and handbooks he co-edited; and thirdly, he had an excellent command

1   Günther Wassilowsky, "Kirchenlehrer der Moderne: Ekklesiologie," in Andreas Batlogg et al. eds, *Der Denkweg Karl Rahners. Quellen-Entwicklungen-Perspektiven* (Mainz: Grünewald, 2003), 229.

2   Andreas R. Batlogg, SJ, "Karl Rahners Mitarbeit an den Konzilstexten," in Franz-Xaver Bischof and Stephan Leimgruber, eds, *Vierzig Jahre II. Vatikanum. Zur Wirkungsgeschichte der Konzilstexte*, 2nd ed. (Würzburg: Echter, 2005), 355–376 at 375.

of Latin, of neo-scholastic theology in which he had been trained,[3] and of the wider theological tradition – both East and West.

The beginnings of his involvement, however, were more modest. The liturgical theologian, Joseph Jungmann, whom Rahner knew from Innsbruck, was one of the leaders of the liturgical renewal movement – the theme of the first and second sessions of the Council. While Jungmann was a member of the liturgical preparatory commission of the Council on the reform of the liturgy, including the use of the vernacular, Rahner had been working on the theme of the permanent diaconate and had made an important contribution in this regard.[4] Thus his work came to the attention of a number of bishops who were interested in the topic. Alongside this was his connection with Cardinal Franz König of Vienna dating back to at least 1937. It was König who invited Rahner to provide feedback on a number of other theological questions that were due for discussion at the Council and who would take him to the Council as his conciliar theologian.[5] These theological themes or "quaestiones theologicae" drafted for the

3   This meant his interventions often found resonance with more traditionally minded, Scholastically trained, curial theologians who recognised how deeply rooted they were in the classical tradition, and Rahner even developed a reasonable working relationship with the leader of this "minority" group, Cardinal Ottaviani.

4   Karl Rahner and Herbert Vorgrimler, eds, *Diaconia in Christo*, Quaestiones Disputatae 15/16 (Freiburg: Herder, 1962). See also Karl Rahner, "The Theology of the Restoration of the Diaconate," *Theological Investigations*, Vol. 5, trans. Karl-H. Kruger (London: Darton, Longman & Todd, 1966; orig. 1962), 268–314, and Karl Heinz Neufeld, *Die Brüder Rahner: Eine Biographie*, 2nd ed. (Freiburg: Herder, 2004), 237–240. In preparation for the Council Rahner was invited by the chairman of the commission on the sacraments to write a position paper on the topic. See *Acta et documenta Concilio Oecumenico Vaticano II apparando*. Series II (Preparatoria), Vol. III/1, (Vatican City: Typis Polyglottis Vaticanis, 1969), 508–511. For his plea to Cardinal König to support the renewal of the diaconate, specifically married deacons, see Karl Rahner, *Sämtliche Werke* (hereafter *SW*), Vol. 21/1, *Das Zweite Vatikanum. Beiträge zum Konzil und seiner Interpretation*, ed. Günther Wassilowsky (Freiburg: Herder, 2013), 86–88.

5   Franz Cardinal König, "My Conciliar Theologian," in *Encounters with Karl Rahner. Remembrances of Rahner By Those Who Knew Him*, ed. & trans. Andreas R. Batlogg & Melvin E. Michalski, Marquette Studies in Theology 63, (Milwaukee: Marquette

Council Fathers included: the sources of revelation, the moral order, the deposit of faith, and a new formula of profession of faith. Neither König nor the other bishops had a clear idea about how the theological discussions would play out at the Council. The draft themes also referred to prior "sources:" the Council of Trent, Vatican I, the encyclicals "Pascendi," "Mediator Dei," and "Humani Generis," and the Decree "Lamentabili." The agenda appeared to be directed against perceived errors of the time – liberalism, rationalism and modernism.[6] Nor did this official preparatory draft square with the tenor of Pope John XXIII's famous opening address to the Council where he spoke about the need for renewal, of the Council as a "new Pentecost," and of how the church should act by "making use of the medicine of mercy rather than severity."[7]

Pope John XXIII appointed Rahner as consultor to the commission on the sacraments in March 1961 in preparation for the Council but there had been difficulties with Rome in the years beforehand over some of Rahner's writings. So although he was at the peak of his career as a theologian – he was fifty-nine when the Council opened – Rahner had been "under observation" by Rome for some time. There had been controversy over a long article published in 1949, "The many Masses and the one sacrifice," where

University Press, 2009) 45–56. Not that Rahner was initially enthusiastic about going to Rome and wondered whether he could be of any use at a Council. See also Franz Cardinal König, "Karl Rahners theologisches Denken im Vergleich mit ausgewählten Textstellen der dogmatischen Konstitution 'Lumen Gentium,'" in *Glaube im Prozess. Christsein nach dem II. Vatikanum*, eds Elmar Klinger & Klaus Wittstadt (Freiburg: Herder, 1984), 121.

6   But, as Yves Congar pointed out, if a Council was merely intended to reiterate prior teachings and condemn errors, there seemed little point in convening one. See Yves Congar, OP, "Erinnerungen an eine Episode auf dem II. Vatikanischen Konzil," *Glaube im Prozess*, 22–32.

7   In the context of guarding and teaching the sacred deposit of Christian doctrine Pope John XXIII stated that "the substance of the ancient doctrine of the deposit of faith is one thing, and the formulation in which it is clothed is another." Pope John XXIII, *Gaudet Mater Ecclesia*, Opening Speech of the Second Vatican Council, 11 October 1962, trans. Joseph Komonchak. <https://jakomonchak.files.wordpress.com/2012/10/john-xxiii-opening-speech.pdf>. Accessed 2 September 2014.

he "raised a variety of questions about the relationship between the Masses celebrated by the church and the sacrifice of the cross they make present, about the 'fruits of the Mass' and the value of multiplying the number of Masses, and about the possibility of concelebration for priests."[8] It was the question of concelebration that would prove problematic and Rahner was forbidden to discuss the issue in the future. He had also been refused permission to publish a manuscript on Mariology in the aftermath of the promulgation of the dogma of the Assumption of Mary by Pope Pius XII in 1950.[9] Further difficulties arose in relation to an article on the virginity of Mary, where Rahner tried to tease out the precise theological content of the doctrine.[10] Finally, in the period leading up to the Council, Rahner delivered an address at the Austrian "Catholic Day" in Salzburg on 1 June 1962 entitled "Do not stifle the Spirit" which alluded to the temptation for the individual and for the church as a whole, including ecclesial authority, to be overly defensive, closed in on itself, and lagging "pitifully behind the

8   William V. Dych, SJ, *Karl Rahner*, Outstanding Christian Thinkers Series (Collegeville, MN, The Liturgical Press, 1992), 11. See Karl Rahner, *The Celebration of the Eucharist* (London: Burns & Oates/New York: Herder & Herder, 1968), esp. the Preface.

9   Rahner tried to decipher the core meaning of this new dogma of Mary's bodily assumption by showing how what happened to Mary will also happen to us – a total redemption in body and soul, a new mode of being, whereby "our own reality itself is transformed and not simply replaced by another." In highlighting the corporeality of the resurrection and Mary's bodily assumption, Rahner moved beyond a conception of the afterlife merely in terms of the continued existence of the isolated soul. See his "The Interpretation of the Dogma of the Assumption," *Theological Investigations*, Vol. 1, trans. Cornelius Ernst (London: Darton, Longman & Todd, 1961; orig. 1954), 215–227, at 223.

10   Karl Rahner, "*Virginitas in Partu*," *Theological Investigations*, Vol. 4, trans. Kevin Smyth (London: Darton, Longman & Todd, 1966; orig. 1960), 134–162. In this article Rahner tries to avoid the danger of Docetism, on the one hand, while "preserving the truth of the real motherhood and birth," on the other (p. 140). For him, the topic brings out the mutual relationship between Scripture and tradition and the development of doctrine, themes taken up by Vatican II's Dogmatic Constitution on Divine Revelation, *Dei Verbum*, 8.

times."[11] Instead – and this would be a recurring theme of his even after the Council – Rahner interpreted Paul's statement (1 Thess. 5:19) not to block the Spirit as recognition of the permanent validity of the charismatic principle in the church and an "imperative for our own particular time, disconcerting, accusing, shocking us out of our complacency" and emboldening us to take risks, especially in ecumenical questions.[12] Almost immediately after this address, and without warning or reasons given, Rahner was informed via his Jesuit superiors that all his subsequent writings had to be submitted to a preliminary censorship in Rome. This was not entirely surprising given the censorious climate in the church at the time. Rahner was in good company: De Lubac, Congar, Chenu, and others were also viewed suspiciously by Rome. Fortunately for Rahner, he was able to enlist the support of three cardinals: Döpfner, König and Frings, who were well disposed to him and who interceded on his behalf with the Pope; he was also able to draw on his association with a group of lay academics and scientists from the *Paulusgesellschaft* who organised a petition on his behalf and sent it to the Pope.[13]

Within a year the Holy Office had backtracked and Rahner was nominated a Council theologian or *peritus* in October 1962, accompanying

11   Karl Rahner, "Do not stifle the Spirit," *Theological Investigations*, Vol. 7, trans. David Bourke (London: Darton, Longman & Todd, 1971; orig. 1966), 72–87, at 78.

12   Ibid. 81. He continues: "Those, therefore, who have the power to command in the church must constantly bear in mind that not everything that takes place in the church either is or should be the outcome of their own autocratic planning as though they belonged to a totalitarian regime. They must keep themselves constantly alive to the fact that when they permit movements 'from below,' this is no more than their duty." (p. 85).

13   The *Paulusgesellschaft*, founded in Germany in 1955, was an international association for the promotion of dialogue between Christianity and society. It became known for its dialogue with Marxism in an attempt to build bridges between East and West in Europe. It continues to support projects that unmask ideologies in religious systems and promote a more humane vision of society. For Rahner's difficulties with Roman authorities including his "preliminary censorship," see Herbert Vorgrimler, *Understanding Karl Rahner: An Introduction to his Life and Thought*, trans. John Bowden (London: SCM, 1986), 87–94, and 148–153.

Cardinal König to many of the commission sessions. As noted, Rahner was
Cardinal König's personal theological adviser even prior to the Council.
His criticisms of the preparatory draft texts (*schemata*) König had received
from Rome reveal the new theological approach Rahner was expecting from
the Council.[14] He complained that at no stage in the drafts was Scripture
used as the foundation for theological thought; rather, it was adduced in
a proof-text manner to prove a particular theological point. Just as weak,
he maintained, was the engagement with the wider theological tradition.
Reference was made only to recent encyclicals. As regards the draft *De
deposito fidei*, Rahner was genuinely shocked with the demand for clear
doctrinal definitions on themes that were still "disputed questions," for
example, on monogenism and limbo. He appealed to Cardinal König to do
all in his power to oppose this doctrinaire tendency towards "definitions"
which, he believed, reflected more the mentality of Vatican I.[15] Instead,
Rahner was looking for a new kind of language, one which tried to identify and engage with people's faith struggles. He wanted the language of
the Council to be more positive and encouraging – helping people rather
than denouncing them.[16] Above all, his hope was that the Council would

14   For what follows, see Günther Wassilowsky, "Als die Kirche Weltkirche wurde. Karl
       Rahners Beitrag zum II. Vatikanischen Konzil und seiner Deutung," 24–27, Rahner
       Lecture 2012, eds, Andreas R. Batlogg, SJ and Albert Raffelt (Munich: Karl Rahner
       Archive/Freiburg: University Library, 2012). Available at: <http://www.freidok.
       uni-freiburg.de/volltexte/8551>. Accessed 1 July 2014. For Rahner's assessments
       (*Gutachten*) of the various drafts, see *SW*, 21/1, 37–214. A summary is available in
       Karl Rahner, *Sehnsucht nach dem geheimnisvollen Gott: Profil, Bilder, Texte*, ed.,
       Herbert Vorgrimler (Herder: Freiburg, 1990), 95–165.
15   Karl Rahner, "Gutachten für Franz Kardinal König," (4 January 1962), *SW* 21/1, 39.
       See also Gerald P. Fogarty, "The Council Gets Underway," in Giuseppe Alberigo and
       Joseph A. Komonchak, eds, *History of Vatican II*, Vol. II (Maryknoll: Orbis/Leuven:
       Peeters, 1997), 72–73, and 79.
16   Here Rahner was in line with the tenor of Pope John XXIII's opening address (see
       note 7) to the Council where he railed against those "who see only ruin and calam-
       ity in the present conditions of human society ... We must quite disagree with these
       prophets of doom who are always forecasting disaster, as if the end of the world were
       at hand." For the theologians and bishops pushing for change, this address would serve
       as a touchstone for their efforts and indirectly "authorised in advance" (Komonchak)

proclaim the "liberating consolation of the Gospel" in a dynamic and attractive way.[17] He succeeded, but not without a struggle, and one that began already with the pre-conciliar *schemata*. Finally, we see in these early criticisms of Rahner an overriding *pastoral* concern, which turned out to be one of the most important legacies of Vatican II.

Rahner at the Council: Towards a Renewed Ecclesiology

The focal point of Rahner's influence on Vatican II was in ecclesiology. He was active in many of the sub-groups of the theological commission which worked on the draft *De Ecclesia*. He wanted the Council to say something positive about the re-introduction of the permanent diaconate, and the Council ultimately decreed that the "diaconate in the future could be restored as a particular and permanent rank of the hierarchy" (*Lumen Gentium*, 29). He also argued for a greater integration of Mariology and ecclesiology. In the second session of the Council, he focussed on the relationship between the Pope and the College of Bishops, namely, on the theme of collegiality, and on the theological significance of the local church. He was involved in the discussions of the famous Schema XIII,

---

their severe critique of the preparatory texts. See Joseph A. Komonchak, "The Struggle for the Council during the Preparation of Vatican II (1960–1962)," in Giuseppe Alberigo and Joseph A. Komonchak, eds, *History of Vatican II*, Vol. I (Maryknoll: Orbis/Leuven: Peeters, 1995), 350.

17   Rahner, *Sehnsucht nach dem geheimnisvollen Gott*, 110. What shocked Rahner was that many of the *schemata* (including "De deposito fidei," "De fontibus revelationis," and "De ordine morali christiano") reflected an out of date, fearful and overly defensive theology which would not connect with Christians of today, many of whom, were struggling with questions of faith and belief. There were few new ideas or creative pastoral proposals, only a repetition of well-worn dogmatic truths (*Selbstverständlichkeiten*) that were not in dispute (pp. 122–123). He was more favourable, however, in his assessment of the schemata on the missions and the mass media (pp. 124–128).

on the relationship between the church and the world today, which culminated in *Gaudium et Spes*. Finally, he had a part in the discussions on the themes of revelation (including the sources of revelation and the issue of the so-called "material insufficiency" of Scripture) and on religious life. So we could say that through his work in the various commissions Rahner had an indirect influence on such Council texts as *Lumen Gentium, Dei Verbum, Gaudium et Spes* and *Perfectae Caritatis*. We say "indirect" because only the bishops could speak in the Council Assembly and only they could vote. Nor did the *periti* determine the themes for discussion; they were more active "behind the scenes" drafting speeches and texts, thus developing and influencing theological opinion. As John O'Malley has pointed out, for many bishops the Council would be "an extended seminar in theology."[18] They tried to update themselves with the latest theological developments and here too Rahner played an important role. During the first two sessions he held at least twenty-three public lectures on various topics connected with the Council. Without such opportunities for discussion and exchange it is hard to see how Vatican II could have been such a learning process for so many of its participants.

At the beginning of the Council's Dogmatic Constitution on the church, *Lumen Gentium*, the church, for the first time at an official doctrinal level, was referred to as a "sacrament:" "The church is in Christ as a sacrament or instrumental sign of intimate union with God and of the unity of all humanity" (*Lumen Gentium*, 1).[19] Behind this new definition of church was, firstly, the rejection by the Council Fathers of the draft

18 John W. O'Malley, *What Happened at Vatican II?* (Cambridge, MA: Harvard University Press, 2008), 126.

19 For Rahner, this statement that the church is the sacrament of salvation of the *world* is the most striking aspect of the Constitution and represented a significant change from a pessimistic and exclusive pre-conciliar understanding of the church as "the small barque on which alone people are saved ... from the *massa damnata*." Karl Rahner, *The Christian of the Future* (London: Burns & Oates, 1967), 82.

schema, "De Ecclesia," and, secondly, the decision by the German-speaking bishops to draw up a completely new text on the church.[20]

Between December 1962 and February 1963 four drafts of what Günther Wassilowsky calls the "German Schema" were drawn up. The key people involved in composing the first draft were Karl Rahner, Otto Semmelroth, Alois Grillmeier, and Rahner's friend, Hermann Volk, Bishop of Mainz. In the preparation of subsequent drafts further important contributors included Cardinal Julius Döpfner, Joseph Ratzinger, Rudolf Schnackenburg and Michael Schmaus. To these were added the "international" voices of Belgian theologians, Gérard Philips and Edward Schillebeeckx, the French Dominican, Yves Congar, and the Dutch Jesuit, Piet Smulders. The end result was a text approved by the entire German-Austrian Bishops' Conference and presented to the Council. Its central idea was the church as the fundamental, universal and eschatological sacrament of salvation for the world.[21] Although there were other schemata on the church presented to the Council, and although those of the Belgian theologian Gérard Phillips (*peritus* to Cardinal Suenens) were ultimately more influential, Wassilowsky has shown that Phillips took over a number of ideas from the German

20 Prior to this decision, Rahner, in collaboration with his Jesuit confrere Otto Semmelroth, drew up some critical observations on the original "De Ecclesia" schema, "Animadversiones de Schemate 'De Ecclesia.'" (*SW* 21/1, 298–339). His criticisms, many of which would later be echoed by senior German-speaking bishops (including Döpfner and König) at the Council, included: the schema resembled a "dissertatio scholastica," lacked a pastoral character and an ecumenical spirit, used Scriptural references only as "dicta probantia" to defend the ecclesiology of recent encyclicals and did not take into account the wider teaching of Scripture and tradition. The schema, moreover, was too "conceptual and deductive," failed to take seriously the reality of sin in the church, and was overly reliant on the image of the church as the "body of Christ" to the neglect of other images, e.g. the church as the people of God. For a comprehensive discussion, see Günther Wassilowsky, *Universales Heilssakrament Kirche. Karl Rahners Beitrag zur Ekklesiologie des II. Vatikanums*, Innsbrucker Theologische Studien 59 (Innsbruck-Wien: Tyrolia-Verlag, 2001, 192–276.

21 For the text of the final draft of the German Schema, see *Acta Synodalia Sacrosancti Concilii Oecumenici Vaticani II* (hereafter *AS*), Vol. I, Part IV, (Vatican City: Typis Polyglottis Vaticanis, 1971), 608–639.

schema, including the notion of the church as the universal sacrament of salvation, and the opening words of its introduction: "Lumen gentium."[22]

Behind this "sacramental" description of the church in the German schema is, firstly, the Greek term *mystērion* (Lat. *mysterium*) found in some Old Latin versions of the Bible and translated as *sacramentum*, and, secondly, Augustine's definition of sacrament as the visible form of invisible grace (*visibilis forma invisibilis gratiae*). The *mystērion* is the "mystery of the kingdom of God" (Mk. 4:11), God's eternal, hidden plan of salvation (1 Cor. 2:1, 7) revealed in Christ (1 Cor. 1:23–24) and fulfilled in the church (Eph. 5:32). The preface (*Prooemium*) of the schema maintained that since the church "understands itself as truly the sacrament of the intimate unity of all humanity with itself and with God, the origin and goal of all, it wants to proclaim its own essence to the faithful and to the whole world with a greater urgency, not to increase its honour before all, but so that it can be more faithful in its mission to the world and connect more easily with the faith of the people."[23] There is a universalising of perspective here: for the first time a draft conciliar text is addressed not only to the *filii ecclesiae* but to all humanity. This perspective would find expression in the final texts of the Council, for example, in the designation of the church as the "light of the world" (*Lumen Gentium*, 1), and the "close link between the church and the whole human family" mentioned in the preface to *Gaudium et Spes*.

Moreover, Augustine's definition of sacrament, when applied to the church, meant going beyond a merely juridical model to argue that the essence of the church is not confined to the visible. In the schema Rahner and his colleagues wanted to show how the "invisible," namely, God's grace or plan, takes historical and concrete form primarily in Christ and subsequently in the church, which is "at the same time the *fruit* and an active *medium* of salvation."[24] According to Wassilowsky this stress on the

---

22   Wassilowsky, *Universales Heilssakrament Kirche*, 277–356. Wassilowsky notes (p. 295, n. 45) that in the German schema the church is not presented as an independent source of light but reflects only what it has received from God through Christ.

23   *AS* I/IV, 610, Translation mine.

24   "... simul est *fructis* salutis et *medium* activum." *AS* I/IV, 614, Translation mine. This notion would later find expression in the terms "signum et instrumentum" of *Lumen Gentium*, 1.

sacramentality of the church would have wider ecumenical implications at the Council. It prepared the shift from the exclusive "est" to the more open "subsistit" in *Lumen Gentium*, 8. The church of Christ would no longer be exclusively identified with the Catholic church; there are elements of the *ecclesia Christi* to be found in other Christian communities.[25] Further, the schema's use of a variety of biblical images to ground its ecclesiology goes beyond the proof-text approach to scripture, is more ecumenically sensitive, and would be reflected in the final conciliar text itself (*Lumen Gentium*, 6–7).

Alongside the sacramentality of the church, the German schema contains a number of other Rahner-inspired theological convictions which would permeate many of the Council documents. The first is what Rahner terms God's universal salvific will. Prior to treating membership and ministries in the church, the schema starts out from a soteriological perspective (*Ecclesia in oeconomia salutis divina*) expressed in trinitarian terms. God the Father invites all to share in the divine life. God's universal salvific will in turn grounds the universal meaning of the incarnation and the universal mission of the church. Rahner wanted the church to be less preoccupied with itself, less defensive, and to see its raison d'être in terms of service to the world.[26] Gone are the church-world dualisms expressed in terms of the sacred versus the profane. God's grace is ubiquitous and also at work outside the church.

25 Wassilowsky, "Als die Kirche Weltkirche wurde. Karl Rahners Beitrag zum II. Vatikanischen Konzil und seiner Deutung," 28.

26 "John XXIII wanted a conversation; he did not want to aggressively defend the faith. He wanted to open up the windows. The Roman Catholic church in Europe ... was defensive: afraid of the sciences, afraid of the Protestants, afraid of modern movements, of the historical method, the struggle with the liberals and so on. The church somehow limped along; she lagged behind recent developments. This was the situation in which Fr. Rahner began his theological career. His work met with approval in circles that were ready for reform. As a matter of fact he did what the pope had expressed in his metaphor, open windows. He did not respond with anxiety and defensiveness." Franz Cardinal König, "My Conciliar Theologian," 49.

The key contribution, therefore, of the German-speaking Bishops' *schema* (and of Rahner and his colleagues who drafted it) was the now commonly accepted notion of the sacramentality of the church. The church, with its message of grace, is the *sacramentum* of salvation for the world.[27] To trace the complicated development of how the draft was received in the Council and how it would be superseded by the Philips schema would take us beyond the scope of this chapter.[28] Nevertheless, the key concerns of Rahner and the German bishops that the Dogmatic Constitution on the church have a strong pastoral and soteriological thrust, be ecumenically sensitive, biblically grounded, and not be restricted to its juridical or mystical dimensions would subsequently find expression in the Constitution's final form.

27   Aside from its opening paragraph, the term is found in *Lumen Gentium*, 9 (Chapter 2: The People of God) and 48 (Chapter 7: The Eschatological Character of the Pilgrim church and its Union with the Heavenly church), where the church is explicitly described as "the universal sacrament of salvation." See also Karl Rahner, "The New Image of the church," *Theological Investigations*, Vol. 10, trans. David Bourke (London: Darton, Longman & Todd, 1972; orig. 1967), 12–15.

28   See Joseph A. Komonchak, "The Initial Debate about the church," in Étienne Fouilloux, ed., *Vatican II Commence … Approches Francophones* (Leuven: Bibliotheek van de Faculteit der Godgeleerdheid, 1993), 329–352, and Wassilowsky, *Universales Heilssakrament Kirche*, 357–390. Phillips' draft was in effect a compromise – attempting to salvage as much as possible from the original schema while expressing these elements "in a more biblical and pastoral style" (349). This reflected the plan of Cardinal Suenens who wanted the Council to centre on a single theme, the church. The Germans, on the other hand, wanted to *substitute* many of the schemata prepared by the Preparatory Theological Commission with those of Rahner, Ratzinger, Daniélou, etc. Congar considered this a "rather naïve" strategy that had little chance of success. He was correct while at the same time accusing himself of being "too tolerant" of many of the original schemata from the Central Commission. Yves Congar, OP, *My Journal of the Council*, trans. Mary John Ronayne, OP, M.C. Boulding, OP, and Denis Minns, OP (Dublin: Dominican Publications, 2012), 144–145.

Other Ecclesiological Themes

We also find a number of other ecclesiological concerns of Rahner reflected to varying degrees in the final texts of the Council. These include: the relationship between the episcopacy and the primacy (the issue of collegiality), the importance of the local church, the theme of the church of sinners, the relationship between Scripture and Tradition, and Mariology. For reasons of space we will confine our comments to the first three of these.

Rahner reflected on the relationship between the episcopate and the primacy prior, during and after the Council. At the outset of the Council and at a time when there was not yet a Constitution on the church we find him reflecting on how to reconcile a "monarchical" understanding of the church (and the papacy) with the fact that the episcopate is itself of divine right.[29] It is clear in their contribution to the debate on what the Council might say about the hierarchy that Rahner (and his co-authors Joseph Ratzinger and Gustave Martelet) wanted to see the structure of leadership in the church expressed in both the primacy and in the episcopal college.[30] Rahner tried to shift the emphasis away from the church conceived as a "perfect society," with the pope envisaged as a kind of absolute monarch, to a more collegial vision of a united episcopate with and under the Pope. While he conceded that it was not always possible to have "a clear-cut demarcation of the respective powers of pope and bishop," his concern was "the danger of over-centralisation in the church."[31] He

29   Karl Rahner, "The Episcopate and the Primacy," in Karl Rahner, Joseph Ratzinger, *The Episcopate and the Primacy* (Freiburg: Herder, 1962), 11–36. See also *Lumen Gentium*, 20, where the Council speaks of the bishops as successors of the apostles "*ex divina institutione.*"

30   Karl Rahner, Gustave Martelet, and Joseph Ratzinger, "De Primatu et Collegio Episcoporum in Regimine Totius Ecclesiae," *SW* 21/1: 341–342. The text is dated October 1963, i.e. at the beginning of the Second Period of the Council and the debate on the church, and includes pointers about how to deal with possible objections to their proposed teaching on collegiality (342–344).

31   Rahner, "The Episcopate and the Primacy," 33, 36.

considered the teaching on the episcopacy, i.e. on the collegial structure of the church, to be the most important section of *Lumen Gentium*.[32] In other words, the church is episcopal in its constitution: the pope possesses plenary power precisely *as* head of the college of bishops.[33] The corollary of this is that the bishop, though subject to the pope, is not a mere functionary without responsibility of his own, but, as successor to the Apostles, is a true shepherd called to feed and guide the flock entrusted to him.[34] In

32   Karl Rahner, "Pastoral-Theological Observations on Episcopacy in the Teaching of Vatican II," *Theological Investigations*, Vol. 6, trans. Karl-H. & Boniface Kruger (London: Darton, Longman & Todd, 1969; orig. 1965), 361. While the doctrine of the primacy was associated with Vatican I, Rahner acknowledged that this Council also implicitly included the teaching on the authority of the episcopal college. See his commentary on *Lumen Gentium*, nn. 18–27 in Herbert Vorgrimler, ed. *Commentary on the Documents of Vatican II*, Vol. 1 (London: Burns & Oates, 1967), 105, n. 10.

33   Rahner was aware of how this statement could be misconstrued as a denigration of "the Roman Pontiff's plenitude of power," as the "Preliminary Explanatory Note" to *Lumen Gentium* put it. His point is that there are not two subjects of supreme power in the church: "*There is only one subject endowed with supreme power in the church: the college of bishops assembled under the pope as its head. But there are two modes in which this supreme college may act: a 'collegiate act' properly so-called, and the act of the pope as head of the college* ... The pope acts *as* head of the college whenever he makes use of his primatial power," a power entrusted to him not by the college of bishops but by Christ. Karl Rahner, "On the Relationship between the Pope and the College of Bishops," *Theological Investigations*, Vol. 10, 55 and 64.

34   "He cannot therefore consider himself to be the mere recipient and executor of commands received from higher quarters. He has an independent duty and responsibility which he cannot simply shirk. He would therefore not be fulfilling his office fully, if he regarded himself as the mere executive organ of universal ecclesiastical laws or of initiatives emanating from Rome." Rahner, "Pastoral-Theological Observations on Episcopacy in the Teaching of Vatican II," *Theological Investigations*, Vol. 6, 362–363. Rahner eschewed any kind of paternalism in the exercise of authority which he believed reflected a too hasty recourse to one's formal authority and led to poor decisions. Writing towards the end of the Council, and pre-empting recent moves by Pope Francis, he suggested "a consultative board around the pope ... drawn from the universal episcopate [would be] a good constitutional concrete expression of the theological unity of pope and universal episcopate in the government of the church." Rahner, "The Episcopal Office," *Theological Investigations*, Vol. 6, 359.

effect, Rahner wanted the Council to bring out the intrinsic unity between the monarchical and collegial aspects of the church, where there exists a "harmony" – inspired by the Spirit – between the Pope and the college of bishops.[35] Behind his views on collegiality was the church's mission to the world (Mt 28:18ff), a mission entrusted both to Peter (Mt 16:18) and to the apostolic college (Mt 18:18) and exercised in the threefold exercise of teaching, sanctifying and governing.[36]

Rahner was aware of course that the episcopacy united with the pope does not exhaust the nature of the church. During the Conciliar discussions there was criticism of what was considered a too one-sided emphasis on the church universal to the neglect of the local, i.e. to the church as it actually exists in the concrete. He called this the tensive relationship "between the *theoretical* and the *real* structures of the church."[37] He saw it exemplified in the Council's teaching on the episcopacy where "the whole official action of the church in the transmission of truth and grace is concentrated in him [the bishop]" whereas in reality, the real care of souls is carried out by priests in the parish.[38] In a letter to Herbert Vorgrimler in October 1963 Rahner refers to a draft that he and Hans Küng prepared on this theme, namely, the importance of the local church, which was delivered in a speech to the Council by the Auxiliary Bishop of Fulda, Edward Schick, on behalf of the German-speaking and Scandinavian bishops.[39] In his address Schick (and Rahner behind him) urged the Fathers not to let their high regard for the episcopacy "to neglect or undervalue the local church and

---

35   The "Preliminary Explanatory Note" to *Lumen Gentium* used the phrase "hierarchical communion" between the bishops and their head and maintained: "Everywhere it is a question of *union* of the bishops *with their head*, and it is never a question of the bishops acting *independently* of the pope." *Decrees of the Ecumenical Councils*, Vol. 2: *Trent to Vatican II*, ed. Norman P. Tanner (London: Sheed & Ward, 1990), 900.

36   Rahner et al., "De Primatu et Collegio Episcoporum," *SW* 21/1,340. See also *Lumen Gentium*, n. 21.

37   Rahner, "Pastoral-Theological Observations on Episcopacy in the Teaching of Vatican II," *Theological Investigations*, Vol. 6, 366.

38   Ibid.

39   Vorgrimler, *Understanding Karl Rahner*, 175.

the priesthood."[40] Following Paul and his use of the term *ekklesia* to designate not so much the universal church but the Christian community of some city, e.g. Corinth, (1 Cor 1:2) or even a community of Christians gathered at home to celebrate the Eucharist (Rom 16:5), Rahner's point is that the parish or community of Christians gathered together around the altar (*Altargemeinschaft*) is not merely an administrative division but an authentic representation and manifestation of the universal church, where Christ is truly present. *Lumen Gentium*, 26, would subsequently acknowledge these concerns stating that: "In these communities [Rahner's *Altargemeinschaften*], although frequently small and poor, or dispersed, Christ is present by whose power the one, holy catholic and apostolic church is gathered together." Nevertheless, Rahner, in his commentary on *Lumen Gentium* 26, maintained that "the other approach [the emphasis on the episcopacy and the universal church] was more or less imposed on the Council by the traditional theology" but yet, as a result of his and Schick's intervention, the second approach was not excluded.[41]

Against a backdrop of the Council's image of the church as a pilgrim community (*Lumen Gentium*, Ch. 7), Rahner also developed the concept

---

40   For an English version of Schick's address, see Yves Congar, Hans Küng, and Daniel O'Hanlon SJ, eds, *Council Speeches of Vatican II* (London and New York: Sheed & Ward, 1964), 22–24. For the Latin version, see *AS* Vol. II, Part II (Vatican City: Typis Polyglottis Vaticanis, 1972), 396–399. For the similarity between Rahner's original draft and *Lumen Gentium*, 26, see Wassilowsky, "Als die Kirche Weltkirche wurde …," 34–37.

41   "One *can* start with the concrete community, where the word of Christ is preached and his saving death is proclaimed in the Eucharist, where, therefore, Christ himself is present in the word and the sacrament … and which is, therefore, church in the true sense of the word." Rahner, "The Hierarchical Structure of the church, with Special Reference to the Episcopate," in Vorgrimler, ed. *Commentary on the Documents of Vatican II*, Vol. 1, 216. While Rahner acknowledged that the Council did not definitively resolve the relationship between primacy and collegiality, he "concluded that the relationship between the Pope and the bishops remained too strongly weighted in favour of the central authority." Richard Lennan, "Ecclesiology and Ecumenism," in Declan Marmion and Mary E. Hines, eds, *The Cambridge Companion to Karl Rahner* (Cambridge: Cambridge University Press, 2005), 138.

of the sinful church or the church of sinners, a theme though present in *Lumen Gentium* and in the Decree on Ecumenism, was treated with a certain "reserve" by the Council.⁴² At one level Rahner was reacting to Vatican I's *Dei Filius* and its exaltation of the church's "eminent holiness, and inexhaustible fruitfulness in everything that is good" (DS 3013). But at another level he claimed that "a church of sinners is itself a piece of the church's consciousness of her faith."⁴³ *Pace* the various heresies from Donatism to Jansenism and their idealistic conceptions of the church, it is not only the justified person but also the sinner who belongs to the church, albeit not in the full sense.⁴⁴ The church does not just stand over against sinners as an institution of salvation; "she is the community of these sinners."⁴⁵ In this context Rahner referred to a speech at the Council by the Austrian bishop, Stephan László, who spoke of a "penitent church," "a communion of sinners" always in need of God's mercy, and who encouraged the Council not to be silent about sin in the church, even in its hierarchy.⁴⁶ Of course sin is a fundamental contradiction of what the church is and

---

42 Karl Rahner, "The Sinful Church in the Decrees of Vatican II," *Theological Investigations*, Vol. 6, 281–288, at 281.

43 Karl Rahner, "The Church of Sinners," *Theological Investigations*, Vol. 6, 255.

44 Rahner distinguishes between the church as a visible sign of grace and as a reality filled with grace and thus "between a (merely) 'valid' and a 'fruitful' membership of the church. The sinner has the first kind of membership ... but not the second." Rahner, "The Church of Sinners," 259. In a similar vein *Lumen Gentium* 14, following Augustine, distinguished between a "heartfelt" (*corde*) and merely "corporal" (*corpore*) membership of the church.

45 Rahner, "The Sinful Church in the Decrees of Vatican II," 291. The church "must regard these sinners as a part of herself, as her members," (p. 284), "containing sinners in its own bosom" as *Lumen Gentium*, 8 puts it. The church is "in a certain sense the subject of the guilt of her members." (p. 286).

46 Ibid., 280, n. 24. For László's speech, "Sin in the Holy Church of God," see *Council Speeches of Vatican II*, 29–31. Rahner rightly notes the influence of Hans Küng here, whose work prior to the Council had drawn attention to this theme. See his *The Council and Reunion* (London and New York: Sheed and Ward, 1961), 34–52. Another influential voice prior and during the Council on renewal in the church was Yves Congar. See his "Comment l'Église sainte doit se renouveler sans cesse," in *Sainte Église*, Unam Sanctam 41 (Paris: Les Éditions du Cerf, 1963), 131–154.

is called to be, namely, the manifestation of God's grace and holiness in the world. Rahner also acknowledged the frequent references to the "holy church," the "holy people of God," and the "holy priesthood" in *Lumen Gentium*, 5, 10, 12, and 26. The holiness of the church, therefore, is not on a par with its sinfulness but, because of God's grace, constantly triumphs over sin. Nevertheless the Council would acknowledge that the church is "always in need of purification and unceasingly pursues penance and renewal" (LG, 8).

Conclusion: The Council, a New Beginning

Rahner viewed the Council as a "process of the collective finding of the truth" (*kollektive Wahrheitsfindung*).[47] This involved dialogue and collaboration not just among the *periti* themselves but also between theologians and bishops in the various commissions and through formal and informal contacts inside and outside the Council. What struck him was the atmosphere of freedom and openness in which the business of the Council was conducted.[48] Not that he was politically naïve. From the beginning of the

47   Karl Rahner, "A Small Fragment 'On the Collective Finding of Truth,'" *Theological Investigations*, Vol. 6, 82–88.

48   "It was a Council in freedom and love. The Council ... explored the growing understanding in faith of the dogmas of the church while remaining equally loyal to the already accepted faith of the church ... The truly miraculous and astonishing thing about this Council was that genuine unanimity was reached in freedom. Common declarations and common agreement were achieved. It is not just to be assumed that this sort of unanimity can be expected in the present day. One can easily get the impression nowadays that freedom has caused, at least in the field of theology, discord, and that only by the show of authority can one make any appreciable advances in thought or activity. But the Council demonstrated that with the grace of God this is not necessarily so." Karl Rahner, *The Church after the Council* (New York: Herder and Herder, 1966), 13–14.

second session he realised that the outright rejection of official draft texts was no longer feasible and he devoted himself instead to textual improvements (*Textverbesserungen*), describing his contribution as a theological service to the Council.[49] In a letter from Rome to his brother Hugo in the autumn of 1963 he noted how there was no one at the Council who had an overview of all that was happening or who could be said to be driving the agenda, not even the moderators.[50] Yet, to his surprise, it was the "synodal-collegial principle" that won out at the Council, a Council that "marked the decisive beginning of the *aggiornamento*" required of the church, its self-understanding and mission *ad extra*.[51] Thus the Council became "*the* life-long theme" (Karl Lehmann) of Rahner as he enthusiastically promoted ecclesial and theological renewal. His fear was that the Council's inner call to the church [would] be smothered and the Council rendered 'harmless.'"[52] But as a Council of the world-church, it retains a permanent significance.[53] We have seen something of how Rahner helped the Council engage with key ecclesiological themes (e.g. the relationship between primacy and collegiality, the importance of the local church, etc.),

49 As the Council was primarily an assembly of bishops, they were free to, accept, reject, amend or rewrite any texts drafted for them, while the two-thirds majority required for decisions ensured compromise solutions had to be found. See Andreas R. Batlogg, SJ and Nikolaus Klein, SJ, "Kollektive Wahrheitsfindung auf dem Zweiten Vatikanum. Zu einer Momentaufnahme von Karl Rahner, SJ," *Stimmen der Zeit* 230 (2012), 582. See also Karl Rahner, "Die Zweite Konzilsperiode," *SW* 1, 408–411.

50 Ibid., 594.

51 Rahner, *The Church after the Council*, 19.

52 Karl Rahner, "The Second Vatican Council's Challenge to Theology," *Theological Investigations*, Vol. 9, trans. Graham Harrison (London: Darton, Longman & Todd, 1972, orig. 1967), 3. However, he became increasingly frustrated in the post-Conciliar era at what he regarded as a retrenchment and an increased centralisation, where the new openings envisaged by the Council were being undermined.

53 See Karl Rahner, "Basic Theological Interpretation of the Second Vatican Council," *Theological Investigations*, Vol. 20, trans. Edward Quinn (London: Darton, Longman & Todd, 1981; orig. 1980), 77–89 and "The Abiding Significance of the Second Vatican Council," *Theological Investigations*, Vol. 20, 90–102.

issues which the Council left largely unresolved.[54] Above all, the church at Vatican II attempted to forge a new relationship with the world, engaging humanity "through acceptance and solidarity, through dialogue and cooperation," a pastoral Council, "orientated neither toward dogma nor toward theological controversy."[55] The church, as a mystery or sacrament of salvation existing in a diaspora situation in a pluralistic society, will continue to offer a message of grace to the world all the while acknowledging that this grace is also at work beyond its sacramental mediation (*Lumen Gentium*, 16 and *Gaudium et Spes*, 22). Such "salvation optimism" (*Heilsoptimismus*) was not intended by Rahner or by the Council as a form of cheap grace or "ecclesiological relativism" but is another unresolved conciliar tension between the "optimism with regard to salvation and the inalienable duty of Christians to be missionaries of the gospel."[56]

Finally, what is striking is Rahner's prescience in that many of the themes we have discussed (including the synodal-collegial principle in the church, the church of sinners, the importance of the local church and the priority of the pastoral), have only become more urgent today. Granted much work has been done in developing diaconate programmes, especially in the English-speaking world. And in Ireland the structured dialogue between faith communities and the Government (arising from the Lisbon Treaty in 2007) will facilitate the engagement between church and world advocated by the Council. On the other hand, the clerical sexual abuse scandals have highlighted the need for a radical reappraisal of how authority

---

54   For a comprehensive list of these themes, see Rahner, "The Second Vatican Council's Challenge to Theology," *Theological Investigations*, Vol. 9, 14–17.

55   Karl Rahner and Adolf Darlap, "Vatican Councils. Vatican II," *SW* 21/2, 1057.

56   Rahner, "The New Image of the Church," *Theological Investigations*, Vol. 10, 19. "The Catholic must think of and experience the Church as the 'vanguard,' the sacramental sign, the manifestation in history of a grace of salvation which takes effect far beyond the confines of the 'visible' church as sociologically definable (at 15–16) ... [While] the Christian hopes for salvation for others also ... he possesses a grace of which those others are deprived – are *still* deprived, precisely the grace namely of belonging to the church *corpore* and not merely *corde*" (at 17 and 19).

and power are exercised in the church. An overly centralised and defensive ecclesial institution suspicious of the world does not correspond with the ecclesiological vision of Vatican II. These scandals have revealed a "defensive institutional culture" in the church, a climate of fear and conformity, and an uncritical deference to authority.[57] The crisis has led to calls for ecclesial renewal on both the personal/communal and on the structural levels – aspects which should not be played off against each other.[58] In a similar vein, Rahner could describe the Christian of the future as a mystic – someone whose faith decision will be rooted in a personal experience of God even when the societal supports for Christianity have disappeared – the church of the diaspora or little flock,[59] while, at the same time, teasing out possibilities for structural change in the church – calling, for example, for the "deliberative and not merely consultative collaboration of the people in the decisions of the institutional church."[60] Further, the principle of autonomy for regional churches or "the pluralism of churches within the one church" highlighted for him the importance of the bishop's role in empowering the voice and effective participation of the laity.[61] Structural

57 See Gerry O'Hanlon, SJ, *A New Vision for the Catholic Church: A View from Ireland* (Dublin: The Columba Press, 2011), 76–93, at 82. See also, Brendan Callaghan, "On Scandal and Scandals: The Psychology of Clerical Paedophilia," *Studies* 99 (2010), 343–356, and Sean Ruth, "Responding to Abuse: Culture, Leadership and Change," in John Littleton and Eamon Maher, eds, *The Dublin/Murphy Report: A Watershed in Irish Catholicism?* (Dublin: The Columba Press, 2010), 102–112.

58 For a fuller development of a response in the Irish context including the proposal for a series of national assemblies or synods, see O'Hanlon, op. cit., 94–114. See also his "The People of God: Towards a Renewed Church," in Suzanne Mulligan, ed., *Reaping the Harvest: Fifty Years after Vatican II* (Dublin: The Columba Press, 2012), 63–87.

59 Karl Rahner, "The Spirituality of the Church of the Future," *Theological Investigations*, Vol. 20, 149–150. See also *The Christian of the Future*, 78–81.

60 Karl Rahner, "Structural Change in the Church of the Future," *Theological Investigations*, Vol. 20, 124. The two other issues Rahner mentions in this article are: the question whether the seat of primacy in the church has to remain in Rome, and the urgent task of ecumenism (p. 127).

61 Karl Rahner, "On the Theology of a 'Pastoral Synod'," *Theological Investigations*, Vol. 14, trans. David Bourke (London: Darton, Longman & Todd, 1975, orig. 1972), 119.

change for Rahner was also linked to the *style* and mentality in which the church should operate in the world – again inspired by the Council – where it becomes possible "to speak of a declericalised, serving, caring church, preaching morality without moralising, being open to secular society, boldly giving concrete directives for public life without always declaring these to be permanently valid dogma or part of the unchanging content of natural law, socially critical without seeking to dictate to secular society or restrict its autonomy."[62] The only "tutiorism" admissible in the church was a "tutiorism of daring" (*Tutiorismus des Wagnisses*): we must have the courage to take risks.[63]

Rahner did not regard the *aggiornamento* undertaken by the church at the Council as a way of making it "more attractive to, and comfortable for, the world."[64] Rather, it was a way of preparing the church to be a more effective witness to the mystery of a God who is "close to us, saving, loving and forgiving,"[65] and who overcomes the sin and tragedies of human exist-ence. This meant focussing on the core of Christian faith – "the real self-communication of God to creation in God's innermost reality and glory."[66] Ultimately, Rahner believed the true significance of the Council would be in how it was received, in the "history of its effects" (*Wirkungsgeschichte*). In a somewhat depressing image, he likened the efforts of the Council to extracting radium from pitchblende: "One must refine a ton of ore

See also O'Hanlon, *A New Vision for the Catholic Church*, 98–101. In the diocese of Limerick, plans are currently underway for a diocesan synod in 2016. For Bishop Brendan Leahy's Pastoral Letter convoking the Synod, outlining the process, and how it might enable the diocese to meet the challenges facing it and facilitate ecclesial renewal, see <http://www.limerickdiocese.org/uploads/Diocesan%20Synod%20 2014/FINAL%20synod%20booklet%20text.pdf>. Accessed 14 November 2014.

62   Rahner, "Structural Change in the Church of the Future," *Theological Investigations*, Vol. 20, 126. See also his *The Shape of the Church to Come*, trans. Edward Quinn (London: SPCK, 1974). See also O'Malley, *What Happened at Vatican II*? 43–52.

63   Rahner, "Do not stifle the Spirit," *Theological Investigations*, Vol. 7, 81.

64   Rahner, *The Church after the Council*, 27.

65   Rahner, *The Christian of the Future*, 99.

66   Karl Rahner "Experiences of a Catholic Theologian," trans. Declan Marmion and Gesa Thiessen in *The Cambridge Companion to Karl Rahner*, 301.

to recover 0.14 gram of radium, yet it is worth the effort ... *so that* in *our* hearts ... there can be extracted a tiny bit of the radium of faith, hope and charity."[67] The Council was only a beginning, a service to the church, as it "seeks to be the guide of humanity into the mystery of God."[68]

67   Rahner, *The Church after the Council*, 30–31 (Translation altered). Rahner continues "Every subtle theology, every dogma, every church law, ... every institution, every bureau and all its powers, every holy liturgy and every brave mission has as its only goal: faith, hope, and love towards God and neighbour" (p. 31).

68   Rahner, *The Christian of the Future*, 101. "The most important thing about Vatican II is not the letter of the decrees, which in any case have to be translated by us all into life and action. It is the spirit, the deepest tendencies, perspectives and meaning of what happened that really matter and which will remain operative. They may perhaps be submerged again for the time being by a contrary wave of caution, fear of one's own courage, terror of false conclusions which people may like to draw ... But the real seeds of a new outlook and strength to understand and endure the imminent future in a Christian way have been sown in the field of the church. God himself will provide the climate in which this crop will grow – the future historical situation of the church which he, as Lord of history, will bring about" (pp. 100–101).

14   The Extremely Important Issue of Education

The exponential increase in educational provision throughout the twentieth century is one of the great stories of human achievement. At pre-school, primary and second level, in colleges and universities and, more recently, through programmes of adult education, societies throughout the world have invested in greater education provision. The sad fact remains that even today fifty-eight million children of school-going age worldwide are not in school.[1] That said, the general unease with which most people view such a reality is testament to the widely held consensus that all children have a right to schooling.

The Catholic church has a long history of involvement in schools, colleges and universities. It was appropriate then that one of the sixteen documents of the Second Vatican Council should deal with this central issue. Its Latin title – *Gravissimum educationis* – indicates that education is an extremely important issue. Initially this article comments on the Council's text before analysing three themes more closely: (1) parental rights; (2) the meaning of a holistic, integral education and (3) looking to the future.

Gravissimum Educationis

The Declaration on Christian Education was promulgated on 28th October 1965. During the preparatory phase of work for the Council it was clear that most bishops and leaders of religious congregations wanted the issues of education and schooling addressed. Both Pope Pius XI and Pope Pius XII

1   This is according to figures published by Unicef and UNESCO; see <http://www.unicef.org/education/bege_61659.html>.

had included such in their draft schemes for the completion of Vatican I. Further, the extraordinary increase in the numbers attending school in the first half of the twentieth century and the expanding role of the state in the provision and oversight of schools raised important questions for Catholic leaders.[2]

It should be noted that it is a declaration rather than a decree and that the title is "Christian education" rather than "Catholic schools". As work on a draft text developed it became clear that the task was overly ambitious. The initial title was "Catholic schools". But what of Catholic pupils who attend non-Catholic schools? What of countries where there are almost no Catholic schools? What of the role of the church in university and other third-level institutions? What of education across the life cycle, especially in adulthood? Given the pastoral agenda of the Council and the tone and contents of the documents already promulgated, it was surely necessary to address these real questions that formed part of the life of Catholic communities throughout the world. The result, after many debates, was a decision to issue a declaration on Christian education.

A declaration is a more general statement of principles than is a decree. That the title is "Christian education" allowed the framers of the text to deal with a range of issues that went beyond Catholic schools. These issues emerge from the pastoral challenges that the local churches face throughout the world. Such challenges vary significantly as countries are at different levels of social and economic development while the relationship with the civil authorities covers a wide spectrum from close co-operation to legal prohibition of Catholic institutions.

Key themes emerge in the document. Among them are:

- All people have a right to education based on enlightened pedagogy. This is especially true of those who live in economic poverty.

---

2   The process of agreeing the text of the declaration is analysed in detail in Herbert Vorgrimler, *Commentary on the Documents of Vatican II, Volume IV* (London: Burns & Oates, 1969), 1–48.

- Education is about the formation of mature and free human persons. It must not be reduced to a purely functional service of society.
- Christians should engage fully in the world, not least through schools and other educational structures, so that co-operation between people can be fostered in the service of peace and the common good. The church's aim in education should be to make the world more human.
- A biblical anthropology must inform Christian education. The human person is created in God's image, falls into sin, is redeemed by Christ and is called to share in the fullness of God's own life. Hope is the guiding virtue in Christian education because God, in Christ, has redeemed all.
- Parents and families have inalienable rights with regard to the education of their children. The role of the state is subsidiary.
- Schools are inseparable from the overall good of the human community. They are a work of partnership that serves the moral, intellectual, cultural, civic, religious and professional development of human persons.
- The state has important responsibilities with regard to the education of all children, including the establishment of state schools. In exercising its proper powers it should not seek a monopoly with regard to school provision but respect the principle of subsidiarity.
- The moral and religious education of children should seek the same standard as that expected in secular subjects.
- Catholic schools have a particular role in bearing witness to the gospel. While pursuing educational and cultural goals they are also a leaven in human society anticipating the coming of God's kingdom.
- Teaching is a noble vocation that can be properly understood as an apostolic ministry in the church.
- The destiny of society and the church is intimately linked to the intellectual development of students in universities.
- Theology should be made available as an academic subject to lay students.

All of these themes must be read through the social, political, religious, scientific and educational contexts of the early 1960s. Furthermore, the debates that led to the final approval of the declaration made clear that much of the work that the Council could not undertake in the area of education would need to be addressed by a post-conciliar commission and by the local episcopal conferences. Since the Council, the Vatican's Congregation for Catholic Education has published the following documents:

> *The Catholic School* (1977);
> *Lay Catholics in Schools: Witnesses to Faith* (1982);
> *Educational Guidance in Human Love – Outlines for Sex Education* (1983);
> *The Religious Dimension of Education in a Catholic School* (1988);
> *The Catholic School on the Threshold of the Third Millennium* (1997);
> *Consecrated Persons and their Mission in Schools* (2002);
> *Educating Together in a Catholic School* (2007);
> *Circular Letter on Religious Education in Schools* (2009);
> *Educating to Intercultural Dialogue in Catholic Schools* (2013).

There have also been two Apostolic Constitutions on third-level education: *Sapientia Christiana* on ecclesiastical universities and faculties (1979) and *Ex corde ecclesiae* on Catholic universities (1990). In addition, the episcopal conferences throughout the world and various national bodies representing religious congregations have published a large volume of documents on Catholic schools and education in particular national contexts. Such an array of publications is not surprising given the importance of education in all societies and the diverse legal realities that must be addressed. From this broad range of material this article looks at three particular issues.

Parental rights

The declaration's emphasis on the inalienable rights of parents in the education of their children is based on the earlier work of Pope Pius XI. In his encyclical *Divini Illius Magistri* (1929) he insists that the state must not force parents to send their children to schools in contravention of their consciences.[3] He even quotes a notable case from the United States Supreme Court in support of his argument for a subsidiary role for the

---

3   Pope Pius XI, *Divini Illius Magistri*, Encyclical on Christian Education, 31 December 1929, 32–35.

state in service of the common good.⁴ But this vision was sorely tested by the behaviour of the Hitler regime in Germany that flouted the terms of a concordat throughout the 1930s. This led Pope Pius XI to write to the German bishops warning of the danger of an absolutist state, not least in the area of schools and education.⁵

By the early 1960s the reality of communist rule all over Eastern Europe and the trend among many democratically elected governments to direct most funding to state schools animated the renewed conciliar emphasis on the rights of parents. It was clear to all that many parents wanted an education for their children based on their religious beliefs but that legal prohibition in some countries and the financial cost of accessing such an education in others effectively nullified this right. It is not surprising then that the declaration expresses thanks to those countries that do fund religious-run schools on a similar basis to all other schools.⁶

The ecclesial emphasis on parental rights in education found strong echoes in the civil sphere from the Universal Declaration of Human Rights to various UN and European legal instruments. The principle of subsidiarity also informed these approaches. The origins of the term are found in Catholic social teaching where it famously emerged in the encyclical letter of Pope Leo XIII, *Rerum Novarum*, in 1891.⁷ Seldom used for many decades outside of Catholic circles it became very important in the development of the European Union as a principle for understanding the relationships between the competencies/rights of the nation states vis-à-vis the centralised structures (Council, commission, parliament). As a result it is now an important legal principle in EU law and in international human rights law while it remains a key theme in Catholic social teaching. The principle holds that rights and responsibilities should be exercised at the most local level possible. If individuals, families and communities can undertake socially

---

4   Pope Pius XI, *Divini Illius Magistri*, 37.
5   Pope Pius XI, *Mit Brennender Sorge* ("It is with deep anxiety"), Encyclical letter on the church and the German Reich, 14 March 1937.
6   *Gravissimum educationis*, 7.
7   While *Rerum Novarum* does not use this term specifically, it refers to the basic principle.

progressive activities (like schooling) then the state should facilitate them rather than seek to replace them. The state has a key role through its laws and structures to do that which exceeds the capacity of local endeavour. With regard to schooling this includes the setting of standards, the structure of curriculum and assessment, the qualifications of teachers and the provision of schools where necessary.

The revised Code of Canon Law published in 1983 is notable for its emphasis on parental rights and responsibilities in education.[8] It states clearly that parents are the primary educators of their children and that all church bodies, especially schools, assist parents with the function of education. The understanding of Catholic schooling that emerges from Canon Law is a liberating one based on the foundation of a partnership between parents and other Catholic church bodies in service of a holistic education.

Fifty years after the Council there is growing acceptance of the principle of parental rights in education. In response to parental demands some countries that have an effective state monopoly in school provision are amending their structures to allow for more local, school autonomy. Many studies demonstrate that such autonomy can be a key driver of improved performance. However, the role of the state must remain central in the establishment of shared standards and adequate funding for all the schools that it recognises. In most countries schools that are not provided by the state itself, including Catholic schools, receive significantly less funding than state schools and are therefore dependent on parental contributions. This means, almost inevitably, that such schools draw more of their students from families who can afford to make a financial contribution to children's education.

In Ireland the situation evolved differently to other countries. The Irish Constitution of 1937 recognises parents and the family as the primary educators of children.[9] The role of the state is subsidiary. This was in accord with Catholic social teaching at the time. While the constitution bestows rights on parents it was the churches, both Catholic and Protestant, that

8   Code of Canon Law, 793–806.
9   Bunreacht na hÉireann (Constitution of Ireland), article 42.1.

effectively exercised such rights. This reality worked well as long as the vast majority of citizens perceived the churches as legitimate guarantors of their rights. In a more secular age when this social-religious consensus begins to break down some parents seek to give alternative expression to their rights concerning the education of their children. This is what has happened in Ireland and the system will continue to evolve in response to parental demand. In Ireland any individual or group of citizens can establish a school and receive state recognition once a sufficient number of parents are convinced of the merits of sending their children to such a school. Given these notable rights afforded to parents in its constitution Ireland will be an interesting social experiment in how a school system evolves in response to changes in parental opinions.

Despite the importance of parents in education many can't or won't exercise their rights and responsibilities. Therefore, since the Council there has been a growing awareness of the need to heighten parents' understanding of their role in education. Many church documents emphasise the need for a partnership approach that fosters dialogue between schools and parents.

> It is not a question of convenience, but a partnership based on faith. Catholic tradition teaches that God has bestowed on the family its own specific and unique educational mission. The first and primary educators of children are their parents ... The school is aware of this fact but, unfortunately, the same is not always true of the families themselves ... Every school should initiate meetings and other programmes which will make the parents more conscious of their role, and help to establish a partnership; it is impossible to do too much along these lines. It often happens that a meeting called to talk about the children becomes an opportunity to raise the consciousness of the parents.[10]

In democratic societies there is little doubt but that the future of Christian education in general, and Catholic schools in particular, is dependent on a heightened awareness among parents of the value of such education.

---

10   Congregation for Catholic Education, *The Religious Dimension of Education in a Catholic School: Guidelines for Reflection and Renewal*, Vatican City 1988, 42–43.

A holistic, integral education: The blessed "and"

Gravissimum educationis is committed to an enlightened pedagogy based on the insights of modern science. The central aims of all schools are educational and cultural. What then is specific about Catholic education or schooling? It seeks to bring the worlds of knowledge and culture into dialogue with what was revealed in the person of Jesus Christ so that the free choice for religious belief is not an irrational withdrawal from science and culture but an embrace of a holistic understanding of the human person. This is why the word "and" is very important in understanding Catholicism: faith *and* reason, scripture *and* tradition, grace *and* nature, religion *and* culture, belief *and* science. Contrast this with more fundamentalist readings of religious texts in evangelical Protestantism: faith rejects reason, scripture uproots tradition, grace supplants nature, religion replaces culture, belief disparages science. Note too the contrast with reductionist readings of religious texts in contemporary atheism: faith ridiculed by reason, scripture and tradition reduced to myth, grace displaced by nature, religion excluded from the public square of culture, belief annihilated by science. There are few more important tasks facing Catholic education today that to retrieve this blessed "and". Failure to do so can isolate believers in an intellectual ghetto.

There is a temptation in contemporary discourse to dismiss religious belief as inherently irrational, divisive, and anti-intellectual. This runs completely contrary to the Catholic education tradition which is built on respect for faith and reason. Those who dismiss Catholic schools as little more than proselytising and indoctrinating tools of religious authority show little sense of the long evolution of Catholic schools over many centuries, the rich diversity within the Catholic sector and the principles which underpin such education today. The most important principle of all is the value placed on both faith and reason. It is this principle which helps to explain why Catholic schools are so effective and respected throughout the world.

Catholic schools were and are committed to academic excellence. This is achieved through respecting the autonomy and methodology of different disciplines while challenging students to achieve their potential across the curriculum. The aim is to facilitate the intellectual and emotional development of mature human persons who will have the capacity to draw upon multiple resources in interpreting their lives. As students follow their timetable during the school day the subjects vary but the individual student remains a unique person with a past and a future. Catholic education wants to provide students with the ability to draw from the rich treasures of both faith and reason in creating that future.

The whole intellectual history of the Catholic church involves a critical interaction with human reason. From its encounter with neo-Platonic philosophy in the third, fourth, and fifth centuries to the re-discovery of Aristotle in the twelfth and thirteenth centuries, the dialogue between faith and reason characterises the high intellectual achievement of the Catholic church. Today, in an era often dominated by religious fundamentalism on the one hand and atheistic science on the other, this commitment to dialogue between faith and reason has a greater urgency. This is an era when science and religion might completely diverge from each other as if it was impossible for the same person to be a rigorous scientist and a sincere religious believer. In the English-speaking world this trend is exacerbated by the restriction of the very term "science" to empirical study of the natural world. This goes completely against the history of the term which covers all areas of human knowledge. Thus philosophy and theology are just as surely sciences as physics and biology.

Faith and reason can live and thrive in the same person: while one cannot be reduced to the other they both play a dynamic role in forming and educating a mature person. It is salutary to note that some of the greatest scientific breakthroughs have been made by religious believers. Similarly, Catholic priests have been prominent in the advance of knowledge and civilisation. Think of Nicolaus Copernicus (whose discoveries revolutionised our understanding of planet earth), Pope Gregory XIII (who gives his name to the calendar in use to this day), Matteo Ricci (the mathematician/ cartographer who led the first real encounter between Chinese and western civilisation), Gregor Mendel (father of the modern science of genetics), Georges Lemaître (the creator of the "Big Bang" theory), and numerous others who lived as priests committed to ever deeper knowledge of the world around them. There is no contradiction between being a fully educated person and a committed Christian. There are few more important tasks for Christian educators than to revisit and re-imagine the relationship between faith and reason.

Pope Benedict XVI consistently drew attention to this fundamental issue. At his meeting with representatives of British society in Westminster Hall he said:

> I would suggest that the world of reason and the world of faith – the world of secular rationality and the world of religious belief – need one another and should not be afraid to enter into a profound and ongoing dialogue, for the good of our civilisation.[11]

He has described the Second Vatican Council as dedicated to finding a new definition of the relationships between the church and the modern age, between the church and the modern state and between Christian faith and other religions.[12] Notice again the importance of the word "and". The Council opened up new avenues of dialogue that allowed believers to re-imagine their relationships with modern science, with modern democracy and with adherents of other religions. Catholic schools and colleges are continually re-interpreting these various relationships as they live at the interface of Catholic faith and modern science; they are a living expression of the interaction between Catholic institutions and democractic governments; and, they are a context for the daily encounter with those of other faiths and none.

The ongoing reception and interpretation of Vatican II now takes place in the context of the ministry of Pope Francis. He has challenged all members of the church to reach out again to the world, not least to those who are on the margins of society. He speaks of two temptations: that of seeking to return to a past which no longer exists; and, that of embracing every secular trend. In contrast, hc calls Christians to live out their faith in the world in which they find themselves. The ministry of Pope Francis will give renewed energy to Catholic schools in creating a mature relationship

---

11   Pope Benedict XVI, *Meeting with the Representatives of British Society, including the Diplomatic Corps, Politicians, Academics and Business Leaders*, Westminster Hall, 17 September 2010.

12   *Address of His Holiness Benedict XVI to the Roman Curia*, 22 December 2005.

with modernity, in seeking to be active participants in democratic societies and in fostering dialogue between all people of goodwill.

Francis stresses the importance of the social dimension of the preaching of the Gospel. Christians are called to live with others and for others. This is because God, in Christ, has redeemed human society and not just each individual. Faith is not just a private matter between the individual person and God. This is an important insight for Catholic education. Pope Francis states:

> No one can demand that religion should be relegated to the inner sanctum of personal life, without influence on societal and national life, without concern for the soundness of civil institutions, without a right to offer an opinion on events affecting society. Who would claim to lock up in a church and silence the message of Saint Francis of Assisi or Blessed Teresa of Calcutta? They themselves would have found this unacceptable. An authentic faith – which is never comfortable or completely personal – always involves a deep desire to change the world, to transmit values, to leave this earth somehow better than we found it.[13]

Christian faith is always lived in particular cultures. The dialogue between faith and culture takes place in the heart and mind of the individual believer, in families, in parish communities and, not least, in schools and colleges. Christian schools and colleges stand as a reminder that the Christian faith is not just a private commitment embraced by individuals but, as a philosophically justified act of faith in a transcendent, personal God, it is an intelligent and reasonable response to what was revealed in the life of Jesus Christ. Furthermore, these educational institutions give expression to the public dimension of Christian faith in their commitment to social solidarity, to outreach to those in need and to promotion of the common good. There will always be a certain tension between religious faith and culture: some people reduce culture to religious faith and so withdraw into a fundamentalist sect where everything outside is seen as a threat; others empty culture of all religious reference so that religious belief amounts to nothing more than personal whim and ignorant superstition. A true dialogue between faith and culture allows one to inform the other and calls

---

13   Pope Francis, *Evangelii gaudium*, Vatican City 2013, 183.

individuals, families, communities, and indeed, our schools and colleges, to an ever greater commitment to human maturity. This is the goal of a holistic, Christian education.

Looking to the Future

Inter-cultural dialogue

There are few issues that are more important in education than fostering inter-religious and inter-cultural dialogue. Ever since the 9/11 attacks in the USA the post-enlightenment principle of excluding religion from the public square, including from state schools in countries such as the USA and France, appears increasingly imprudent. What is required is dialogue not isolation. Because of the prophetic approach of the Second Vatican Council the Catholic church has been at the forefront of inter-religious dialogue for the past fifty years. Over that time four types of dialogue have been developed: the dialogue of life; the dialogue of works; theological dialogue; and, the dialogue of religious experience.[14] The dialogue of life reflects on the joys, challenges and sorrows of life especially in the context of the fundamental realities of family, language and culture. The dialogue of works encourages those involved to collaborate in the holistic development of all men and women. Theological dialogue demands knowledge of various religious traditions and their mutual interaction. The dialogue of religious experience is based on the lived encounter of various faiths, not on intellectual abstractions, but rather on the actual lives of the faithful.

The most recent publication by the Vatican's Congregation for Catholic Education is entitled *Educating to Intercultural Dialogue in*

14   Pontifical Council for Inter-Religious Dialogue, *Dialogue and Proclamation*, Vatican City 1991, 42.

Catholic Schools.[15] It provides important reflections on what it is to be a Catholic school in a globalised world characterised by cultural and religious pluralism. Education is the key to mutual understanding and to building a civilisation of peace in such a complex world. The document challenges Catholic schools to engage in dialogue through facing the reality of a diverse cultural situation, by overcoming prejudices and by education through encounter with the other. It notes that "schools are privileged places for intercultural dialogue".[16]

What is this intercultural dialogue? It is not a cultural relativism which suggests that all cultures and traditions are essentially the same and often seeks to quarantine related practices within a purely private sphere of life. Nor is it a religious fundamentalism which denies the other and withdraws into a vacuum sealed in its own unchallenged identity. Rather, it is an invitation to engagement with the other person, the other faith, the other culture based on innovative and courageous fidelity to one's own faith and culture. Such dialogue is not just talking but includes all interreligious relationships with both individuals and communities.[17] It seeks common ethical values which are the foundations of justice and peace. The aim of this dialogue is not to abandon one's own inherited faith and practices but to rediscover them in a deeper way through encounter with the other. This is the opposite of relativism.

> The relativistic model is founded on the value of tolerance, but limits itself to accepting the other person, excluding the possibility of dialogue and recognition of each other in mutual transformation. Such an idea of tolerance, in fact, leads to a substantially passive meaning of relationship with whoever has a different culture. It does not demand that one take an interest in the needs and sufferings of others, nor that their reasons may be heard; there is no self-comparison with their values, and even less sense of developing love for them.[18]

15 Congregation for Catholic Education, *Education to Intercultural Dialogue in Catholic Schools: Living in Harmony for a Civilisation of Love*, Vatican City 2013.
16 *Educating to Intercultural Dialogue in Catholic Schools*, 6.
17 *Educating to Intercultural Dialogue in Catholic Schools*, 13.
18 *Educating to Intercultural Dialogue in Catholic Schools*, 22.

Commitment to a civilisation of love is a challenge to Catholic schools and colleges and to all educators. Educating to inter-cultural dialogue will help to build such a civilisation.

Lay leadership

One of the great developments at the Council was a re-discovery of the significance of baptism. Returning to the scriptural and patristic sources, the documents of the Council open new horizons for lay ministry, lay apostolates and lay leadership.

> The most basic reason for this new role for Catholic laity, a role which the church regards as positive and enriching, is theological. Especially in the course of the last century, the authentic image of the laity within the People of God has become increasingly clear; it has now been set down in two documents of the Second Vatican Council, which give profound expression to the richness and uniqueness of the lay vocation: The Dogmatic Constitution on the church, and the Decree on the Apostolate of the Laity.[19]

This new emphasis on the role of the laity is particularly important in the area of education. There has always been a significant presence of lay teachers in schools but one of the most obvious changes in Catholic schools over the past fifty years has been the declining number of professed religious and the large increase in lay leadership.

The overall result of the move to lay leadership in Catholic schools has been a notable success. Such leaders and teachers have brought new energy, different life experiences and a diverse range of professional expertise to bear in schools. As many have their own children they have created a heightened awareness of the importance of a child-centred pedagogy and spirituality. Given their presence in all spheres of human activity they

19   Congregation for Catholic Education, *Lay Catholics in Schools: Witnesses to Faith*, Vatican City 1982, 2.

can bring faith and culture into renewed dialogue and contribute to the important Christian task of reading the signs of the times.

Lay leaders in Catholic schools need the support of the broader ecclesial community. By definition, they do not have the structured, communal life of professed religious which provided a very effective network in support of schools. Creating relevant, accessible opportunities for the spiritual and intellectual formation of principals and teachers is an important task in all countries. Such undertakings demand the investment of scarce resources but, lacking such, there is a real danger that the whole structure could be hollowed out from within during this secular age.

Another group of lay teachers deserve particular mention and support. These are committed Catholics who work in state schools and other contexts where they provide what might be the only witness to gospel values in the lives of some of their students. The life of such a teacher can be a true example of faith and culture in dialogue.[20]

Theological studies open to all

The history of education and schooling in the western world is inseparable from theology. The great schools of theology of the high middle ages evolved into universities. Theology and philosophy were the foundational disciplines of the new universities of the twelfth and thirteenth centuries. These disciplines were important precisely because of their significance in the first thousand years of western Christianity. They also formed the core of the curriculum for those studying for the priesthood. Sadly, in the post-reformation church and throughout the period of reaction to the enlightenment the study of theology became the preserve of the clergy. It was inseparable from the ordained ministry.

In one of the great signs of throwing the windows open the Declaration on Christian Education called for the teaching of theology to the laity of the

20   *Lay Catholics in Schools: Witnesses to Faith*, 49.

church.[21] Few could have predicted what would transpire. New colleges, institutes, departments and faculties quickly emerged with specialisations in theology, biblical studies, catechetics, religious education and pastoral studies. Long-established universities and colleges opened the doors of theology lectures to lay students. New avenues of dialogue were explored with the social and human sciences as multi-disciplinary insights were brought to bear on Christian belief.

This growing emphasis on adult religious education and the study of theology by large numbers of lay people at university level has been a key characteristic of the post-conciliar church. This means that the priest is no longer the only person in the parish or school who has received a thorough grounding in theological reflection. Society has entered an era in the western world where large numbers of people have received a good general education. Many have attained excellent educational standards in their chosen field. A simplistic and sometimes superstitious approach to faith will not satisfy these people. Many of them find traditional religious answers insufficient for the world in which they live. Consequently, some turn to new spiritualities, eastern religions, and even the occult in search of a liberating message.

In looking to the future the Catholic church is still only beginning to come to terms with the opening up of theology as a discipline to the broad church community. While some of the institutions founded in the heady days of the aftermath of the Council have run their natural course over the succeeding fifty years, the study of theology and related disciplines by a significant number of lay people will continue to be a source of life and renewal. Pope Francis consistently challenges pastors, bishops and priests to support the growth in discipleship of all God's people. In his important address to the leaders of the bishops' conferences of Latin America he asked:

> are we conscious and convinced of the mission of the lay faithful and do we give them the freedom to continue discerning, in a way befitting their growth as disciples, the mission which the Lord has entrusted to them? Do we support them and accompany them, overcoming the temptation to manipulate them or infantilise them? Are we

21   *Gravissimum educationis*, 10.

constantly open to letting ourselves be challenged in our efforts to advance the good of the church and her mission in the world?[22]

A new world of knowledge and information

The horizons of knowledge, information and intelligence are rapidly expanding during the digital revolution that is so much a part of this age in human history. Educators can be dis-orientated by the rapidity of access to information. But some educational principles are surely still true. A fundamental aim of a vibrant school system is to facilitate the emergence of a literate society where individuals learn how to learn so that each person can embark on a life-long educational journey. Literacy impacts on all aspects of life and opens the door to further horizons of knowledge and imagination through literature, mathematics, music, science, religion, art, sport and the whole range of new possibilities that are emerging through information technology. If any education system fails to make students literate and numerate then it closes the door to much that matters in life.

The leaders of tomorrow are in the classrooms of today. All pupils are capable of imagining, creating and exploring. Fostering a commitment to critical thinking and creativity is the heartbeat of any living tradition and Catholic schooling is an expression of just such a living tradition. Today's social commentators often speak of "innovation" and the "knowledge economy". To be truly innovative and knowledgeable is to be more fully human. It is human beings who will create the innovation and knowledge that are needed. The aim of schooling is far greater than job training or qualification for a particular third-level programme – it seeks to create a human person who is knowledgeable and innovative and so can adapt to many different roles and realities in the future. An authentic, contemporary, Christian vision of education will foster an approach to schooling that keeps curiosity alive, nurtures a love of learning, stimulates problem-solving and

22 Pope Francis, *Address to the Leadership of the Episcopal Conferences of Latin America*, Rio de Janeiro, 28 July 2013.

critical thinking and encourages students to become independent learners
while they grow into mature freedom, responsible relationships and commitment to the common good.

Conclusion: The Eucharist as Educator

The Council's Constitution on the Sacred Liturgy, *Sacrosanctum Concilium*,
speaks of the Eucharist as the source and summit of Christian life. As such,
the Eucharist provides a context for a deeper understanding of Christian
education.

Bread and wine are among the most wonderful of human creations.
But they are precisely that: human creations. They do not grow on sheaf
and vine. From sowing the seeds and tending the vine, to harvesting the
grain and grape, to the sharing of bread and the pouring of wine, human
community is created and fostered. Through the work of human hands
the fruit of the earth becomes food and drink. The preparation of bread
and wine and the transformation of these two basic realities into the body
and blood of Christ are a sign and foretaste of the destiny of all reality. All
creation, all human labour and endeavour will be transformed into the
new creation. So the Eucharist teaches.

Christians are called to work with adherents of all faiths and none to
build a world of human justice and dignity. In the same way as with human
hands people create bread and wine so must they struggle with political
ideas and institutions to create a humane world. The church's sacramental
celebration gives shape to a new world and nourishes believers in their
efforts to create it. Thus the Eucharist points the way to overcome the
dichotomies that emerge between the sacred and the secular.

The Eucharist is primarily about the future. Though it is rooted in
events of close to two thousand years ago its true orientation is towards the
future. God has laid hold of human history and has begun to transform it
from within. The Eucharist is bread broken for a new world; it is a prayer
of praise and thanksgiving; it is a foretaste and a promise. The Eucharist is

orientated to the future not as threat but as invitation. In a world that can easily become preoccupied with the present people are invited to open their hearts to the future as God's promise. The Eucharist unites the church in heaven and on earth in giving praise and thanks to God for the gift of creation, for the even greater gift of redemption and for the pledge of future glory. As the bread and wine are transformed into the Body and Blood of Christ so too all of creation will be renewed in Christ "so that God may be all in all" (1 Cor 15:28).

Education provides the key to such a future. Without an enlightened pedagogy humanity is doomed to revisit the past over and over again. In awakening sensibilities and disturbing consciences, education can liberate people from their inherited stereotypes to embrace the future with renewed energy and hope. The Eucharist reveals the wonderful plan that God has in store and it invites humanity to enter into an ever-deeper communion with the Triune God and with all of creation. As Jesus was the greatest of teachers so the Eucharist remains the most trusted educator.

15   The Future of Collegiality

Vatican II still has the capacity to stand in judgment over the state of the church today. This is because the Council did its work well and was so thoroughly and enthusiastically received that it effected a total transformation of the landscape of Catholicism, regrounding liturgy and theology in a broad biblical vision, opening paths of ecumenical and interreligious understanding, and establishing a new framework for Catholic life and thought that has proved impossible to overturn.

Yet in some respects the Council, by its incompletion, also stands in judgment on itself. Inconsistencies, weakness, and vagueness in the "letter" of its texts force us to elicit its "spirit," or its dialectically necessary continuation. To remember Vatican II is to hear the voice of something struggling to be born, and to renew the hope that this something, the "new order of human relationships" promised by John XXIII in his opening speech ("*Gaudet mater ecclesia*"), can become a reality in the church and the world. The church was to become a model of human community, a place marked by joyful discussion and sharing, a network of hospitality, in which everyone could exercise their particular role in an enriching collaboration with the others. On that basis Catholics could undertake a new creative outreach to other churches and religions and to the secular world. Pádraic Conway contributed much in the fifty years accorded him to shape that "new order of human relationships," and his work continues in our present discussions.

Central to this vision is the ideal of collegiality. This is a subject about which theologians have been nagging from the time of the Council. At the risk of falling into a well-worn rut, I shall rehearse here how on the upper level of episcopal collegiality the vision of the Council was thwarted by excessive concern with papal authority, both at the Council itself and in subsequent developments. The papal primacy and the episcopal collegiality should have been regrounded in the concrete life of the local churches as living communities, and then both could have been strengthened together rather than set in opposition. Collegiality was misconceived in an abstract way as something existing between bishops as individuals in a grouping above the church rather than as grounded in the diocesan communities the bishops lead and in the communion between local churches. That abstraction connects with the wider failure to embody collegiality in diocesan and parochial structures allowing greater lay participation and forums for consultation and open discussion.

The New Habit of Mind

In celebrating Vatican II, we invest anew in its mentality, or the much-decried "spirit of the Council" (a phrase used frequently by Paul VI). This remains a bedrock reference and a powerful resource for overcoming any developments that fail to respect it, any modes of thinking that fall short of the broad, biblically grounded vision that the Council opened up. The framework of understanding put in place by the Council was strongly affirmed and elucidated in countless theological works, sermons, papal and episcopal instructions, and a saturation-level of reference to conciliar documents in all Catholic discussions in the 1960s and 1970s. This made it impossible to imagine that the Council could ever become a dead letter, even if its texts, religiously studied and quoted, often seemed rather drab. Indeed it could be claimed that Vatican II was welcomed more generally and more warmly than any Council in the history of the church.

But already the twenty-fifth anniversary of the Council brought to many an eerie sense that this entire epoch was now closed, and that the Council had become a period-phenomenon, or as some seemed happy to think, a blip on the radar-screen of history. Yet, despite ebbing enthusiasm, no counter-movement has succeeded in unseating the postconciliar vision as "the only show in town," theologically speaking. There is no viable path back to a preconciliar framework of thought. Those who treat the Council as merely "pastoral," with no binding force on the way Catholics should think, miss the full power of the conciliar vision, which is more comprehensive than any focus on dogma could have been. Pastoral theology, as the teaching of Pope Francis in *Evangelii gaudium* illustrates, engages the full reality of ecclesial life, placing articles of belief in their integral lived context. Those who play off dogmas against the pastoral horizon of the Council end up cementing a sect rather than building a community.

The triumph of the new "habit of mind" that the Council brought is well described by Massimo Faggioli:

> The theological method of the Council – attention to history, valuation of experience – cannot be renounced. On the plane of lived faith, Catholics worldwide live Vatican II every day, albeit sometimes unconsciously. To choose to celebrate the Council fifty years after its opening implies the possibility of becoming more conscious of our own theological praxis, and also of the questions left unresolved by the Council and which await a response.[1]

There is no "hermeneutic of continuity" that can eliminate the spirit of the conciliar texts, which is a spirit of innovation. The questions left unresolved cannot be repressed but must be thought through in ongoing discussion. The theological method of the Council grows in power and clarity the more it is practised, and provides a long-term warrant for trust in the renewal of the church. It is bound to undergo constant development as it is deployed in every field. The great pioneers of this way of thinking – Congar, Rahner, Schillebeeckx, Küng – offer not a settled body of doctrine but a practice of rethinking truths of faith in exposure to contemporary questioning and the insights of other philosophical and religious traditions. Like Vatican II itself, such theology is not a set of theses and arguments, but has the quality of an event or an encounter. It launches a vast conversation, which is still going on throughout the Catholic world today.

1   *La Stampa*, 4 October 2012.

The Mission of the Church

Vatican II took place amid the warm glow of a rediscovery of what Henri de Lubac called "the splendor of the church." Yves Congar and Hans Küng had portrayed the history of the church as the unfolding of a great communal adventure, in which bishops and laity had a more vital place than was envisaged in the ultramontane mentality prevalent since 1870. "Ecclesial" became a radiant word, replacing the stuffy "ecclesiastical," and theologians vied with one another in having their thought espouse the full dimensions of the church's life instead of sinking back into doctrinal abstraction or morose individualism.

Four magisterial documents mark a high point in the enthusiasm about the church: John XXIII's *Mater et Magistra* (1961), Paul VI's *Ecclesiam Suam* (1963), *Lumen Gentium* (21 November 1964), and *Gaudium et Spes* (7 December 1965). It is perhaps significant that there has been no subsequent papal document devoted to the church as such and that no session of the Synod has been devoted to that topic. A mist seems to have spread again, leaving us with no clear image of what the church is or what it is for. We need a more vibrant enactment of collegiality at all levels to dispel this mist.

One of Vatican II's most original achievements was its unprecedented effort to clarify the notion of church in a profound and exact way (as Paul VI remarked at the opening of the second session of the Council). The scriptural aspect of the Council's method was in evidence in this venture. The appeal to experience was less in evidence, nor were the human sciences drawn upon. The church as such is an elusive object of thought, and theologians have preferred to deal with specific sub-topics that lend themselves to more concrete analysis and juicier controversy, such as the sacraments, authority, the questions of church and State. Notions such as collegiality or the people of God or the *sensus fidelium* shed a benign influence over church rhetoric in the palmy days of the Vatican II period, then they became weapons for rather ineffectual polemic, and now they seem to have been overused and lost their cutting edge.

The Council's vision of the church in *Lumen Gentium* relies too much on an outpouring of scriptural quotes with little strong argumentative framing. Reading this self-confident text fifty years later, the temptation is great to dismiss the glorification of the church as so much empty noise. How can we reassert faith in the church as a divinely instituted instrument of salvation in a period of acute criticism of the church as it has actually existed? Perhaps the answer may be found by following up on what the document's vision of the church as a concrete people, struggling in history, but full of eschatological hope. It is when the Council slogans are brought down from the clouds and translated into the terms of what communities experience in their prayer, reflection, and action, that their true power is glimpsed.

Newman's dying Gerontius cries: "And I hold in veneration/For the love of Him alone/Holy church as His creation/And her teachings as His own." How can we affirm this article of faith convincingly today? Consider what the Buddhist formula, "I take refuge in the sangha," suggests: not a sentimental resort to a reassuring mother-image, but an identification with a creative community engaged in wholesome practice. Individual faith is widened, deepened, made more secure, when it embraces the faith of the community, when "I believe" becomes "We believe." This is more than obedient subscription to official teaching; it is sharing in a vast life of faith that traverses the ages. The doubt and confusion of the individual who broods alone on religious questions is healed and resolved when lifted up into the clear light of the community's faith. This can be troubled by fetishisation of particular points of doctrine. But in a functioning community of worship such issues recede as the core shared gospel vision finds expression anew. When we speak of a collegial and dialogical church we are not just discussing an ordinary human organisation. Rather we are trying to realise more effectively the event of community and communion that the church, as forerunner of the Kingdom, is supposed to be.

Episcopal Collegiality

The call for "collegiality" is not then just a slogan for democratisation. It stems from the desire to realise effectively the nature and mission of the church as envisioned by the Council. The idea of episcopal collegiality came in from the cold fifty years ago, when the bishops expressed their collegiality in its highest form, in a general Council. Some had viewed collegiality with suspicion, as a sleeping giant it would be dangerous to awaken, something like the Estates General in prerevolutionary France. Vatican I had anathematised the view of fifteenth-century Conciliarism and eighteenth-century Gallicanism and Febronianism, that the authority of bishops gathered in an ecumenical Council was above that of the pope. Despite this, the conciliarist ideal continues to haunt the Catholic imagination and was revived by several writers in the 1960s. It can be held at bay only by an effective rethinking of the Petrine primacy in more collegial terms. Vatican II itself did not look back sufficiently to the collegial structures of the past. "The modern practices of representation and consent that characterise secular constitutional government are not alien to the tradition of the church. And if in the future the church should choose to adapt such practices to meet its own needs in a changing world, that would not be a revolutionary departure but a recovery of a lost part of the church's own early tradition" (Brian Tierney).[2]

Both papal primacy and episcopal collegiality are regarded as having scriptural foundation and as being divinely established. The picture of the early churches in the Pauline letters and the account of conciliar debates in Acts 15 provide a model and inspiration to future reflection on church governance, but it has proved difficult to translate this into well-defined principles in canon law. The relationship between episcopal collegiality and papal primacy has been a vexed issue since at least the twelfth century, when the decretalists found contradictions among their sources. Vatican I defined the primacy lucidly, but in doing so sharpened the tension between primacy and collegiality, so much so that some theologians began to regard the task of reconciling the two as one of those exquisite theological paradoxes, like the tension between freedom and predestination, that one must sustain in an act of trusting faith, without itching for a solution.

Mary McAleese tackles these ancient questions on fresh ground, in showing precisely how they affect the 1983 *Code of Canon Law*. Her analysis

---

2   Quoted, Mary McAleese, *Quo Vadis? Collegiality in the Code of Canon Law* (Dublin: Columba, 2012), 44.

of Vatican II's failure to give a concrete profile to episcopal collegiality brings to light a deep structural flaw that lies at the base of so much confusion and anguish in church life today. This flaw has permitted the Curia to increase its control over the church: "the Curia authorities working in conjunction with the Pope have appropriated the tasks of the episcopal college. It is they who now carry out almost all of them" (Cardinal König).[3] The Curia personnel has mushroomed since the Council, and now exceeds the number of diocesan bishops worldwide; about 40% of the world's bishops do not lead a diocese; and John Paul II located collegiality as a relationship between bishops as such, "preceding the fact of presiding over a church" (*Apostolos suos*, n. 11), and in many ways subordinated this collegiality anew to the hierarchical teaching and governing authority of Pope and Curia. Theologians protest that these developments border on the heretical, but the canonists, resisting the new mentality of the Council, continue to define church relationships in a way that ensures continued blockage of the growth of collegiality.[4]

Vatican I, in *Pastor Aeternus*, called the papacy a ministry of unity, not a power above the bishops and alien to them but that of the first among brothers, and it insisted that the immediate and universal power of the Pope could not undercut the power of the bishops. That Council disbanded before the role of the episcopacy could be further clarified. Wrongly interpreted, Vatican I came to mean that bishops derive all their authority not directly from Christ (as Vatican II teaches, in *LG*, n. 26), but from the papal *plenitudo potestatis*, their power of jurisdiction being "immediately communicated by the Sovereign Pontiff" (Pius XII, *Mystici Corporis*).[5] Thus, "the culture of strict primatial authority articulated at Vatican I has a considerable head start over the new concept of conciliar episcopal collegiality, left hanging, ambiguous and uncoordinated after

3   Quoted in ibid., 135.
4   I am indebted to Hervé Legrand, OP, for all these points.
5   Quoted, Hervé Legrand, "Les évêques, les églises locales et l'Église entière", *Recherches de sciences philosophiques et théologiques* 85 (2001), 461–509; 464. See also Legrand, "Roman Primacy, Communion between Churches, and Communion between Bishops", *Concilium* 2103/5: 63–77.

Vatican II."[6] In the time of Paul VI, some already complained that the vision of the Council had found no institutional embodiment (Küng, Rahner). Cardinal Suenens in particular "'resisted Peter to his face,' when *Humanae Vitae* was issued without a shred of episcopal input."[7] Today the urgency of structural reform that would give substance to the ideal of collegiality is ever more widely recognised. Such reform would be a major innovation, but one called for by the unresolved tension in Vatican II and in centuries of church tradition, and one that poses no threat to the doctrinal foundations of church structure.

McAleese is surprised that a 2,000-year-old institution still has not defined its basic structures of governance clearly.[8] But perhaps that is not so surprising in view of the great variety of shapes that the church has taken throughout history, and the degree to which church structures are makeshift arrangements to give expression to the life of the people of God and their organic communion. Take even so relatively well-defined an institution as an Ecumenical Council. In practice, a Council will be a complex event shaped by the forces of its time, and it would be hard to find a series of events bearing the same name that are so extremely diverse as the twenty ecumenical Councils that have punctuated the history of the church. Critics of Roman claims, from Sarpi[9] to Döllinger, have delighted in pointing this out, noting especially that the Councils of the first millennium were convened by the Emperor, not the Pope, while defenders of the full-fledged doctrine of papal primacy, from Bellarmine to Scheeben, have gone to great lengths to square the dogma with the historical facts.[10]

6   McAleese, *Quo Vadis?*, 136.

7   John Wilkins, "Bishops or Branch Managers? Collegiality after the Council," *Commonweal* 139.17 (12 October 2012), 16–21.

8   McAleese, *Quo Vadis?*, *159–160*.

9   See Paolo Sarpi, *Istoria del concilio tridentino*, ed. Corrado Vivanti (Turin: Einaudi, 1974), 5–8.

10   See Hermann Josef Sieben, *Die katholische Konzilsidee im 19. und 20. Jahrhundert* (Paderborn: Schöningh, 1993), 186–214; F.X. Funk, *Kirchengeschichtliche Abhandlungen und Untersuchungen*, I (Paderborn: Schöningh, 1897; repr. Frankfurt: Minerva, 1972), 39–121.

Canon law should not aim to sort out this historical complexity by producing timeless blueprints, but should be at the service of a constructive theological vision meeting the challenges of the church's life and mission today. Sharp definitions of structures of sacramental power and teaching and governing authority must be entirely subservient to this task of promoting the vibrant functioning of the community of salvation. Canon law should be a charter for possibilities of inculturation and creativity in the worldwide church, rather than imposing a narrow uniformity. It can best free the church from dysfunctionality if it modestly avows the largely functional nature of its own prescriptions and seeks constantly to place them in theological perspective, in dialogue with ecclesiologists. The Code of Canon Law should be submitted to the higher judgment of theologians and bishops with a view to its replacement by something more conducive to the flourishing of Christian life.

Episcopal collegiality was supposed to be concretised by the triennial synod in Rome. But as Archbishop John R. Quinn remarked in 1999: "The Synod has not met the original expectations of its establishment and in reality the Curia sees itself as exercising oversight and authority over the College of Bishops and worse still as subordinate to the Pope but superior to the College of Bishops."[11] To a sceptical canonist, "one of the most brilliant chess moves" aimed at out-manoeuvering the progressives at Vatican II was the specification in *Christus Dominus*, n. 5, that the Synod would be created by the Pope himself, thus pre-empting a conciliar establishment of a permanent Synod in Rome, which would have created a more democratic church. The conciliar text here ensures that the papal *plenitudo potestatis* can be limited by the synod only when and insofar as the pope allows it. Its activities are rigorously cut off from any possibility of permanence that might give it the role of a co-determiner of teaching and governance with the pope.[12] The composition of this text was constrained by the *motu proprio Apostolica Sollicitudo*, 15th September 1965, which Paul VI timed for the

---

11 Mary McAleese, *Quo Vadis?* (Dublin, Columba Press, 2013), 123–124.
12 Hans Barion, *Kirche und Kirchenrecht* (Paderborn, 1984), 543–546, cited, Sieben, 331–332.

opening of the last session of the Council. The papal text makes no mention of collegiality and treats the Synod as a practical matter of collaboration with the pope, thwarting both the theology and the concrete demands of the Council fathers.[13] Roman canonists might scramble to stress the power of the synod as an actualisation of the collegial principle, its *potestas ordinaria* as a *subjectum iurium* and a *persona moralis*, with a *fundamentum in iure divino*.[14] But the gap between the expectations voiced by several bishops and the actual shape of what Paul VI set up was apparent.[15]

A great weakness of the Council is that it envisaged collegiality too abstractly, welcoming it as in relationship to the pope, but ignoring its enactment at the regional level at which collegiality was originally developed in the ancient church.[16] The Council did stress the role of episcopal conferences, as expressions of the sense of collegiality. The reception of *Humanae Vitae* by the episcopal conferences in 1968 seems to have raised the spectre of autonomous national churches arrogating authority to themselves and introducing a confusing pluralism into Catholic teaching. In the wake of these events, influential voices (Ratzinger,[17] de Lubac) stressed that the episcopal conferences had no properly theological status, but were little more than a useful practical arrangement. The authority of episcopal conferences has been undercut step by step in a series of Vatican documents and interventions. John Paul II's *Apostolos Suos* (1998) "is the indirect Roman response to the *relatio finalis* of the 1985 Synod, which recommended that the question of the magisterial authority of the conferences be deepened and developed."[18] It reduces their status to that of "a pragmatic construct

13   See J. Grootaers, *Actes et auteurs à Vatican II* (Leuven: Peeters, 1998), 443–450.
14   Wilhelm Bertrams, cited, Sieben, 333.
15   Josef Neumann, "Die Bischofsynode," *Theologische Quartalschrift* 147 (1967), 1–27, 9, cited Sieben, 333.
16   Klaus Mörsdorf, cited, Sieben, 343.
17   *Theologische Prinzipienlehre: Bausteine zur Fundamentaltheologie* (Munich: Wewel, 1982). This contradicts his insistence on the theological standing of episcopal conferences in what he wrote in the 1960s (as quoted in Sieben, 340).
18   Massimo Faggioli, "The Regulation of Episcopal Conferences since Vatican II," *The Japan Mission Journal* 68 (2014), 82–95; 94.

of convenience," denying that they can take on "the collegial nature proper to the actions of the order of bishops as such."[19] Here theological scruple risks leaving the church unable to give concrete contemporary form to the collegiality essential to its identity and its life. If episcopal collegiality is essential to the divinely established structure of the church, it must be given strong juridical and practical form. If neither the synods nor the episcopal conferences can ensure this, and in the absence of any project to convene another ecumenical Council, bishops are forced to conceive of their collegial role as simply one of spiritual unity around the pope and docile transmission of papal teaching.

Some theologians imagined that the impulse toward collegiality would win out over the painfully constructed compromises of the conciliar texts, but in fact "the compromise finally adopted did not end the tension between two projects for the future. They remain juxtaposed and it is not surprising that this tension has resurfaced, inevitably, in the process of reception. Up to now it has not been possible to achieve a synthesis."[20] If developments are blocked or frozen at the level of the hierarchy, the spirit of collegiality has found expression elsewhere in the church. "The broader view of conciliar collegiality has developed most coherently within religious institutes, where ... in the process of reception of the *novus habitus mentis* of the Council, there has been a clear move away from autocratic governance structures towards (the recovery of historically normative) collegially participative, even democratic structures."[21] Such language is also found in the *Code of Canon Law*, but when it comes to episcopal collegiality "that logic is routinely avoided, circumvented or ignored while the word collegiality is

---

19   McAleese, *Quo Vadis?*, 141.
20   Lukas Vischer, "L'accueil réservé aux débats sur la collégialité," in G. Alberigo and J.-P. Jossua, eds, *La réception de Vatican II* (Paris: Éditions du Cerf, 1985), 305–325; 318. Available as "The Reception of the Dabate on Collegiality", *The Reception of Vatican II*, ed. by G. Alberigo, Jean-Pierre Jossua, and Joseph A. Kononchak (Washington: CUA Press, 1987), 233–248.
21   McAleese, *Quo Vadis?*, 30.

liberally used to describe ecclesial structures which would not pass the test of collegiality set down by the General Norms" enunciated in the Code.[22]

What has most stood in the way of building a collegial church in the half-century since the Council is the mystique surrounding the figure of the pope, a mystique given a new lease of life by being conjoined with a modern media cult of personality. This was linked with a huge quantitative inflation of papal teaching (4,000 pages a year from John Paul II). Benedict XVI's courageous *gran rifiuto* struck a blow against this mystification, permitting a more sober understanding of the role of the bishop of Rome. But now we hang pathetically on every word and gesture of another elderly pope, hoping that he can magically summon into being a fully functioning collegial church. The revolution people want him to effect is well prepared in theology and in the now widespread consciousness of the faithful, but it is blocked by the structures in possession. Will Francis have time to tackle this blockage?

As I write, the hope that the Extraordinary Synod for the Family, convened for October 2014, would be a showcase of episcopal collegiality, as well as of consultation of the laity, has been dampened by the publication of a drab *Instrumentum laboris* that seems to be motivated more by worry about threatened official positions than by concern or empathy for the actual life of families. This document follows the format of a rather stilted questionnaire that was widely distributed and that the laity received gratefully. Now one is left wondering if the questionnaire was an inquisition on the cheap, and if, having noted the *dubia* rife among the people of God the bishops will simply provide *responsa* in the time-honoured format, and in the customary negative tones. The credibility of the Synod may be saved by the presence of lay observers. Disheartening is the thought that episcopal collegiality offers no relief from a crushing conservatism, and could even intensify it due to the increased influence of bishops from less enlightened local churches, as has happened in the Anglican Communion.

Another buzzword, "reform of the Curia," underestimates the difficulty of what that task entails. It is not a matter of cornering certain key figures

22   Ibid., 149.

and telling them to "clean up their act." Bishops sometimes call the Curia the "bureaucracy of the void."[23] If it were a well-ordered organisation such as one might imagine the CIA or the KGB to have been, one might be able to change it by appointing strong figures in key positions. But it may be so much in thrall to hallowed dysfunctional routines and so opaque in its operations that to tackle it is like trying to give backbone to a lump of jelly – a jelly that instinctively fights back and stings any hand that would reshape it. But even if the Curia is seen as an admirable bureaucracy, it seems to be one that is set in its ways, relying on authoritative papal and canonical documents that are immunised against the question whether they properly reflect the nature of the church and its faith. A more effective Curia could spell the death knell of a communal and collegial church, subjecting the life of the faithful even more intensively to Roman centralism.

Church and Kingdom

The eschatological relationship between the church and the Kingdom of God is mentioned early in *Lumen Gentium*: the church has a "mission to proclaim and to spread among all peoples the Kingdom of Christ and of God and to be, on earth, the initial budding forth of that kingdom. While it slowly grows, the church strains toward the completed Kingdom" (n. 5). The section on "the eschatological nature of the pilgrim church" calls the church back to its original identity as a community inspired by the teachings and presence of Christ and striving toward their eschatological fulfilment. The presentation of the eschaton is rather flat, however, with drab strings of scriptural quotations: "The pilgrim church in her sacraments and institutions, which pertain to this present time, has the appearance of this world which is passing and she herself dwells among creatures who groan

---

23   See Alberto Melloni, "*Questions from History for Tomorrow's Council,*" *The Japan Mission Journal* 59 (2005), 252–262; 258.

and travail in pain until now and await the revelation of the sons of God" (*n.* 48). The eschatological mission of the church is not strongly enough connected here with Jesus' preaching of the Kingdom, and with the prophetic tradition of Israel, nor is it sufficiently linked with justice and peace and the task of building up the Kingdom in the earthly city. Generally speaking, the prolix Council documents content themselves with sketching an ideal, using biblical rather than contemporary terms, and do not address at all the forces the militate against the ideal, for instance, the tension between charism and power signaled by Leonardo Boff and many others.

Although the image of God's people on their way sets the church and its history in perspective and does equal justice to its human and divine dimensions, it, too, has remained rather vague and has not found convincing concrete embodiment. Thomas O'Loughlin remarks: "I think we may have missed the boat in thinking of renewal in terms of the church or the people of God – we tried that in the 60s and 70s and nothing much happened – stymied by inertia long before the reactionary backlash. I think now the only way forward for Christian faith is by way of discipleship and building small communities from the bottom up – and the whole ecclesia empowering and resourcing these gatherings of disciples."[24] The New Testament has some scenes of high church politics, as in the "Council of Jerusalem" in Acts 15, but on the whole the model of churchhood it gives us is that of small groups engaged in prayer, worship, charitable works. Here is where the church stands or falls. Unity in faith and in church order among a vast population of 1,200,000,000 believers must entail some controlling mechanisms, but these should be empowering resources, not a repressive police. Much greater liberty and freedom to create must be accorded to the local communities, each in their particular circumstances producing an original variation on the gospel themes.

Steeping oneself in the culture of the early church one comes to envisage a network of local communities, all striving together toward the Kingdom, bound by communion and friendship, and reaching out too in friendship to communities from other denominations or other faiths,

24   Personal communication.

continuing the Christian tradition with a new maturity, preserved from disaggregation by their pastors but not bruised by them or processed into conformist routine. Vatican II's image of the people of God on their way to the eschatological goal seemed too open to the guardians of orthodoxy, and Vatican II's glorification of the church was hijacked not only for reassertion of papal authority but for blatant amalgamations of the sort the Council has prised open – the church of Christ no longer merely "subsisted in" the Catholic church (*LG*, n. 8), but *was* that church; the church no longer strove toward the Kingdom, but *was* that Kingdom on earth; a fortiori Jesus was not a prophet of the Kingdom but the Kingdom in person, the *autobasileia*, a phrase of Origen picked up by Henri de Lubac and Benedict XVI. Thus existential and historical realism is lost and the church becomes once again an inscrutable mystery to be preserved intact; inevitably this was accompanied by an effort to restore the pre-Vatican II liturgy. But beautiful images of the Mystical Body or the Bride of Christ, lack reality if dissociated from the actual life of the people and their struggles in history.

Critics of lay movements in the church or of the basic communities favoured in liberation theology see their efforts at creative renewal as a bid for power. The Congregation of Bishops expressed the fear in 1997 that diocesan synods might be placed in opposition to the bishop on the grounds of representing the people of God. The Irish church has held no diocesan synods since the Council, and though the idea of a national synod was mooted in the 1970s, nothing came of it. A national synod in Britain in 1980 ruffled feathers by a declaration against *Humanae Vitae*, and there was little follow-up. The agendas of lay movements do sound like a laundry list of complaints rather than a concrete plan for action, and when the abolition of celibacy and the ordination of women head the list, bishops are all too likely to protest, as Archbishop Diarmuid Martin did a few years ago, that everything cannot be "up for grabs."

While the Council envisaged primarily a lay apostolate in the secular sphere, the collapse in vocations to ordained ministry has had the effect of drawing laity increasingly into ministerial roles, such as presiding at funerals. Theological qualifications are now found among lay people to an unprecedented degree. These new lay competences and responsibilities should be expressed in structural reforms, for instance in giving the laity a voice in the choice of priests and bishops. If bishops need to courageously claim and express their collegial dignity, their equal co-exercise of the power of teaching and governing with the bishops of Rome, so do lay people need to claim their charisms and give them full expression. Much can be learned from the example of Anglican parishes, where every Sunday one can hear a well-prepared and engaging sermon, where the music (organist, choir, congregation) is of high quality in terms of piety and theology, where the congregation report on their works of charity and are empowered to continue them, where bible study groups and book groups abound, where new or visiting worshippers make themselves known and are welcomed with a round of applause, where over coffee the togetherness of the service is continued, where members make long journeys to be present and former members revisit with gratitude and nostalgia, where the Eucharist is celebrated reverently and in appropriate language. Of course there are also very many vibrant and happy Roman Catholic parishes, but I strongly believe we should be consulting our fellow-Christians about the dynamics of worship. It is together with them that we advance on the pilgrim path to the Kingdom.

The Ambiguities of Communion

A church pervaded by the spirit of communion, celebrated in warm exchanges at every level, would give an attractive face both to episcopal collegiality and Petrine primacy, correcting the legalistic, hierarchical model of churchhood. But in recent decades, the ecclesiology of communion has been heavily promoted in a rather distorted form, no longer nourishing the dynamic forward movement of the people of God but morphing into an ideology of communion with the past, proven by seamless continuity. The popularity of this notion of "communio" in theological schools and with the papacy has not promoted a capacious theological vision of the church, for it is much less well-founded in a grasp of the church's biblical foundations and historical development than the vision of Vatican II, and also because the architects of the communio-ecclesiology seemed to pit it against the conciliar ecclesiology of Congar and Küng. When we are told that an "ecclesiology of communion" is "the central and fundamental idea of the documents of the Second Vatican Council," and when this communion is described abstractly as meaning that "the church is called during her earthly pilgrimage to maintain and promote communion with the Triune God and communion among the faithful" (John Paul II, *Ecclesia de Eucharistia*, n. 34), it is hard not to suspect that communion is invoked here to play down collegiality, once hailed as "the backbone of the Council" of its "centre of gravity."[25]

John Paul II's document *Pastor Bonus* (1988) "exudes a strong sense of primatialism, with *communio*, unity and service the updated language for describing the subsidiary and subordinate role played at universal governance level by the episcopal college."[26] "It looks as if *communio* is believed to thrive through passive obedience and silence on any subject of controversy. Yet many commentators think the opposite, that the church is being weakened by the absence of healthy flows upwards and downwards of information and opinion."[27]

John Paul II deplored that "in some places the practice of Eucharistic adoration has been almost completely abandoned ... abuses have occurred, leading to confusion with regard to sound faith," and that the Eucharist is "celebrated as if it were simply a fraternal banquet," leading to "ecumenical initiatives which, albeit well-intentioned, indulge in Eucharistic practices contrary to the discipline by which the church expresses her faith" (*Ecclesia de Eucharistia*, n. 10). This may miss the real depth of our eucharistic crisis, which has less to do with theology than with the lack of vitality, meaning, and a true sense of community in our liturgies. The alleged ambiguities of intercommunion are as nothing in comparison with the ambiguities of a celebration in which language and body language negate real communication and community. More than 80 per cent of the footnotes to

25 Legrand, "Les évêques," 464.
26 McAleese, *Quo Vadis?*, 134.
27 Ibid., 156.

this encyclical are to Vatican documents, particularly those composed by John Paul II himself. Such self-referentiality undercuts the persuasiveness of these documents, giving the impression that the author wants to draw his hearers into his own circle of ideas with not enough effort to open up to ideas coming from other sources.

Communio also describes the group feeling of the new Catholic movements, who look only to the pope as the embodiment of authority. However, the church has failed to provide a broad tent under which lay movements of many kinds could flourish, in a truly pluralistic fellowship or *koinōnia*. Of the new movements promoted by Rome, such as Opus Dei, the Focolare, Comunione e liberazione, Faggioli writes: "The post-Vatican II, anti-modern anguish embodied by the movements has contributed to the failure of the conciliar and synodal institutions in the church and to the suppression of subsidiarity in the relations between Rome and the local churches, in favor of a modernistic presidential style of leadership that is not traditional and not Catholic."[28] Communion thus, in a painful irony, becomes a codeword for a short-circuiting of the true flow of teaching and governance in the church, which is marked by participation, dialogue, and collegiality.

The basic texture of Christian life, communion in the broadest and best sense, must be recovered before the meaning of Eucharist and ministry becomes perspicuous again. The Bible, especially in Genesis, begins not with institutional structures, but with the texture of ordinary human community, friendships, family, earthly society. It is on this foundation that it then expounds the idea of a holy people, the people of the Mosaic Covenant, the people renewed and inspired by the message of the Prophets. The primary concern of church renewal should be the authenticity of human relationships in the church. Parishes should, of course, always be places of warmth, welcome, sharing, and the upper echelons of church bureaucracy should be at the service of this, and should bathe in its glow. The texture of human community centers not on animal warmth but on free and intelligent communication, and nothing brings more joy to a Christian community

---

28   Massimo Faggioli, "The New Catholic Movements, Vatican II and Freedom in the Catholic Church," *The Japan Mission Journal* 62 (2008), 75–84.

than successful events of communication within its ranks or of respectful debate with those outside them. Here models of community developed in the modern world have much to teach the church. There should not be a painful mismatch between the eucharistic community and what is liberating and enriching in contemporary, democratic experience of community. If the church community is to be a model for warmer, more just, and more inclusive relationships in society at large, it must speak a language of community that makes sense outside its precincts.

The Challenges of Governance

The Catholic church is the largest and oldest organisation in the world, and cannot be run without thorough discipline. The degree of theological and liturgical uniformity among its more than a billion members remains a remarkable phenomenon. But does it justify an excessive concentration of power and responsibility at the very top? Authorities that are complied with rather than obeyed, without a warm relationship of listening (*ob-audire*) and willing cooperation, will fail to win real respect, which means not only that John XXIII's "new order of human relationships" has not materialised, but that a breakdown of real discipline has already begun.

A peculiarly sensitive area of church governance concerns the regulation of theological thought, expression, and teaching. The Congregation for the Doctrine of the Faith is faulted for slighting due process and for failing to adopt the constructive and helpful role envisaged for it by Paul VI after the Council. But a deeper source of unease is the clash between the modern culture of free thought, with its sacred rights of freedom of conscience, of opinion, of expression, of publication, and academic freedom, and the obligation to subscribe to a detailed set of tenets under pain of excommunication or loss of livelihood.

Since the Fathers of the church devoted a huge amount of their energy to defending the faith against heretics, it can hardly be denied that the defence of sound teaching is a valid form of serving the church. But zeal for orthodoxy can be destructive, not only when it fails to respect the consciences of the erring, but when it is exercised through structural channels that are too narrow. Effectiveness in detecting and punishing error is no guarantee that the growth of truth is being encouraged; the wheat may in fact be plucked with the tares. Here again collegiality supplies a possible solution: let the cultivation of orthodoxy be a praxis of the entire people of God, in a climate of discussion and free exchange of thought.

To be sure, we must be wary of an angelistic idea of the church as a community that has banished conflict. Doctrine and discipline cannot be maintained by a rosy consensus, allowing freedom of conscience and freedom of thought to flourish unchecked. In the early church, bishops gathered in synods to thrash out controversies about such disciplinary matters as the date of Easter or such doctrinal matters as the heterodox teaching of Paul of Samosata, bishop of Antioch (deposed in 268 CE). It is not clear that the authority to bind and to loose (Mt 16:19; 18:18; Jn 20:23) will be any easier to accept when it is exercised by local hierarchies, say in the USA, Australia, or the Philippines, rather than by the CDF. While defenders of orthodoxy are often theologically backward, it can hardly be denied that the task of upholding core convictions on the Trinity, Christ, the Atonement, and the Eucharist is as urgent today as ever. Dialogue and cooperation between theologians and bishops has a crucial importance here, and its absence is something in which neither group can take any comfort.

Vatican II is to some extent spoilt by its uncritical retention of a vocabulary of inerrancy and infallibility that carries modern associations of Cartesian certitude and suggests a clutching at epistemological control. Still under the spell of Vatican I, the Council accorded infallibility not only to the Pope but to the bishops and the laity: "The entire body of the faithful, anointed as they are by the Holy One, cannot err in matters of belief. They manifest this special property by means of the whole people's supernatural discernment in matters of faith when 'from the Bishops down to the last of the lay faithful' they show universal agreement in matters of faith and morals." (*LG*, n. 12). Here the prophetic role of the laity is reduced to the discernment of dogmatic truth: the assurance that they cannot err in matters of belief is on the same plane as the rigid view of scriptural inerrancy, which *Dei Verbum* could not overcome. The cult of "universal agreement" suggests a noetic paradise where all minds magically accord. A heritage of certitudes about the nature of the church, carried over from the Tridentine period, or expanded by the addition of the Roman scholastic doctrine of the infallibility of the universal magisterium (*LG*, n. 25), is amalgamated with the biblical vision with no effort to problematise critically the pluralism of ecclesiological ideas over the centuries. The privilege of infallibility, though so rarely exercised by a pope, is now extended to all bishops, and defining faith and morals is presented as the chief activity of bishops. Whatever their underlying meaning, the terms "infallibility" and (biblical) "inerrancy" convey to the modern ear a misleading view of theological truth. The Council could have made an act of radical trust by sticking with the term "indefectibility," the indefectibility of the Holy Spirit which has little to do with foolproof automatic guarantees.

The claim that Catholics alone enjoy the fullness of truth, and alone enact that truth in an integral way, leads to a bullying insistence that anyone who refuses to join the church is guilty, indeed damnable: "Whosoever, therefore, knowing that the Catholic church was made necessary by Christ, would refuse to enter or to remain in it, could not be saved" (*LG*, n. 14). Conservative Catholic theologians today still solemnly debate the conditions under which non-Catholics or atheists may be saved, suggesting for example that God may give them a final illumination in limbo after death before sending them on to purgatory. What is needed here is a broader perspective on the religious history of humankind, and a more optimistic vision of how divine truth and grace is at work in it, within which the Catholic claims could come into focus more persuasively. Here is a case where obsessing about the letter of the Council is not a guarantee of orthodoxy but rather a falling away from the breadth of perspective which is essential to true orthodoxy.

It is another mark of the lack of courage and imagination of post-conciliar Catholicism, and the paralysing effects of the urge to control, that the phrase "ecumenical dialogue" is likely to conjure up not a joyous and stimulating sharing of traditions in a renewed quest for deeper understanding of the Scriptures, but rather a cautious, scruple-ridden negotiation around doctrinal niceties. Indeed, Benedict XVI at one point was saying the there is no possibility of theological dialogue with religions outside the Christian fold; we can collaborate on them only on ethical and social projects.

Fear of compromising orthodoxy has kept ecumenism on a tight leash. Any idea or gesture that suggests a yielding or a laxity meets a nervous reaction. Thus Paul VI's generous reference to the church of England as "our sister church" was disowned by a note from the CDF in 2000. The only vision of church unity that effectively operates is still one in which all Christians will offer obeisance to Roman authority and its claims. The family of Christian churches, as a pluralism of traditions, is seen as a reality *de facto*, but not *de iure*, and the fear of letting it proliferate at the expense of the *de iure* status of the church of Rome has meant that little of the potential for sharing and mutual instruction between the churches has been realised. Missing in all this is a sufficient sense that if the Catholic church enters into real dialogue with the other churches, it is bound to be radically changed in the process. Dialogue entails mutuality, and parity among the discussants – which inevitably creates tensions for all claims of authority and superiority.

We can hope that the next Council will adopt a more radically trusting, kenotic stance, learning to let go of all these encumbrances. In doing so, it may complete and rescue Vatican II as Vatican II completed Vatican I. There is a dialectic that points forward, a tension that can be resolved only in a deeper commitment to the spirit of Vatican II, and it is becoming increasingly clear that the only alternative to this path of life is one of regression and decay. The surprise of the "Francis effect" may be the harbinger of a Catholic revival in the true key of the Council. He will not meet "the imperative of expectation" unless he takes daring structural steps, such as to use a "possibility allowed by the Council, and designate the Synod of Bishops as a standing decision-making body representative of the College of Bishops."[29] But he has made encouraging programmatic statements: "A juridical status of episcopal conferences which would see them as subjects

---

29   Mary McAleese, "Pope Francis and Collegiality," *The Japan Mission Journal* 68 (2014), 75–81; 81, 79; see also Juan Masiá, "Reviewing Synodality: Walking Together with the Bishop of Rome," ibid., 97–104.

of specific attributions, including genuine doctrinal authority, has not yet been sufficiently elaborated. Excessive centralisation, rather than proving helpful, complicates the church's life and missionary outreach" (*Evangelii gaudium*, n. 32). Perhaps the spirit of the Council will blossom afresh, not only in these upper echelons, but in a culture of constructive open discussion and creative innovation in all our communities and assemblies.[30]

30   See also J.S. O'Leary, "Vatican II: The Unfinished Council," *The Japan Mission Journal* 66 (2012), 273–282.

PART VII

Unfinished Business:
Ongoing Challenges for Irish Catholicism

FAINCHE RYAN

16   Vatican II and the Question of Ministry

Every ecumenical Council manifests or puts on display, to some extent, what the church really is.

That those who gather at a Council carry lofty titles (pope, patriarch, cardinal, archbishop, bishop, religious superior, theologian) and wear somewhat unusual garb should not distract us from the fact that, at heart, they are brothers and sisters (women did play their part, however circumscribed it may have been) in the faith to all other Catholic Christians. Their deliberations represent, in a dramatic form, what the church is called to be.[1]

Richard Gaillardetz's reflection, influenced by his reading of the work of Yves Congar, indicates where any discussion of ministry must begin – in the context of a discussion of "what the church really is". For this reason the first task of the essay is to recall the ecclesiology of Vatican II, in particular as expressed in *Lumen Gentium* 26. Secondly, we shall consider how this ecclesiology has been expressed or perhaps more correctly been allowed to express itself, in the fifty years since Vatican II. In this regard attention will be paid to ministerial expressions which were virtually non-existent before the Council, and thus unimagined in the eras immediately prior to the Council. The "revival" of the permanent diaconate shall also be critiqued. Finally, in the third section, we shall look at the Irish context, to see how the universal movements of the Spirit find particular expression.

---

1   Richard R. Gaillardetz, "Conversation Starters: Dialogue and deliberation during Vatican II" in *America*, February 13, 2012. <http://americamagazine.org/issue/5128/article/conversation-starters> accessed 5/6/2014.

Part One: "This church of Christ", *Lumen Gentium* 26

Ministry is an ecclesial activity, and thus the foundational issue is which
vision of the church is operative. From this point of view, the key conciliar
text is *Lumen Gentium*, the Dogmatic Constitution on the church,[2] for this
Constitution has things to say with influence into the future. One must
learn from the ecclesial perspectives developed in *Lumen Gentium* in order
to properly interpret the theology of ministry found in the decree on the
ministry and life of priests *Presbyterorum ordinis*,[3] or indeed the decree on
the apostolate of the laity, *Apostolicam Actuositatem*.[4]

In *Lumen Gentium* is found the most radical remembering of what
the church is called to be – the "new People called by God" (LG 26). The
opening of this document is replete with descriptions of the church. The
church is a mystery, it "is in Christ like a sacrament or as a sign and instrument both of a very closely knit union with God and of the unity of
the whole human race" (LG 1) ... "The church, or, in other words, the
kingdom of Christ now present in mystery, grows visibly through the
power of God in the world." (LG 3) In *Lumen Gentium* paragraph four
there is a particular emphasis on the presence of the Holy Spirit dwell-
ing "in the church and in the hearts of the faithful as in a Temple ...
By the power of the gospel the Spirit permits the church to keep the
freshness of youth". (LG 4) The universal church is seen to be a "people
brought into unity from the unity of the Father, the Son and the Holy
Spirit" (LG 4).

2   <http://www.vatican.va/archive/hist_councils/ii_vatican_council/documents/
     vat-ii_const_19641121_lumen-gentium_en.html>.
3   <http://www.vatican.va/archive/hist_councils/ii_vatican_council/documents/
     vat-ii_decree_19651207_presbyterorum-ordinis_en.html>.
4   <http://www.vatican.va/archive/hist_councils/ii_vatican_council/documents/
     vat-ii_decree_19651118_apostolicam-actuositatem_en.html>.

In paragraph 26 of *Lumen Gentium* a profound vision of Church is articulated. A central passage states:

> In any community of the altar, under the sacred ministry of the bishop, there is exhibited a symbol of that charity and "unity of the mystical Body, without which there can be no salvation." (ST III q. 73 a. 3) In these communities, though frequently small and poor, or living in the Diaspora, Christ is present, and in virtue of His presence there is brought together one, holy, catholic and apostolic Church. (LG 26)

In this paragraph we have a rich understanding of how the local church is to be understood. The church is fully present wherever legitimate local congregations (*legitimis fidelium congregationibus localibus*) are gathered together by the preaching of the gospel, to celebrate the mystery of the Lord's Supper. The full mystery of Christ is present here, signified by the ministry of the Bishop (and priest) in a congregation gathered, a community. In this ecclesiology Bishop and congregation are relational concepts – no matter how small a gathering, the whole Christ prays where the people are gathered with their Bishop, and the Holy Spirit is active in the gathering.

It is, as a *whole*, as a charismatically gifted community, that we are church. This newly recovered understanding of Church necessitated new discussions on ministry. If, as the ecclesiology of Vatican II suggests, the Holy Spirit breathes life into the church as a whole, and not just some parts, in exploring questions of ministry we need to open new doors, and windows. The community are a gifted people. One of the main struggles since Vatican II has been to try and recognise how the Holy Spirit continues to sanctify the church, to renew it, and how the Spirit equips and directs with hierarchical and charismatic gifts so that the church may grow in the "way of all truth" (LG 4).

In parallel with this emphasis on the entire community *Lumen Gentium* is concerned to present the church as an ordered community. In this way it maintains a distinction between the ordained and the laity:

> Though they differ from one another in essence and not only in degree, the common priesthood of the faithful and the ministerial or hierarchical priesthood are nonetheless interrelated: each of them in its own special way is a participation in the one priesthood of Christ. (LG 10)

The document thus retains the language of "hierarchy" first introduced by the work of Dionysius the Areopagite, probably in the late fifth century.[5] At the same time it modifies this top down model by using in parallel ministerial or hierarchical, the word ministerial indicating a service *among* the community of the baptised. This tension between the two models remains evident in *Presbyterorum ordinis*. In general then it must be said that when Vatican II speaks of the gifts of the non-ordained members of the charismatic community we tend to hear of a lay *apostolate* rather than the language of ministry. The vocabulary of ministry in Vatican II documents is mostly associated with bishop, priest, deacon.

Part II: Developments in the Fifty Years Since Vatican II

In the aftermath of Vatican II these distinctions did not serve well the needs of the ecclesial community. As new gifts began to appear, and new needs became apparent, the importance of correct theological language came to be seen as crucial. Indeed just as there were many creative developments in ministerial gifts and activities so too theology, and theological language had to develop in innovative ways. Some people speak of the lay apostolate, and others of lay ministry, some see these terms as synonymous, others not. Language carries a theological vision, and so expresses a particular vision of the church, a particular vision of God. It is crucial we strive to get language right ... with the help of the Holy Spirit.

Hans Küng, in his post Vatican II work, *The Church*, articulated well the phenomenon of a church in growth. He expressed the belief that God calls us, the church of Christ, "constantly to new decisions of faith, to a free responsibility, to loving service ... (for) Changing times demand

5   <http://plato.stanford.edu/entries/pseudo-dionysius-areopagite/#CelEccHie>. Accessed 9 July 2014.

changing forms."[6] At the same time he is well aware that not every change in form is "in accordance with the church's nature. Here we come to the problem of what criteria we have to help us distinguish whether the church is true or false."[7]

All developments, changes within the church have to subject themselves to constant appraisal to ascertain if in this way, with this change, the People of God are facilitated to grow more deeply into the "way of all truth".

This applies no less to the question of ministry. *Lumen Gentium* 26, cited above, is clear: The church of Christ is present in all legitimate local congregations of the faithful ... united with their pastors ... Christ is present in these communities, and it is in virtue of Christ's presence there is brought together one, holy, catholic and apostolic church. The text continues, "For 'the partaking of the body and blood of Christ does nothing other than make us be transformed into that which we consume'" (LG 26).

These ecclesial insights were in many ways ground breaking. They spoke of a gifted people, of the Spirit indwelling and inspiring the whole people, they spoke of church as community gathered with its bishop around a communion table. The decree on the ministry and life of priests *Presbyterorum ordinis*, teaches that it is Christ's whole Mystical Body, the church, which shares "in the anointing of the Spirit with which he himself is anointed ... Therefore, there is no member who does not have a part in the mission of the whole Body" (PO 2). For this reason many believed that ministries were to be shared more widely with suitable people amongst whom it was discerned the Holy Spirit was calling ... or so the teachings of the Second Vatican Council seemed to imply.

Developments at the local church, in very many places, expressed in a variety of ways this new vision of the wider church, to a greater or lesser extent. These developments, for the most part, far outran church documents and theological articulations. *Ministeria quaedam* (Pope Paul VI, 1972) was an effort to bring stability and order, as well as to foster an orderly

---

6   Hans Küng, *The church* (London: Search Press, 1968), 263.
7   Hans Küng, *The church* (London: Search Press, 1968), 263.

ecclesiological advance.[8] This Apostolic Letter (On first tonsure, minor orders, and the subdiaconate), gives hope when it declares "What is obsolete in these offices will thus be removed and what is useful retained; also anything new that is needed will be introduced and at the same time the requirements for candidates for holy orders will be established."[9] It speaks of the Christian people as "a chosen race, a royal priesthood, a holy nation, a purchased people" (I Pt 2:9; see 2:4–5) who have a right and duty by reason of their baptism to full and active participation in the liturgy. The document is eloquent in its discussion on "the ministries of the word and of the altar" "that in the Latin church are called the offices of *reader* and *acolyte* and the subdiaconate" (MQ). These ministries, in accordance with the contemporary outlook, are no longer to be called minor orders and so "their conferral will not be called *ordination*, but *institution*" (MQ).

This significant change indicates that change is possible when deemed desirable. This arrangement, the document insists, will bring out more clearly the distinction between clergy and laity, between what is proper and reserved to the clergy and what can be entrusted to the laity. Citing *Lumen Gentium* 10, *Ministeria quaedam* suggests that this change will also help to express more clearly that mutuality by which the universal priesthood of believers and the ministerial or hierarchic priesthood, though different, are "nonetheless interrelated", each sharing in the one priesthood of Christ. All very interesting thus far, and for the most part positive. The teachings indicate a people moving ever more deeply into the ecclesial reality which emerged from Vatican II.

Reading on, however, one discovers that "in accordance with the ancient tradition of the church, institution to the ministries of reader and acolyte is reserved to men". (MQ no. 7) This astounding statement should give us pause from the perspective of today's ecclesial realities. As we pause, and think again, we recall that there is no explicit treatment of the role of

8   <http://www.vatican.va/holy_father/paul_vi/motu_proprio/documents/hf_p-vi_
     motu-proprio_19720815_ministeria-quaedam_lt.html>.

9   Pope Paul VI, *Ministeria quaedam*, Apostolic Letter given *Motu Proprio*: On first
     tonsure, minor orders, and the subdiaconate (1972) Hereafter as MQ. <http://www.
     ewtn.com/library/papaldoc/p6minors.htm>. Accessed 16 June 2014.

women in ministry in any of the Vatican II documents. To judge from the way in which *Ministeria Quaedam* developed its teaching, it seems that in church documents the term "laity" may frequently be read as meaning men, i.e. males. This seems extraordinary. As one is no longer ordained but rather instituted as a reader or an acolyte there is no danger of a "creeping ordination" here. Yet even these ministries are not to be opened to women except in extraordinary circumstances. It follows that for women to read in mass, or to distribute communion (while frequent today in many places) is not to be deemed "normal" to the official church but is happening only because of extraordinary necessity.[10]

It is no surprise then that the question of women's involvement in ministry remains a vigorous topic of theological discourse, and simultaneously an area where church discipline seems to lack theological informing. It also does little to enamour the church to the world of many Irish women today. Tension is evident.

The current code of Canon Law offers little comfort. Canon 230 §1 allows for lay men (*Viri laici*), to be admitted to the ministries of lector

10   Indeed the official teachings pertaining to the use of male or female "extraordinary" ministers of the Eucharist are insightful as to a particular vision of church and ecclesial ministry, which it might be argued, is not totally at one with the ecclesiology emanating from Vatican II. The General Instruction on the Roman Missal is clear: "In the distribution of Communion the Priest may be assisted by other Priests who happen to be present. If such Priests are not present and there is a truly large number of communicants, the Priest may call upon extraordinary ministers to assist him, that is, duly instituted acolytes or even other faithful who have been duly deputed for this purpose. In case of necessity, the Priest may depute suitable faithful for this single occasion./These ministers should not approach the altar before the Priest has received Communion, and they are always to receive from the hands of the Priest Celebrant the vessel containing the species of the Most Holy Eucharist for distribution to the faithful." [162]. <http://www.usccb.org/prayer-and-worship/the-mass/general-instruction-of-the-roman-missal/girm-chapter-4.cfm>. Accessed 14 June 2014. See also *Interdicasterial Instruction on certain questions regarding the collaboration of the non-ordained faithful in the sacred ministry of Priests, Ecclesiae de mysterio*, August 15, 1997, art. 8: Roman Missal, Appendix III, *Rite of Deputing a Minister to Distribute Holy Communion on a Single Occasion*.

and acolyte, lay persons (this seems to include women) can fulfil these functions only "by temporary designation" (Can. 230 §2) and

> When the need of the church warrants it and ministers are lacking, lay persons, even if they are not lectors or acolytes, can also supply certain of their duties, namely, to exercise the ministry of the word, to preside over liturgical prayers, to confer baptism, and to distribute Holy Communion, according to the prescripts of the law. (Can. 230 §3)

There seems to be no theological warrant for the teaching, simply a matter of need. If women can perform duties in case of necessity, why can they not undertake these roles as ministries? The whole thing really is quite extraordinary.

The issue of female altar servers is also extraordinary. For a long time prohibited and yet active in many parishes, where parish priests permitted, now many young girls are privileged with the ability to serve at the Eucharistic table. It is truly astonishing to be reminded that, as with (male and female) extraordinary ministers of the Eucharist, women or girls serving at the altar happens by way of exception. Canon 230 §2 lays down that: "Lay persons can fulfil the function of lector in liturgical actions by temporary designation. All lay persons can also perform the functions of commentator or cantor, or other functions, according to the norm of law" [*Laici ex temporanea deputatione in actionibus liturgicis munus lectoris implere possunt; item omnes laici muneribus commentatoris, cantoris aliisve ad normam iuris fungi possunt.*]

In 1992 the Pontifical Council for the interpretation of Legislative Texts, were approached for clarity in the interpretation of this text. In short, they were asked to address the following issues: 1) can the liturgical functions which the canon teaches may be entrusted to the lay faithful, be carried out equally by men and women, and 2) if these liturgical functions include serving at the altar. The answer affirmed these interpretations, (*laici, sive viri sive mulieres*) with the following clarifications:

> 1) Canon 230 #2 has a permissive and not a preceptive character: "*Laici ... possunt.*" Hence the permission given in this regard by some Bishops can in no way be considered as binding on other Bishops. In fact, *it is the competence of each Bishop*, in his diocese, after hearing the opinion of the Episcopal Conference, *to make a prudential*

judgment on what to do, with a view to the ordered development of liturgical life in his own diocese.[11] [emphasis mine]

The clarification continues. If, "for particular reasons" a bishop in a diocese decides that women may also serve at the altar, this decision must be clearly explained to the faithful, making clear that women frequently do serve at altar, and indeed frequently serve as lectors and distribute Holy Communion as Extraordinary Ministers of the Eucharist. "These liturgical services mentioned above are carried out by lay people *ex temporanea deputatione*, according to the judgment of the Bishop, without lay people, be they men or women, having any right to exercise them."[12]

This way of understanding lay participation in ministry lies in tension with the theological vision of Vatican II, and indeed with the actuality of church life in many parts of the world today.

church discipline, rather than theology seems to provide the guiding principal. The following incident perhaps indicates the reason for the tension, and restrictions. On 5th November 1995 in the Parish of Santi Mario e Famiglia Martiri in Romanina, a suburb on the outskirts of Rome, John Paul II celebrated Mass. Among the altar servers were four eleven-year-old girls, Michela, Eleonora, Giovanna, and Serena. One year after the issuance of the Vatican Communication on Female Altar Servers, John Paul II was seen to lend concrete support to altar girls. The Holy See responded to this event with a statement which recognised that while it was "normal for girls to serve mass beside the Pope, because it is prescribed by a Vatican document" ... "this does not mean that the church is willing to review its rejection of female priesthood."[13]

---

11   Vatican Communication on Female Altar Servers. Congregation for Divine Worship Rome, 15 March 1994 <http://www.ewtn.com/library/curia/cdwcomm.htm>. Accessed 6 June 2014.

12   Vatican Communication on Female Altar Servers. Congregation for Divine Worship Rome, 15 March 1994 <http://www.ewtn.com/library/curia/cdwcomm.htm>. Accessed 6 June 2014.

13   <http://vaticaninsider.lastampa.it/en/inquiries-and-interviews/detail/articolo/chierichette-altar-girls-monaguillas-gesuiti-jesuits-jesuitas-8698/>. Accessed 10 July 2014.

So, positively there is change. My son and daughter can both serve at mass, but my daughter or mother or sister or wife can only do so for particular reasons, if the Bishop permits. While church teaching counsels that this norm is "already being widely applied" and women "frequently serve as lectors in the Liturgy and can also be called upon to distribute Holy Communion as Extraordinary Ministers of the Eucharist and to carry out other functions", the restriction of the "Bishop permits" still applies.[14] While similar restrictions apply to "lay" men, the possibility for formal institution of men to the roles of acolyte or lector exists. Again, in practice this is rare. So, while it is normal practice for the church to have men and women serving as lectors and as ministers of the Eucharist, and to have girls as altar servers, our teachings tell us this is all exceptional and extraordinary. In summary then, it is normal practice to have men and women serving at mass, and distributing communion, and girls as altar servers. All the while the official position is that this is exceptional and extraordinary.

The restoration of the deaconate was another major initiation undertaken under the aegis of the Second Vatican Council, "in complete continuity with ancient Tradition and the specific decision of the Council of Trent".[15]

Although the Council of Trent disposed that the permanent Diaconate be restored, this prescription was not carried into effect. It was left to the second Vatican Council to "to restore the diaconate as a proper and permanent rank of the hierarchy … (and confer it) even upon married men, provided they be of more mature age, and also on suitable young men for whom, however, the law of celibacy must remain in force" [2].[16] Three reasons are identified as underpinning this decision: "(i) a desire to enrich the church with the functions of the diaconate, which otherwise, in many

---

14   Congregation for Divine Worship Rome, <http://www.ewtn.com/library/curia/
      cdwcomm.htm>. Accessed 6/6/2014.
15   *Joint Declaration, Congregation for Catholic Education Congregation for the Clergy*,
      <http://www.vatican.va/roman_curia/congregations/ccatheduc/documents/
      rc_con_ccatheduc_doc_31031998_directorium-diaconi_en.html>. Accessed 14
      June 2014.
16   *Joint Declaration, Congregation for Catholic Education Congregation for the Clergy*.

regions, could only be exercised with great difficulty; (ii) the intention of strengthening with the grace of diaconal ordination those who already exercised many of the functions of the Diaconate; (iii) a concern to pro-vide regions, where there was a shortage of clergy, with sacred ministers".[17]

John Paul II also saw it important to insure that the permanent deaco-nate was recognised as helping to "complete the picture of the ecclesiastical hierarchy".[18] Deacons are ordained. "It is both convenient and useful" that men called to this ministry "be strengthened by the imposition of hands, which has come down from the Apostles, and more closely united to the altar so as to exercise their ministry more fruitfully through the sacramental grace of the diaconate".[19]

Many questions arise from the restoration of the permanent diaconate. The fact that the deacon is ordained marks the first time in a millennium, in the church of the Latin Rite, that one could be ordained to a clerical order whose identity is not directly linked to *leadership* of the Eucharistic celebration. The distinct identity of the deacon is yet to be satisfactorily described. In the above quotation John Paul has linked the identity to a service closely united to the altar, other theological reflection emphasises that the deacon is called to serve.[20] J.V. Taylor asserts that those who "hope

17   The Joint Declaration continues: "Such reasons make clear that the restoration of the permanent Diaconate was in no manner intended to prejudice the meaning, role or flourishing of the ministerial priesthood, which must always be fostered because of its indispensability." Here again there is an expression of felt need to "protect" the ministerial priesthood.

18   Deacons are called to Life of Holiness, Pope John Paul II Catechesis at the General Audience of October 20, 1993 <http://www.ewtn.com/library/PAPALDOC/JP931020.htm>.

19   Joint Declaration, Congregation for Catholic Education Congregation for the Clergy, paragraph 3 <http://www.vatican.va/roman_curia/congregations/ccatheduc/documents/rc_con_ccatheduc_doc_31031998_directorium-diaconi_en.html>. See also *Lumen Gentium* 29.

20   The ministry of the deacon is characterised by the exercise of the three *munera* proper to the ordained ministry: the *munus docendi* (proclaim the Scriptures, instruct the people; the *munus sanctificandi* (he assists in the administration of baptism, in the custody and distribution of the Eucharist, in assisting at and blessing marriages, in

to build a service-theology ... on the actual use of words like *diakonos*" will be disappointed.[21] John N. Collins, in his *Diakonia. Re-Interpreting the Ancient Sources*, also challenges the idea of deacons as ordained to serve.[22]

Nathan Mitchell's assertion that the distinctiveness of the renewed permanent diaconate lies in "pastoral leadership":

> By restoring the diaconate as a permanent role with the church's ordained leadership, Paul VI implicitly broke the long-standing connection between ordination and "sacramental power." ... Theirs is a ministry, rooted like all others in a recognition of baptismal charism, that places pastoral leadership before sacramental power. The diaconate represents, then, those New Testament qualities of ministry which Schillebeeckx has aptly described as "the apostolic building up of the community through preaching, admonition and leadership." The restoration of the diaconate is thus important not because it resurrects an ancient order that had all but faded in the West, but because it affirms the principle that *recognition of pastoral leadership is the fundamental basis for calling a Christian to ordained ministry.*[23] [Emphasis in the original.]

This brings us to the crux of the matter. Today, in all parts of the world, a variety of people exercise pastoral leadership in the church. Similarly many, women and men, assist with service at the altar.

---

presiding at the rites of funeral and burial, in the administration of sacramentals); the *munus regendi* involves works of charity and the direction of communities or sectors of church life, especially as regards charitable activities. According to the norms, this latter is "most characteristic of the deacon". Basic Norms for the Formation of Permanent Deacons, Congregation for Catholic Education *ratio fundamentalis institutionis diaconorum permanentium* 9. <http://www.vatican.va/roman_curia/congregations/ccatheduc/documents/rc_con_ccatheduc_doc_31031998_directorium-diaconi_en.html>. Accessed 14 June 2014.

21   J.V. Taylor, *The Go-Between God: The Holy Spirit and the Christian Mission (London: SCM 1972)*, 141.

22   John N. Collins, *Diakonia: Re-Interpreting the Ancient Sources* (Oxford: Oxford University Press, 2009).

23   Nathan Mitchell, OSB, *Mission and Ministry: History and Theology in the Sacrament of Order* (Wilmington, DE: Michael Glazier, Inc., 1982), 304.

This points toward a tension inherent in the documents of Vatican II. There is a clear desire to recognise the church as a pneumatological reality (LG 4) wherein developments in ministry would be seen as rooted in and dependent on the charismatic nature of Christ. Ministry is ecclesial, it is an activity of the church. Side by side with this lies an ecclesiology which recognises the importance of order in the church, an hierarchical order. These two visions need to speak to one another, for both are important for a Catholic church. The documents rediscovered the centrality of the People of God, the importance of collegiality and the ecclesiology of *communio*. They recognised the activity of the Spirit in the church, not just in parts of the Body, but in the whole Body of Christ. At the same time the hierarchical structure of the church was reemphasised, as was the distinctive nature of the ordained minister. The fact that little was done to develop a theology of orders which could flourish in the renewed ecclesiology has left us with many unanswered questions. This is clearly a real challenge for contemporary theology of ministry.

Many of the complexities of the post 1960 church receive clearest visibility in the area of Lay Ecclesial Ministry. Since Vatican II there has been a virtual explosion in the area termed pastoral leadership or lay ecclesial ministry, to use just two of the myriad of terms currently utilised. That many terms are used to describe this ministry of the non-ordained indicates perhaps a great richness of ministry, or alternately indicates a confusion of what we are trying to describe.

This form of ministry is new. Vatican II only opened the door a little to this vision of a church in which not only ordained people are recognised as ministers. The appreciation of *Lumen Gentium* 37 that lay people have a right "to receive in abundance from their spiritual shepherds the spiritual goods of the church, especially the assistance of the word of God and of the sacraments" and that they are to "openly reveal to them their needs and desires with that freedom and confidence which is fitting for children of God and brothers in Christ" is wonderful. Alongside it helps accentuate recognition of the inability of the traditional church structures to meet these needs.

The context of the church, in many places throughout the world is one of scarcity, and need. Joan Chittester's question daily becomes more pertinent:

> "What do they really need?" ... The question haunts me. What do the people really need in a period when the sacraments are being lost in a sacramental church. But all approaches to the question – even the consciousness that there is a question to be asked conscientiously about the nature and meaning of priesthood – is being blocked, obstructed, denied, and suppressed. "What do they really need?" becomes a haunting refrain in me for more reasons than the philosophical.[24]

Lumen Gentium paragraphs 35 and 41 indicate openness to, and a realisation of the spiritual giftedness of the lay person when it comes to apostolic work. *Apostolicam Actuositatem* continues on in this vein, seeing the lay apostolate as essential to the wellbeing of the church, and confirming the Spirit's action amongst all peoples (see AA 3). In its third chapter, *Apostolicam Actuositatem* gives numerous examples of the opportunities for pastoral work, work that might be termed ministry, that lie open for lay people.

The existence of Canon 517.2 of the 1983 Code indicates an official recognition of the necessity of these ministries: "If, because of a lack of priests, the diocesan bishop has decided that participation in the exercise of the pastoral care of a parish is to be entrusted to a deacon, to another person who is not a priest, or to a community of persons, he is to appoint some priest who, provided with the powers and faculties of a pastor, is to direct the pastoral care." Increasingly the church needs these people as there is "a lack of priests". The question a paper on ministry needs to ask is – does the good of the church not need these people *simpliciter*?

---

24   Joan Chittister, "Discipleship for a priestly people in a priestless period" Dublin 2001, <http://www.womenpriests.org/wow/chittist.asp>. Accessed 10 July 2014.

Part Three: Developments in Ireland Since Vatican II

In the years following Vatican II much happened. In the English speaking world the bishops in the United Kingdom and the United States produced some excellent documents.[25] These documents show a clear recognition not only of the need for active lay participation but also for its desirability if the church is to flourish. In the United States many parishes are managed and animated by laypeople, again most of whom are well qualified. In Germany and Switzerland people with excellent qualifications in theology have for many years now entered the work of ministry.

While these developments have had some influence in the Irish church, on the whole things have developed much more slowly. While religious sisters have, since Vatican II become increasingly active in parish ministry their work has frequently been "unofficial" and the conditions of their working environment have often been less than good. Voluntary work has helped enable some parishes to flourish, and increasingly dioceses have employed lay people in a variety of posts; more often administrative than actively pastoral it must be admitted.

In 2008 a new initiative was started in the Archdiocese of Dublin. It comprised of a selection process, followed by the training and employment of Parish Pastoral Workers.[26] This initiative, which was quite successful, now seems to have come to an end. Currently there are no more people in formation for this programme. At the same time the Archdiocese, together with many other dioceses in Ireland, has begun a programme for the permanent diaconate. The First Ordination of Permanent Deacons in the

---

25   The Bishops' Conference of England and Wales. *The Sign We Give*. Report from the Working Party on Collaborative Ministry (1995); Cardinal Roger Mahoney, and the Priests of the Archdiocese of Los Angeles, *As I Have Done for You* (2000); Committee on the Laity of the United States Conference of Catholic Bishops (USCCB) *Co-Workers in the Vineyard of the Lord: A Resource for Guiding the Development of Lay Ecclesial Ministry* (2005).

26   <http://www.kandle.ie/dublin-parish-pastoral-workers/>. Accessed 10 July 2014.

Archdiocese of Dublin took place in the Pro-Cathedral on 4 June 2012.[27]
The Parish Pastoral Worker initiative ended as a new form of ordained
ministry took root in the Irish church. Those entering Parish Pastoral Work
were required to have a primary degree in theology/religious education,
or equivalent, as well as relevant experience (and some applicants were
very highly qualified theologically).[28] The level of theological formation
required of the Deacon seems to be less.

An important issue here is canonical regulations about preaching.[29] As church teaching stands at present "presbyters and deacons possess the faculty of preaching everywhere" (Can. 764) while "lay persons
can be permitted to preach in a church or oratory, if necessity requires
it in certain circumstances or it seems advantageous in particular cases"
(Can. 766). The homily, a preeminent form of preaching, is reserved to a
priest or deacon (Can. 767 §1). Thus the situation is that some with high
level theological formation, together with pastoral experience, cannot
preach except by way of exception, those with diaconate training can
preach by right. While indeed preaching is a charism, it is one that normally requires theological formation. The Irish church, as it struggles to
find its way forward in a challenging environment, could not but benefit
from theologically informed preaching.

Apart from these significant developments, there have been many
creative advances in Ireland in these fifty years. The effects can be seen
in practically every parochial Eucharistic gathering. There will be readers and ministers of the Eucharist at nearly every parochial celebration

27   <http://vocations.dublindiocese.ie/documents/IHaveGivenYouAnExample_
      2ndEd__000.pdf> indicates that vocations to the Permanent Diaconate are still
      actively been sought, and welcomed.
28   <http://www.kandle.ie/dublin-parish-pastoral-workers/>. Accessed 10 July 2014.
29   Can. 766: "Lay persons can be permitted to preach in a church or oratory, if neces-
      sity requires it in certain circumstances or it seems advantageous in particular cases,
      according to the prescripts of the conference of bishops and without prejudice to
      can. 767.1." Can. 767.1: "Among the forms of preaching, the homily, which is part of
      the liturgy itself and is reserved to a priest or deacon, is preeminent; in the homily
      the mysteries of faith and the norms of Christian life are to be explained from the
      sacred text during the course of the liturgical year."

of the Eucharist. This is no longer extraordinary. Many have benefited from theological education, either at parish level, or in third level colleges. Many dioceses and religious congregations have employed lay people to participate in their core ministries. In some dioceses this is much more encouraged and flourishes better than in others. At the same time many people have found the lack of openness to the formal ministry of women in the church, discouraging. In parallel the lack of any genuine welcome to informed open debate on ministerial questions of great urgency is lamentable. Most seriously it has been evident for a long time that there will not be adequate priests to lead the assembly in Eucharistic liturgies, and yet no real openness to develop an adequate strategy, in consultation with all the faithful has been attempted. A younger generation is easily discouraged, and turns away, in the face of these realities.

A Way Forward?

The situation today is complex. Vatican II opened the possibility for a new vision of the church.

Some issues need clarification, ideally resolution, if the church is to move forward as a priestly people gathered round the Eucharistic table.

The first concerns the distinction between charism and ministry. While the distinction is not one that is mutually exclusive the key question as to who does what in the church is a central ecclesiological issue. Since Vatican II much has been written. Many align themselves with the thought of Hans Küng who suggests that people are baptised into ministry: "baptism ... initiates a person into charism and diaconal action, into a community that is essentially ministerial."[30] This idea of universal ministry seems to be rooted in German Protestant theology of the post Second World War

30　Hans Küng, *The Church* (1968), 247.

era.[31] Nathan Mitchell, following the same line of thought, noted that the entire ecclesial community is charismatic, and goes on to situate ministry as belonging to all the baptised. When Catholic theologians followed this vision of the church, confusion was encountered as it became clear that to call everything ministry is to call nothing ministry. Some theologians sought to overcome the confusion by speaking in terms of apostolate for the unordained and ministry for the ordained. However this line of thinking leaves us essentially back in the pre Vatican II era where the lay apostolate was a recognised entity, and without the resources to give a proper theological articulation to the new developments in pastoral leadership. The church, the People of God, is indeed a charismatically gifted community, but not everyone has a vocational call to ministry.

A second area where confusion has arisen concerns how ministry is to be properly understood. Theologians have found themselves immersed in a linguistic conundrum. The reinstatement of the permanent diaconate resulted in much discussion on the meaning of the Greek term *diakonia*.[32] This term has tended to be translated into English quite simply as "service". Many began to read this as saying all ministry is service, and thus the concept of service, or servant leadership becomes of great importance in the theologies of ordained ministry that developed at this time. But the concept of service, or indeed of servant leadership, cannot be the distinguishing characteristic of ordained ministry for the simple reason that all Christians are baptised into the commandment of love of neighbour. The vocation of the common priesthood all the baptised share is one of love and service. The call to ecclesial ministry is a call to something more. The

31   The essay by Ernest Käsemann, "Ministry and Community in the New Testament", in his *Essays on New Testament Themes*, trans. W.J. Montague (London: SCM, 1964), 63–94 was very influential here. Käsemann's ideas concurred with those of Eduard Schweizer originally published in 1946, reworked and presented in *church Order in the New Testament*, trans. F. Clarke (London: SCM, 1961), 100–101, 180. For more on this see John N. Collins, *Ordained and Other Ministries: Making a Difference in Ecclesiology* 3.1 (2006), 11–32: 12–17.

32   John N. Collins, *Diakonia: Re-Interpreting the Ancient Sources* (Oxford: Oxford University Press, 2009) is a key text here.

question that needs to be addressed is whether ecclesial ministry is limited to the ordained, or can some group of the baptised have a vocation that is ministerial, though not ordained.

In sum a number of ecclesiological anomalies in the area of ministry have arisen since Vatican II. Bernard Sesboüé identifies what he terms is a new kind of crisis of priestly identity and this is accompanied by a crisis when considering the ecclesial status of permanently employed lay ecclesial ministers. In line with this it seems evident that it is only when we rightfully conceive of how ordained ministry is to be understood, with its accompanying theology, can we properly develop a theology for permanent, and ordinary, lay ministry in the church. As things stand, when the church warrants it and ordained ministers are lacking lay persons can supply and fulfil certain tasks. "However, the exercise of such tasks does not make Pastors of the lay faithful: in fact, a person is not a minister simply in performing a task, but through sacramental ordination," (CL 23) It is clear that this is not a satisfactory solution to current ecclesial realities. It is difficult to justify theologically.

It seems to me that what is needed today is a profound revisiting of the ecclesial understanding of ordained ministry in the Catholic church. Following from this there will be the theological space for a proper theological articulation of other forms of ministry that have come to birth in the post Vatican II era. As the church attempts to address this issue theologically and practically, Joan Chittester's thoughtful vocational question comes to mind again: "What do the people really need in a period when the sacraments are being lost in a sacramental church?" Surely the Spirit is calling us to take that question seriously. We do not need to be fearful. We cannot afford to be fearful.

ENDA MCDONAGH

17 A New Style of Church and Theology After Vatican II

Debates abound and grow more divisive about the interpretation and implementation of Vatican II, its letter and spirit, its continuity and discontinuity with prior Councils and the earlier Christian tradition. Fresh light, at least for me, has been shed on these debates by other contributions in this collection. I have no desire to repeat or to evade the debates in this short reflection. In seeking some further understanding of Gospel and church in the light of Vatican II, I will be guided not just by its debates and documents but by my own "faith-wrestling" with "poetry and politics", as I sometimes describe the wider if secular sources of "revelation", which have preoccupied me for a life-time. One of the fruits of that struggle has been a growing acceptance of the significance of "style" or form in appreciating a particular art object, scientific discovery, communications or political system. While context and content are important they are always interdependent with, and sometimes simply dependent on, the style and method involved from which they may never be separated, without serious loss to the observer or participant.

Literary and art critics, writers and artists, very properly to my mind, emphasise the primacy of form in discerning content or meaning. The form shapes even determines the content for many. I encountered, to me, an unusual example of this in preparing a few thoughts for a recent Conference in Maynooth on the Bicentenary of the Birth of August Welby Pugin, Architect of the Main College Building. In his most significant written work, "The True Principles of Pointed or Christian Architecture" (1841), he stated. "The two great rules for design are these: 1st, that there should be no features about a building which are not necessary for convenience, construction, or propriety; 2nd, that all ornament should consist of enrichment of the essential construction of the building ... In pure architecture the smallest detail should have a meaning or serve a purpose". In this building (Newman House) it may be worth mentioning that John Henry Newman described Pugin as a genius (but a bigot because he was intolerant of any architecture other than Gothic). More relevantly Pugin's insistence on attending to form, content and context and his ruling out of ornamentation not enhancing the main construct, are also applicable/appropriate to works of literary and visual art. It is taking them a step further perhaps to apply them to a community and its communications. Yet in the case of church as community and of its structure and communications, the dominant form has for a long time been impersonal and juridical. And so the language of church self-presentation and of internal communication has been the legal language of command and obey, and the language of truth-presentation as that of propositions to be accepted by subjects in obedience. All this ignores the basic structure of teaching as one of persuasion, illumination and truth sharing.

Vatican II may seem an unlikely subject for a discussion of style. Applying the term style to a large organisation could seem far distant from its application to a person ("The style is the man"), a personal achievement such as a poem or other artistic objects, or ways of human behaviour, including of course modes of dress and address. The church for all the limitations of its visible structures is more deeply and fruitfully a set of relationships, a community, much more akin to a family than to organisations such as a commercial corporation or even to a political state. At least this is what the New Testament in its various descriptions like the community of Jesus' disciples or images such as the Body of Christ make clear. It is what Vatican II in its Constitution on the Church (*Lumen Gentium*) emphasises in so many ways from its crucial opening chapter on the Mystery of the Church.

Introduced in this way by its properly divine dimension the Mystery is then located in Chapter Two in the whole company of the Faithful, the People of God. The ordering of the community is reserved to Chapter Three on the Hierarchical Structure with its own divine stamp and new insight in its emphasis on Collegiality. This applies first of all to the College of Bishops with the Pope, in leading and ruling the church Universal. It also applies in diverse ways to the local church at parish, diocesan and regional levels. So the document continues in its illumination of the divine and human aspects of the church.

With that vision of community of disciples of Jesus, of brothers and sisters in Christ, the basic relationality in equality of all the People of God seems evident, and beyond that in the whole human community as has recently emerged. The ecclesial community calls for a language and style of communicating appropriate to its own relationships internally with Christ and one another. These may not be reduced to the aforementioned juridical forms with their superior and inferior implications and suggestions of authority and subject, command and obey, characteristic of some purely human and political societies. Vatican II is unique among Councils in its pervasive use of terms such as dialogue, in its adopting a dialogical style in its long debates among the bishops in the Aula and between the bishops and other consultants in the various commissions and committees preparing the documents to be debated. All this was underlined by the refusal of the Council to issue definitive documents usually associated with Councils of the past and invariably accompanied by the condemnatory "*Anathema sit*" directed at those who refused to accept the doctrine as defined.

In the church's communications style, where more than two or three or more are gathered together in His name, conversation in the presence of and about Jesus and His God, may be more appropriate a term than dialogue by reason of numbers and of the need to pay due respect to all the participants. In this context it may also apply more readily to participants beyond the community of Catholic believers. This had already begun at the Council as with the presence and very description of the "Separated Brothers and Sisters" in Christ, and to the members of the Jewish community and other religions in the very significant and innovative document "*Nostra Aetate*". More radically still it extended its conversational style to the whole human family in its Address (another significant and including word) to the Modern World in *Gaudium et Spes*.

The range of addressees, the respectful invitations voiced, the rejoicing in the human achievements and the sharing in human tragedy of so many, exposed further, deeper dimension of this conversational style. A real conversation demands a partnership, a real turning to the other as its common lineage with conversion already suggested. This is at the heart of all real talk about God and divine revelation, about and with human beings, their gifts and achievements, their failures and needs: all real theology. In conversing then with other Christians and beyond, we are not primarily, for example, trying to win arguments, a usually self-defeating project. We are trying to understand their position with heart and head, to be enriched and enlarged by their commitment and understanding as well as sharing our own with them. Such conversation involves mutual conversion, a loving relationship in community that deepens our relationships in and with Christ, even if it does not and should not remove all our differences. This applies beyond our Christian or even religious horizons as *Gaudium et Spes* clearly heralded.

Before exploring this more fully in terms of sacred and secular in the context of the present hostility so often manifested between some exclusivist advocates of both traditions (and in the light of my own preoccupations with poetry and politics and other human activities,) I need to step back a bit and analyse the differing poles in community/communion and difference/otherness, conversation and conversion.

Community is formed by the bonding in developing relationships of the different or other human beings, in which continuing mutual enrichment depends on respecting and preserving the continuing otherness in basic equality. So it is in marriage and family, in friendship and various forms of collegiality and collaboration. So it was among the early disciples with Christ and one another; so it was at the high-points of Vatican II. Only thus could you have such vigorous debates without breaching the fundamental unity or community. Only thus could you achieve such near unanimous agreement on so many controverted matters. Unfortunately that agreement and respect for otherness did not carry forward into succeeding decades for reasons too complex to be addressed here or perhaps anywhere in the present divisive atmosphere. For now I wish to confine myself briefly to a couple of particular points of sharp disagreement under the rubric of otherness and communion within the ambit of the two great Conciliar themes of the church and the modern world.

The first of these is gender difference or otherness of human beings as male and female. From the creation story to the Pauline image of Christ and the church as Bridegroom and Bride, this basic human otherness has offered particular forms of enrichment to the communion of humanity. Of course it involves the equality of man and woman not only in marriage but also in friendship, as colleagues in various professions, in citizenship in civil society and even in sainthood in the communion of saints. The equality has only slowly emerged in the secular world, the "City of Man", and still more slowly in the communion of the historical church as distinct from the communion of saints. This continuing failure in the Catholic church has deprived the community of the richness in worship and governance which such acceptance would inevitably bring. A very telling example is that of the breakthroughs in Catholic theology, which over the last fifty or sixty years women theologians have achieved. Many of our best Catholic theologians world-wide are now women and their number and achievements continue to grow in Ireland as elsewhere. Their exclusion from leadership has greatly impoverished the church's mission and its true sense of communion and discipleship. In this as in so many other areas the present Catholic leadership might well take a lead from its fellow-Christians as well as from its contemporary secular societies as suggested by the ecumenical and secular thrust of the Council documents.

In this connection it is not enough to speak of the potential of women in the prophetic activity of the church, which has historically been significant and is continued by many women-theologians today, not least because in practice it is subordinate to the priestly and kingly or ruling roles. Without the participation of women in these roles the equality and potential of women is neglected in their dignity as, equally with men, images of the Creator God and members of the Incarnate God, Christ. Indeed the image of the church as composed of such equal members of Christ by faith and Baptism is distorted.

The discrimination against women as candidates for ordination offends against the style of community and communications which Jesus initiated in the community of disciples and of the witnesses to the Resurrection. The New Testament accounts of Jesus' friendship with, love of women, even or perhaps especially and of public sinners like Mary of Magdala, or otherwise estranged from the Jewish community such as the Samaritan woman, sets a precedent, a binding precedent, which their exclusion from leadership in the church denies. The women's fidelity on Calvary after the male disciples had betrayed or denied and eventually all but the beloved disciple had deserted him, embodied their reciprocal loving leadership. It in turn was rewarded in their being called to be the first witnesses of the Resurrection. In so far as the traditional restrictions on women's roles in the church were cultural in origin and maintenance, they are now recognised as outmoded and unworthy. The willingness of Vatican II to learn from such contemporary developments should surely apply here.

Fuller reflection on the leadership of Jesus as expressed in the image and practice of the Good Shepherd rather than king or ruler and on the role of pastor in the world today, stretches well beyond that of the conventional reigning and ruling. Indeed the very qualities which Jesus exemplified as Good Shepherd, his compassion and his weeping with the wounded and bereaved, his mercy and readiness to forgive, his going in search of the lost sheep fit with regular female style, characteristics and behavior at least as well as with male.

The Jesus style of governing or ruling is illuminated by its merging with the wisdom tradition which underlines the loss of feminine wisdom and experience from the regular pastoral care and governance of the church. In this context the denial of ordination to women not only distorts the Jesus style of leadership. More obviously the confining of the priestly pastoral role to celibates reduces once more the pastoral range and style of the ordained priest's activity and too easily results in the clericalisation which has had such a negative influence. Of course there is the danger evident in some sister churches already of the clericalisation of women priests where they remain a small and restricted minority.

The need for married priests and the readmission of those already married to serve as priests is becoming more widely accepted in the church and can temper the move to clericalism. It must not be used to strengthen the opposition to the ordination of women. In terms of the style of community which Jesus initiated the inclusion of women in its pastoral and worshipping leadership has become increasingly essential.

The Council's opening to the secular world and its culture applied more sharply still to religious freedom and the integrity of conscience, personal entitlements denied or distorted through the nineteenth and first half of the twentieth centuries. The personal liberation which these implied appeared still very threatening to some of the Council Fathers. Today as we have so recently experienced in Ireland they continue to be at least distorted. So the the richness to Gospel understanding and living, which genuine theological diversity would bring, is being lost to us. Healthy difference as English theologian Kevin Kelly reminds us and on which Vatican II thrived, is being lost, labeled unacceptable dissent or even heresy without the kind of fair debate which is so valued in the best secular societies. We have had many sad examples of this unjust treatment of theologians and others in Ireland recently. The consequent damage to the church as teacher and exemplar of truth and justice and love after the manner of Jesus grows apace.

Various diagnoses of these failures to recognise and accept otherness in its enriching capacity are possible and at least partly true. Fear of the other and the otherness or strangeness is undoubtedly one. That is at least partly due to a failure of imagination. Otherness and its potential to enrich demand a lively and sympathetic imagination schooled in the larger world of beauty or style as well as unity, truth and goodness. It was that that kind of imagination which enabled the Council Fathers to move beyond the recent distortions of faith and practice by learning from such a variety of others, religious and secular, contemporary and historical. Some of these enriching others were not exclusively Christian or even religious. The Council's respect for human cultural achievements, in the arts and sciences as well as in the more traditional discipline of philosophy and the more pressing practice of politics, made demands on the imagination not entertained by even recent church leaders, at least outside the confines of a rather restricted range of religious topics. And so was that openness to contemporary art and culture that influenced the Council Fathers, consciously or unconsciously, their words and images, their attitudes and approaches, their style of address which formed the basic style of Vatican II. That style is under threat if not already eclipsed. It is for this and future generations to relearn that humane and Christian style of thought, address and imagination in the kinds of conversations and community which Vatican II symbolised. Our immediate responsibility is to strive to promote that style, integral to the Scriptures, particularly to the New Testament, in church and theology.

It should be acknowledged that these reflections were composed long before the advent of Pope Francis whose initial attitudes and activities with a new style of papacy suggest something of a new style of church and theology as advocated here. But that is a task for another conference.

PATRICK HANNON

18   Church and State in Ireland:
      Perspectives of Vatican II

Our title will have evoked the expectation of a piece about debates concerning the impingement of Catholic beliefs on the law of the land, and in the
fifty years since Vatican II there has indeed been much discussion of what
is fairly characterised as a Catholic influence on the Irish Constitution
and laws.[1] Practical matters at issue seem on the whole to have been settled: there has been a gradual loosening of the hold of "the church", as the
standard narrative has it, evidenced especially in the liberalisation of laws
on divorce, contraception, abortion, and homosexual relationships. But
some issues still await debate: it's unlikely that we've seen an end to argument about the law on abortion; a referendum on same-sex unions is in
the offing; and it may be supposed that assisted suicide and euthanasia will
come in question before long.

Moreover, discussion has now broadened beyond Irish domestic law.
For one thing, membership of the European Union, together with Ireland's
subscription to the European Convention on Human Rights, has meant
an impact of enactments of the European Parliament and of decisions
of the European Court of Human Rights. A Declaration appended to
the Treaty of Amsterdam (1997) provides that the Union "respects and
does not prejudice the status under national law of churches and religious

---

1   The Catholic church in Ireland extends over the entire island and church-state rela-
     tions at a juridical level differ as between the North and the Republic. An adequate
     treatment of both is impossible here, and attention is confined to the situation in
     the Republic.

associations or communities in the Member States".[2] This has no direct bearing on the jurisprudence of the Human Rights Court, which is an institution of the Council of Europe, and though the Court employs the doctrine of what's called the "margin of appreciation", which requires it to take account of cultural and philosophical differences in signatory states, its decisions may prompt legislative changes when a state is found in breach of the Convention.[3]

Catholic influence has not been confined to law, and there's still a strong Catholic presence in the patronage and management of education, albeit that most religiously owned post-primary schools are now staffed and managed by lay persons, and that the extension of patronage of primary schools to other interests is now well in train. Similarly, hospitals once managed and staffed by religious have passed to predominantly lay governorship, and a decline in vocations to religious life means that there is little or no religious representation on hospital staffs. But church ownership has meant that schools and hospitals are from time to time the sites of public controversy, when a professed Catholic ethos comes in conflict with employment policies or, in the case of hospitals, with some practice or procedure at odds with Catholic health care ethics.[4]

Changes in the Public Square

Controversy in either of these arenas is not new: think of Noel Browne's Mother and Child scheme in 1951, or of John McGahern when as a primary teacher in 1965 he was faced with dismissal following controversy

2   Official Journal C 340, 10 November 1997 p. 133. Further, "The European Union equally respects the status of philosophical and non-confessional organisations". Ibid.
3   For current law see Gerard Hogan and Gerry White, *J. M. Kelly: The Irish Constitution*, 4th edition (Dublin: Bloomsbury Professional, 2003).
4   *Religion, Education and the Constitution*, ed. Dermot Lane, Dublin: Columba Press, 1992, remains a valuable introduction to key issues.

over his novel *The Dark*. What is new is two-fold: first, Irish society has become religiously more plural and, second, Catholic practice has declined during the past several decades. Islam is now a significant presence, and membership of the Orthodox church has increased noticeably, thanks mainly to immigrants from Eastern Europe.[5] The significance for belief of the decline in Catholic practice is difficult to measure, and to what extent Irish society can be said to have become secularised is difficult to say, not least because of the protean character of the term secular and its cognates. But it looks as if that debate is moving gradually toward a question more fundamental than that of church-state relations, the question of the role of religion – any religion – in society.[6]

That question is live in the anglophone world in the United States especially, in main part owing to the emergence of what has come to be called the Christian Right, the outcome of an increased membership of evangelical Christian churches, and of an informal alliance between these and Catholic church leadership in face of certain moral and political problems in US society. In Europe the question is canvassed most prominently in

5   According to the 2011 census the church of Ireland remains the second largest religious grouping, showing some increase in membership since the census of 2006. Professed adherence to Buddhism and Hinduism has also increased slightly.

6   See Dermot Keogh, "The Catholic Church in Ireland since the 1950s", in Leslie Woodcock Tentler ed., *The Church Confronts Modernity: Catholicism Since 1950 in the United States, Ireland, and Quebec* (Washington DC: Catholic University of America Press, 2007), 93–149; also Lawrence Taylor, "Loss of Faith or Collapse of Empire?", Tentler op. cit. 150–173; and Michele Dillon, "Catholicism, Politics, and Culture in the Republic of Ireland", in Ted Jelen & Clyde Wilcox, *Religion and Politics in Comparative Perspective* (Cambridge: Cambridge University Press, 2006). John H. Whyte's *Church and State in Modern Ireland* 1923–1979 (2nd ed., Dublin: Gill and MacMillan, 1984), is authoritative for the period covered. Relevant theological issues are treated in, e.g., Enda McDonagh, *Vulnerable to the Holy* (Dublin: Columba Press, 2004), chapters 2–5; Gerry O'Hanlon SJ, *Theology in the Irish Public Square* (Dublin: Columba Press, 2010); Thomas O'Loughlin, "The Credibility of the Catholic Church as Public Actor", *New Blackfriars* 94 (1050), March 2013, 129–147; Patrick Hannon "Religion, the Constitution, and the New Ireland", *Irish Theological Quarterly* 74 (3) 2009, 258–271; also, "Christian Values in a Pluralist Society" in Hannon, *Right or Wrong: Essays in Moral Theology* (Dublin: Veritas, 2009), 85–100.

France, where an influx of Islamic peoples has challenged the church-state doctrine known as *läicité*. Controversy over the wearing of the burqa or niqab – both involving full face covering – in schools and various public places has provoked a response on the state's part which is hard to reconcile with mainstream interpretations of religious freedom and the rights of minorities.[7]

7   A judgment of the European Court of Human Rights dated July 1st, 2014 held that France's ban on the wearing of the burqa or the niqab is not in breach of Article 9 of the European Convention of Human Rights and Fundamental Freedoms. Article 9 states a right to freedom of religious belief and practice, "subject only to such limitations as are prescribed by law and are necessary in a democratic society in the interests of public safety, for the protection of public order, health or morals, or for the protection of the rights and freedoms of others" (§2). The Court found the ban justified inasmuch as its intent is "to guarantee the conditions of 'living together' as an element of the 'protection of the rights and freedoms of others'", thus necessary in a democratic society, making it a legitimate exception under §2. See *France v S.A.S.*, Grand Chamber, European Court of Human Rights, 1 July 2014, at <http://hudoc.echr.coe.int/sites/eng/>. In addition to its narrative of Court jurisprudence the judgment provides a legislative history of the statute, an account of comparable legislation in Belgium, the Netherlands and Spain, and a summary of relevant international law and practice. Thus it affords an introduction both to the issue of full-face covering in France and to the approach of the Court to issues of religious freedom at the interface of human rights law under the Convention and the domestic law of signatory states. See also *Lautsi v Italy* (2011), involving the display of a crucifix in the classrooms of a state school: judgment at <http://hudoc.echr.coe.int/sites/eng/>. A summary of this and other cases concerning religious symbols and clothing is available on a fact sheet published by the Court's Press Unit at <http://www.echr.coe.int/Documents/FS_Religious_Symbols_ENG.pdf>. See also M.D. Evans, "Freedom of religion and the European Convention on Human Rights: approaches, trends, and tensions" in P. Cane, C. Evans, and Z. Robinson, eds, *Law and Religion in Theoretical and Historical Context* (Cambridge: Cambridge University Press, 2008, 291–315. On the controversy over the wearing of the niqab at school, three important books are anthropologist J.R. Bowen's study *Why the French Don't Like Headscarves: Islam, the State, and Public Space* (Princeton: Princeton University Press, 2008), historian J. Wallach Scott's *The Politics of the Veil* (Princeton: Princeton University Press, 2009), and *Critical Republicanism: The Hijab Controversy in Political Philosophy* (Oxford: Oxford University Press, 2008) by Cécile Laborde, professor of Political Theory and director of the Religion and Political Theory Centre at the University of London.

Underlying philosophical issues are debated extensively at an academic level in both the United States and Europe, John Rawls and Richard Rorty being two of the most influential thinkers in the US, Jürgen Habermas and Marcel Gauchet among the most notable in Europe. On both continents discussion is usually conducted under the heading "religion in the public square" or "religion and the public sphere", or "public reason", and the net question has been whether it's proper to allow religious argument a place in civic debate. An initially negative answer was premised on the notion that secular discourse is neutral, but this approach has over time been undermined, both directly and by way of fall-out from a wider epistemological critique. Rawls, Rorty, and Habermas all came to modify their views, eventually conceding that religious argument is admissible, so long as the conclusion can also – and will eventually – be articulated in non-religious terms.[8]

So the way in which questions about law and morality are framed in the future will be against a background much changed from that of the decades after Vatican II. An added factor, of course, is the problem of credibility resulting from the child abuse scandal; the difficulty of recovering trust in Catholic institutions can scarcely be overstated. The concept of church reflected in the Council's deliberations and decisions stresses the role of laity. Yet the bishops, individually and collectively, remain charged with oversight of Catholic witness to the Gospel, and their presence in the public square remains important. I hope to show here that the legacy of the Council furnishes the makings of a constructive church contribution for the future, and there is much of pastoral value to be derived from a careful attention to both Constitutions on the church.

---

8   See J. Rawls, "The Idea of Public Reason: Postscript," in J. Bohman and W. Rehg, eds, *Deliberative Democracy: Essays on Politics and Reason* (Cambridge, MA: Harvard University Press, 1997), 131–141; R. Rorty, "Religion in the Public Square: a Reconsideration", *The Journal of Religious Ethics* 31, 1 (2003), 141–149; J. Habermas, "Religion in the Public Sphere", *European Journal of Philosophy* 14 (2006), 1–25. Especially noteworthy for Catholic theology is J. Habermas and J. Ratzinger, *The Dialectics of Secularization: On Reason and Religion*, tr. B. McNeil (San Francisco: Ignatius, 2006). See the section "Further Reading" at the end of this chapter.

Past Debates

But what of church intervention in such debates in Ireland since the Council? It's anachronistic to criticise past episcopal statements for lack of awareness of dimensions of their context that hadn't yet come properly into view, and in any case my interest here is not in finding fault. There is something to be learned from the interventions of the past few decades and their reception, and a brief review will serve. The essence of what I have to say is that whereas the Conference's statements generally accorded well with the Council's Declaration on Religious Freedom (*Dignitatis humanae*), they suffered from insufficient attention to some themes of the Constitution on the church (*Lumen gentium*) and of the Constitution on the church in the Modern World (*Gaudium et spes*).

The Declaration on Religious Freedom proposed a new way of looking at the meaning of religious freedom, seeing it as grounded in the dignity of the person and in the nature of the search for truth. On this basis the Council declared a right to religious freedom, meaning that no-one is to be forced to act in a manner contrary to conscience, or prevented from acting according to conscience, "within due limits". These limits are later said to be the requirements of the common good and, in a formula familiar now in Catholic social teaching, the requirements of the common good are summarised as those of peace, justice, and public morality.[9] The freedom that the Council had primarily in mind concerns religious as distinct from moral matters, though a wider conscience freedom seems to be be intimated in paragraph 3.[10] But in any case the argument on which the principle of religious freedom rests – the dignity of the person and the nature of the search for truth – can found a principle of freedom of conscience in moral

---

9   The foregoing is a summary of the Declaration's teaching as set out in paragraphs 2, 3, and 7. For background see G. Alberigo & J.A. Komonchak, *History of Vatican II*, vol. 4, Maryknoll, NY and Leuven 2004.

10   *Dignitatis humanae*, par 7. All translations are as at the Vatican website <http://www.vatican.va/archive/hist_councils/ii_vatican_council/index.htm>, adapted where necessary in favour of inclusive language.

matters too, for human dignity and the nature of the search for truth as the Declaration understands it are at root not different as regards morality.

The Irish Bishops' Conference statements on law and morality, beginning with their reaction to the decision in the *McGee* case in 1974,[11] have taken their cue from the Council's declaration that people must be free to follow conscience, subject to the requirements of the common good. And the bishops have evolved a mode of address of these issues having three characteristic components. Adverting to a distinction between morality and law, they reiterate Catholic teaching on the morality of each; acknowledge the right and responsibility of the lawmaker or the citizen to decide what form legislation might take; and set out the Conference's view of the measure in question, in terms of its likely impact on the common good.

A look at all of the Conference's statements shows that the balance of the components varied somewhat as between one topic or another, indeed as between one statement and another on the same topic. The reason for the variation isn't evident on the face of the statements themselves. It can't be traced to "growing conservatism", for its incidence isn't chronologically linear. Nor is it relatable to the gravity of the issues: the first statement on abortion (1982) contains the clearest affirmation of a legitimate autonomy of the political sphere, the second statement on contraception (1978) the least clear.

What are we to make of this? Perhaps the first thing to say is that the statements are not academic accounts of the relationship between law and morality. They are, rather, the concrete response of the bishops to a concrete pastoral situation as this was perceived by the Conference at the time. Whether a perception was valid, whether a particular response was in the circumstances the most apt, is no doubt debatable, and debated even among the bishops themselves. The point is that each was an exercise in the concrete application of principle, from which we should never expect the neatness of a text-book treatment. Hence we needn't be surprised if at one time there was a strong emphasis on the substantive morality of (say) abortion; at another, more attention given the lawmaker's right to

11 *McGee v. The Attorney General* [1974] IR 284.

decide on forms of legislation; yet another time, much stress on what the bishops thought would be the impact of certain kinds of law. The differing emphases reflected the Conference's perception of the requirements of its pastoral function at a particular time. But no doubt they also answered to assumptions on the bishops' part about the nature and style of the leadership required of them. So for example if a Conference's sense of its role is paternalistic, its stance will be anxious and protective. It's likely to dwell upon the hazards which a proposal appears to entail, and to be forceful in warning agains it. It must, if it's not to be unfaithful to principle, grant the right of citizens and legislators to make up their minds as to what law is best. But the stress will be on a negative appraisal, and its recognition of the lawmaker's freedom will be pro tanto muted.

And to some extent this kind of anxiety has marked the hierarchy's handling of the debates in question here. It appeared in an extreme form in their second statement on contraception, which came close to discounting the lawmaker's right to decide what the law should be. To be fair, this wasn't typical: an explicit acknowledgment of the rights of lawmakers and voters is normally made. One would have to say, though, that the dominant impression left by the statement is of the bishops' resistance on the several issues in debate. No doubt this is what was intended. After all, if the Conference is persuaded of the undesirability of a legislative measure it's only to be expected that it will register its objections. And I am far from suggesting that there is no place for a critique of policies or legislation which a society or its governors may have in mind. But a stance and style that seems anxious and protective is inappropriate when one is addressing an adult people.

Then there's the matter of the content. It may be, as some of the statements say or imply, that but for the bishops some aspects would receive insufficient attention. Yet most of the considerations that the bishops highlight are of a kind that will surface in any civic debate. Of course it may be replied that that's not the point: what's important is that the bishops are seen to support or oppose a contemplated development, the influence of "the church" brought to bear on the course of events. But this raises questions of theology that are more fundamental still. For it seems to presuppose a view of the church as composed of the leaders and the led, with the led being said by the leaders in religious and civic matters alike; and that conception is simply untrue to the self-understanding of the Catholic church today.

As it turned out, the bishops' caveats seldom if ever had the desired effect. An exception was the first referendum on abortion, and it can be surmised that the bishops' opposition, anticipated or actual, delayed the introduction of legislation on the availability of contraceptives, to take an obvious example. But on the only other occasion on which the result coincided with the Conference's view – the 1986 referendum on divorce – it's not unlikely that the amendment's rejection owed more to fears about property ownership and inheritance than to religious or moral conviction or church allegiance. In any case, and whatever the reasons for past rejection of their views, it's important, in terms of the bishops' own teaching objectives, that citizens and legislators are encouraged to take responsibility for the shaping of Ireland's future.[12] The moral and political maturity which this bespeaks won't be achieved in an ethos which is experienced as negative and untrusting. And this is where attention to themes of *Lumen gentium* and *Gaudium et spes* can help.

A Fresh Start

The first of these themes concerns the place of the lay member of the church. As early as the opening chapter of *Lumen gentium*, entitled The Mystery of the church, the Council drew attention to the fact that all the faithful are members of the body of Christ which is the church. Moreover, "in the building up of Christ's Body various members and functions have their part to play".[13] In chapter 2 on The People of God, the

---

12   For important observations from the vantage-point of political philosophy see Patrick Riordan SJ, "The Purpose of the Law: the Case of Same-Sex Marriage", *Studies* 103, no. 409 (2014), 10–20.

13   *Lumen gentium* (hereinafter *LG*), paragraph 7.

Council affirmed every lay member's share in the priesthood of Jesus.[14] And, it continues, "[t]he holy people of God shares also in Christ's prophetic office; it spreads abroad a living witness to Him, especially by means of a life of faith and charity and by offering to God a sacrifice of praise, the tribute of lips which give praise to His name".[15] However, "[i]t is not only through the sacraments and the ministries of the church that the Holy Spirit sanctifies and leads the people of God and enriches it with virtues but, allotting His gifts to everyone according as He wills, He distributes special graces among the faithful of every rank. By these gifts He makes them fit and ready to undertake the various tasks and offices which contribute toward the renewal and building up of the church".[16]

These passages refer in the first place to the life of the church *ad intra*, but they are relevant here because they affirm the dignity of each member of Christ's church, and they honour the variety of gifts among the faithful in consequence of the indwelling of the Holy Spirit; for it can hardly be said that that dignity and the variety of gifts are any the less to be honoured when the faithful follow their baptismal calling in the world. In fact "[w]hat specifically characterises the laity is their secular nature", the Council later says,[17] and "by their very vocation, [they] seek the kingdom of God by engaging in temporal affairs and by ordering them according to the plan of God".[18] "Therefore ... it is their special task to order and to throw light upon these affairs so that they may come into being and then continually increase according to Christ, to the praise of the Creator and the Redeemer."[19]

---

14   *LG* 10. "Though they differ from one another in essence and not only in degree, the
       common priesthood of the faithful and the ministerial or hierarchical priesthood
       are nonetheless interrelated: each of them in its own special way is a participation
       in the one priesthood of Christ."
15   *LG* 12.
16   Ibid.
17   *LG* 31.
18   Ibid.
19   Ibid.

In view of the high calling of lay members of the church, it's not surprising to find the Council enjoining pastors to cherish and take heed of their potential. In chapter three, bishops are instructed to listen to all the faithful,[20] and chapter four on the laity contains a summons: "Let the spiritual shepherds recognise and promote the dignity as well as the responsibility of the laity in the church. Let them willingly employ their prudent advice. Let them confidently assign duties to them in the service of the church, allowing them freedom and room for action. Further, let them encourage lay people so that they may undertake tasks on their own initiative. Attentively in Christ, let them consider with fatherly love the projects, suggestions and desires proposed by the laity".[21]

Secularity Graced

The secularity of the lay calling is the theme too of a well-known paragraph of *Gaudium et spes*, where it blends with two other typically conciliar emphases. "It is to the laity, though not exclusively to them, that secular duties and activities properly belong", says the Council; "Therefore acting as citizens in the world, whether individually or socially, they will keep the laws proper to each discipline, and labor to equip themselves with a genuine expertise in their various fields".[22] Here is echoed an idea already mooted in an earlier paragraph, what the document calls the autonomy of earthly affairs.[23] The Council Fathers were at pains to stress that this doesn't mean independence of the Creator's purposes; but "[i]f by the autonomy of earthly affairs we mean that created things and societies themselves enjoy their own laws and values which must be gradually deciphered, put

---

20 *LG* 27.
21 *LG* 37.
22 *Gaudium et spes* (hereinafter *GS*), paragraph 43.
23 *GS* 36.

to use, and regulated by human beings, then it is entirely right to demand that autonomy".[24] This is no mere fad of modern times, therefore; rather it harmonises with the will of the Creator.[25] "For by the very circumstance of their having been created, all things are endowed with their own stability, truth, goodness, proper laws and order. The human person must respect these as they are isolated by the appropriate methods of the individual sciences or arts."[26]

That theme blends with one caught elsewhere in a sentence: Catholics "will gladly work with others who seek the same goals".[27] This follows from the secularity of the disciplines by which humans try to understand and order the material world and society, and is in tune with a note struck earlier: "Respect and love ought to be extended also to those who think or act differently than we do in social, political and even religious matters. In fact, the more deeply we come to understand their ways of thinking through such courtesy and love, the more easily will we be able to enter into dialogue with them".[28]

The theme of the secularity of the lay vocation blends also with a remark later in the paragraph: "Let the laity not imagine that their pastors are always such experts, that to every problem which arises ... they can readily give a concrete solution, or even that such is their mission".[29] This recalls a point made in the paragraph immediately preceding: "Christ ... gave His church no proper mission in the political, economic or social order. The purpose which He set before her is a religious one".[30] And it leads naturally to an observation of great practical importance. Often, says the Council, a Christian view of things will suggest a specific solution in certain circumstances: "Yet it happens rather frequently, and legitimately so, that with equal sincerity some of the faithful will disagree with others

24   Ibid.
25   Ibid.
26   Ibid.
27   Ibid.
28   *GS 28.*
29   *GS 43.*
30   *GS 42.*

on a given matter."[31] The Council Fathers were concerned lest solutions proposed on one side or another be confused with the Gospel's implications, saying that no-one may appropriate the church's authority for any particular opinion. By the same token, it's misguided to expect the bishops to attach more authority to a view than it's capable of bearing in mainline Catholic theology.

These themes of Vatican II provide pointers to the requirements of leadership at every level in the church of today and tomorrow, and I shall later draw some conclusions about the requirements of an effective church presence in the public square. I've reproduced the Council's own words because the passages quoted happen to illustrate, if only in an inevitably limited way, a valuable insight of the historian John W. O'Malley SJ. O'Malley refers to the "spirit"[32] of Vatican, and whilst acknowledging the term's vagueness he shows how it can be given content if one attends to the genre of the Council's documents. He is able to identify the genre as "epideictic", a mode of discourse found in patristic writing, and studied by Aristotle, Cicero and Quintilian among others, and explicitly distinguished by them from the discourse proper to the legislator or the judge.[33]

31 *GS 43.*
32 A recent fashion in some quarters of the church for disparaging Vatican II displays a special contempt for any reference to the Council's spirit. The nay-sayers seem unaware of the term's acceptability to the 1985 Extraordinary Synod (cf. *Origins* 15, no. 27, 19/12/85), and to theologians of the distinction of Karl Rahner, Yves Congar, Walter Kasper, and Avery Dulles.
33 J.W. O'Malley, *Vatican II: Did Anything Happen?* New York and London 2008, 76–83. O'Malley prefaces an analysis of the vocabulary of the documents with the observation: "As with the traditional genres used by Councils, the most concrete manifestation of the character of this genre, and therefore an important key to interpreting its import, is the vocabulary it adopts and fosters. Nowhere is that vocabulary more significant than in Vatican II and nowhere is the contrast greater between it and all preceding Councils. Nowhere is the vocabulary more indicative of what the genre stands for and therefore of the style of church the Council promoted by means of it." See also O'Malley, "The Style of Vatican II", *America* 188 (24/2/03).

Persuasion ...

The epideictic genre, O'Malley explains, is a form of the art of persuasion. "While it raises appreciation, it creates or fosters among those it addresses a realisation that they all share (or should share) the same ideals and need to work together to achieve them. This genre reminds people of what they have in common rather than what might divide them, and the reminder motivates them to cooperate in enterprises for the common good, to work for a common cause."[34] Those are the traits that characterise the discourse of Vatican 2, O'Malley says: "The Council was about persuading and inviting. To that end it used principally the epideictic genre. I am, of course, not saying that the bishops and theologians self-consciously adopted a specific genre of classical rhetoric as such. I am saying that the documents of the Council, for whatever reason, fit that pattern and therefore need to be interpreted accordingly".[35]

Turning to more specific implications of the Council's dicta, one might mention first the unmistakeable recognition of the dignity of each member of the church, a recognition that by itself should be enough to preclude an attitude of paternalism or condescension.[36] The same can be said of the injunction to bishops to listen to the lay faithful, and to all pastors to take note of the laity's "prudent advice";[37] and there is the salutary reminder that pastors can't give concrete solutions to every problem, "or even that such is their mission.[38] The particular competence of lay men and women, and the distinctiveness and secularity of their vocation, are emphases of the Council's ecclesiology which demand an unequivocal place in pastoral leadership now.

---

34   Op. cit., 76.
35   Op. cit., 77. It will no doubt have occurred to the reader that this applies also to the style of Pope Francis's letter *Evangelii gaudium*.
36   It may be perhaps taken for granted that authoritarianism is nowadays out of the question.
37   *LG* 37.
38   *GS* 43.

Since "Christ ... gave his church no proper mission in the political, economic or social order",[39] and granted a due autonomy of earthly affairs, and what *Lumen gentium* calls the secular nature of the lay vocation, it is especially important to recognise "that with equal sincerity some of the faithful will disagree with others on a given matter".[40] This has a bearing on the distinction drawn in moral theology, and acknowledged explicitly by some episcopal conferences, between general moral principle and the "prudential application" of principle to the facts of a situation. In the Catholic repertoire of moral values there are some principles said to hold always and without exception;[41] but not all are; and whether or how a moral principle is to be translated into law is a separate question again.[42] Judgments about concrete application of principle, and especially those about the embodiment of moral value in the law of the land, are apt to disclose differences of opinion, and opinions are often heavily coloured by political preferences. It has been a merit of the Irish Conference's statements that on the whole they have avoided any semblance of political partisanship.

39   *GS* 42.
40   *GS* 43.
41   *Gaudium et spes* itself at par. 27 gives a list of the evils envisaged in these principles. See also Pope St John Paul II's encyclical *Veritatis splendor*, par. 80 (<http://www.vatican.va/holy_father/john_paul_ii/encyclicals/documents/hf_jp-ii_enc_06081993_veritatis-splendor>).
42   Catholic moral theology possesses valuable resources on which to draw in regard to morality and law, notably the so-called Tract on Law of St Thomas Aquinas (*Summa Theologiae* 1a 2ae, qq 90–97); see "Aquinas, Morality and Law" in P. Hannon, *Right or Wrong? Essays in Moral Theology*, Dublin 2009, 123–136. The casuistry developed in Catholic moral-pastoral tradition under the heading "Cooperation in Evil" is useful for the practical application of principle; that it doesn't provide neat answers and is open to misuse are no reasons to overlook its potential.

... And Pacific Argument[43]

One other of the Council's themes is important for the future in Ireland; as expressed in words quoted earlier: "Respect and love ought to be extended also to those who think or act differently than we do in social, political and even religious matters. In fact, the more deeply we come to understand their ways of thinking through such courtesy and love, the more easily will we be able to enter into dialogue with them".[44] The reach of this injunction extends to other churches and faiths but not only to them, and if we heed the fact that census returns show an increase in the number of people not declaring affiliation to a religion, or declaring atheist or agnostic, suggests that religious leaders will henceforth have to take account of a secular presence in the public square.

This may not come easily to bishops, given that the ranks of the unbelieving or unaffiliated must include many former Catholics, some of whom will have little good to say for "the church". But the Council's injunction to respect those who think or act differently in social, political or religious matters applies to people outside of the religions as well as to those within, and it's wrong to dismiss the conscientiously held values of others just because they no longer subscribe to ours. Catholics in Ireland, moreover, have been learning painfully to pay attention to voices that tell of the sinfulness that is in the church. In any case it's unlikely that those who have relinquished allegiance to a religion will no longer have values in common with Catholic Christians, given the humanism of the Christian moral vision, a direct implication of belief in the incarnation of the Word in Jesus Christ.

---

43   "Persuasion and pacific argument" is how John Courtney Murray somewhere
      described the mode of discourse appropriate to church voices in the public square.
44   *GS* 28.

A New Question?

At the outset I suggested that our debates about church-state relations may be moving toward questions about the role of religion in society. If that is so we'll be joining, somewhat late in the day, a conversation that has been taking place in the United State over several decades, and intensively in some member-states of the European Union more recently. And we are not well prepared, if one can judge by debate up to now. The secularisation of Irish society tends to be viewed in terms of a waning of the influence of "the Catholic church", identified with church institutions and governance, a development welcomed or lamented depending on which "side" a commentator is coming from. But this is a superficial view of the concept and process, and distinctly unhelpful in practice.[45]

Owen Chadwick, writing of what he called the secularisation of the European mind, has maintained that the term secularisation describes "an objective process, still obscure in its causes and consequences but a matter of history".[46] He offers a definition: "the relation (whatever that is, which

45 It must be hoped that Ireland is spared any version of the culture wars which have bedevilled US debate on secularisation and religious freedom; high feeling and heated rhetoric generate tensions and conflicts which have little to do with the merits of positions in debate.
    A scholarly challenge to widely held assumptions regarding "liberal" attitudes toward religion is presented by Steven H. Schiffrin in *The Religious Left and Church-State Relations*, Princeton 2009. Schiffrin's focus is on US constitutional jurisprudence, but the argument of Part III, "Religion and Progressive Politics" could enrich thinking in most other parts of the West. See also Michael Perry, *The Political Morality of Liberal Democracy* (Cambridge: Cambridge University Press, 2010). For "conservative" perspectives see the *Catholicism and Religious Freedom: Contemporary Reflections on Vatican II's Declaration on Religious Liberty*, ed. K.L. Grasso and R.P. Hunt (Lanham: Rowman & Littlefield Publishers, 2006). A thought-provoking proposal for re-envisaging the issues is M. Scherer, *Beyond church and State: Democracy, Secularism, and Conversion* (Cambridge: Cambridge University Press, 2013).
46 O. Chadwick, *The Secularization of the European Mind in the Nineteenth Century* (Cambridge: Cambridge University Press, 1975), 264.

can only be known by historical enquiry) in which modern European civilisation and society stands to the Christian elements of its past, and the continuing Christian elements of its present".[47] The reflections which led Chadwick to favour this approach merit reproducing. "The word *secularisation* began as an emotive word, not far in its origins from the word *anticlericalism*". Sometimes it meant a freeing of the sciences, of learning, of the arts, from their theological origins or theological bias. Sometimes it meant the declining influence of churches, or of religion, in modern society. Then the sociologists, heirs of Comte, aided by certain historians and anthropologists, did a service by showing how deep-seated religion is in humanity and in the consensus which makes up society. They therefore made the word unemotional; a word used to describe a process, whatever that process was, in the changing relationship between religion and modern society, a process arising in part out of the industrial revolution and the new conditions of urban and mechanical life, in part out of the vast growth in new knowledge of various kinds."[48]

Chadwick remarks that modern sociologists – and others – haven't always restricted the term to neutral usage, and that it's sometimes used as a word of propaganda – propaganda, one fears, on both sides of the type of debate that's likely to erupt in Ireland when certain items of socio-moral import are broached. Strong feelings about moral values and deeply held convictions are natural, but they are not well served by a rhetoric which disrespects people who hold a different view.[49]

47   Ibid. The definition is in quotation marks and a footnote cites Lübbe, *Säkularisierung*, Freiburg 1965.
48   Ibid.
49   Words of Karl Rahner are apposite: "If Christians take seriously *as* Christians their socio-political task ..., then as individuals and as groups they cannot fail to work out ideas for the future ... which will be rejected by other Christians appealing to the same ultimate Christian principles and motivations ... But when Christians are opposed to Christians in this way there is bound to be a great deal of bitterness. They are fighting one another while appealing to what is for both sides an absolute criterion of living". For Rahner the answer is not to avoid the fray but "to learn, particularly in the church of the future, to maintain the church's unity and mutual love", something that "must be constantly learned and practiced". *The Shape of the church to Come*,

A Healthy Secularism

Owen Chadwick's observations present a starting-point for constructive discussion, and the discussion must also benefit from an awareness of the experience of other societies on both sides of the Atlantic. A proper study calls for interdisciplinary exchange between social and political theorists, sociologists of religion, philosophers and theologians, and religious and political leaders; and one might hope that Catholic bishops will recall the Council's stress on consultation and conversation with lay members of the faithful, not to mention other churches and faiths. But perhaps we can hope to take for granted what Josef Ratzinger as cardinal and as pope more than once described as a "healthy" secularism, a mentality and practice that accords proper autonomy to politics and its institutions whilst recognising the value of religious faith in answering to "an awareness of something missing", to borrow the title – and the theme – of an essay by Jürgen Habermas.[50]

The working out of this in practical terms is itself a process, involving tensions which arise from competing views of the common good, as we've seen from the recent experience of France, or the controversy in the US over the provision by employers of insurance cover for contraceptives when the employers think that the use of artificial contraceptives is morally wrong. Such controversy often originates in a legal problem, and a resolution depends on whatever constitutional theory underpins the decisions of the courts. But it may also challenge prevailing legal and political orthodoxies, as the French example shows.

The French thinking is one of the reasons that prompted Charles Taylor to argue that Western systems operate with a mistaken concept of secularism: "[w]e think that secularism (or *läicité*) has to do with the

---

tr. E. Quinn, London 1974, 126; from a chapter entitled "Socio-critical Church", all of which is pertinent to the our concerns here.

50 See e.g. J. Habermas et al., *An Awareness of What Is Missing: Faith and Reason in a Post-secular Age*, tr. C. Cronin (Cambridge: Cambridge University Press, 2010).

relation of the state and religion; whereas in fact it has to do with the (correct) response of the democratic state to diversity".[51] Taylor points out that the state and religion have three goals in common: "that they are concerned with 1. protecting people in their belonging to and/or practice of whatever outlook they choose or find themselves in; with 2. treating people equally whatever their choice; and 3. giving them all a hearing".[52] There is no reason, he says, to single out religion as against non-religious, "'secular' (in another widely used sense), or atheist viewpoints". Indeed, he concludes, the point of state neutrality is to avoid favouring or disfavouring not just religious positions but any basic position, religious or nonreligious: "[w]e can't favour Christianity over Islam, but also religion over against nonbelief in religion, or vice versa".[53]

The validity of Taylor's concept of secularism is at one level a question for the specialist in political or legal theory, but from a standpoint in Catholic tradition his argument is attractive. Especially engaging is his account of its practical implications, in elaborating which he glosses what he calls "the French Revolutionary trinity" – liberty, equality, and fraternity: 1. No-one is to be forced in the domain of religion or basic belief ... 2. There must be equality between people of different faiths or basic belief; no religious outlook or (religious or areligious) Weltanschauung can enjoy a privileged status, let alone be adopted as the official view of the state. Then 3. all spiritual families must be heard, included in the ongoing process of determining what the society is about (its political identity, and how it is going to realise these goals ... This ... is what corresponds to "fraternity".[54] The three goals can conflict, he acknowledges, and this suggests a fourth goal: "that we try as much as possible to maintain relations of harmony and

---

51   C. Taylor, "Why We Need a Radical Re-definition of Secularism", in Judith Butler, Jürgen Habermas, Charles Taylor, and Cornel West, *The Power of Religion in the Public Sphere*, New York 2011, 36. An expanded version of this, entitled "What Does Secularism Mean?", is included in Taylor's collection of essays *Dilemmas and Connections*; see note following the asterisk.

52   Ibid. and 37.

53   Ibid. Taylor's "basic belief" corresponds to Rawls's "comprehensive view of the good".

54   Op. cit. 34–35.

comity between the supporters of different religions and Weltanschauungen (maybe this is what really deserves to be called "fraternity").[55]

That fourth goal is idealistic, but Taylor's career has included active participation in politics in Quebec, so his thinking isn't to be dismissed as the high-minded theorising of a stereotyped inhabitant of the academy. And his fourth goal won't be alien to people of faith, least of all to people whose faith tradition goes back to Jesus of Nazareth. Pastoral leadership in the Christian tradition is not reducible to an exchange of ideas, and Christian values are kept alive through the living witness of all the baptised, not just through the ministry of those who have Gospel oversight. But a presence of the church in the public square is required by the church's mission, and Irish society will be impoverished if the challenges this presents in a secular age are not met.

Further Reading

The several layers of debate on secularisation have generated a vast and growing literature. This may be sampled in W.H. Swatos Jr. & D.V.A. Olson (eds), *The Secularization Debate*, Oxford and Lanham Md 2000; R. Bhargava (ed.), *Secularism and its Critics*, Oxford 2005; T. Gelen & C. Wilcox, *Religion and Politics in Comparative Perspective*, Cambridge 2006; J.R. Jakobsen & A. Pellegrini, *Secularisms*, Durham NC and London 2008; E. Shakman Hurd, *The Politics of Secularism in International Relations*, Princeton 2008; P. Cane, C. Evans, and Z. Robinson (eds), *Law and Religion in Theoretical and Historical Context*, Cambridge 2008; H. Joas & K. Wiegandt, *Secularization and the World Religions* (tr. A Skinner), Liverpool 2009; G.B. Levey & T. Modood (eds), *Secularism, Religion and Multicultural Citizenship*, Cambridge 2009; M. Warner, J. van Antwerpen, C. Colhoun (eds), *Varieties of Secularism in a Secular Age*, Cambridge MA

---

55   Ibid. and 35.

2010; C. Bender & and P.E. Klassen, *After Pluralism: Reimagining Religious Engagement*, New York 2010; C. Calhoun, M. Juergensmeyer, J. van Antwerpen (eds), Oxford 2011; B.S. Turner, *Religion and Modern Society: Citizenship, Secularisation and the State*, Cambridge 2011. Authorities in their fields such as Talal Asad, Robert Bellah, Rajav Bhargava, Steve Bruce, José Casanova, William E. Connolly, Grace Davie, Hans Joas, Danièle Hervieu-Léger, Saba Mahmood, Tariq Modood, Rodney Stark and Charles Taylor are among those whose work is represented in the collections, and perspectives other than western can be found in essays in nearly all of them.

In the sociology of religion the work of Peter Berger has aroused great interest, and not only because of his abandonment of the so-called secularisation theory – roughly, that with modernity and enlightenment the decline of religion was inevitable. For an introduction and evaluation see L. Woodhead, with P. Heelas and D. Martin, *Peter Berger and the Study of Religion*, London and New York 2001. Berger, with Grace Davie and Effie Fokas, explores a much discussed question in *Religious America, Secular Europe? Theme and Variations*, Farnham UK and Burlington VT 2008.

Charles Taylor's work in social and political theory is of course internationally acknowledged, and *A Secular Age* (Cambridge MA 2007) seems destined to achieve classic status. Section III of his *Dilemmas and Connections: Selected Essays* (Cambridge MA and London 2011) is called "Themes from *A Secular Age*", and the essays chosen, together with his *Varieties of Religion Today* (Cambridge MA 2002), are a preparation for engaging with the thesis of the larger work. A thought-provoking book by a political theorist is M. Scherer, *Beyond Church and State: Democracy, Secularism, and Conversion*, Cambridge 2013.

The most recent scholarly contribution from Catholic theology is a fine study by Kenneth R. Himes, *Christianity in the Political Order*, Maryknoll NY 2013. Important too, especially for bridging theology and law/jurisprudence, is Kathleen Caveny's, *Law's Virtues: Fostering Autonomy and Solidarity in American Society*, Georgetown 2012, and Caveny's work generally; as is the thinking about human rights and about the common good of David Hollenbach SJ: see *The Common Good and Christian Ethics*, Cambridge 2002; also, with Bruce Douglass (both eds), *Catholicism and Liberalism:* Contributions to American Public Policy; and Hollenbach's work generally. Bridging law and theology from the law side is their Law School colleague in Boston College Gregory Kalscheur: see his "Conscience and Citizenship: The Primacy of Conscience for Catholics in Public Life", *Journal of Catholic Social Thought* 6 (2009): 319–336. The writings of John Courtney Murray SJ retain a quasi-canonical status, especially "The Problem of Religious Freedom", published in *Theological Studies* in September 1964, almost exactly a year before the Council's discussions which led to the Declaration on Religious Freedom. Lesser-known but significant articles by Murray are collected, with a useful introduction and notes, in J. Leon Cooper (ed.), *Religious Liberty: Catholic Struggles with Pluralism*, Louisville KY, 1993. Cooper has also edited, with Todd David Whitmore, *John Courtney Murray and the Growth of Tradition*, Kansas MO 1996, essays by leading US theologians who comment on and develop Murray's key themes. Karl Rahner, Yves Congar, and Henri de Lubac were among the European theologians whose work assisted the Council's thinking in this area, and their writings may still be read with profit, as of course may the writings of Josef Ratzinger from before and after he became Pope Benedict XVI.

Christian theologians other than Roman Catholic, and scholars of the philosophy of religion, are also participants in the secularisation debate. In the UK they include Nigel Biggar, John Finnis, Duncan Forrester, David Fergusson, and Rob Warner; in the US, Martin E. Marty, Nicholas Wolterstoff, Paul Weithman, Jeffrey Stout, Christopher Eberle, Jeremy Waldron (US and UK). See Nigel Biggar, Linda Hogan (eds), *Religious Voices in Public Places*, Oxford 2009. Required reading in the vein known as Radical Orthodoxy, even for those of different theological leanings, is John Milbank, *Beyond Secular Order: the Representation of Being and the Representation of the People*, Oxford and Malden MA 2013.

The New York based Social Science Research Council has a programme called Religion and the Public Sphere, which includes a project dealing specifically with religion, secularism, and related topics, entitled *The Immanent Frame*, after a phrase of Charles Taylor's: <http://www.ssrc.org/programs/the-immanent-frame-blog/>.

Notes on Contributors

JIM CORKERY is an Irish Jesuit who has been teaching Systematic Theology at the Milltown Institute, in Dublin, for more than twenty years. In 2009, he published *Joseph Ratzinger's Theological Ideas: Wise Cautions and Legitimate Hopes* and a year later he co-edited, with US Jesuit Thomas Worcester, a collection of essays entitled *The Papacy Since 1500: From Italian Prince to Universal Pastor*. His current areas of research and writing are: the Second Vatican Council, on which he has lectured in Ireland and in South Africa; contemporary approaches to the resurrection; and the almost 500-year life-span of the Society of Jesus. In the autumn of 2014, he joined the Faculty of Theology at the Gregorian University in Rome.

GABRIEL DALY is an Augustinian priest. One of his areas of specialisation is Catholic Modernism, having published *Transcendence and Immanence: A Study of Catholic Modernism and Integralism* (1980). He is also author of *Creation and Redemption* (1988). He taught Theology in Milltown Institute and Trinity College Dublin and is a founder member and lecturer in the Irish School of Ecumenics and Honorary Fellow of TCD. His most recent publication is *The Church: Always in Need of Reform*, due to be published in 2015, preceded by a reprint of *Asking the Father* on prayer of petition.

MICHAEL DRUMM, a priest of Elphin Diocese, is the Chairperson of the Catholic Schools Partnership. This body provides support for all of the partners in Catholic schools in a changing Ireland. He has published several books and articles on the role of religion in Irish society. He is an assistant priest in the parish of Esker/Adamstown in Dublin.

GABRIEL FLYNN is Senior Lecturer in Systematic Theology at Mater Dei Institute, Dublin City University. He completed his doctorate at the University of Oxford in 2000. He was lead editor of *Ressourcement: A Movement for*

Renewal in Twentieth-Century Catholic Theology (2012). He is also editor of *Leadership and Business Ethics*, Issues in Business Ethics 25 (2008) and *Yves Congar: Theologian of the Church* (2005)/*Yves Congar: théologien de l'Église* (2007). He has been Guest Editor at *Louvain Studies*, and has also contributed to *La vie spirituelle*, *New Blackfriars*, *Concilium* and the *Journal of Business Ethics*.

SEÁN FREYNE (d. 2013) was Emeritus Professor of Theology in the School of Religions and Theology in Trinity College Dublin, Fellow of Trinity College Dublin, member of the Royal Irish Academy and a trustee of the Chester Beatty Library of Oriental Art. He was the author of many books and an acknowledged expert on the geography and religious significance of Galilee. His most recent publication was *The Jesus Movement and Its Expansion: Meaning and Mission* (2014).

PATRICK HANNON is a priest of the diocese of Cloyne and Emeritus Professor of Moral Theology at Maynooth College. He holds doctorates in theology (Maynooth) and law (Cambridge) and is a member of the Irish Bar. He has written extensively on issues at the intersection of religion, law and politics, and his publications include *Church, State, Morality, and Law* (1992). *Right or Wrong? Essays in Moral Theology* (2009) is his most recent book. At present he is parish chaplain in Donabate, Co. Dublin, and teaches at Mater Dei Institute, Dublin City University, and the Loyola Institute, Trinity College Dublin.

LINDA HOGAN is Vice-Provost and Chief Academic Officer and Professor of Ecumenics at Trinity College Dublin. As Vice-Provost/CAO she has overall responsibility for education and research at the university and deputises for the Provost as required. She is a theological ethicist whose primary research interests lie in the fields of theological ethics, human rights and gender. She has published widely on the ethics of human rights, intercultural ethics, and gender. She has been the lead academic on a number of research projects focussing on religious pluralism and inter-religious ethics.

DERMOT A. LANE is Parish Priest of Balally in Dublin 16 and former President of Mater Dei Institute of Education, Dublin City University. He has published several books, most recently *Stepping Stones to Other Religions: A Christian Theology of Interreligious Dialogue* (2011) and *Religion and Education: Reimagining the Relationship* (2013). He was awarded an Honorary DPhil from DCU in 2014.

ENDA MCDONAGH is Emeritus Professor of Moral Theology at St Patrick's College, Maynooth. He has published some twenty-five books. He is author of *Theology in Winter Light* (2010), joint editor with Vincent Mc Namara of *An Irish Reader in Moral Theology: The Legacy of Fifty Years*, 3 vols. (2009–2013), and sole editor of *Performing the Word: Festschrift for Ronan Drury* (2014).

DECLAN MARMION is a Marist Priest and Professor of Systematic Theology in St Patrick's College, Maynooth. He is the author of *A Spirituality of Everyday Faith: A Theological Investigation of the Notion of Spirituality in Karl Rahner* (1998) and joint editor with Mary E. Himes of *The Cambridge Companion to Karl Rahner* (2005).

PATRICK MASTERSON is former President and Emeritus Professor of Philosophy of Religion at University College Dublin. He is author of many books and articles, including *Atheism and Alienation* (1973), *The Sense of Creation* (2008) and *Approaching God: Between Phenomenology and Theology* (2013).

GERARD O'HANLON is a former Provincial of the Irish Jesuits. He works in the Jesuit Centre for Faith and Justice, and is Associate Professor of Systematic Theology in Milltown Institute, Dublin. Among his publications are *Theology in the Irish Public Square* (2011) and *A New Vision for the Catholic Church: A View from Ireland* (2011).

JOSEPH O'LEARY is a priest of the diocese of Cork and Ross. He studied literature and theology in Maynooth, Paris and Rome, and taught theology in the USA. Since 1983 he has been living in Japan, working on Buddhist-Christian theology and as Professor of English Literature at Sophia

University. His publications include *Religious Pluralism and Christian Truth* (1996) and *Philosophie occidentale et concepts bouddhistes* (2011).

ANDREW PIERCE is Assistant Professor in Ecumenics in the Irish School of Ecumenics, Trinity College Dublin. Between 2010 and 2012 he was president of the *Societas Oecumenica*, the European Association for Ecumenical Research. He currently serves as a member of, and a consultant to, the Inter-Anglican Standing Commission on Unity, Faith and Order (IASCUFO). His current research is concerned with the connections – in late nineteenth- and early twentieth-century theology – between modernism, ecumenism and so-called religious fundamentalism.

JACINTA PRUNTY is Senior Lecturer in History at the National University of Ireland Maynooth and a Holy Faith sister. Her research interests include urban historical geography, the history of cartography, and the history of religious life in Ireland in the nineteenth and twentieth centuries. Her most recent publication is *From Magdalen Asylums to Small Group Homes: The Sisters of Our Lady of Charity in Ireland, 1853–1970* (2015).

ETHNA REGAN is Senior Lecturer and Head of the School of Theology in Mater Dei Institute, Dublin City University and a member of DCU's Institute for International Conflict Resolution and Reconstruction. A Holy Faith sister, she previously taught at the University of the West Indies, Trinidad and worked with Credo Foundation for Justice in Port of Spain. She also taught for five years in Samoa in the Pacific Islands. She has published in the areas of ethics, liberation theology and theological anthropology, and is the author of *Theology and the Boundary Discourse of Human Rights* (2010).

FAINCHE RYAN is currently Assistant Professor of Systematic Theology at the Loyola Institute, Trinity College Dublin. Her doctoral thesis was on the theology of Thomas Aquinas. This was published in the series of the Thomas Instituut te Utrecht as *Formation in Holiness. Thomas Aquinas on Sacra doctrina* (2007). Her present research interests include the theology of Eucharist and the theology of ministry. She is currently preparing a book in this area.

Select Bibliography

The literature on Vatican II is vast and impossible to control. A selection, therefore, will be just that, and therefore, subjective to some degree. The following texts have become, or are becoming, standard references:

Histories of Vatican II

Alberigo, Giuseppe, and Komonchak, Joseph A., eds, *History of Vatican II*, Five Volumes, New York: Orbis Books, 1995–2006
Faggioli, Massimo, *Vatican II: The Battle for Meaning*, New York: Paulist Press, 2012
O'Malley, John W., *What Happened at Vatican II?*, Cambridge, MA: Harvard University Press, 2008

Theological Commentaries

Heft, James L., with O'Malley, John, *After Vatican II: Trajectories and Hermeneutics*, Grand Rapids, MI: W.B. Eerdmans Publishing Company, 2012
Hünermann, Peter, and Hilberath, Bernd J., eds, *Herders Theologischer Kommentar zum Zweiten Vatikanischen Konzil*, 5 volumes, Freiburg im Breisgau: Herder, 2004–2005
O'Collins, Gerard, *The Second Vatican Council: Message and Meaning*, Collegeville, MN: Liturgical Press, 2014
Ratzinger, Joseph/Benedict XVI, *Theological Highlights of Vatican II*, New York: Paulist Press, 1966/2009
Vorgrimmler, Herbert, ed., *Commentary on the Documents of Vatican II*, Five Volumes, London: Burns and Oates, 1967–1969

Interpretations

"Address of His Holiness Benedict XVI to the Roman Curia", 22 December 2005, available: <http://www.vatican.va/holy_father/benedict_xvi/speeches/2005/december/documents/hf_ben_xvi_spe_20051222_roman-curia_en.html>

Clifford, Catherine E., *Decoding Vatican II: Interpretation and Ongoing Reception*, Madeleva Lecture in Spirituality, New York: Paulist Press, 2014

Dadosky, John, "Has Vatican II been *Hermeneutered*? Recovery and Developing its Theological Achievements following Rahner and Lonergan", *Irish Theological Quarterly*, 2014, no. 4: 327–349

Dadosky, John, "Towards a Fundamental Theological *Re*-interpretation", *Heythrop Journal*, 2008: 742–763

Rahner, Karl, "Towards a Fundamental Theological Interpretation of Vatican II", *Theological Studies*, 1979: 716–727

Rush, Ormond, *Still Interpreting Vatican II: Some Hermeneutical Principles*, New York: Paulist Press, 2004

Rush, Ormond, "Towards a Comprehensive Interpretation of the Council and Its Documents", *Theological Studies*, 2012: 547–569

Schultenover, David G., ed., *Vatican II: Did Anything Happen?*, New York: Continuum, 2007

Theobald, Christoph, *La réception du concil Vatican II: I. Accéder a la Source*, Paris: Cerf, 2009

Theobald, Christoph, *Le concile Vatican II: Quel avenir?* Unam Sanctam, Nouvelle Série, Paris: Les editions du Cerf, 2015

Diaries

Chenu, Marie-Dominique, *Notes quotidiennes au concile*. Paris: Cerf, 1995.

Congar, Yves, *My Journal of the Council*, Translated from the French by Mary J. Ronayne, OP, and Mary C. Boulding, OP. English translation editor Denis Minns, OP, Dublin: Dominican Publications, 2012

De Lubac, Henri, *Carnets du Concile I et II*, Paris: Cerf, 2007

Goldie, Rosemary, *From a Roman Window: Five Decades of the World, the Church, and the Catholic Laity*, Blackburn: HarperCollinsReligious, 1998

McEnroy, Carmel Elizabeth, *Guests in Their Own House: The Women of Vatican II*, New York: Crossroad, 1996

Stacpole, A., ed., *Vatican II by those who were There*, London: 1986

Chronology of Significant Moments before, during and after the Second Vatican Council

25 January 1959	Announcement by John XXIII of his intention to hold a Council
25 December 1961	Letter convoking the Council (*Humanae Salutis*)
11 October 1962	Address of John XXII opening the Council (*Gaudet Mater Ecclesiae*)
12 December 1962	Closure of the First session
11 April 1963	Encyclical of John XXIII, *Pacem in Terris*
3 June 1963	Death of John XXII
21 June 1963	Election of Paul VI
29 September 1963	Opening of the Second Session
4 December 1963	Conclusion of the Second Session
4–6 January 1964	Pilgrimage of Paul VI to Jerusalem and meeting with Patriarch Athenagoras
14 September 1964	Opening of Third Session
21 November 1964	Conclusion of the Third Session
14 September 1965	Opening of the Fourth Session
7 December 1965	Final meeting of the Fourth Session
8 December 1965	Closure of the Council, with a message address to Humanity
25 July 1968	Encyclical Letter of Paul VI, *Humanae Vitae*
30 September– 6 November 1971	Third Synod of Bishops on *Justice in the World* and *Ministry*

16 October 1978	Election of Karol Wojtyla as Bishop of Rome. John-Paul II
25 November 1981	Appointment of Archbishop Joseph Ratzinger (Münich) as Prefect of the Congregation for the Doctrine of the Faith
25 January 1983	Promulgation of the New Code of Canon Law
24 November–8 December 1985	Extraordinary Synod of Bishops commemorating the Twentieth Anniversary of Vatican II
2 April 2005	Death of John-Paul II
19 April 2005	Election of Cardinal Ratzinger as Bishop of Rome, Benedict XVI
22 December 2005	Christmas Address of Benedict XVI to the Curia about the interpretation of Vatican II
7 July 2007	*Motu Proprio* on the Liturgy: *Summorum Pontificum* (greater use of the Latin Tridentine Mass)
24 January 2009	Lifting of the excommunication of four bishops from the Society of St Pius X ordained by Archbishop Marcel Lefebvre
25 March 2010	Approval of new English translation of the Roman Missal
11 February 2013	Resignation of Benedict XVI
13 March 2013	Election of Cardinal Jorge Bergoglio as Bishop of Rome, Francis

Index

STUDIES IN THEOLOGY
SOCIETY AND CULTURE

Religious and theological reflection has often been confined to the realm of the private, the personal or the Church. In Europe this restriction of religion and theology can be traced back to the Enlightenment and has had long-lasting and pernicious consequences for the understanding of religious faith and society. On the one hand, there has been a rise in religious fundamentalisms around the globe, while, on the other hand, so-called advanced societies are constructed mainly along economic, pragmatic and rationalistic lines. Added to this is the reality that religious faith is increasingly lived out in pluralistic and multi-faith contexts with all the challenges and opportunities this offers to denominational religion.

This series explores what it means to be 'religious' in such contexts. It invites scholarly contributions to themes including patterns of secularisation, postmodern challenges to religion, and the relation of faith and culture. From a theological perspective it seeks constructive re-interpretations of traditional Christian topics – including God, creation, salvation, Christology, ecclesiology, etc. – in a way that makes them more credible for today. It also welcomes studies on religion and science, and on theology and the arts.

The series publishes monographs, comparative studies, interdisciplinary projects, conference proceedings and edited books. It attracts well-researched, especially interdisciplinary, studies which open new approaches to religion or focus on interesting case studies. The language of the series is English. Book proposals should be emailed to any, or all, of the following:

SERIES EDITORS:

- Dr Declan Marmion, St Patrick's College, Maynooth (Declan.Marmion@spcm.ie)
- Dr Gesa Thiessen, Trinity College, The University of Dublin (gesa.thiessen@tcd.ie)
- Dr Norbert Hintersteiner, University of Münster (norbert.hintersteiner@uni-muenster.de)

Vol. 12   Dermot A. Lane (ed.):
            Vatican II in Ireland, Fifty Years On: Essays in Honour of Pádraic Conway.
            421 pages. 2015. ISBN 978-3-0343-1874-7.